The château of

Chantilly

The château of

Chantilly

Jean-Pierre Babelon
Photographs by Georges Fessy

Domaine de Chantilly
nouvelles éditions scala

Acknowledgements
Jean-Pierre Babelon, Georges Fessy and Éditions Scala would like to express their warm thanks to Madame Nicole Garnier-Pelle, head curator of the Musée Condé at Chantilly, for her continual and illuminating help in producing this book.
Jean-Pierre Babelon and Georges Fessy wish to thank Catherine Berthoud for her collaboration and efficiency in carrying out the picture research.
Georges Fessy and Éditions Scala thank Monsieur Ramdane Manseur, librarian at Chantilly library, and all members of staff at the museum and estate of Chantilly for their courteous welcome.

Translation from French: Judith Hayward
Editing: Scott Steedman
Layout and production: Robaglia design, Virginie Leroux
Picture research: Catherine Berthoud

www.editions-scala.fr
ISBN 978-2-35988-109-7

Author's note

No book on the château of Chantilly has been published since the appearance in 1910 of Gustave Macon's standard reference work *Chantilly et le musée Condé*, who made successful and meticulous use of the abundant archives preserved at the château as did the books by Henri Malo (1938) and Raoul de Broglie (1964) published subsequently.

While knowledge of the superb collections of paintings and drawings in the museum at Chantilly has been brought completely up to date by the publications of Nicole Garnier-Pelle, the head curator, research in architecture has mainly related to particular points or periods, and has been restricted to articles published in specialist journals.

There was no complete, in-depth study. For the first time this work offers a synthesis, bringing together the château, gardens and estate of Chantilly in the context of a historical and art historical continuum.

The photographs are all original and the choice of iconography exceptionally rich, as a result of very thorough research into private and public collections extending as far as the United States.

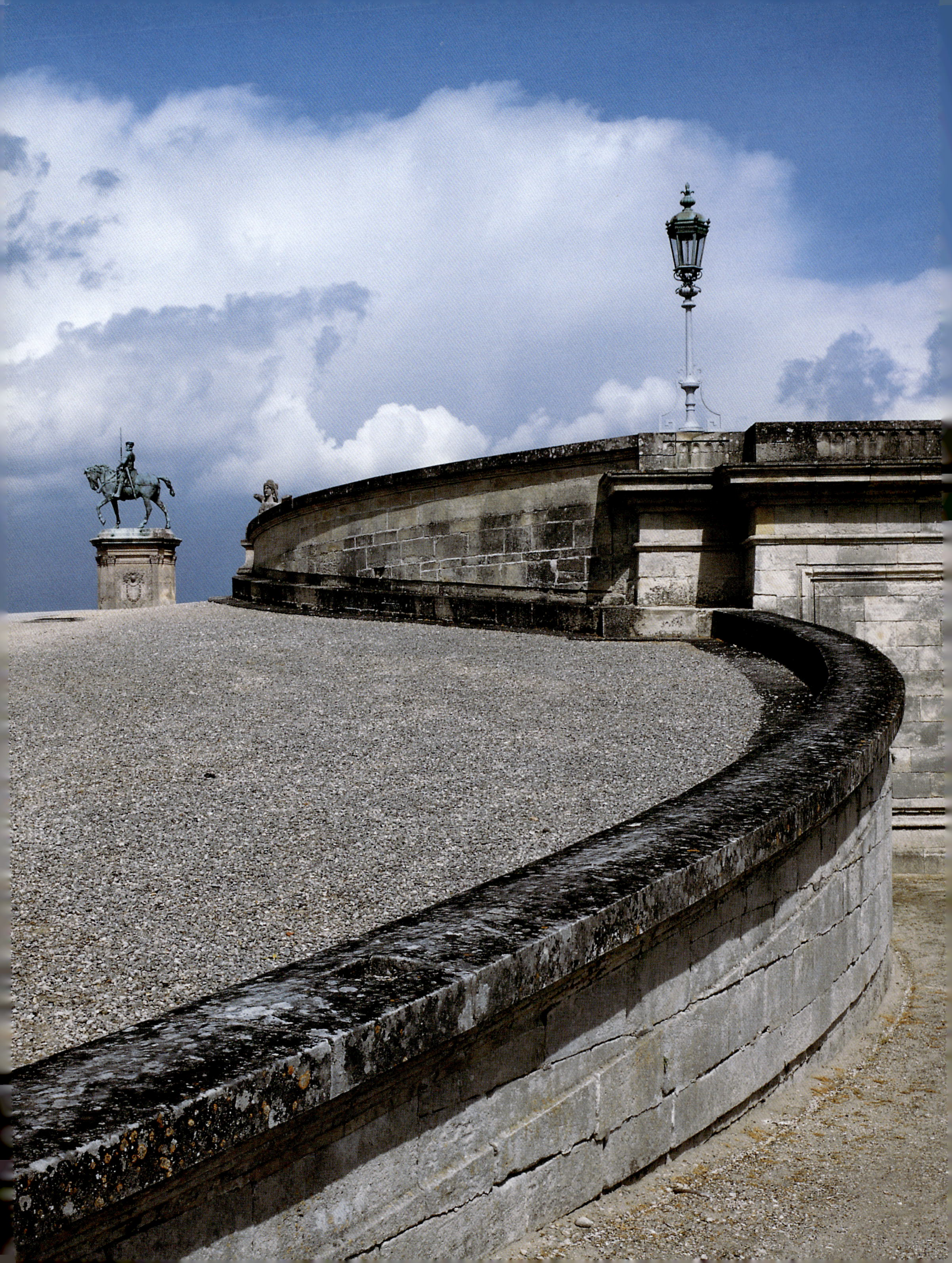

LIST OF CONTENTS

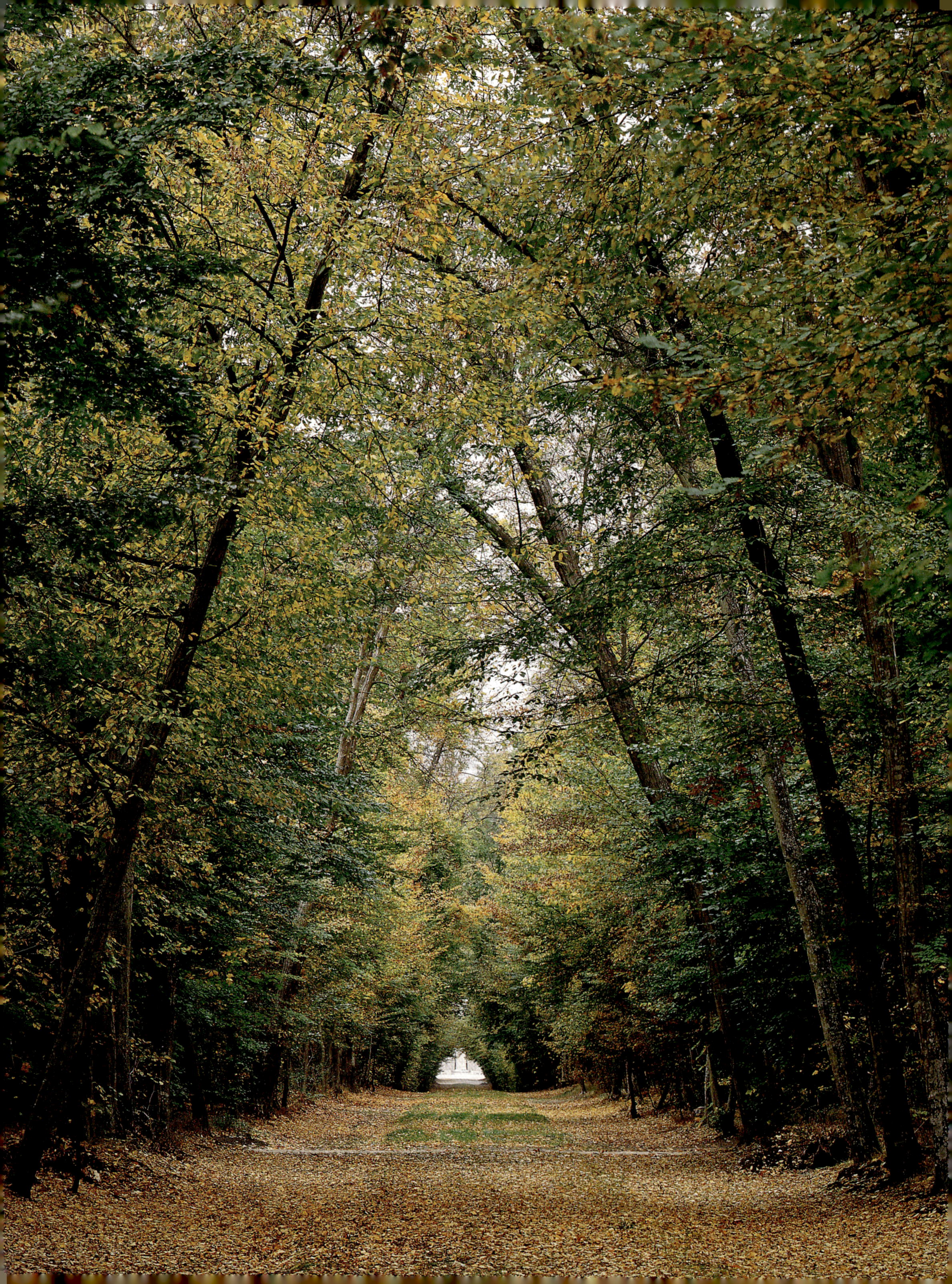

Introduction

Report has it that when Emperor Charles V visited Constable Anne de Montmorency in 1540 he was so taken with Chantilly that he would willingly have given one of his provinces in the Low Countries in exchange for it – they were in fact causing him a lot of problems! Half a century later Henri IV, who did not hesitate to describe Chantilly as "the most beautiful house in France", offered to grant his comrade Constable Henri any one of his royal châteaux in its place. This is sufficient indication of the magic of the place which has deeply affected all those who have visited it over the centuries. The Valois and Bourbon kings, all except for Henri III and Louis XVI, took particular delight in staying there, sometimes for long periods, and sometimes regularly. Thus Francis I, Henri II, Charles IX, Henri IV (who regularly booked in for the month of March), Louis XIII, Louis XIV and Louis XV came here to enjoy real holidays – at the owner's expense, and sometimes even in his absence – as the setting was so beautiful, life so sweet, and the hunt so varied and rewarding.

Chantilly is most striking in its originality, the ways in which it differs from the other great houses of France. It is a masterly exception, a status characterised and expressed in the layout of its natural site, the genius of its creators and the story of the men and women who fashioned it and dwelt there. So a kind of permanent paradox is associated with the site and buildings we admire: while Chantilly is obviously one of the finest creations of French classicism, thanks to the admirable mastery of space developed here by Le Nôtre, it nonetheless contradicts the principles that normally govern the organisation of a French-style château, in the relationships between the house and gardens, the forecourt area and the stables, and the junction between town and château. These articulations, crucial to the handling of the landscape as a whole, have been drawn along lines that reject the choice of a single axis passing through the centre of the château – the Versailles system – replacing it with a dispersed order made up of a subtle network of parallels, tangents and diagonals. By virtue of this new optical and kinetic system which was introduced to allow visitors to appreciate Chantilly's qualities, at each focal point they gradually discover the natural pictures that have been prepared for their delectation.

After emerging from the great forest surrounding the gardens, a protective, nurturing cover into which they have been incised as in a wood engraving, visitors will see a side view of the château site before approaching it along its axis. On the left side the large grassy expanse of the Pelouse unfolds, encircling the base of the imposing architecture of the Écuries like a sea, right up to the triumphal arch that serves as an introduction to the town. At the gilded railing of the main gate, before crossing the bridge leading into the enclosed inner sanctum, they will be able to take in the whole composition, balanced with such consummate skill. At the centre, instead of the fullness we would traditionally expect, there is emptiness: the high terrace where the statue of the Constable stands like a beacon, a lighthouse for lost landlubbers. Behind it, as visitors climb the gentle slope of the ramp, a panoramic view of the vast wooded amphitheatre emerges, held back at a respectful distance by the Grand Canal and constituting the backdrop of the stage set. On the left, very much to the side, the mass of the château rises, reflected in the glinting water of the moats, lodged on its triangular islet since time immemorial, and kept there by all the generations up to and including the duc d'Aumale, refusing to emerge from that site, as if the old road to Picardy which used once to bisect the site from south to north still traced its age-old path.

This history has left its mark on the architecture. The château on its misshapen, awkward little island has been reconstructed time and again, and these buildings can be numbered like the succession of cities of Troy rediscovered by archaeologists: the Chantilly I of the Bouteillers of Senlis, the Chantilly II of the d'Orgemonts, the Chantilly III of the Montmorencys, the Chantilly IV of the Condés and the Chantilly V of the duc d'Aumale. The enduring nature of the bases of the round towers, the general configuration of the triangle and the weight of history have made these successive châteaux seem in a way like the continuous germination of a single seed without any violent transformation, and the last on the scene skilfully combines all its architectural references to the past in a complex and lively composition, a sort of syncretism of the masses and accents where the tall cylinders of the towers and the tapering silhouettes of the pinnacle turrets still stand out, like a last token of loyalty demonstrated by an heir towards his ancestors.

At the foot of the fortress, the low islet has housed the Petit Château since the sixteenth century, more of a country house, low-lying and vulnerable, since the banks of the pond had not been properly stabilised. Like the Grand Château it has suffered in the storms of history, and yet – and here is another paradox – it has survived virtually intact, ensuring the true permanence of Chantilly from age to age, welcoming its lords, generation after generation, in suites of rooms that still exist.

The exceptional nature of Chantilly also lies in the history of France. The château and its huge surrounding estate had a place in that history right from the origins of the Capetian Dynasty, which was loyal to the Senlis region, one of its most reliable sources of support.

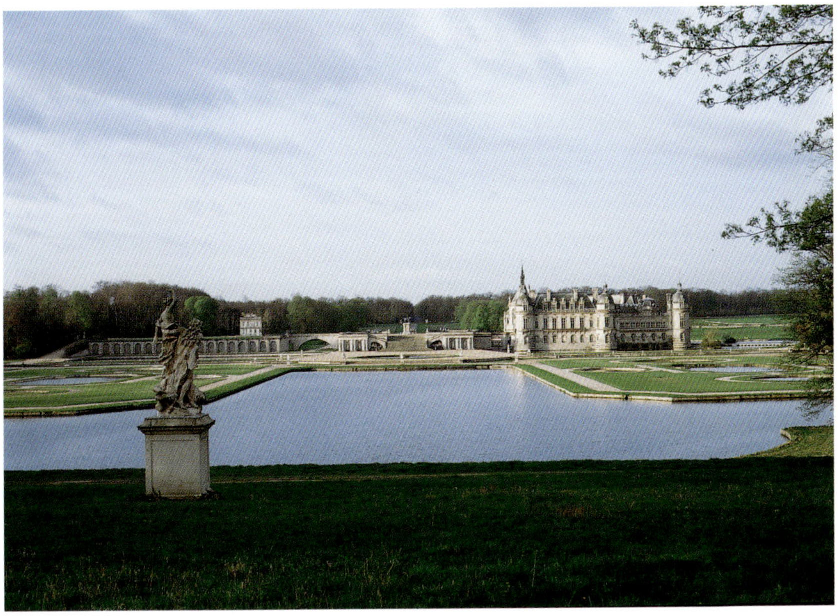

The site of Chantilly viewed axially from north to south
Behind the statue of *Hercules abducting Deianira* by René Frémin installed on the Vertugadin around 1820, the eye takes in the whole composition: the canal, the *parterres* and the château.

Then it constituted a considerable strategic stake when the Armagnacs and the Burgundians confronted one another. As time went by, it passed into the hands of leading figures who were closer and closer to the power of the monarchy, and then to the royal family itself: Pierre d'Orgemont, chancellor to Charles V, then Anne and Henri de Montmorency, constables and very close advisers to Francis I, Henri II and Henri IV, next the Great Condé, cousin to Louis XIV and winner of many laurels, followed by his descendants, one of them the prime minister of Louis XV, and finally, in the last chapter, the duc d'Aumale, the actual son of a king of France.

This progress of the lords of Chantilly to the summit of the state went hand in hand with the inevitable alternation between favour and disgrace that characterises the careers of great favourites, especially when their membership of the highest nobility leads them to claim some share of power. On two occasions tension rose to the point where it culminated in a dramatic rupture: Henri II de Montmorency was condemned to death and executed for armed rebellion, and history repeated itself with the Great Condé, who also rebelled against his king during the Fronde. He too was condemned to death in absentia, and his property confiscated. Owned by these great champions of aristocratic power, Chantilly played the part of an independent planet, and it became something of a habit to see it as a kind of rival domain to Versailles, with its splendid festivities, its artists and men of letters regularly in attendance, and a whole host of courtiers. The House of Condé was also visited by European sovereigns travelling through France, from Kristina of Sweden to Gustav III, from Emperor Joseph II to the future Tsar Paul I, all eager to admire its new beauties as celebrated by the poets. At the end of the seventeenth century and right through the eighteenth, Le Nôtre's gardens, the Écuries, the Hameau, the legendary hunts, the illuminations and the plays all contributed towards making Chantilly one of the brightest beacons of princely civilisation, one on which kings cast looks of envy.

Finally, the exceptional nature of Chantilly lies in the epilogue to its destiny. Like so many other châteaux of prime importance, it could have fallen victim to one of the various revolutionary episodes, suffering the fate of Marly or Meudon, Saint-Cloud or Les Tuileries. It would seem that the fact it belonged to a princely dynasty and not to the Crown saved it from being lost, despite the destruction of the Grand Château in 1799. When the Condés returned from exile at the time of the Restoration they were very keen to reconstitute their estate as a means of asserting their identity, and the same feeling led them to look for an heir who would ensure that the family inheritance was safeguarded. Their choice – an Orléans prince who became a royal prince as a result of the July 1830 Revolution – could not have been better.

The duc d'Aumale, who like the last Prince de Condé had the painful privilege of experiencing exile twice, was smitten by a true passion for Chantilly, and after losing the closest members of his family it became the main interest of a long life devoted to patriotic duty and the arts. He focused his exceptional intelligence and sensitivity on resurrecting the estate, château and gardens. The course of history was one of the major themes underlying his inspiration and the programme he dictated to Honoré Daumet, the man he had chosen to succeed the great exponents of French architecture who had gone before him: Pierre Chambiges, Jean Bullant, Jules Hardouin-Mansart and Jean Aubert. But Daumet's Chantilly is nonetheless a major work of its day, and the most ambitious private building to be constructed in France during the Republic, at the period when the last châteaux were built.

Chantilly had long since achieved great renown for the quality of the porcelain manufactured there in the eighteenth century, not to mention its lace, or Chantilly cream; it is still one of the places where horses are venerated and racing carries on, honouring a long equine tradition that can be traced back to the Montmorencys and the Condés. The duc d'Aumale wanted to add a new dimension, and this is another aspect of that exceptional nature that makes Chantilly so outstanding. He was unquestionably one of the greatest collectors of all time, possessed by a passion that never left him in peace, from his youth to his very last days, in France and in exile. That passion enabled him to turn his château into one of the foremost museums in France, if not Europe, a museum above all of paintings, bringing together masterpieces by Italian, Flemish, Dutch and French masters: Fra Angelico, Lippi, Raphael, Van Dyck, Enguerrand Quarton, Clouet, Poussin, Champaigne, Watteau, Ingres and

Delacroix; but he also assembled an exceptional collection of drawings, ranging from Pisanello to Michelangelo, Holbein to Rembrandt, Clouet to Poussin, as well as sculptures, objets d'art and furniture. The illuminated manuscripts are among the finest in the world: the *Très Riches Heures du duc de Berry*, the miniatures by Fouquet for the *Livre d'heures d'Étienne Chevalier*, the *Psalter of Queen Ingeborg*, the *Lorsch Sacramentary*, the *Bréviaire de Jeanne d'Évreux* and countless other manuscripts, rare editions and splendid bindings. At the express request of the duke, Daumet's palatial architecture was thus transfigured into a sophisticated yet functional setting, suitable for housing and displaying to the public one of the finest collections of works of art that has ever existed.

All that remained was for the duke's final decision to be implemented, the gift to France of the treasure in its entirety through an institution endowed with immortality and standing above political crises: the Institut de France. Thus through the good offices of Louis-Philippe's son, the efforts lavished by generations to maintain and embellish Chantilly ultimately enriched the national heritage. So it was now up to the Institut de France to continue the unremitting efforts made over the centuries. Among the succession of members of various academies appointed to keep the project on course and make decisions, some extremely conscientious men have devoted themselves to the task with passionate enthusiasm: tribute should be paid to them collectively, and particularly to the memory of Maurice Schumann, the last to leave us. He has been succeeded as head of the college of curators by the historian Alain Decaux, from 1998 to 2009, another member of the illustrious band to which the prince was so devoted, the Académie Française, by Pierre Jean Rémy, in 2009-2010, and by Marc Fumaroli, since 2010. Maurice Schumann liked to recall the undertakings given to the testator of 1884, and he continued to feel that he had to account to the dead prince for the proper management of the treasures he had left, remaining faithful to what he called the "Chantilly ethic", the product of both nature and history: the eternal values of an exceptional site.

To ensure the restoration and the upkeep of this national heritage, in full observance of the Duc d'Aumale's will and in collaboration with the college curators, the Fondation pour la sauvegarde et le Développement du Domaine de Chantilly was created in 2005 by His Highness the Aga Khan. From January 1, 2006 and for a period of 20 years the Foundation is responsible for managing the estate and museums.

Following pages

Chantilly as an island
The two châteaux that have stood on their island for centuries are reflected in the mirror of the ponds; on the left stands the château rebuilt for the fourth time by the duc d'Aumale, on the right that constructed by Anne de Montmorency..

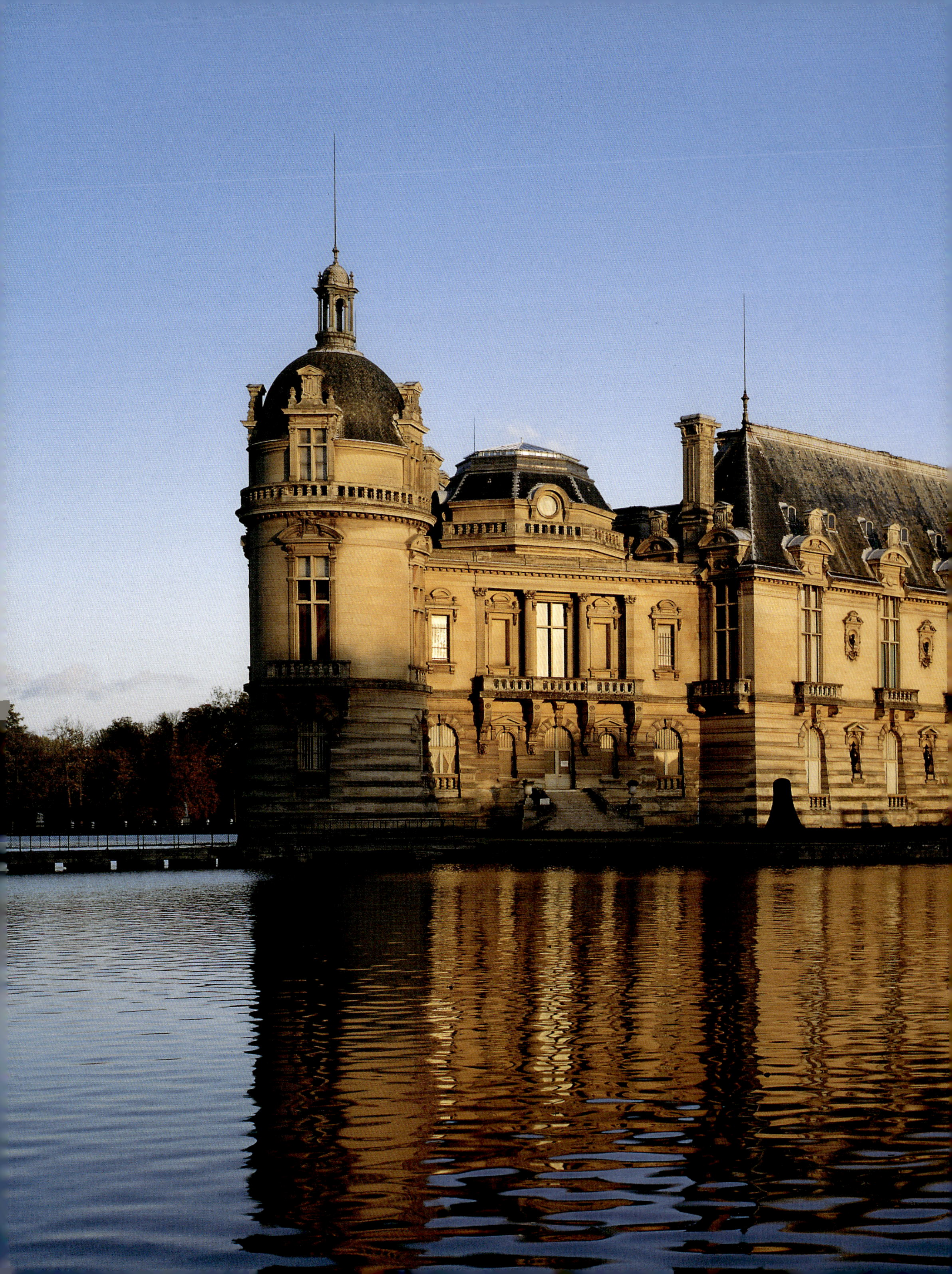

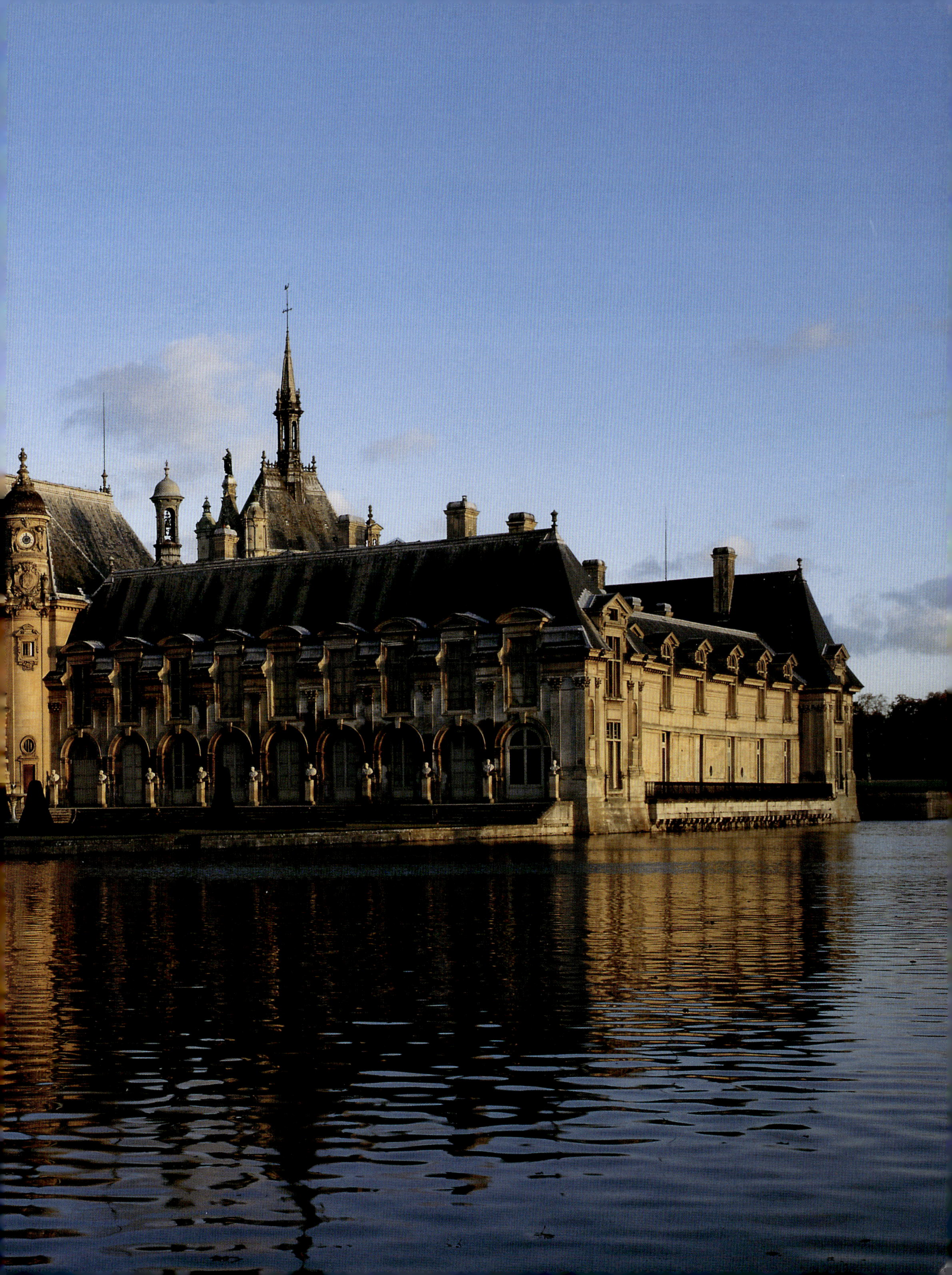

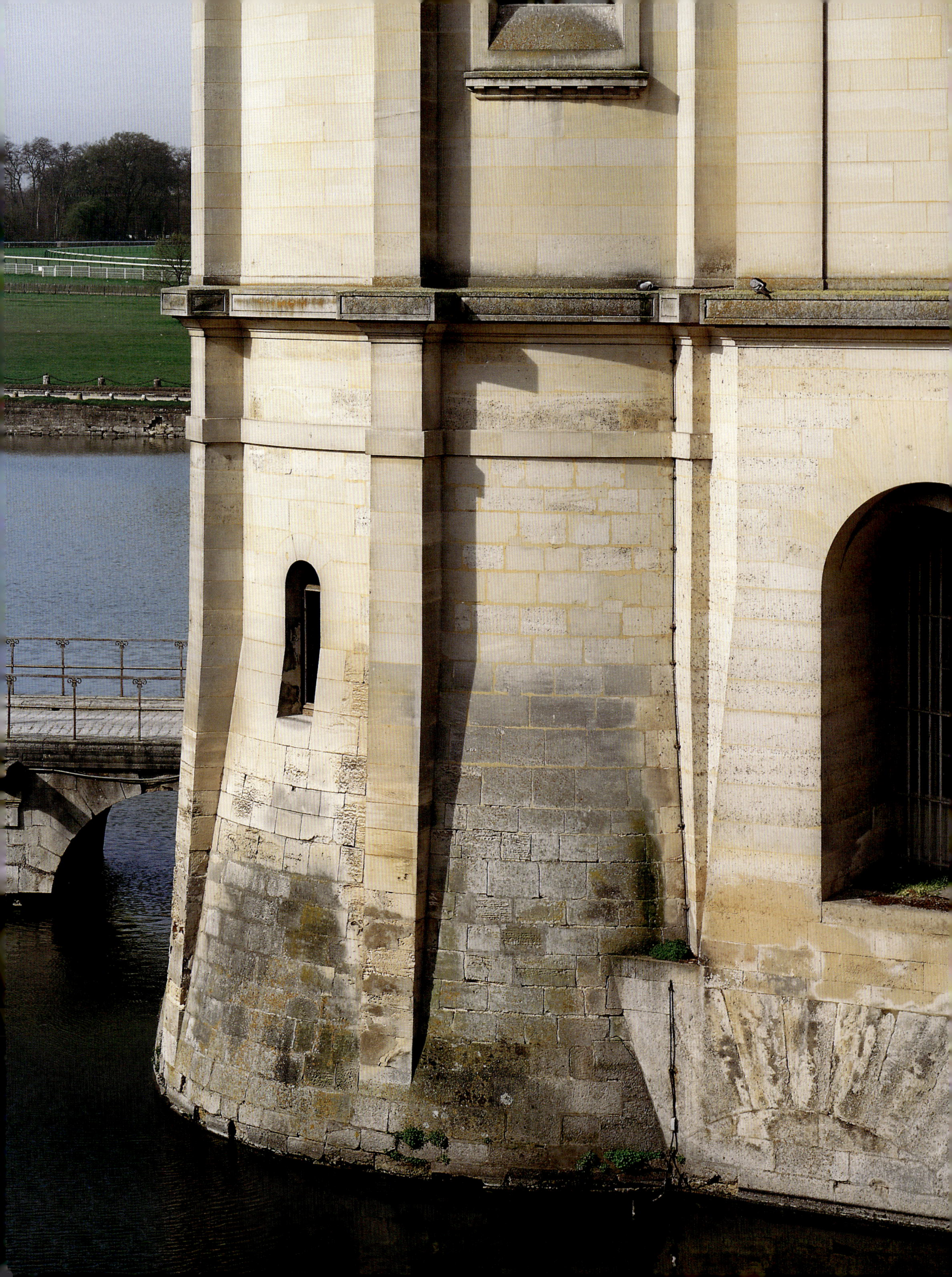

From cup-bearer to the king to chancellor of France

A special site

Ten leagues (40 km) from Paris on the outer edges of the Île-de-France, Chantilly came into being beside the old road to Picardy which passed through the forest on its way from Luzarches and Lamorlaye, crossing the Thève and the Nonette, tributaries of the river Oise, and further on the Oise itself. Castles were constructed at crossing points: Creil was built by Charles V on an island in the Oise, whereas at Chantilly the fortification was perched on a rocky massif ringed by ponds. From its earliest days the road passed over these on stone-built causeways before crossing the Nonette via a bridge. The valley of that bright, fast-flowing river, stocked with trout and freshwater crayfish, harmoniously articulates the movements of the site, and had a decisive influence on the birth and development of the estate.

Quite early on a few clusters of houses were built on its southern slopes, the hamlets of Les Fontaines and Quinquenpoit on the area currently occupied by the town of Chantilly, and further west the hamlet of Gouvieux. To the east, just over a league (4 km) away by the path skirting the ponds, is the old Roman fortified town of Senlis, the capital of a lordship that was very attentively watched over by the kings of France as it was part of the personal estate of Hugh Capet at the time of his accession to the throne. This was royal land from the start of the Capetian monarchy: the rock on which Chantilly stood was part of the diocese of Senlis (the parish of Saint-Léonard of Avilly), while the three neighbouring hamlets came under the diocese of Beauvais.

It was in the late tenth century at the time of Hugh Capet that the place known as Chantilly – the name suggests it once belonged to a Gallo-Roman by the name of Cantilius – emerged from anonymity and made its appearance in documents[1]: it then belonged to Rothold, lord of Senlis and Ermenonville.

The base of the Tour de Paris
The ground plan and foundations of the round towers that punctuated the fourteenth-century château have survived the successive reconstructions, even if their facework has had to be repaired over the centuries.

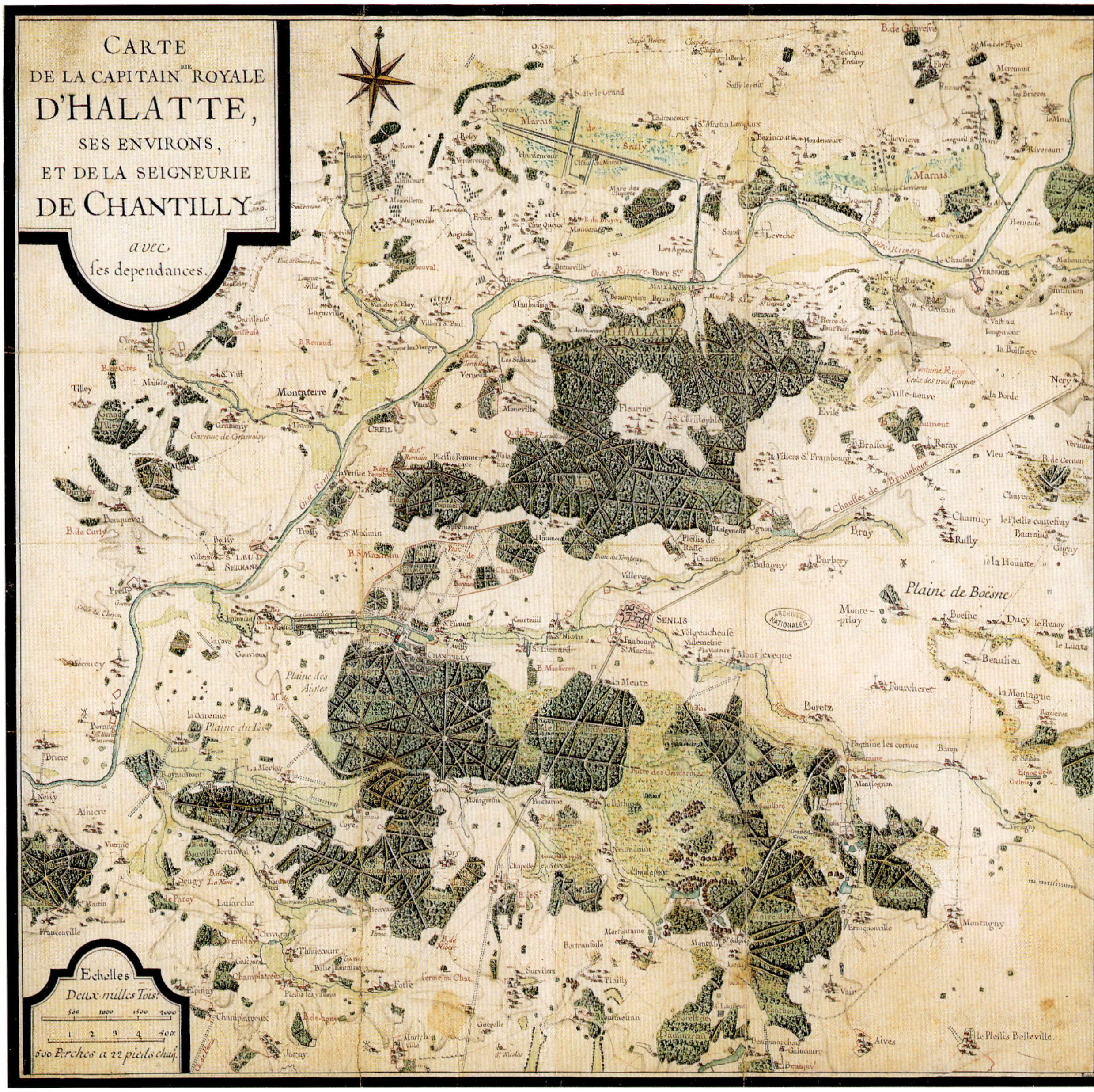

The Capitainerie of Halatte and the lordship of Chantilly

This eighteenth-century map shows the great extent of the forested highlands that lent themselves so well to hunting, criss-crossed by the tributaries of the Oise and a dense network of roads.

A century later it was in the hands of one of his successors, Gui, a loyal servant of King Louis VI, who honoured him by appointing him an officer of the Crown, with the office of "bouteiller" or cup-bearer, and the name of that office was flatteringly added to the family surname, so that they became the Bouteillers of Senlis.[2] The first castle built amidst the waters was their work. Study of the rocky plateau in which the cellars of the castle and the galleries of the terrace facing it were dug seems to prove that originally there was just a single massif rising from the pond, and the first builders blocked off the spur by digging out a straight moat to isolate the building from the road to Paris, which climbed over the east end of the mound; they may also have dug out the moat to the south to cut off a low-lying islet, so preventing the enemy from striking at the foot of the wall.

On all sides the castle was surrounded by the great clumps of trees forming the ancient forest of Cuyse[3], part of the tree canopy formerly covering Gaul that first started to be cleared in the twelfth and early thirteenth century: north of Senlis the forest of Halatte, and south of the river Nonette the forests of Ermenonville and Chantilly. The latter extending over no less 6,275 hectares did not belong only to the lord of Chantilly; at the whim of gifts, especially royal gifts, it was divided among the great abbeys of the region, Saint-Denis, Chaalis[4], Saint-Nicolas d'Acy and Hérivaux, as well as the priory of Saint-Leu-d'Esserent. The forest constitutes the profound, eternal nature of this place; it was the hunting estate that afforded the nobility their supreme, favourite pleasure pursuits, but along with the fishing in the ponds it also generated a considerable income. Over the centuries claims regarding the right to hunt led to often violent confrontations between the monks and the lords of Chantilly, unremitting in their endeavours to enlarge the extent of their forest domain.

Chantilly I - The Bouteillers of Senlis

Initially the Bouteillers of Senlis owned only the immediate vicinity of the castle at Chantilly, the wooded part of the present park, meadows north of the Nonette from below Avilly, a few hectares of land to the south, and nothing to the west, on the other bank of the pond (the site of the English garden), where the monks of Saint-Leu-d'Esserent built a farm known as the Grange Saint-Leu, or Petit Saint-Leu. From the fifteenth century on it was known as Bucan – later changed to Bucamp – from Buchan, the name of a Scottish soldier who lodged

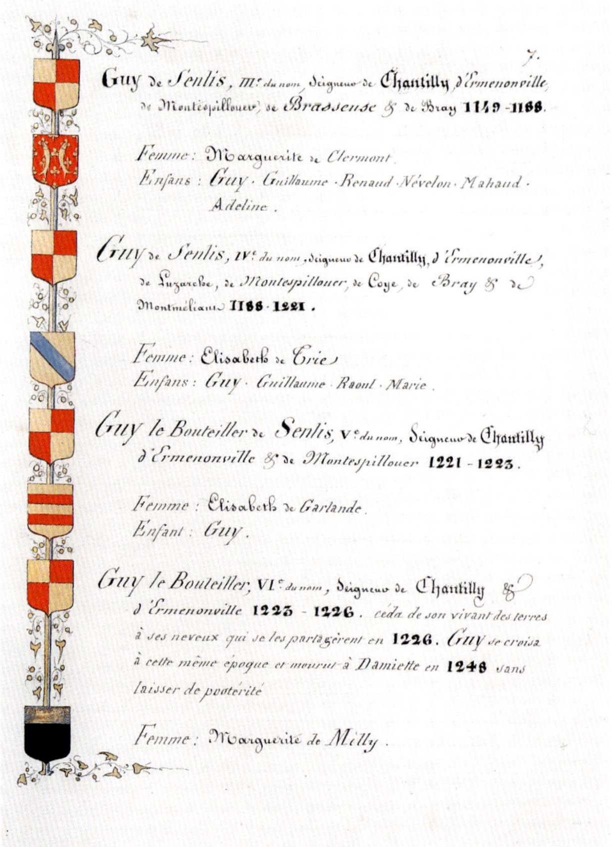

7.

Guy de Senlis, III.e du nom, Seigneur de Chantilly, d'Ermenonville, de Montespillouer, de Brassense & de Bray 1149 - 1188.

Femme : Marguerite de Clermont.
Enfans : Guy · Guillaume · Renaud · Névelon · Mahaud · Adeline.

Guy de Senlis, IV.e du nom, Seigneur de Chantilly, d'Ermenonville, de Luzarche, de Montespillouer, de Coye, de Bray & de Montmélian 1188 · 1221.

Femme : Elisabeth de Trie.
Enfans : Guy · Guillaume · Raoul · Marie.

Guy le Bouteiller de Senlis, V.e du nom, Seigneur de Chantilly, d'Ermenonville & de Montespillouer 1221 - 1223.

Femme : Elisabeth de Garlande.
Enfant : Guy.

Guy le Bouteiller, VI.e du nom, Seigneur de Chantilly & d'Ermenonville 1223 - 1226. céda de son vivant des terres à ses neveux qui se les partagèrent en 1226. Guy se croisa à cette même époque et mourut à Damiette en 1248 sans laisser de postérité.

Femme : Marguerite de Milly.

Arms of the Bouteillers of Senlis
The Bouteillers were the lords of Chantilly in the twelfth and thirteenth centuries. The château which had been sacked thirty years earlier was sold to Pierre d'Orgemont in 1386.

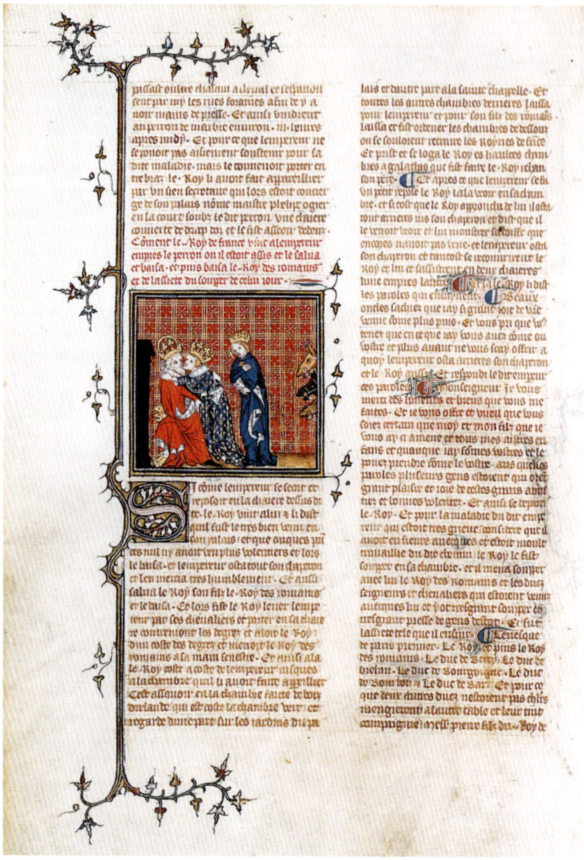

The meeting between King Charles V and Emperor Charles IV in Paris
Pierre d'Orgemont, lord of Chantilly and formerly a Councillor to Charles V, gave an account of this famous 1378 meeting, which he attended, in his *Grandes Chroniques de France.*

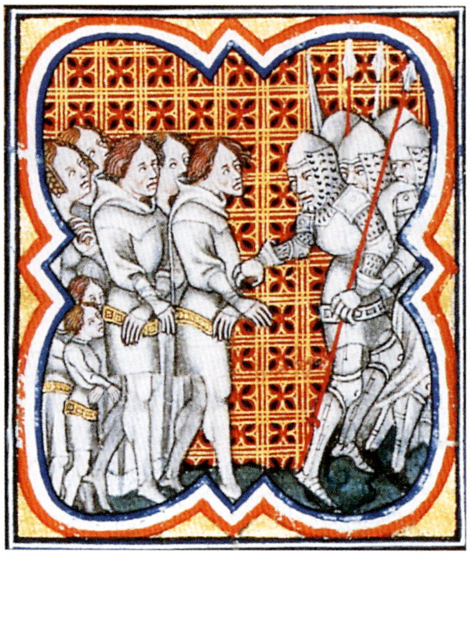

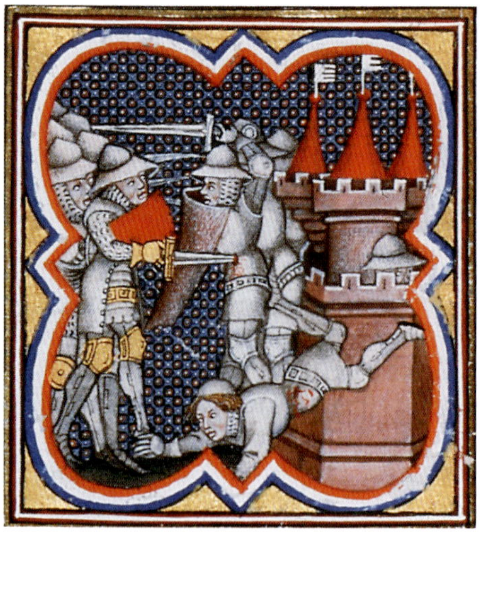

there during the Hundred Years' War. Behind that in the hamlet of Quinquenpoit a tower which was mentioned in 1280 was built by lords allied to the Bouteillers, as was a chapel of ease, in 1219 referred to as "the church of Saint-Germain at Chantilly", which suggests that no place of worship was yet present in the castle. In 1227, when the property left by Gui III (who had an abundance of possessions in the region) was divided, it was his second son, Guillaume, who became the owner of the domains of Chantilly, Courteuil and Montmélian; he travelled to the Holy Land and died a prisoner in Egypt around 1240. His son Jean decided to create the first chapel in the castle, but died in 1286 without fulfilling his vow. Instead the chapel was built at the end of his life by Guillaume III, and he was buried there in 1340. His body was rediscovered in the crypt in 1718 when the chapel was reconstructed, at the point where the staircase known as the Escalier d'Honneur rises today.[5] Chantilly endured the full force of the troubles that racked the kingdom in the second half of the fourteenth century. The strategic importance of its position prompted the Valois king, Philip VI, to take the necessary measures to ensure its defence when the hostilities of the Hundred Years' War began, to make up for the deficiencies of Guillaume IV le Bouteiller, its incompetent and debt-ridden lord.

As the price of this assumption of responsibility, Chantilly was given in 1347 to the Duke of Normandy, later to become John the Good,[6] but the misfortunes of war did not really allow the transaction to be implemented. In 1356 King John was beaten and taken prisoner by the English at Poitiers, and the Jacquerie uprising which flared up two years later at Saint-Leu-d'Esserent spread like wildfire through the entire Beauvaisis district, with exception being taken to landowners and the nobility in general. The castle was sacked. Once again royal power had to intervene, with the regent Charles seeing no other alternative than to install a cousin of the incompetent lord in his place, for fear "that the enemy may take the said fortress, which would be very prejudicial and harmful to our good town of Senlis, the surrounding country and the entire kingdom".

Chantilly II - Chancellor Pierre d'Orgemont

In 1386, after long years of disputes and proceedings between the heirs of the Bouteillers, Chantilly was finally sold for eight thousand *livres* to Pierre d'Orgemont, lord of Méry-sur-Oise, who immediately set about reconstructing it.[7] D'Orgemont, the son of a burgher of Lagny[8], had had a brilliant career as a

Opposite

Bottom left

Violence during the Jacquerie

This miniature from the *Grandes Chroniques de France* shows the crushing of the peasant uprising in 1358.

Bottom right

The attack on the market of Meaux

Another episode from the Jacquerie which caused bloodshed in Beauvaisis and the Paris area, related in the *Grandes Chroniques de France.*

jurist which took him to the position of First President of the Paris *Parlement*, before being appointed to the foremost legal office in the kingdom: he became Chancellor of France in 1373. He was a very valued adviser to Charles V, and at his request oversaw the writing of the chronicle of events that had taken place during the reigns of John and Charles in the *Grandes Chroniques de France*, a real monument of historiography. On the king's death in 1380, d'Orgemont decided to hand in his seals of office, retaining only one office as President of the Audit Chamber. He was a great builder; the historian Henri Sauval writing in the seventeenth century[9] said he had built at Méry "a country house that was fairly well proportioned as to size for a person of his rank; and as to beauty, what may be imagined and expected from an uncouth, coarse century such as his. He also enlarged Chantilli adding several buildings that can still be seen there."

The former Chancellor wasted no time. On 4 March 1386, before he had even signed the contract of sale, he instructed five masons so that he could get an estimate of the expense entailed in building "the stretch of wall – that is the whole curtain wall – and four towers abreast in front of the castle of Chantilly"[10], but that first phase had hardly been completed when he died on 3 June 1389. It fell to his son Amaury, a jurist like his father and Chancellor to the king's brother, duc Louis d'Orléans, to complete the rebuilding. After the east face, the masons were ready for work the following 25 November to construct the north face – "a stretch of wall and a tower in the middle on the side facing Vineuil" – then it was the carpenters' turn to set to work on the whole castle from 1391 to 1393, and the whole thing was completed the following year. As the work undertaken in the sixteenth century by Anne de Montmorency did not alter the lower parts of the castle[11], we can rely on the engraved views of it given by Du Cerceau in his *Plus Excellents Bâtiments de France*, as well as the various drawings and engravings made in the seventeenth century before the alterations by Hardouin-Mansart, to make a mental reconstruction of the castle of the d'Orgemonts: its plan can still be read in the buildings erected by the duc d'Aumale, since the bottoms of the towers which are bathed by the waters of the moat belong to that fourteenth-century building, in spite of repairs to their facings over the centuries. The castle took the form of an irregular polygon approximately triangular in shape, punctuated by seven towers with a circular ground plan topped by ramparts with

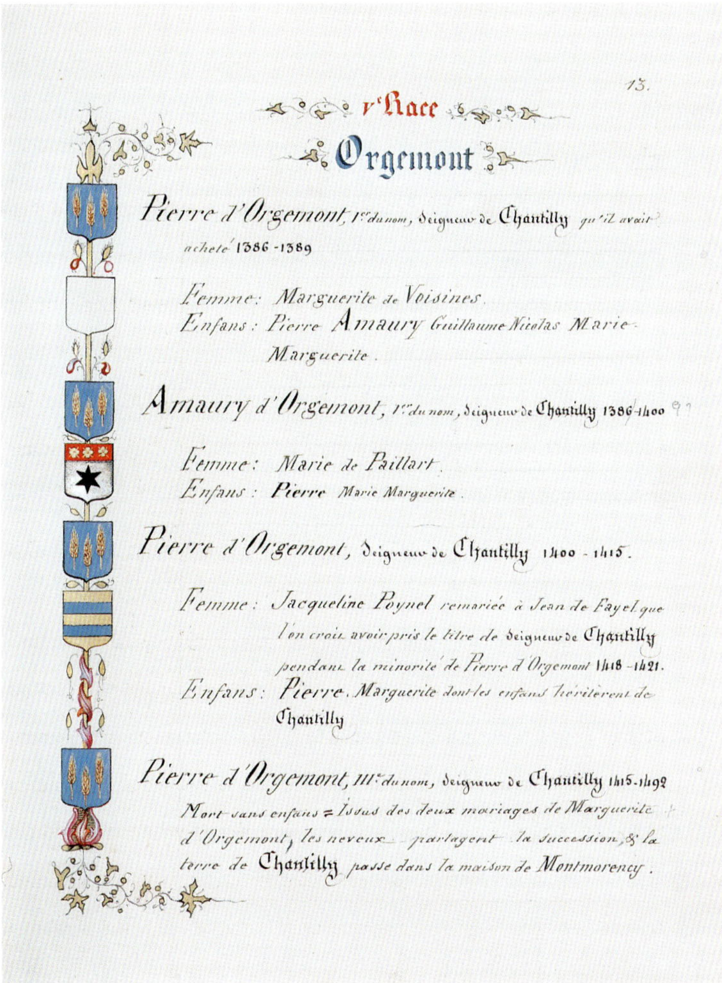

13.

1ʳᵉ Race

Orgemont

Pierre d'Orgemont, 1ᵉʳ du nom, seigneur de Chantilly qu'il avait acheté 1386-1389

Femme: Marguerite de Voisines.
Enfans: Pierre Amaury Guillaume Nicolas Marie Marguerite.

Amaury d'Orgemont, 1ᵉʳ du nom, seigneur de Chantilly 1386-1400

Femme: Marie de Paillart.
Enfans: Pierre Marie Marguerite.

Pierre d'Orgemont, seigneur de Chantilly 1400 - 1415.

Femme: Jacqueline Poynel remariée à Jean de Fayel que l'on croit avoir pris le titre de seigneur de Chantilly pendant la minorité de Pierre d'Orgemont 1418 - 1421.
Enfans: Pierre. Marguerite dont les enfans héritèrent de Chantilly

Pierre d'Orgemont, IIIᵉ du nom, seigneur de Chantilly 1415-1492

Mort sans enfans = Issus des deux mariages de Marguerite d'Orgemont, les neveux partagent la succession, & la terre de Chantilly passe dans la maison de Montmorency.

Arms of the d'Orgemonts

The last descendant of the fourteenth- and fifteenth-century lords of Chantilly was Pierre III d'Orgemont.

machicolations and crenellations under a conical roof. At the centre of the east face were two of these towers, forming the outer façade of a "keep", probably used as a place of residence by the lord; it had a straight façade on the side facing the court. It was in the lower part of the keep that the entranceway was arranged, controlled by a portcullis inserted behind a pointed equilateral arch that could be reached via a drawbridge from the rocky platform. Two further towers reinforced either end of the east face, later known as the Tour de Paris and the Tour du Connétable. The centre of the north façade was occupied by the Tour de Vineuil, and at its western extremity at the point of the acute angle was a small corbelled tower known as the Tour des Prisons. Finally, coming back round, in the middle of the south side one last tower had no doubt been preserved from the castle of the Bouteillers, backing on to the old chapel where services were conducted by "grey friars" (Franciscans).

Through the contracts for carpentry work we still know of the existence of two galleries and a "house that is over the stoves", arrangements that matched the new requirements for comfort in everyday castle life. A well was dug in the courtyard, at the foot of the Tour de Vineuil.

External access to the drawbridge and a symmetrical bridge leading to the road to Senlis was controlled from a fortified forecourt at the bottom of the mound, where the Paris road emerged; as we have said, it passed obliquely through the *viviers* or fishponds, as a causeway: on the right the "fishpond of the val de marchié" which we call the Étang de Sylvie, on the left the "fishpond behind the castle"[12], the pond encircling the low island where the Petit Château would later stand. The road to Picardy carried on northwards over a second causeway leading to Vineuil, which passed between the moats of the castle on the left and "the new pond along the park in the direction of the river" Nonette – later referred to as the Pièce du Serrurier – on the right.

Pierre and Amaury d'Orgemont had embarked on a major policy of acquisition to increase the size of their estate: Chavercy, Montjay, Vineuil, Saint-Firmin, Montgrésin. This was the first stage of the great expansion which would be pursued for the next six centuries, during which time no land was ever disposed of; in 1398 it took the form of the creation of a park enclosed by walls, work carried out by the mason Jean Quatrehommes.[13] To the west, an agreement reached with the monks of Saint-Leu made it possible to use the barn once it had been rebuilt. The castle could breathe, it had gained the vital space it needed. But insecurity threatened already. On Amaury's death in 1400, Chantilly went to his young son Pierre II, cup-bearer to the Duke of Burgundy, then to Pierre's widow Jacqueline Paynel after he was killed at Agincourt in 1415. When she wanted to claim custody of her niece, a rich heiress, it was quite useful to declare "that she is very well housed at the château of Chantilly, which is beautiful and strong". The war between the Armagnacs and the Burgundians raged in this region of tremendous strategic importance, and Chantilly passed from one camp to the other: it was handed over to the English-Burgundian side in 1421, but retaken in the name of Charles VII in 1430 by Antoine de Chabannes. Peace finally returned. Having no direct heirs, the last descendant of the d'Orgemont family, Pierre III, decided in 1484 to divide his property between his two nephews in his own lifetime, and Chantilly passed to his sister's son, Guillaume de Montmorency, who took up residence there straight away.[14]

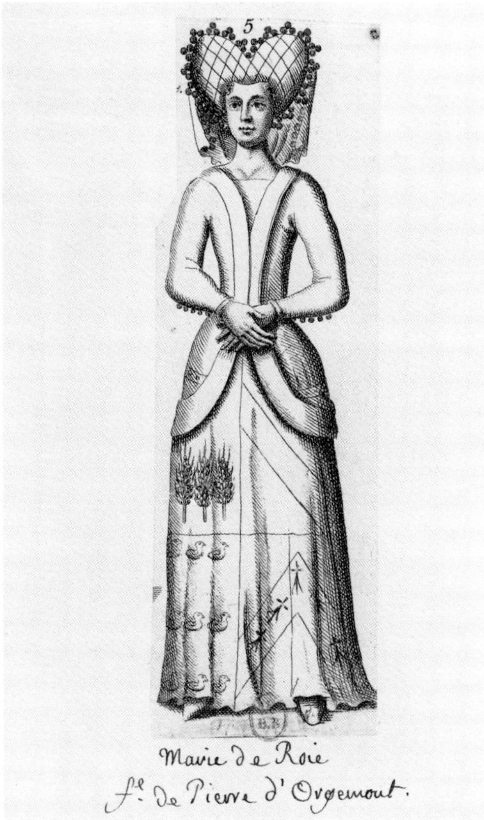

Marie de Roye
This recumbent statue adorned the tomb occupied by Marie de Roye and her husband Pierre III d'Orgemont in the Chapel of Our Lady at the church of the Cordeliers in Senlis. As their marriage, which took place in 1422, was childless, Chantilly passed to the Montmorencys.

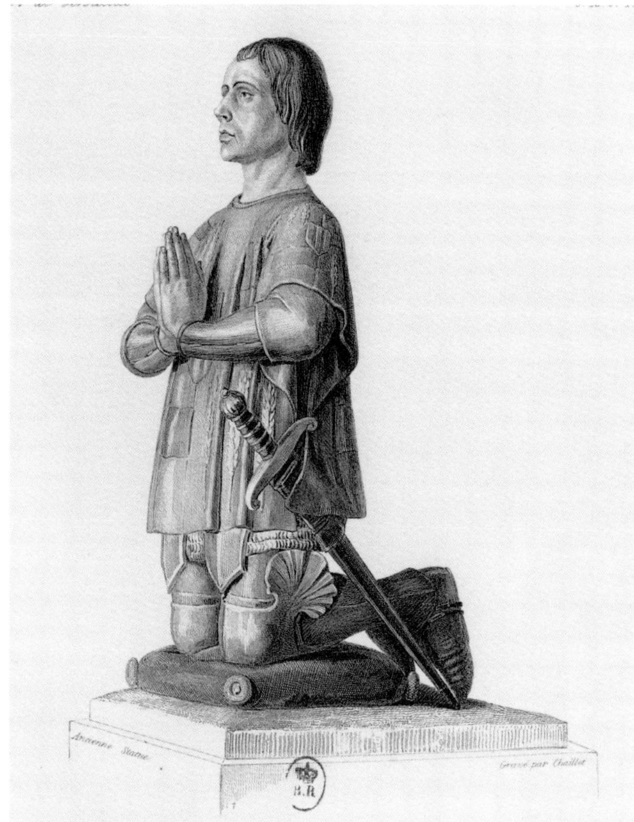

Pierre I d'Orgemont
This statue of the Chancellor once stood on his tomb in the d'Orgemont chapel in Sainte-Catherine-du-Val-des-Écoliers in Paris. The original has been lost, but the museum in Versailles has a casting.

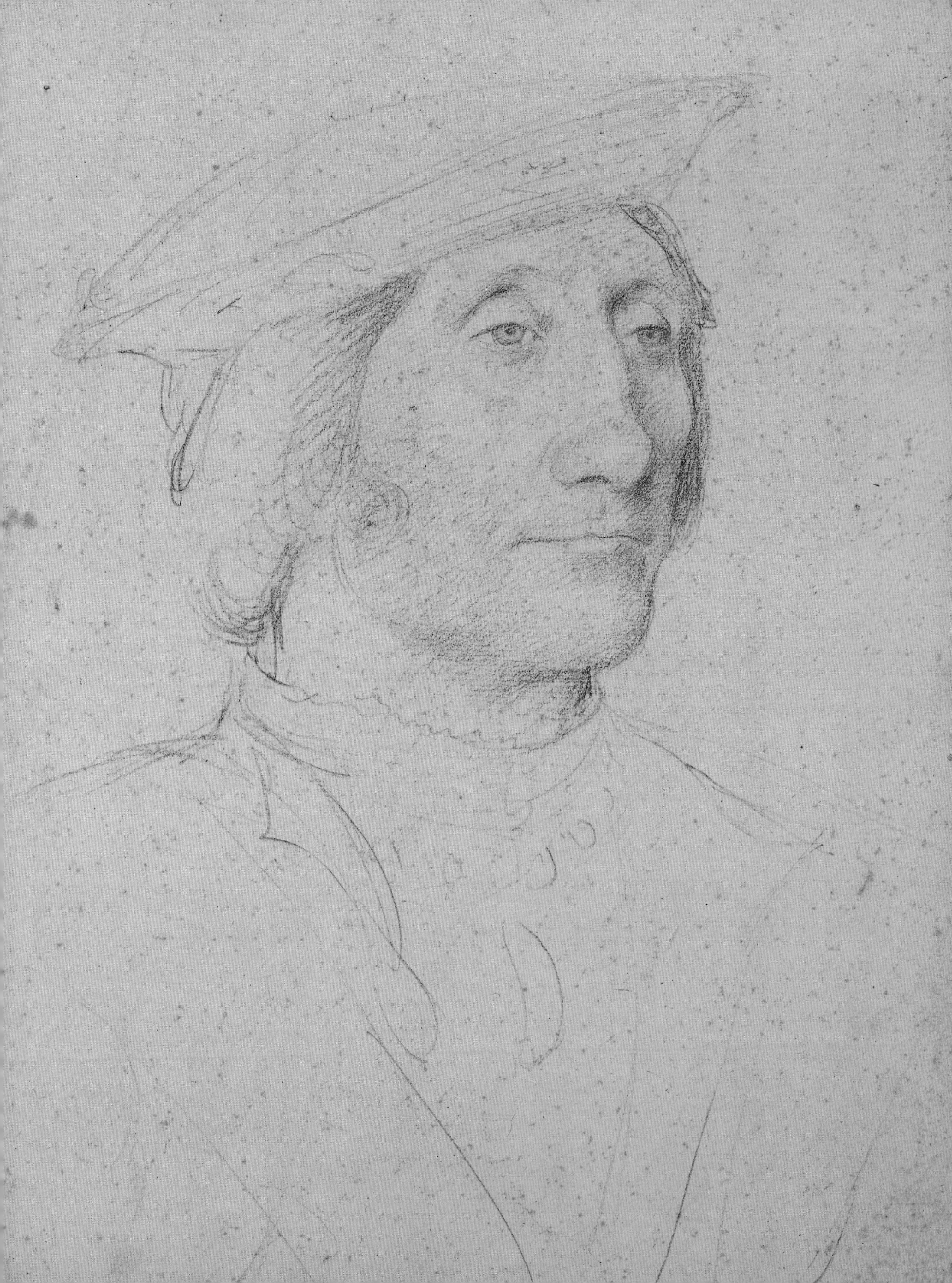

The Montmorency period

The foremost barons of France

It was once again a lineage originating from the northern fringe of the Île-de-France close to Picardy that took over at Chantilly in 1484, but a far more illustrious family than the Bouteillers of Senlis – not to mention the d'Orgemonts with their recent bourgeois origins. The Montmorencys were one of the oldest and most famous feudal houses in France. From the time of Bouchard le Barbu – who emerged in 1005 as a close associate of King Robert the Pious, who made him a gift of Montmorency castle – throughout the Middle Ages, members of the family had held the highest offices at the French court: four Constables, one Cupbearer, one Gentleman of the Bedchamber, one Grand Chamberlain, one Grand Pantler, one Field-Marshal, one Governor of Picardy. One of the Constables, Matthieu I, married the widow of King Louis VI, while another, Matthieu II, was the main force behind the victory of Bouvines; Charles I was the godfather of the child who became King Charles VI, and Jean II fought alongside Joan of Arc. In 1472, displeased with his elder sons who had sided with the Burgundians, Jean II transferred the barony of Montmorency and the lordship of Écouen to his youngest son Guillaume. Twelve years later Guillaume added Chantilly and its dependencies – given to him by his uncle Pierre d'Orgemont – to his possessions, then the magnificent Burgundian estates assigned to him by his brother-in-law René Pot: La Rochepot, Châteauneuf, Thorey… These gifts enabled him to occupy a leading position in the kingdom. After accompanying Charles VIII on the first Italian expedition, Guillaume de Montmorency provided the most dependable support to Queen Anne of Brittany during Louis XII's expedition, as he did later to Louise of Savoy when she was acting as Regent while Francis I was held captive. As the general administrator of a financial district and governor of several royal castles, he showed extraordinary vitality right up to his death in 1531 at the age of eighty. He was both

Guillaume de Montmorency
This portrait in the Musée Condé at Chantilly is attributed to Jean Clouet. It depicts the nephew and heir of Pierre III d'Orgemont.

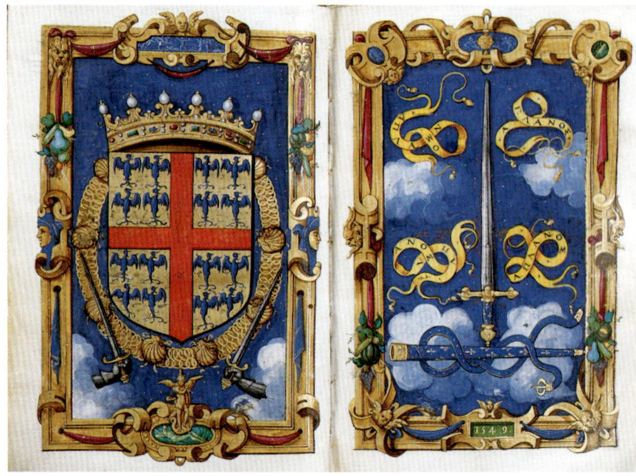

Livre d'heures du connétable de Montmorency
On the left is the coat of arms of the Montmorencys, the cross gules surrounded by the famous "alerions" (the sixteen imperial eagles won at the battles of Soissons and Bouvines), and on the right the sword of the Constable of France standing in pale, with the mottoes chosen by Anne.

a passionately keen huntsman and a sophisticated scholar, amassing a very rich library at Chantilly, the first in a distinguished line of libraries. As early as 1522, as was customary in great families, he divided his possessions in his own lifetime between his two remaining sons, Anne and François, but throughout his life he continued to preside with keen enthusiasm over the preservation and enrichment of the family fortune. At Chantilly, which continued to be his main residence, in 1494 he bought the ruins of the farm of Bucamp, along with the land now forming the Pelouse and the meadows lying between the castle and Vineuil. At the castle he demolished the old chapel of the Bouteillers of Senlis in 1507, replacing it with a new sanctuary dedicated to St James and St Christopher, embellished with two stained glass windows on one of which he was depicted with his five sons, while his wife Anne Pot was featured on the other with their three daughters.[1] It is not known whether the work he undertook stopped there. The buildings adjoining the chapel to the south occupying the tip of the triangle to the west, as we see them depicted in the seventeenth-century drawings[2], appear to be in a Late Gothic style in the Flamboyant manner, which might well mean they should be attributed to the work carried out by Guillaume de Montmorency in the period 1490-1510[3], contrary to the evidence of Sauval quoted above, which suggests they dated from a century earlier, to the time of Pierre d'Orgemont. These buildings occupied the best position in the castle in terms of air, view, and peace and quiet for those living there, and it may be surmised that Guillaume had his accommodation there; in any case that is where his successors were lodged, first and foremost his grandson Constable Henri in the early seventeenth century: his bedroom overlooked the Jardin de la Volière on one side, and the meadow stretching towards Vineuil on the other.[4]

The chapel of Chantilly
For the building he erected in 1882, Honoré Daumet drew inspiration from the chapel of Écouen and had the masterpieces that had been torn out of it at the French Revolution reinstalled: the altar, the wood panelling and the stained glass panels depicting the Constable's sons on one side, and his wife and daughters on the other.

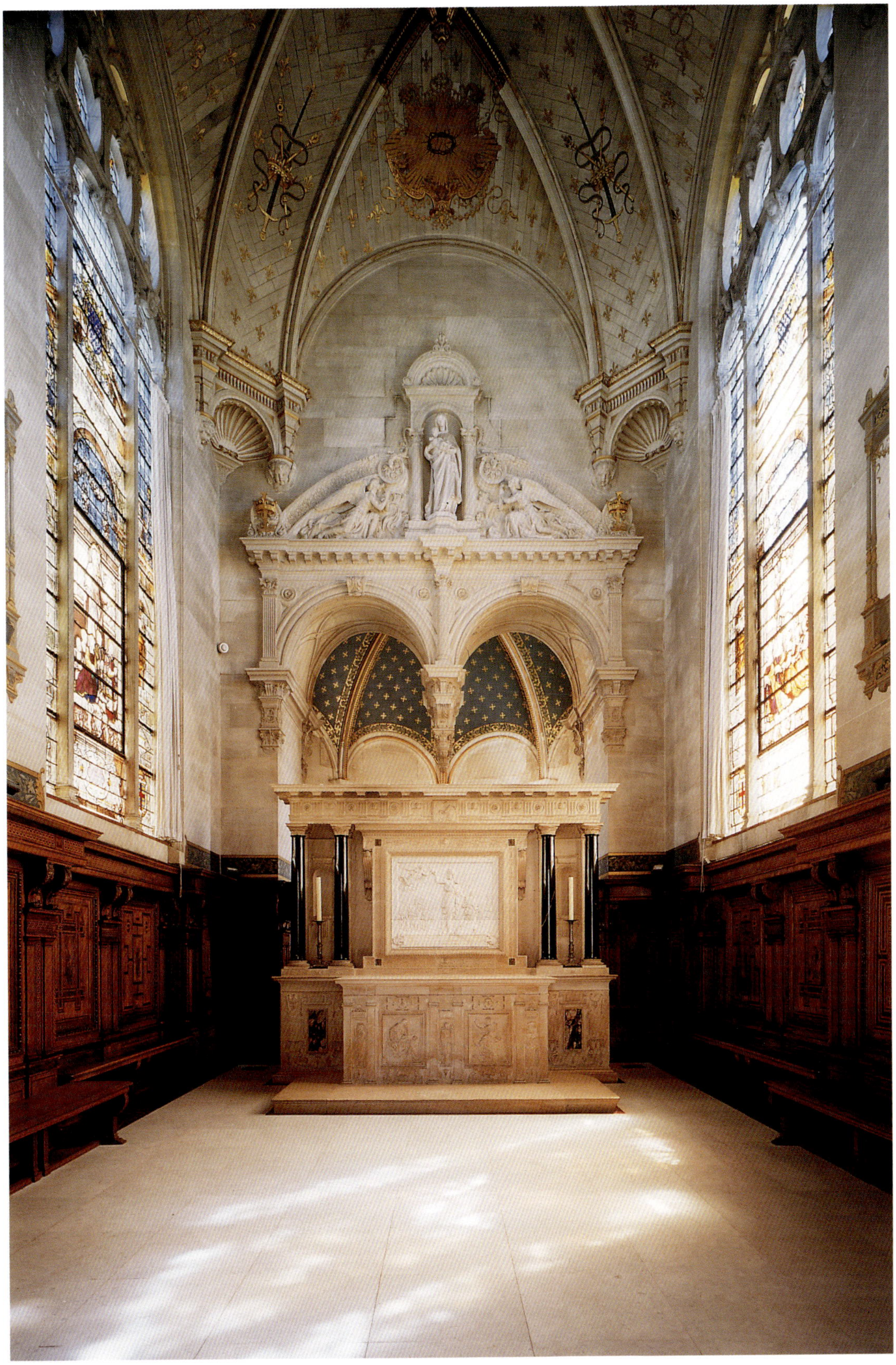

Anne de Montmorency, a Renaissance prince

Destiny had reserved an eminent place in the history of his century for Anne de Montmorency, even more than for his father. Throughout his career, marked by a close familiarity with his kings which brought him a succession of favours and falls from grace, Anne established himself as the foremost statesman in the kingdom, in particular at the end of his life when he became the main person to whom Catherine de' Medici turned to save the monarchy, during the disastrous religious conflicts that were bathing the country in blood.[5]

Born at Montmorency – or Chantilly? – on 15 March 1493, the godson of Queen Anne whose Christian name he bore, he spent his childhood in his father's castles at Chantilly and Écouen before going on to the royal château at Amboise, where he was educated alongside the future King Francis I under the attentive eye of Louise of Savoy, so forming a youthful bond that guaranteed his career. On his mother's death in 1510 he enrolled as a volunteer in the troops leaving for Italy, and fought at Marignano. He then experienced a lightning rise: Gentleman of the Bedchamber in 1514, First Equerry to the king – an office that enabled him to be very close to the sovereign – in 1520, then Field-Marshal and Knight of St Michael in 1522, the year when he came into possession of Chantilly. Through gifts, purchases, confiscation and legacies, Anne amassed a huge estate, a virtual principality spread right across France, from the Île-de-France to Berry, from Burgundy to Normandy, 600 fiefdoms, 130 castles, properties and lordships, four town houses in Paris…

His political authority and immense wealth enabled him to be at the forefront of the great builders in France, and each of his promotions triggered a new campaign of improvements at his many castles. His choice of architects and the originality of the schemes he called for reveal him as a man of enlightened, modern personal tastes, fully worthy of a Renaissance prince. However, his military or diplomatic activities constantly kept him away from his estates, and even from the kingdom, and he had to conduct his business from a distance by calling on men he could trust, first and foremost his father.

Anne de Montmorency as a young man
In this magnificent likeness from 1514 attributed to Jean Clouet, one of the treasures from the collection of graphic portraits by the Clouets and their followers held at Chantilly (362 items), the young hero has all the good looks and ardour of a 21-year-old.

The first building work - The gardens - The Galerie des Cerfs

The first operations undertaken by the future Constable at Chantilly related to the gardens. This is normal procedure and there is nothing surprising about it: before tackling the building the gardens are created and they in turn influence

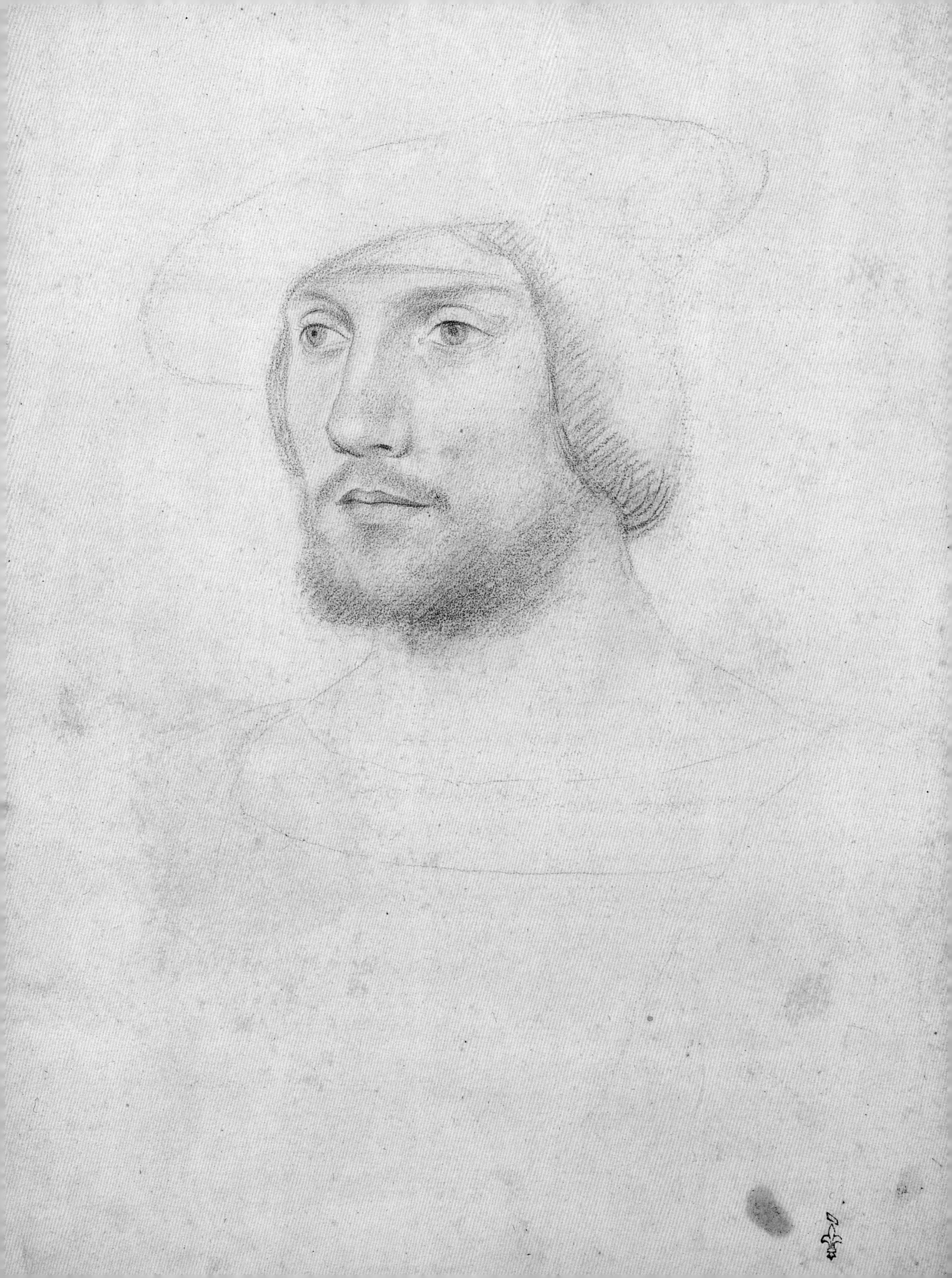

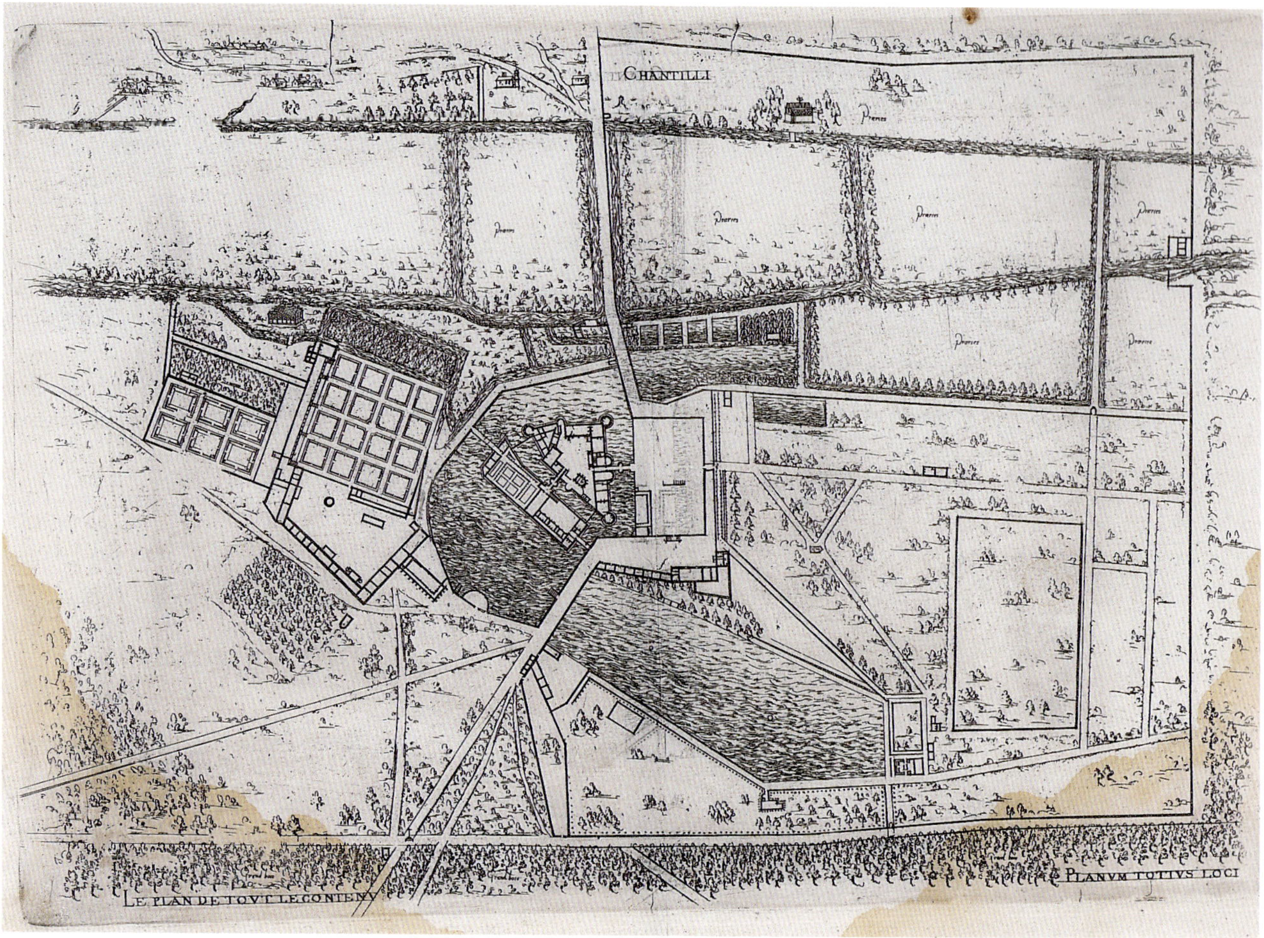

The site of Chantilly
In the centre of this engraving from the *Plus Excellents Bastiments de France* by Jacques Androuet Du Cerceau (1579) can be seen the road from Paris to Picardy, skirting the chapel of the Montmorency's château.

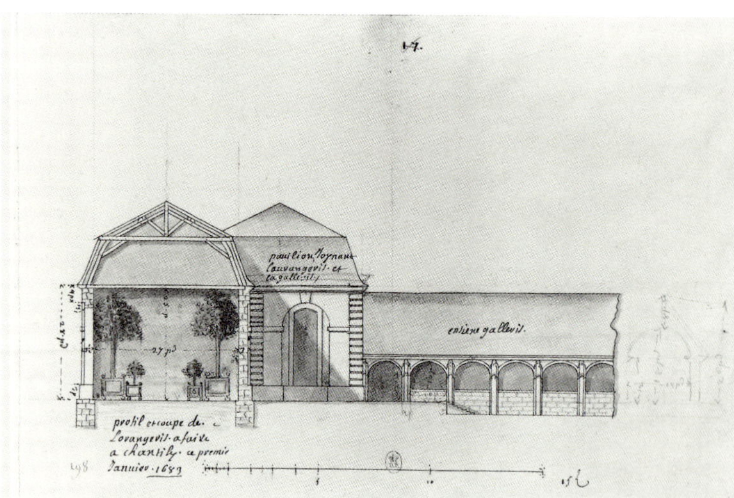

The Galerie des Cerfs
This drawing for the Orangerie produced by Jules Hardouin-Mansart's office (1683) shows on the right an elevation and section of the gallery constructed by Anne de Montmorency from 1524 to 1530.

the architecture. At this period in the early sixteenth century, ever since Charles VIII had returned from Naples dazzled by all he had seen on the shores of the Mediterranean, gardens were more fashionable than they had ever been, even in the days of King René of Anjou. Among the artists and skilled craftsmen the king had brought back to France was a gardener, Pacello da Mercogliano, who was immediately asked to work at Amboise and Blois for the king, and at Gaillon for his powerful minister, Cardinal Georges d'Amboise. At Amboise it was possible to design new parterres directly beside the buildings erected by Charles VIII, but at Blois and Gaillon the smallness of the castle site made it necessary to plant the gardens beyond the fortified mound, choosing a position where they could be seen very well from the living quarters. It was this option that was adopted by Guillaume de Montmorency at Chantilly, on behalf of his son Anne.

On the other side of the water opposite the buildings on the west tip of the triangle, which as we have seen probably housed the rooms used by the master of the house, was the meadow of the former farm of Bucamp which had just been bought back from the monks. The flat, open space lent itself to being laid out as a large, square garden; the ground plan engraved by Du Cerceau enables us to visualise the sixteen regular squares arranged like a chessboard, separated by a network of perpendicular paths, with the central intersection widened by a section cut out from each square. As both a pleasure garden and one used to grow produce, in 1524 it was planted with white mulberry, plum, cherry and apricot trees ordered from Normandy and Languedoc. To shield it from the wind, close the view opposite the castle and make it pleasanter to walk in, the construction of an arcaded gallery was undertaken at the same time, shutting the garden off to the west. Work had begun in March 1524, and Francis I probably visited the site the following month when he went there to hunt stags, so inaugurating the ever-rising number of visits made by kings to Chantilly, even in its owner's absence, to enjoy the beauty of the spot and take advantage of its outstanding hunting. Serious events soon put an end to the period of euphoria that had marked the beginning of the reign. Confronted by Emperor Charles V and defeated at Pavia in 1525, Francis I turned out not to be the invincible hero people had liked to think him at the time of Marignano. The king's captivity was reminiscent of the sad days of King John, and plunged the kingdom into consternation, putting the devotion and capabilities of his most loyal of all comrades, Anne

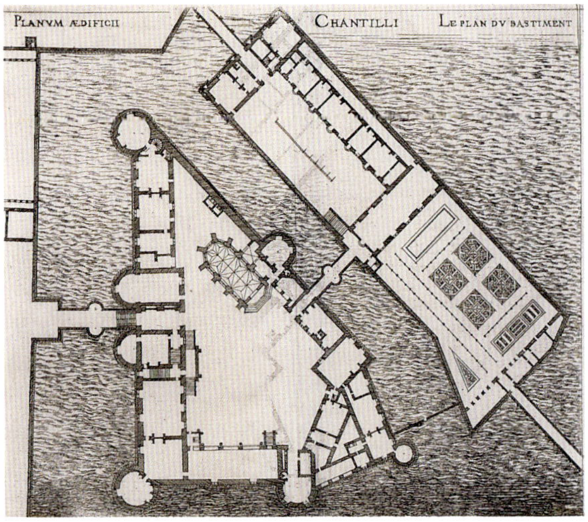

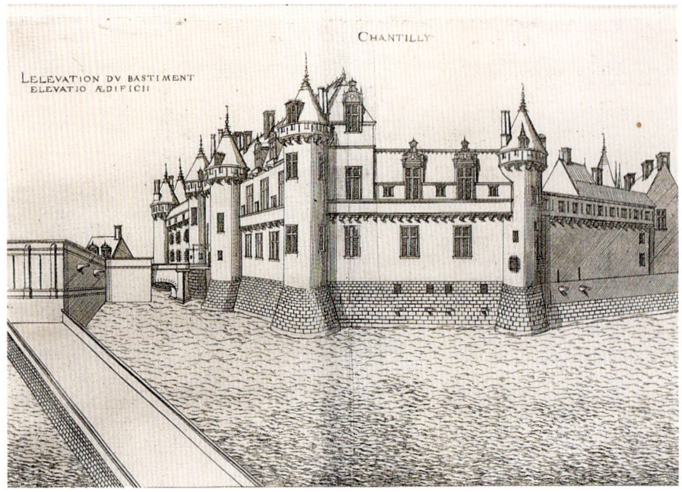

The ground plan of the two châteaux
This engraving by Jacques Androuet Du Cerceau shows the wide moat separating the old triangular château rebuilt by Pierre Chambiges and the Petit Château designed by Jean Bullant on its rectangular island.

The north façade of the Grand Château
The engraving by Jacques Androuet Du Cerceau has the same orientation as the ground plan beside it, with the north facing the viewer. On the left, the entrance wing and drawbridge; on the right, the gallery as far as the Tour de Vineuil and the Tour des Prisons.

The main court
From left to right: the gallery, the spiral staircase, the new residential block, the loggia, the back of the entrance keep, the chapel, and the wing overlooking the moat. Engraving by Jacques Androuet Du Cerceau, 1579.

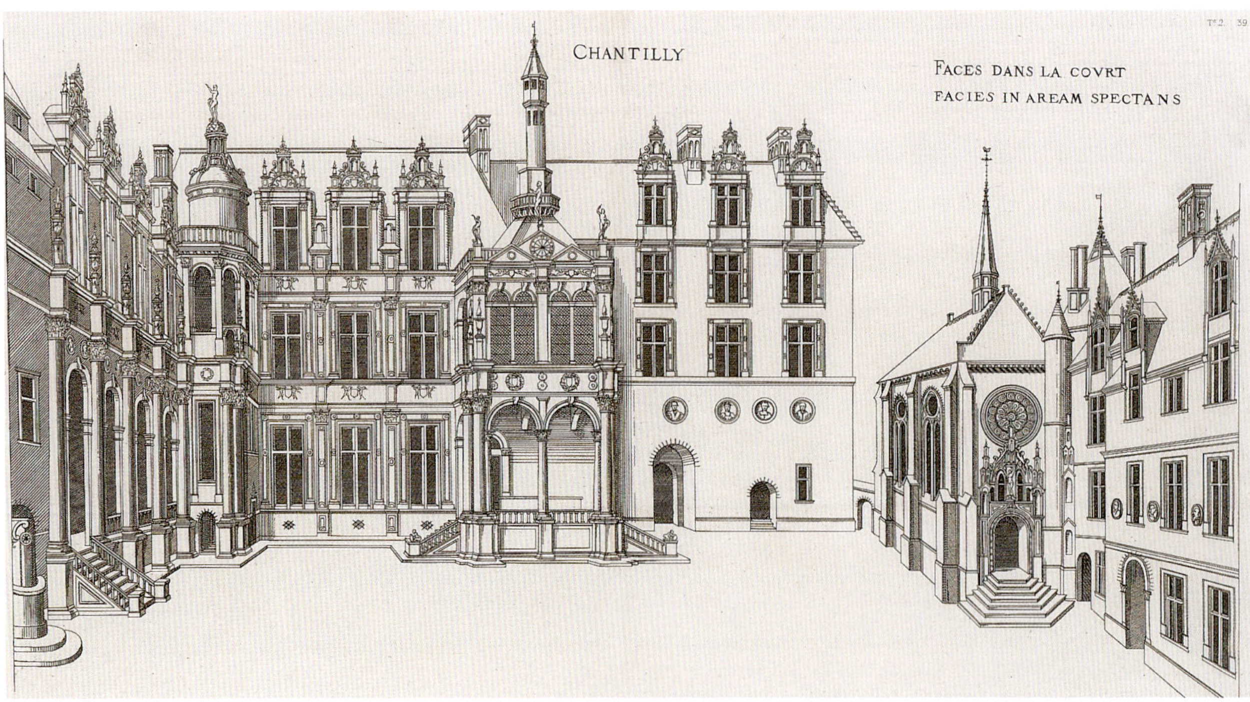

de Montmorency, to the test. After accompanying the king to his prison in Madrid, Anne negotiated the terms for his release – the captivity of the young royal princes until the Treaty of Madrid was implemented – and at the same time laid the foundations of an alliance with England in order to restore France's position within Europe. He made a brilliant job of these ticklish tasks and in 1526 the king, who was not ungrateful, appointed him Grand Master of France and Governor of Languedoc. The first of these titles gave him overall authority over the king's household, artistic commissions and work in the royal buildings – Fontainebleau and Saint-Germain, for example – while the second marked the start of the Montmorency's involvement in the south; they would be detained there for a long time by the duties of their office, and were to play a crucial role. As a third signal favour, Anne was admitted into the king's family circle through his marriage to Madeleine of Savoy, the daughter of Louise of Savoy's brother, and a first cousin of Francis I. The wedding, celebrated in the presence of the entire court at Saint-Germain-en-Laye in January 1527, was final confirmation of the high esteem in which the great favourite was held.

That same year work at Chantilly was resumed: it related to the "gallery and house in the garden of Bucamp" which was completed in 1530. This was inserted between two pleasure pavilions, one of them paved with tiles made of Rouen faience[6] to add to its attractions, the other assigned to "boilers and baths".[7] The walls of the gallery were decorated with cynegetic (hunting) scenes, all the rage in the similar buildings at Blois, Gaillon or the ducal castle at Nancy and especially justified at Chantilly: here stags could be seen depicted in a natural manner by a painter called Martin de Meilles, their heads fitted with real antlers – the search to track down the finest specimens extended as far as Germany.[8] The Galerie des Cerfs continued in existence until 1785; a seventeenth-century drawing[9] enables us to picture the basket arches and pillars with their Gothic mouldings. Nearby stood a close tennis court built beside the pond in 1527-29, a heronry opposite the Jardin de la Volière[10], as well as the agricultural buildings associated with the farm and lodgings for household servants.

In 1527, a year of euphoria, the decision was made partially to reconstruct the castle, as we learn from a letter from Pierre de Garges, the steward at Chantilly, who assisted Guillaume de Montmorency with the building work. On 9 August, stones were quarried to "work on the keep". Availing himself

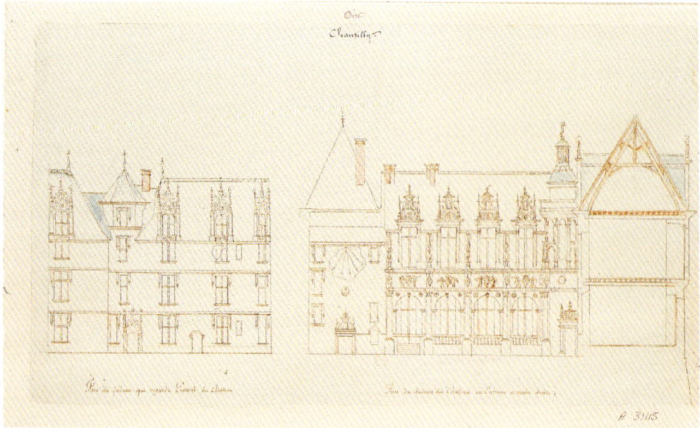

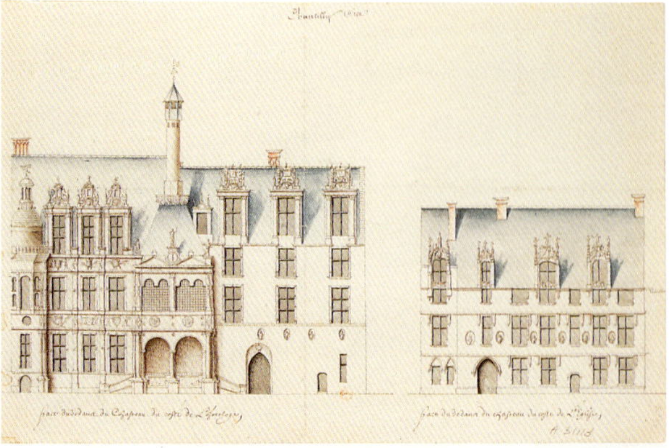

The buildings on the court, to the west and north
This drawing shows the state of the château before 1687: on the left, the buildings in the Flamboyant style occupying the tip of the triangle, with their staircase tower; on the right, the back of the Tour de Vineuil, decorated with a sundial, and Chambiges's gallery.

The buildings on the court, to the east and south
On the left stand the spiral staircase, the new residential block, the loggia with its clock and campanile, then the back of the keep; on the right, the building that went along the south moat, beside the chapel (state prior to 1687).

of his authority as Grand Master, Anne made sure of the collaboration of royal experts to oversee his construction sites – Villeroy, the Financial Secretary, and Jean Grolier, Treasurer of France; it was the latter, a distinguished book-lover, who in October sent him the estimate "for the building you wish to have erected at the lodge at your gateway at Chantilly". But until then the Montmorencys had only ever called on local masons who followed normal practice and the traditional way of doing things. A mistake had been made in building the gallery; it was pointed out on 27 September 1527 in a letter from the bishop of Soissons, M. d'Iverny, who added sententiously: "It would be a good idea for you to have some knowledgeable masons come and see what your people are doing." The lesson was heeded. The time for architects and new art had finally arrived at Chantilly, just as at had at Fontainebleau, which Francis I was starting to modernise at the same time, beginning as at Chantilly with the irregular court of the old castle, the Cour Ovale.

Chantilly III - Pierre Chambiges's work at the Old Château

In spite of his offices at court and the various missions which kept him far from home, it did not take Anne long to decide on his architect. At Senlis cathedral in the immediate vicinity, Pierre Chambiges[11] was continuing building in the manner of his father Martin, whose work could be seen at the cathedrals of Sens, Beauvais and Troyes. It was his name that was chosen for the reconstruction of Chantilly, and the patronage of the Grand Master was soon to enable him to attract royal commissions. Appointed master builder to the city of Paris, he was entrusted with building the Hôtel de Ville (based on plans by Domenico da Cortona), then with building Francis I's châteaux at Saint-Germain-en-Laye, Fontainebleau (the Cour du Cheval Blanc) and La Muette.

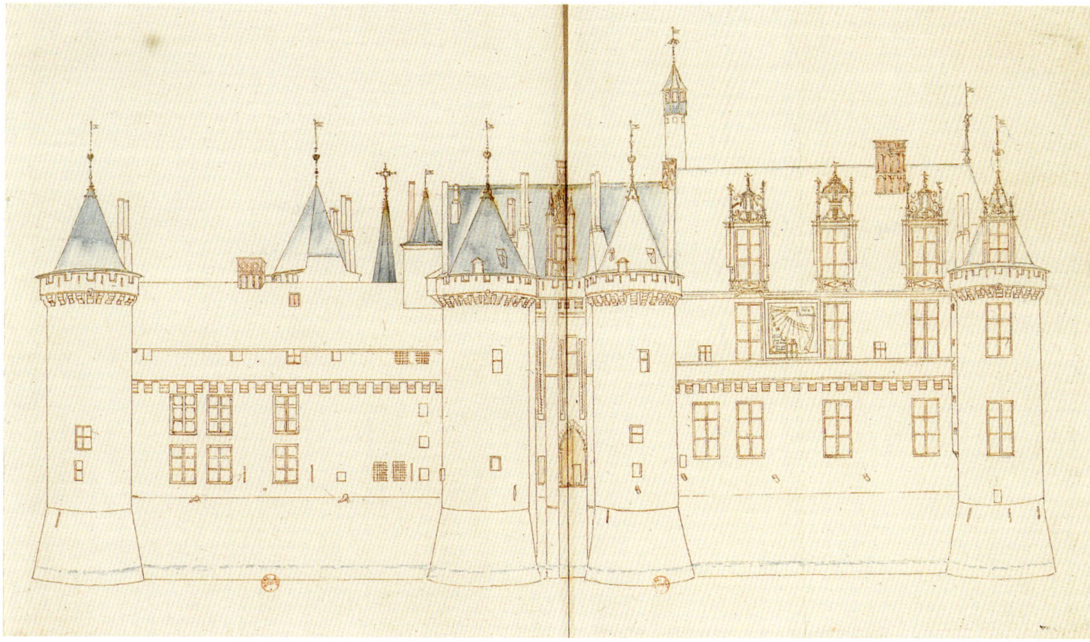

The entrance façade, facing east
From left to right can be seen the Tour des Cuisines (or Tour de Paris), an old residential block, the keep and its two towers, the residential block rebuilt by Chambiges, decorated with a sundial, and the Tour du Connétable (state prior to 1687).

The south façade facing the moat of the Petit Château
This drawing shows, from left to right, the Tour Rouge (or Tour des Prisons), several residential blocks occupying the west tip of the triangle, the drawbridge to the Petit Château, the south tower, the chapel and the curtain wall along to the Tour des Cuisines (state prior to 1687). Two more sundials adorn these façades.

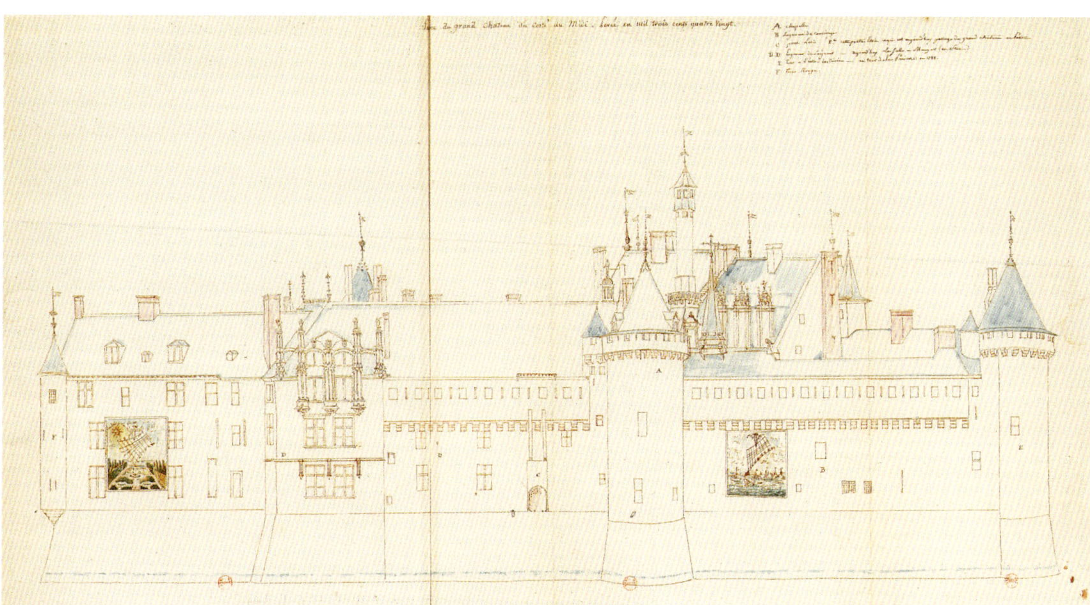

At Chantilly, Chambiges's presence was first mentioned on 10 February 1528. The building work started with the "keep", i.e. the two towers and the entrance block, and Anne spent the summer and autumn on the spot to oversee its completion. Work carried on until 1530 in accordance with a well-defined programme: the towers were preserved, and residential blocks were built between them, using the old curtain walls as external walls. First of all a residential wing was built north of the keep, extending as far as the corner tower (the Tour du Connétable), then another building containing an open gallery with columns was erected along the northern rampart. The letters sent by Guillaume and Grolier make it possible to follow progress at the site in detail, until the letter of 28 October 1530, where the completion of the perron of the staircase is broached: "You will find it beautiful, and quite different from the masonry-work you have seen up to now." All the writer's delight at the novelty of the solution shines through these words. Externally, that novelty was perceptible only in the tracery of the high dormers with semi-circular pediments topped by niches, but internally all the gracefulness of the early Renaissance was spread over the wings round the triangular court, which really needed to be brightened up.

By combining the engraved views by Du Cerceau and the drawings from the Bibliothèque Nationale[12], we are fortunate enough to be able to reconstruct all the buildings in our mind's eye. On the east side the entrance keep had only been spruced up by the insertion of new openings, fitted out with dormers and decorated chimney stacks, and embellished on its lower parts with antique medallions or copies of antiquities, always a convenient procedure for adapting an old building to the taste of the day. Numerous examples of this can be found in the Loire area (Meillant, Le Lude), Normandy (Gaillon, Fontaine-Henry), Île-de-France (Sarcus) or much further afield (Pau). But in this case the addition was more particularly appropriate, given Anne de Montmorency's very strong love of antiquities, a taste he developed during the time he spent in Italy and which led him while Governor of Languedoc to issue instructions for the preservation of the antiquities at Nîmes through an order promulgated in 1548. It was probably those medallions he was referring to in a letter he addressed to Cardinal Du Bellay in July 1535, when the cardinal was on a mission to Italy: "I must not forget to let you know that I have had all my heads and medals arranged at Chantilly, and it is really marvellous to see them; but there are still some empty spaces; you know what I mean, and you will please

me greatly if while you are over there you would like to help me fill them."[13]
To the left of the keep, Chambiges erected the grand set piece that gave the court all its character, projecting from the normal building line; Anne followed its construction attentively. This aedicule consisting of two bays – on the ground floor housing a large perron with straight flights on either side giving access to the principal staircase inserted inside the main building, and on the upper floor containing a wide, open loggia – was liberally decorated with columns, pilasters, candelabras and statues. Two twin pediments framed a clock, the matrimonial coats of arms of the Montmorencys adorned the supports, and a high lantern roof topped the building like a beacon. The idea for this pavilion, handled as a projecting bay and establishing the move away from the large projecting staircase towers of the previous age, was probably borrowed by the architect from a more modest arrangement, still Gothic in spirit, that can be seen not far from Chantilly at Nantouillet, the château of Antoine Duprat, Chancellor of France.[14]
Continuing towards the left, we come to the new building, three bays in length and richly decorated using the articulation seen on the façades of Chambord, pilasters, casement windows opening above a double band of mouldings and high dormers topped by niches.[15] The escutcheons of France repeated on the two upper storeys suggest that this building was intended to house the royal apartments. At the corner a spiral staircase is located in a small tower decorated with columns and pilasters; its ground plan alters subtly from one level to the next, square on the ground floor, octagonal on the first, and circular for the culminating *tempietto* which juts out above the roof behind the balustrade. This graceful arrangement was repeated in precise detail by Chambiges for Francis I in the courtyard at Saint-Germain-en-Laye, where it can still be seen.
On the north wing with which the staircase turret is articulated we can admire another architectural set piece, a gallery at raised ground-floor level, with four round arches opening off it, and above it a storey of high partial dormers – i.e. dormers that intersect the cornice – decorated like those on the previous building, and separated by candelabras. Anne had given instructions for the old curtain wall on the north to be broken through and two casement windows inserted to bring air and daylight not only to the gallery, but the whole courtyard, which thus benefited from an unusual effect of transparency towards the outside world, an indication of the modern ideas of the master of

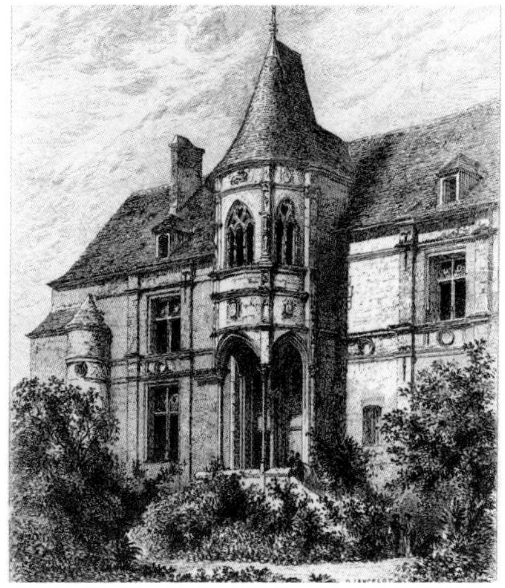

The loggia of the château of Nantouillet
It houses the chapel on the first floor, and on the ground floor provides access from the residential block to the garden.

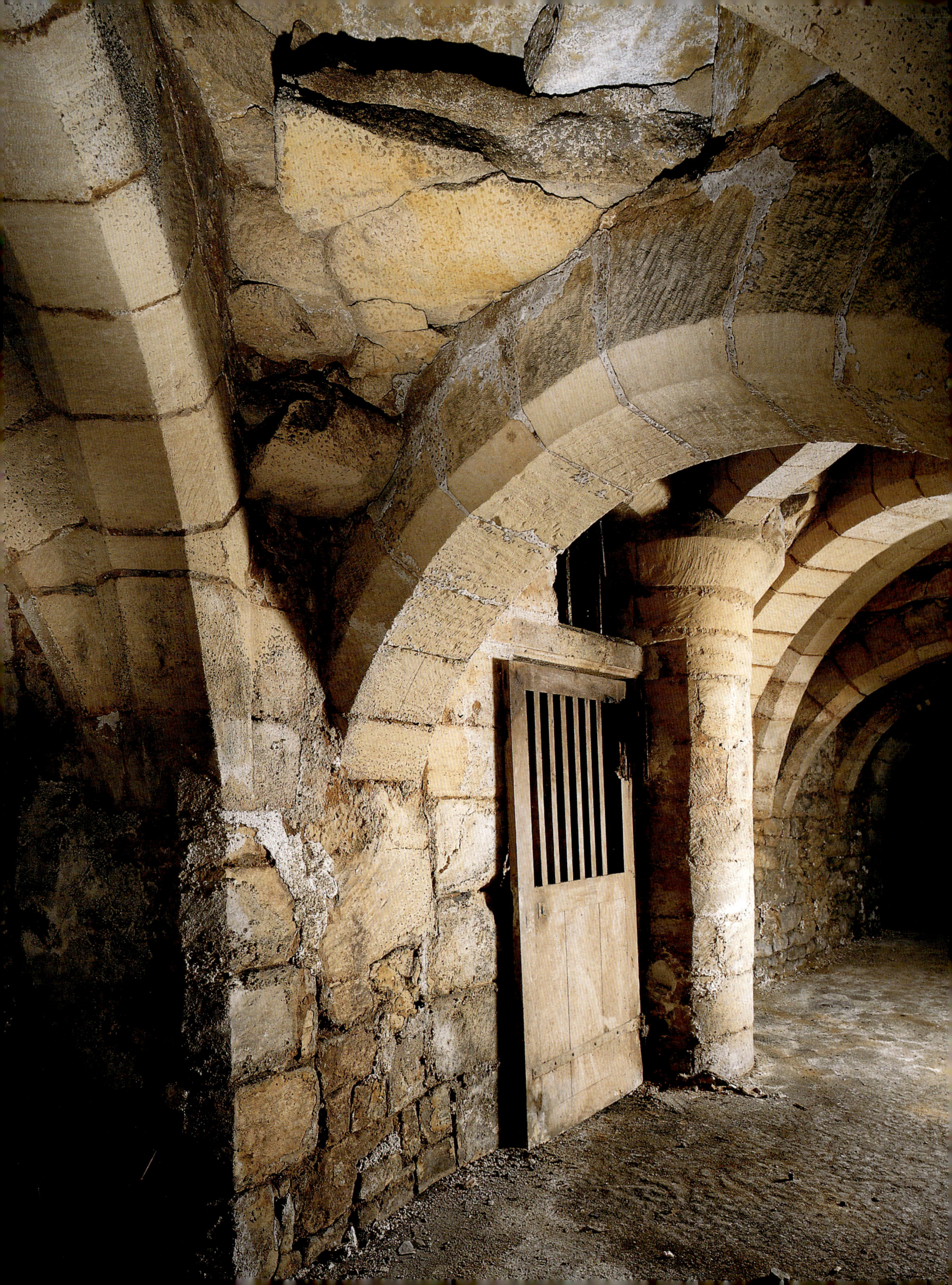

the house. A letter from Grolier dated 23 September 1530 informs us that his opinion was also sought regarding the handling of the columns on the gallery and the perron, "some of which are full, and the others fluted lengthways, the grooves as wide as the fillets, and you only have to say if you want them all to be the same, or one worked, and the other not, which can still be done". Further on was a large gable decorated with a sundial corresponding to the Tour de Vineuil, overhanging the well which was useful to the nearby kitchen; then to the west and south the succession of buildings in the Gothic style already described, which were preserved; then the passage towards the bridge leading across the moat to the low island; next the reverse side of the south tower; and finally the 1507 chapel.

All that remains of Chambiges's work today is the invisible part, the great network of "cellars, storerooms and pantries" that was dug out of the rock below the courtyard in 1529. Du Cerceau did not fail to mention them in the commentary on his engravings: "two-storey cellars more reminiscent in their organisation of a labyrinth than a cellar, there are so many corridors leading between them, all vaulted". Grolier had also taken care of procuring for his friend, detained in Bayonne to negotiate the release of the king's sons, all that was needed to fit out the house: decorated windows and furniture ordered from Paris, tapestries from Antwerp, and so on. By the summer of 1530 everything was ready to provide a princely reception for the Countess of Nassau, then another for the imperial ambassador, soon to be followed by Francis I in 1531, one month before the death of Guillaume de Montmorency, and in 1540 by Emperor Charles V himself.

Throughout this time the improvements continued. Anne wanted to alter the inconvenient layout of the arrival which made it necessary for both his visitors and those using the Picardy road – known as the Route des Postes – to scale the rocky spur. A mason from Senlis, Jean Choquet, was given the job of cutting and flattening it to turn it into terrace of a very roughly rectangular shape, with stone-built side walls (contract dated 21 May 1538). This terrace was reached from the south side by a staircase with a perron leading up to it. As for the road, it was re-routed and passed to the right of the terrace at a lower level, under an arch that was symmetrical to the one on the drawbridge from the castle leading to the wooded park[16] and the road to Senlis: a crucial decision that anticipated the grand scheme by Le Nôtre. A little later Anne and

Pierre Chambiges's cellars
"He is working hard on the vaults of the storerooms and cellars and they will soon be closed over" (23 September 1529). Beneath the courtyard of the Old château, the network of galleries is roofed with bonded arches propping up the rocky ground.

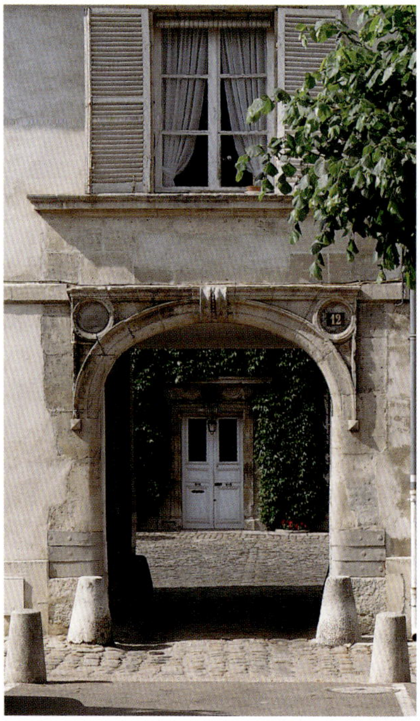

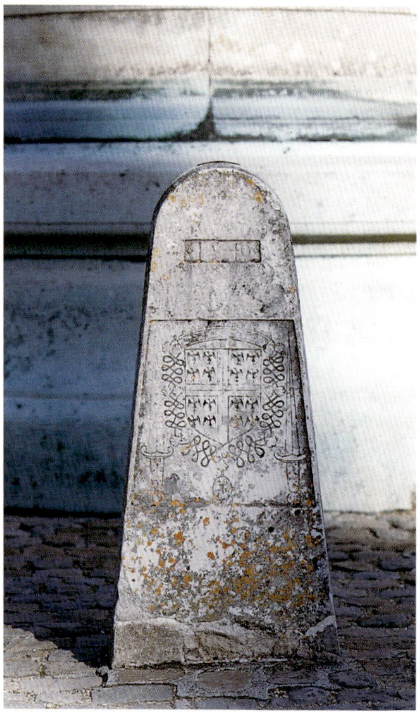

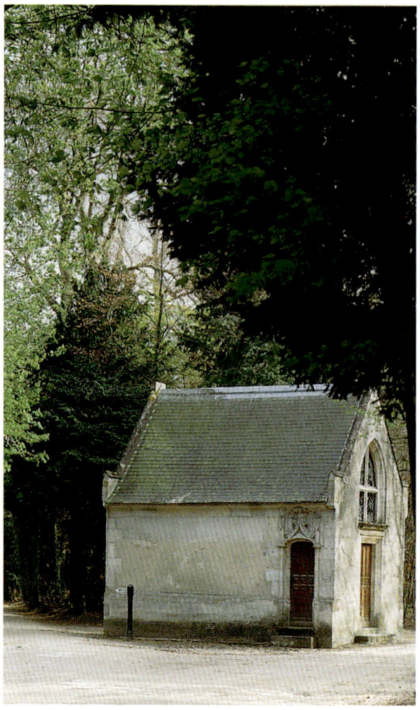

Three reminders of the Constable at Chantilly
On the left, the Hôtel de Beauvais, built in the town in 1540 at the spot where the territory of the bishopric of Beauvais started (12, rue du Connétable); in the centre, one of the boundary stones of the estate with the Constable's arms; on the right, the chapel of Saint-Paul (c. 1535) behind the château of Enghien.

his wife gave proof of their piety by setting up a Roman-style pilgrimage on his estate, with stations in seven chapels constructed by Chambiges; the pilgrimage was endowed with indulgences through papal bull issued by Paul III and Julius III. Four of these chapels are still in existence, Sainte-Croix on the Pelouse, Saint-Paul behind the château of Enghien, Saint-Jean rebuilt in the park, and Saint-Pierre incorporated into a house at Vineuil.[17]

The Petit Château by Jean Bullant - A manifesto of new architecture

Not content with transforming Chantilly, Montmorency had given instructions for major improvements at his other residences during his years in favour, first at Écouen where rebuilding started in 1538, the illustrious year when he was made Constable of France, and at the same time at Fère-en-Tardenois, which had been Francis I's wedding present. However it was the splendour of Chantilly that was widely recognised. To give a comparative idea of the beauty of the Abbey of Thélème, in the first edition of *Gargantua* Rabelais chose only Bonnivet castle in Poitou, but in the 1542 edition he declared his abbey to be "a hundred times more magnificent than Bonnivet, Chambord or Chantilly". By then Montmorency had fallen from favour with the king. The policy of rapprochement with the Holy Roman Empire which he had appositely

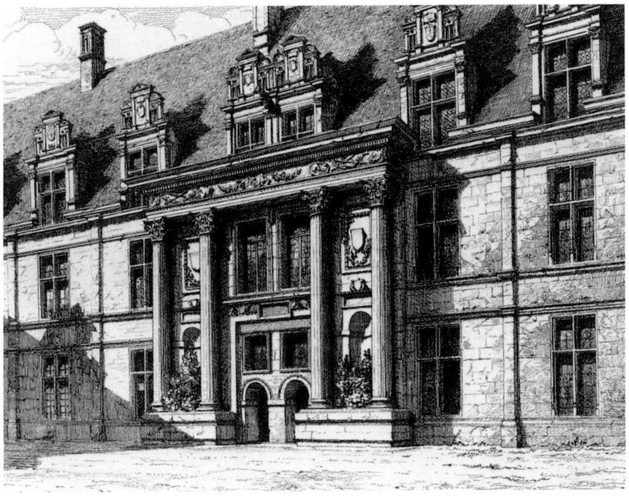

Portico of the château of Écouen
The large portico in the colossal order of the château of Écouen is Jean Bullant's masterpiece.

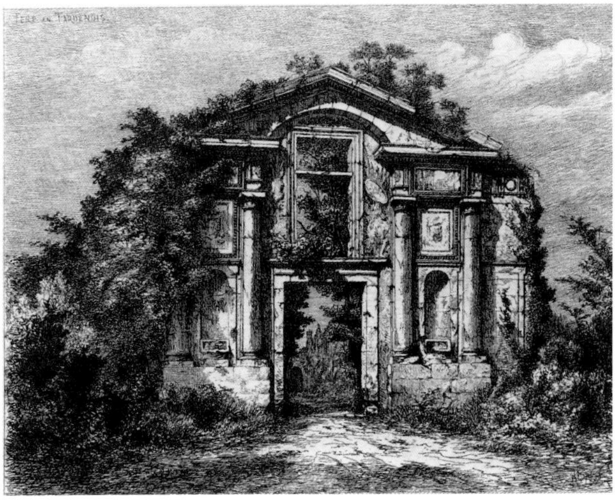

Entrance to the gallery of the château of Fère-en-Tardenois
Another work by Jean Bullant, the large portico leading to the bridge-gallery of the château of Fère-en-Tardenois.

initiated after Pavia to get France out of trouble and end its diplomatic isolation had ultimately been repaid by affronts to national pride that were inflicted with nothing being given in return. His personal links with Emperor Charles V were held against him, as was his lofty obstinacy; Francis I lost patience and in October 1540 ordered him to leave court and withdraw to his estates. This fall from favour lasted until the king's death. On the other hand, on his accession in 1547 his successor Henri II who had felt an almost filial affection for the Constable ever since his captivity in Madrid was only too happy to be able to rely on an experienced adviser, brave soldier and great diplomat who had the rare distinction of being on good terms with both Catherine de' Medici and Diane de Poitiers. As soon as Anne resumed a leading role in state affairs, being made a duke and a peer of the realm in 1551, we note a resumption of activity at his châteaux. He had already demonstrated his taste for modernity through his links with Jean Goujon; as his new architect he no longer chose a builder of Flamboyant cathedrals influenced by the Loire style like Chambiges, but a new-style theorist, a man who had read Vitruvius and examined the monuments of Rome in situ, so acquiring perfect practical knowledge of the classical orders which he would apply in France with the authority of a master: Jean Bullant.

Following page

The Pelouse seen from the Petit Château
The quality of the proportions and profile of Jean Bullant's Corinthian order mouldings is admirable.

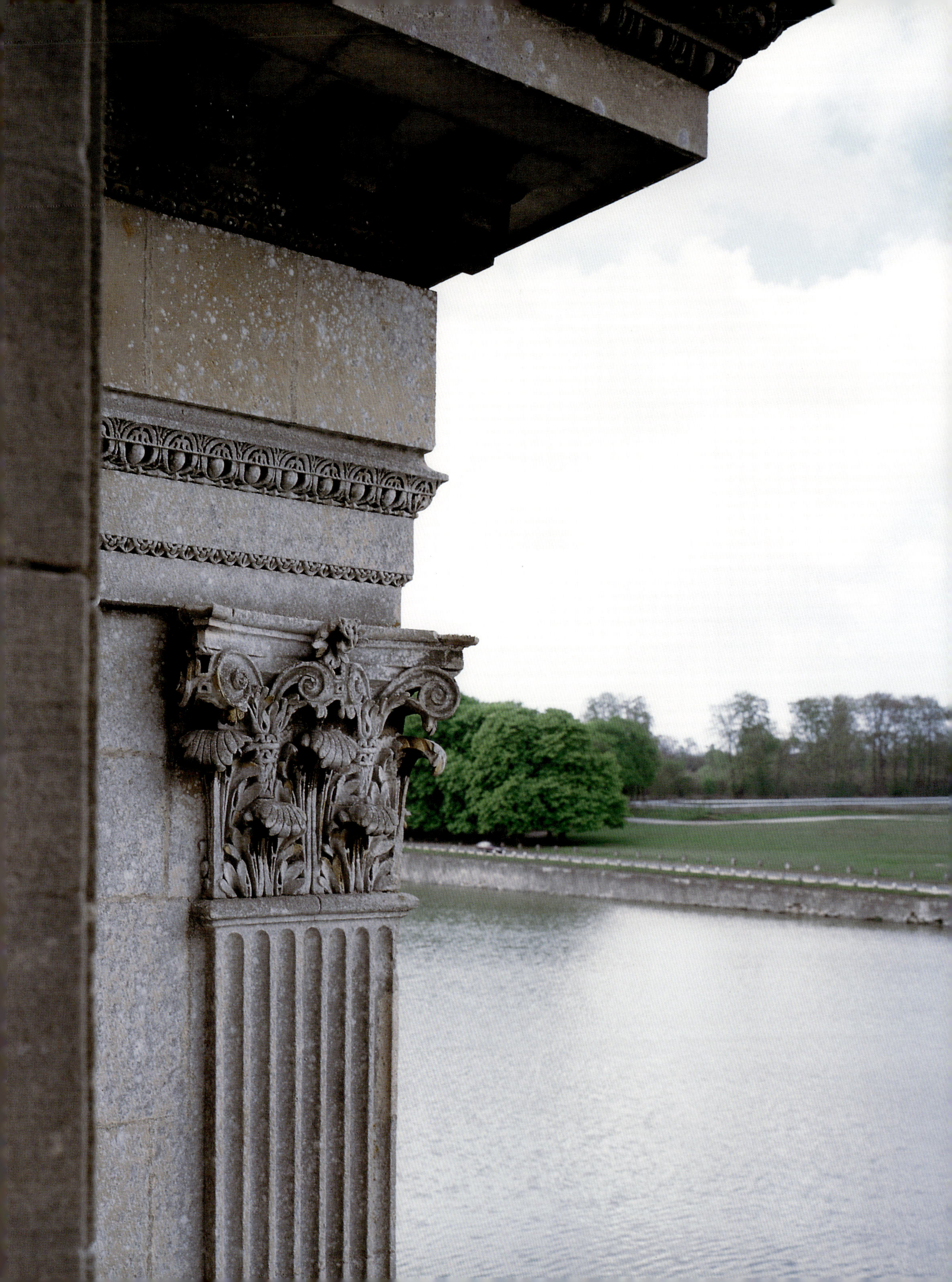

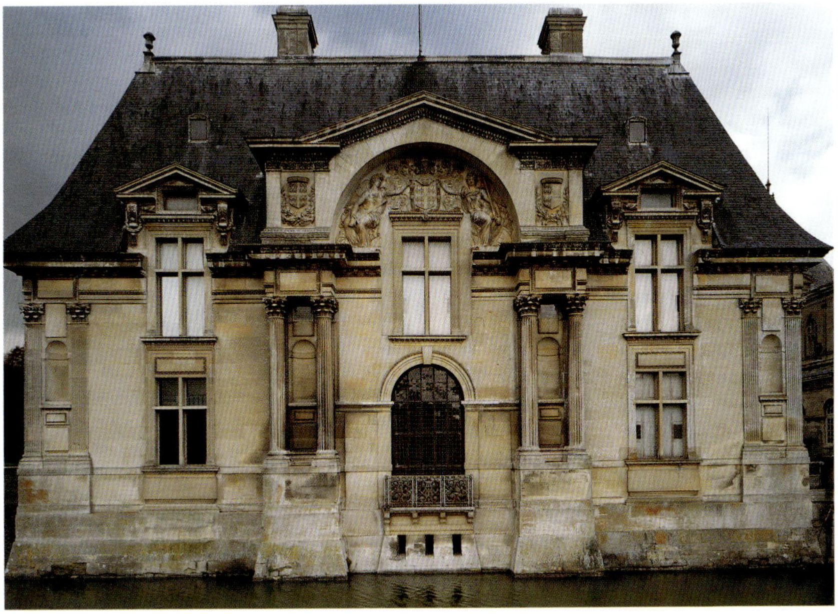

The entrance wing of the Petit Château
The central opening of the portico which gave access to Bullant's château via the drawbridge was blocked up in 1875.

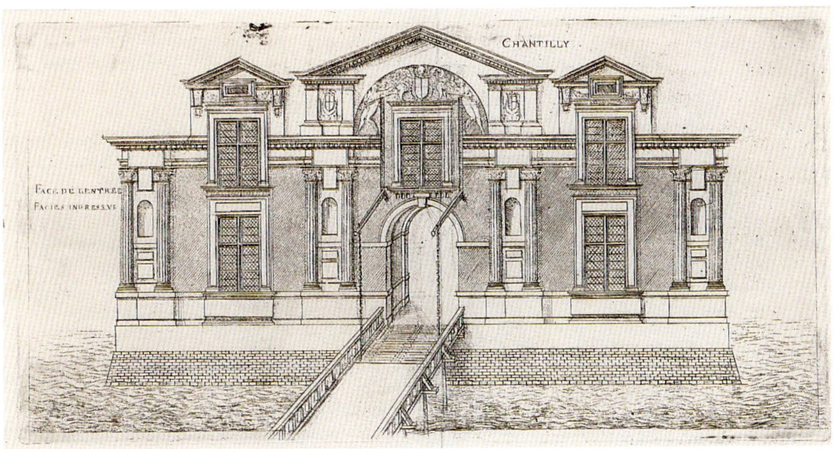

The entrance wing of the Petit Château
The façade by Jean Bullant, engraved by Jacques Androuet Du Cerceau in the *Plus Excellents Bastiments de France*, 1579.

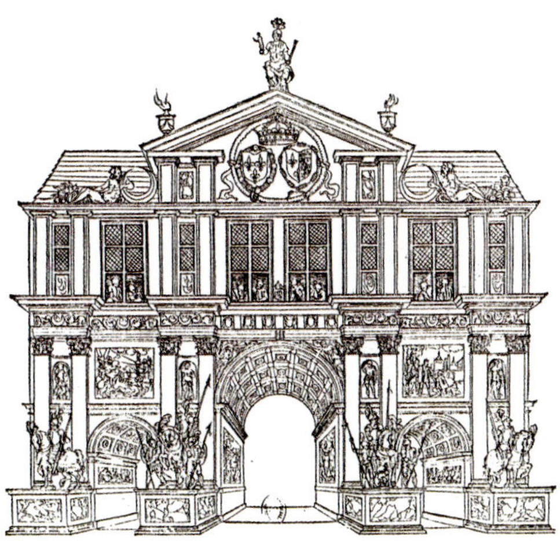

The triumphal arch on the rue Saint-Antoine
This temporary structure was put up for King Henri II's entrance into Paris in 1549.

Following pages

The Petit Château seen from the Pelouse
This view shows the Petit Château in front of the buildings put up by the duc d'Aumale.

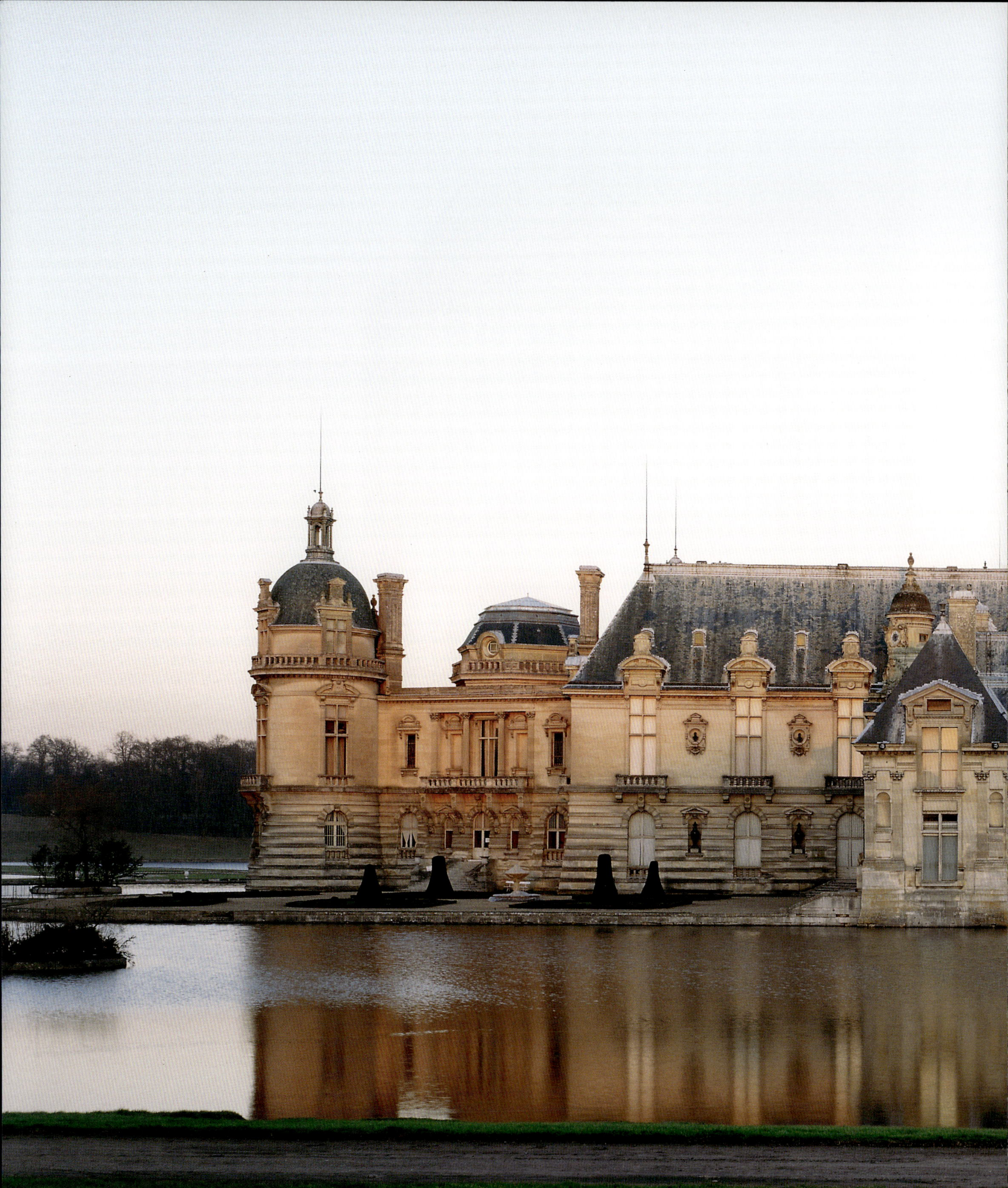

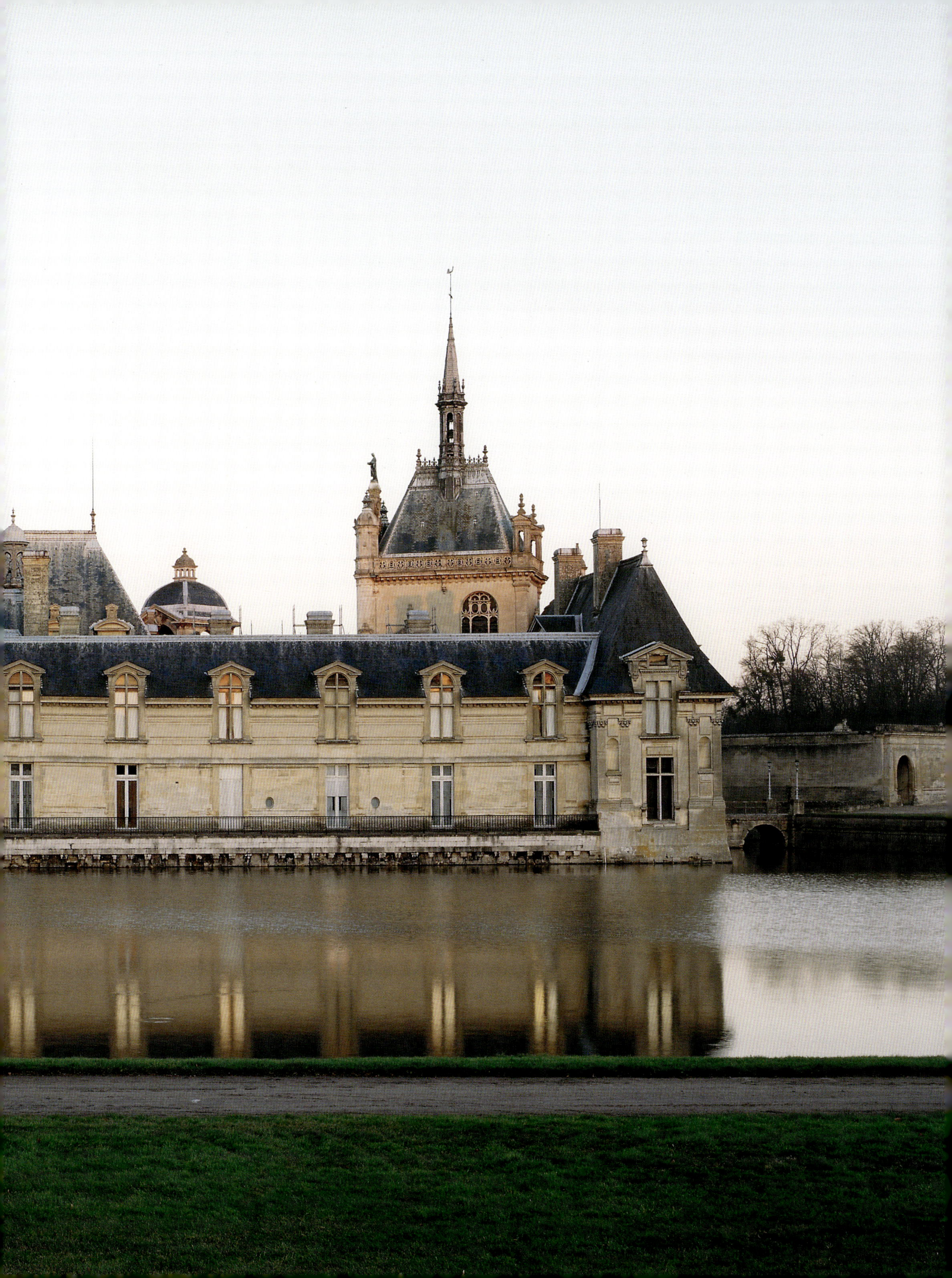

The court of the Petit Château
A carriage entrance used to pass through this wing at the back. On the right is the wing that housed the servants' quarters, since 1848 lined by the wooden gallery designed by Félix Duban.

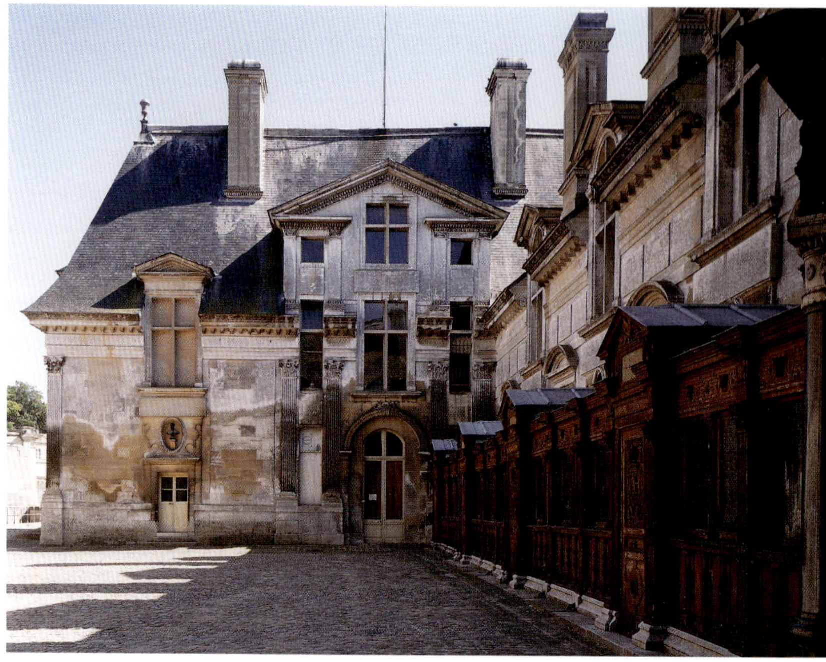

The wing housing the servants' quarters
Engraving by Jacques Androuet Du Cerceau, 1579. The jerky rhythm of the doors and windows is remarkable. On the right, the gallery wing had a blind wall on the courtyard side.

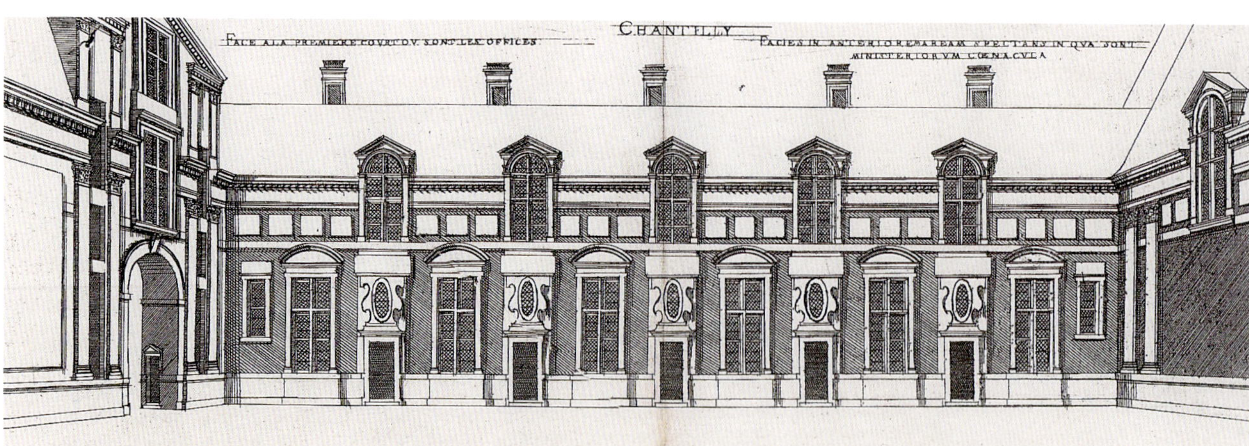

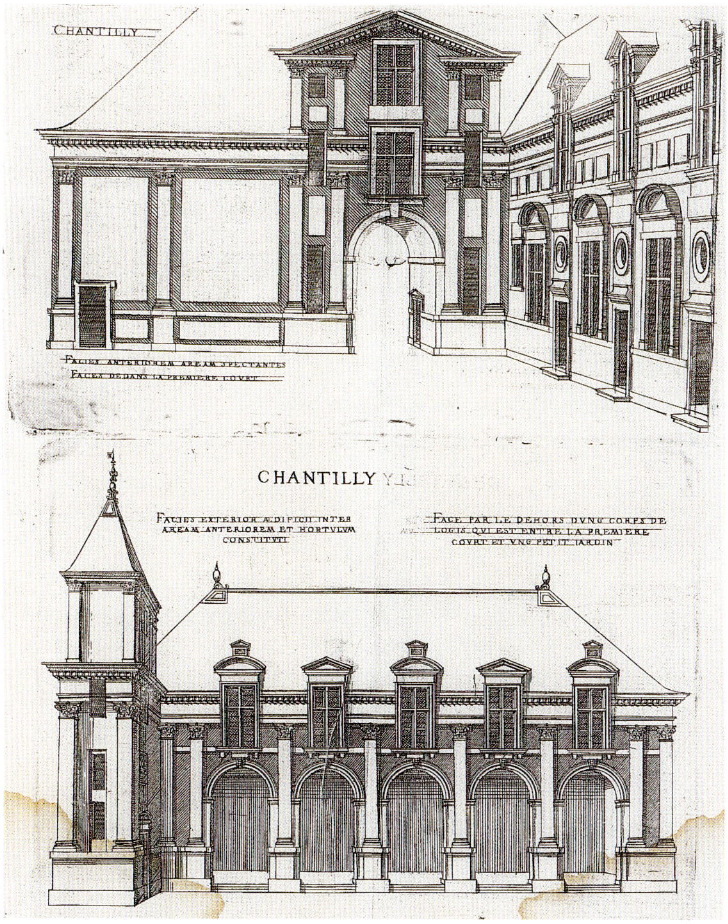

The two wings of the Petit Château
Above, the back of the entrance wing;
below, the gallery facing the Jardin de la Volière, with its five open arches and its little staircase tower.

The south façade of the Petit Château
The long balcony-terrace cantilevered over the water on beams was then edged with a masonry parapet, which was replaced by a wrought-iron railing at the time of the building work carried out by Mansart.

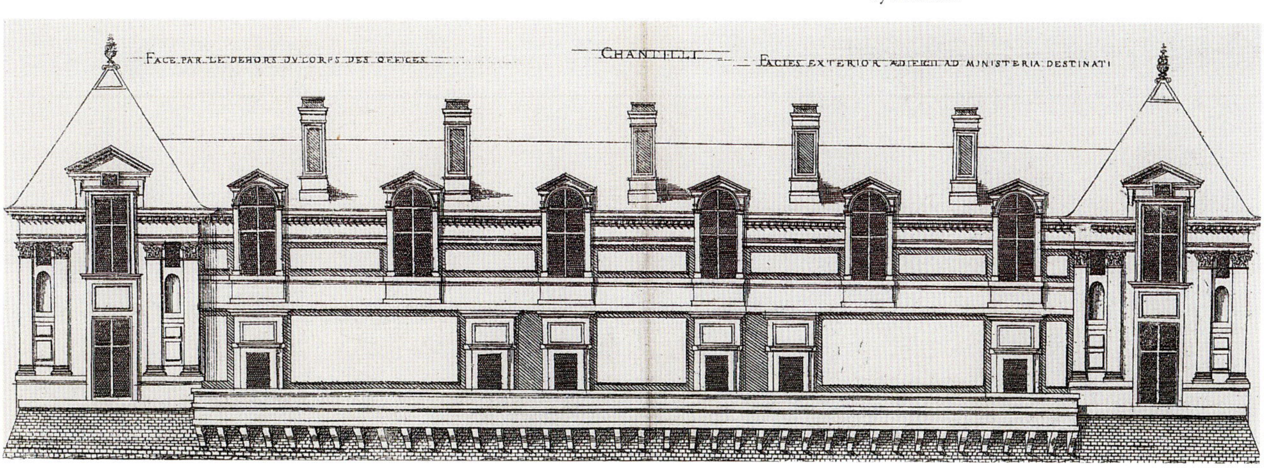

Bullant was born in Amiens between 1515 and 1520 to a family of Picardy masons, and had spent some time in Italy before establishing his reputation in Paris around 1550.[18] In that year he was recruited by the Constable to work on all his buildings, first and foremost at Écouen where he took up residence in 1556 and lived until his death in 1578. He profoundly altered the appearance and spirit of the château, finishing his interventions with the famous projecting bay with colossal columns in the court and the pedimented projecting bay on the terrace side. At Fère he built the amazing two-storey bridge-gallery that crosses the ravine leading to the château (1555-60). He also rebuilt the château of Gandelu (1560 – no longer in existence), produced plans for the château of Offémont (1567-69), and enlarged the Hôtel Neuf de Montmorency in the Marais in Paris.

Meanwhile the Constable had yet again fallen from favour. After being the hero of the armed struggle against Spain, he was then defeated and taken prisoner at Saint-Quentin in 1557. Henri II's accidental death two years later struck him with full force. A new party dominated by the Guise family had influence with the young king, Francis II, and Montmorency was side-lined, accused of laxness towards Protestants because of his family links with Admiral de Coligny and his brothers – his sister's own children. His fall from favour led him to speed up the work undertaken by Bullant at Chantilly. The fashion of the time was for houses built for enjoyment, not very tall and with regular architecture, standing on open sites surrounded by gardens and running water like the Florentine villas or the vineyards of the Roman cardinals. Cardinal Jean Du Bellay at Saint-Maur, Henri II at the Château Neuf at Saint-Germain and the Guises at Joinville had led the way. So Bullant built a new house at Chantilly on the low island at the foot of the south face of the castle, where a garden had just been laid out. The building scheme coincided with an expert survey of all his châteaux which in 1558 the Constable had entrusted from afar to the king's First Architect and Superintendent of Buildings, Philibert de l'Orme, while he was being held prisoner by the Spanish after Saint-Quentin. From the terms in which his report[19] is couched, we can sense the esteem in which the artist held the statesman, the extent to which he valued his taste and his capabilities, and his desire to construct for him "a fine building of a completely new kind". In the report mention is made of Jean Bullant, who was in charge of buildings; de l'Orme had asked him about everything to do with the Constable's plans. Thus de l'Orme had been informed of the new design for Chantilly, one which was very much in line with his own approach. We lack information regarding the date when work on the Petit Château started, in 1557 or 1558, as we know of only one contract, for the "roof of the gallery at Chantilly", made at the end of 1559 between the roofer Pierre Gobert and the mason Pierre Desilles[20], responsible for carrying out Bullant's drawings. But we know that work was finished in 1563, to go by the mention of the "living quarters in the new house" in a letter addressed to the Constable's wife, Madeleine of Savoy.

If all that remains of Chambiges's work are the vaulted cellars, the main part of what Bullant did is still in existence, in spite of the alterations it underwent in the seventeenth century, then again in the nineteenth. The new building was intended to provide its occupants with certain conveniences they had lacked in their old quarters: first of all, a gallery directly accessible from the château (unlike the Galerie des Cerfs) and opening onto a garden, then accommodation for the "officiers" (servants), and finally a gatehouse worthier of a ducal residence than two mediaeval towers framing a drawbridge. This represented a real revolution in the layout of a princely residence, which hitherto, as at the Louvre, had concentrated on safeguarding entrances by means of fortification. Thus Du Cerceau in his comments on his architectural plates of Chantilly gives us to understand that the Petit Château was now the entrance to the main castle.

The building occupies the south-east half of the island and follows a horseshoe-shaped ground plan: on the side facing the pond is the long building containing the domestic quarters, with two shorter buildings forming perpendiculars on either side, the entrance wing to the east, and the gallery to the west. The entrance building was reached by a drawbridge from the lower court of the castle located at the foot of the terrace, a court enclosed by walls containing surveillance and policing buildings: the Capitainerie and the prisons.[21] It was on the external façade that the new architectural solution chosen to draw the eye to the entrance of the princely residence was expressed, just as at Écouen, Anet, Saint-Maur and La Tour d'Aigues. For a man as keen on antiquity as Montmorency, the door must have called to mind Roman triumphal arches. Indeed a monument erected in Paris for the entry of King Henri II in 1549, the arch of the rue Saint-Antoine, may have served as an inspiration. When we realise that these ephemeral architectural structures had been designed by Jean

Goujon and Philibert de l'Orme, we can better appreciate the learned style strongly tinged with Mannerism which Bullant employed here, having already used it in 1554 on the doorway of the bridge-gallery at Fère-en-Tardenois.

The large central portico consists of a round arch supported by pairs of Corinthian columns of the colossal order surmounted by small attic pilasters, and is placed under a broad pediment, intersecting its lower cross-beam. Allegorical figures[22] surrounding the Constable's large coat of arms adorn the tympanum, on either side of the high window above the great door. On the side two vertical bays with casement windows accompanied by partial dormers topped by pediments are structured by pairs of pilasters separated by niches. The large entablature, interrupted again and again as if in play, is copied from the entablature of the temple of Jupiter Serapis on the Forum Romanum.

A similar spirit, but odder and more jerky in the placing of the casement windows and pediments, imbues the façades on the inner court, at the back of the entrance pavilion and on the servants' wing, which lines up five small lodgings, *ministeriorum coenacula*, with low doors alternating with high rectangular casement windows, under a roof intersected by partial dormers with arched openings, arranged above the doors. On the pond side, Bullant's structuring was given a more classical appearance by Hardouin-Mansart in the following century, but he kept the quite exceptional continuous balcony-terrace cantilevered above the water, which affords a magnificent view of the Pelouse and the forest. Henri d'Albret, inspired by the same desire to capture a view – the Pyrenean landscape – had built the large balcony on the château of Pau in 1529. Finally the last wing, which was doubled in depth and lengthened in Mansart's day, housed a gallery, closed towards the court but open on the garden side, just like the Petite Galerie of the Louvre built a few years later for Charles IX by Pierre II Chambiges from drawings by Lescot. Its five round-arched openings, separated by Corinthian pilasters, and above them partial dormers topped by alternating triangular and curvilinear pediments, formed an unusually well-balanced and harmonious composition with its reduced dimensions and intimate appearance, before it was extended by one bay at the end of the seventeenth century, then by three more in the early nineteenth.

On the side, a small pavilion with a lantern indicates the presence of a spiral staircase and gives access via a perron to the bridge that crosses the moat and makes it possible to reach the main château. In front of the gallery there was a

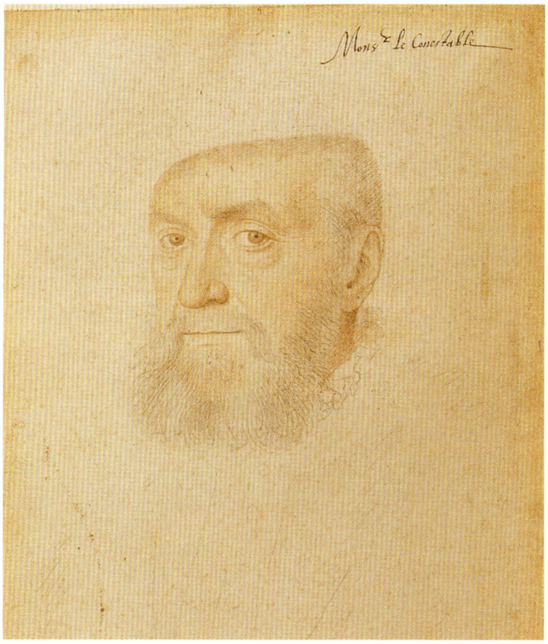

Anne de Montmorency
This portrait attributed to François Clouet (c. 1560) shows the Constable looking old, at the time when the regent Catherine de' Medici asked him to take up service again, on both the political and the military fronts.

garden arranged as a *parterre*, at the far end of which an aviary had been built as early as 1528. A lightly constructed footbridge known as the Pont de la Volière gave access to the Bucamp gardens and the Galerie des Cerfs across the pond. The circuit was thus complete, with the Petit Château serving as a pivot for circulation for practical and leisure purposes, while at the same time affording the maximum enjoyment of the most beautiful views of the site. This really was the new age: the 1560s were the period of Catherine de' Medici, and the Tuileries built for her brought together the genius of Philibert de l'Orme and Jean Bullant, both of them builders as well as theorists, Bullant having published his famous treatise on the orders, *Reigle generalle d'architecture*, in 1564. Just as with Pierre Chambiges, it was the Constable's patronage that had led to Bullant receiving royal commissions. The 1560s were also the years of the first Wars of Religion. After the death of Francis II, Anne de Montmorency resumed his service, backed by the queen mother who relied on his authority. While the Petit Château was being completed, the old man continued to command the royal armies and fight against the Huguenots with unfailing gallantry. When he finally succumbed to his wounds, on the evening of the battle of Saint-Denis in November 1567, he was seventy-four years old.

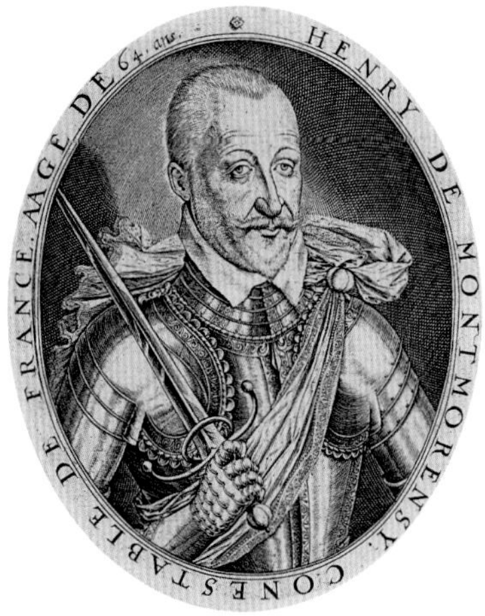

Henri de Montmorency
Engraving by Thomas de Leu.
The new Constable was a faithful companion of Henri IV.

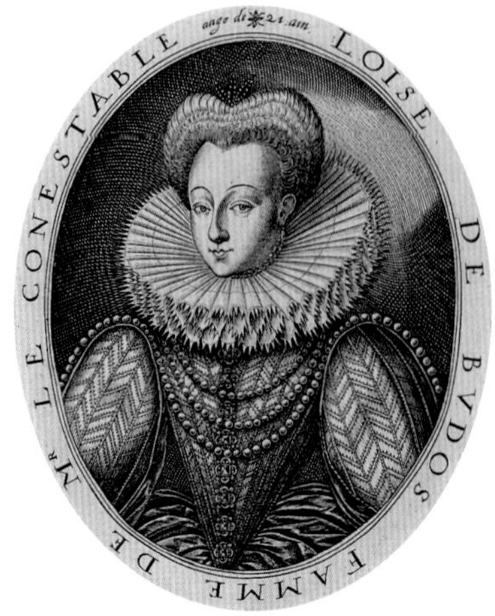

Louise de Budos
Engraving by Paul de la Houve, after J. de Weert.
The second wife of Henri de Montmorency came to a sad end, dying in unexplained pain.

The last Constable de Montmorency

On his death, Anne de Montmorency left Chantilly to his eldest son, François, a Field-Marshal like his father, who died in 1579 leaving no children.[23] His property reverted to his younger brother Henri, due de Damville, also a Field-Marshal, born at Chantilly in 1534. He was a colourful personality who as Governor of Languedoc, a role he had taken over from his father in 1563, had succeeded in handling the Protestants skilfully and in forming a sort of autonomous principality that remained peaceful and tolerant throughout the sad days of the Wars of Religion. Because of this, it was for many years impossible for him to leave the south, and Chantilly was left in the care of three relatives: his mother Madeleine of Savoy, until her death in 1586; Diane de France, the widow of his brother François and the natural daughter of King Henri II; and his youngest brother Guillaume, sieur de Thorey.

In these northern districts where the Catholic League was constantly strengthening its position, the property of the Montmorencys, a moderate family with links to the Protestants, was at the mercy of Catholic extremists. There was a resurgence of violence in 1589 when the execution of the Guise brothers at Blois was announced. To ensure her safety, Diane requested a garrison, which was in position in January, but the League immediately reacted by sending a force under the command of a cousin of the Guises: the duc d'Aumale, a portentous name. The Catholics made their way into the park through breaches in the wall enclosing it, but did not succeed in investing the castle and were soon routed by the royal troops. Diane immediately had

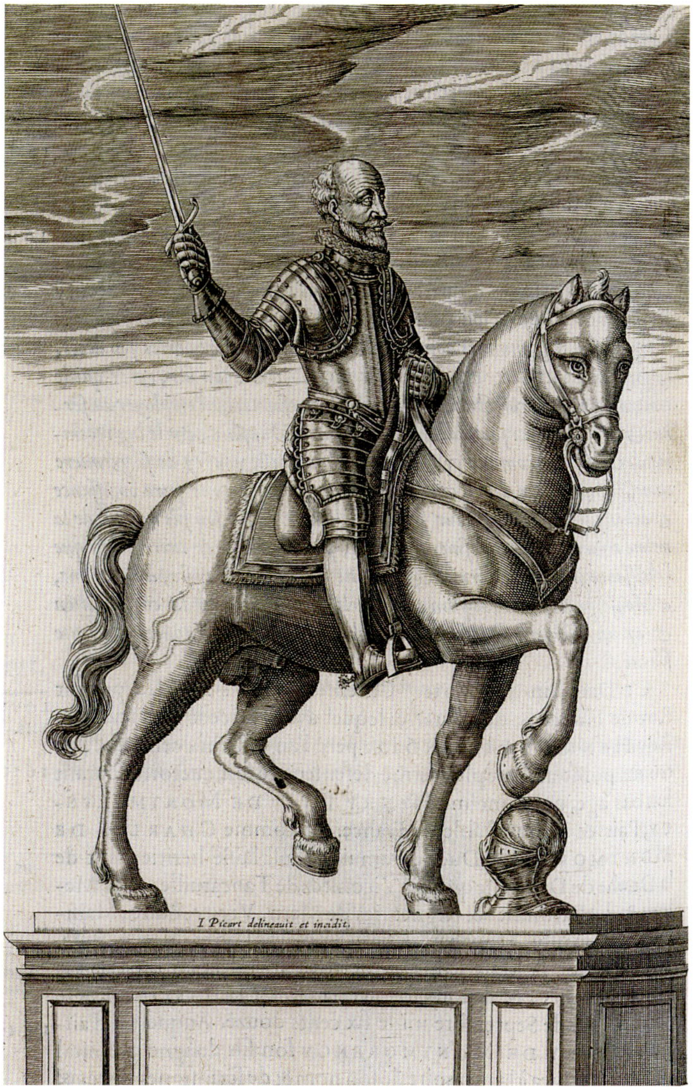

The equestrian statue of Constable Henri
Engraving by J. Picart, 1624.
This statue was erected in 1612 on the terrace at Chantilly.

the breaches filled in and the approaches to the castle fortified with gabions. A new chapter in the history of France then opened, with the reconquest of the kingdom by Henri IV, in which Henri de Montmorency played an active part. As a loyal ally who had kept Languedoc obedient to royal power, whether Catholic or Protestant, Anne's son received the sword of Constable de France from the hands of the king in 1594; it had been left in its sheath since 1567. His missions to Lyons, Dauphiné and Provence still prevented him from coming north, but the time soon came in late 1595 when hostilities started to die down, after the victory of Fontaine-Française against the Spanish and the first transfers of allegiance by the leaders of the League. On 6 November, Henri IV wrote to him from Chauny: "Knowing that your long travels merit rest, and not wanting to deprive you of the pleasure you will feel at seeing your house at Chantilly, my cousin your wife and your son, I am allowing you ten or twelve days rest, requesting that you come and join me when this period has elapsed."[24]

At Chantilly the Constable was received with transports of joy by those living there, rejoining his wife, the beautiful Louise de Budos, whom he had married three years earlier after the death of his first wife, the daughter of the duc de Bouillon, as well as his legitimate and illegitimate children, all brought up in the same nursery, following the style of Henri IV. A bolt from the blue was to strike at his affections on 26 September 1598. The death of Louise at the age of twenty-three, overcome by terrible pains, deeply upset the king and the court, and the strange circumstances of her death inflamed popular imagination which saw it as a mysterious intervention by Satanic forces.[25] A year later, the king's mistress Gabrielle d'Estrées died in identical circumstances – heavily pregnant – and suffering the same pains, which were interpreted in a similar manner. Modern science has diagnosed the cause of both these tragic deaths as the dreadful effects of puerperal eclampsia.

The work carried out by Pierre Biard

Once peace had returned to the kingdom, the Constable could stay at Chantilly more often, and at Écouen and Mello too; from 1599, in spite of the pitiful state of his finances, he embarked on a series of consolidation and improvement schemes that are a credit to his taste and discernment. They relate to the châteaux, the outbuildings, the park, and something that still contributes to the fragile beauty of the location today: the moats and ponds, the banks of which had to be continually repaired. He too chose a true artist to implement his designs: Pierre Biard (1559-1609), an architect, engineer and sculptor, a Parisian who had distinguished himself through his work at the Louvre and the Hôtel de Ville.[26] The building work related first and foremost to the Petit Château and its surroundings. Thus the south-west pavilion, established by Bullant on a poorly reinforced bank[27], had to be rebuilt and its foundations welded together by iron bars (1601). The lower garden was walled in by a stone parapet (1601) and the ruined aviary was reconstructed (1603), as was the footbridge leading to Bucamp (1604). Later on, in 1611, the gallery was embellished by a painted decoration commissioned by the Constable from his usual painter, Guillaume Heaulmé, who also worked on the town house

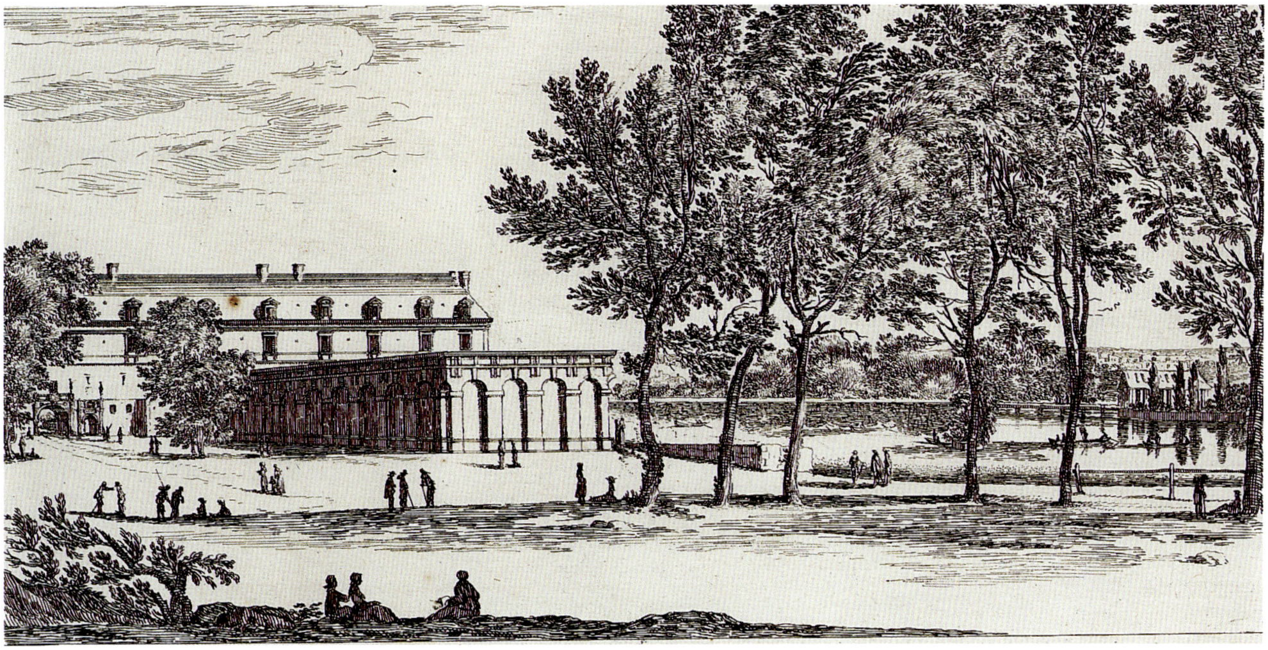

The old Jeu de Paume
Engraving by Israël Silvestre.
A close tennis court had been built beside the pond opposite the aviary by Anne de Montmorency in 1527-29, and it was rebuilt by his son Henri around 1604.

in Paris: it took the form of four large paintings on canvas depicting powerful Barbary horses from his stable, with bay or dapple-grey coats, two barebacked, the two others carrying King Henri IV and the Constable, sword in hand. These powerful images of the horses of Chantilly, unfortunately lost[28], were intended to bring to mind those commissioned by Federigo Gonzaga around 1530 for the Sala Grande of the Palazzo del Te at Mantua.

On the Bucamp side, Biard had the decoration of the Galerie des Cerfs restored by a sculptor brought in to "mend your broken stags" and by duchesse Diane's painter who was instructed to colour them. The bath-house pavilion was reconstructed (1604) and all the outlying buildings restored: the armoury, the heronry, the large kennel and the close tennis court. In the upper garden, behind the gallery (the site of the present-day Jeu de Paume, or close tennis court), white mulberry, peach and cherry trees were planted, along with muscat vines. In honour of Henri IV who took it upon himself during one of his visits to order the digging of two canals, a new garden known as the Jardin du Roi was laid out. Finally in 1601 the Constable laid the first stone near the Maison de Beauvais of a Capuchin monastery intended to house his tomb, although in the end Biard's plans were carried out in Languedoc.[29]

However the great novelty lay in landscaping a sector of the wooded park in the very near vicinity, turning it into a pleasure area that the next generation

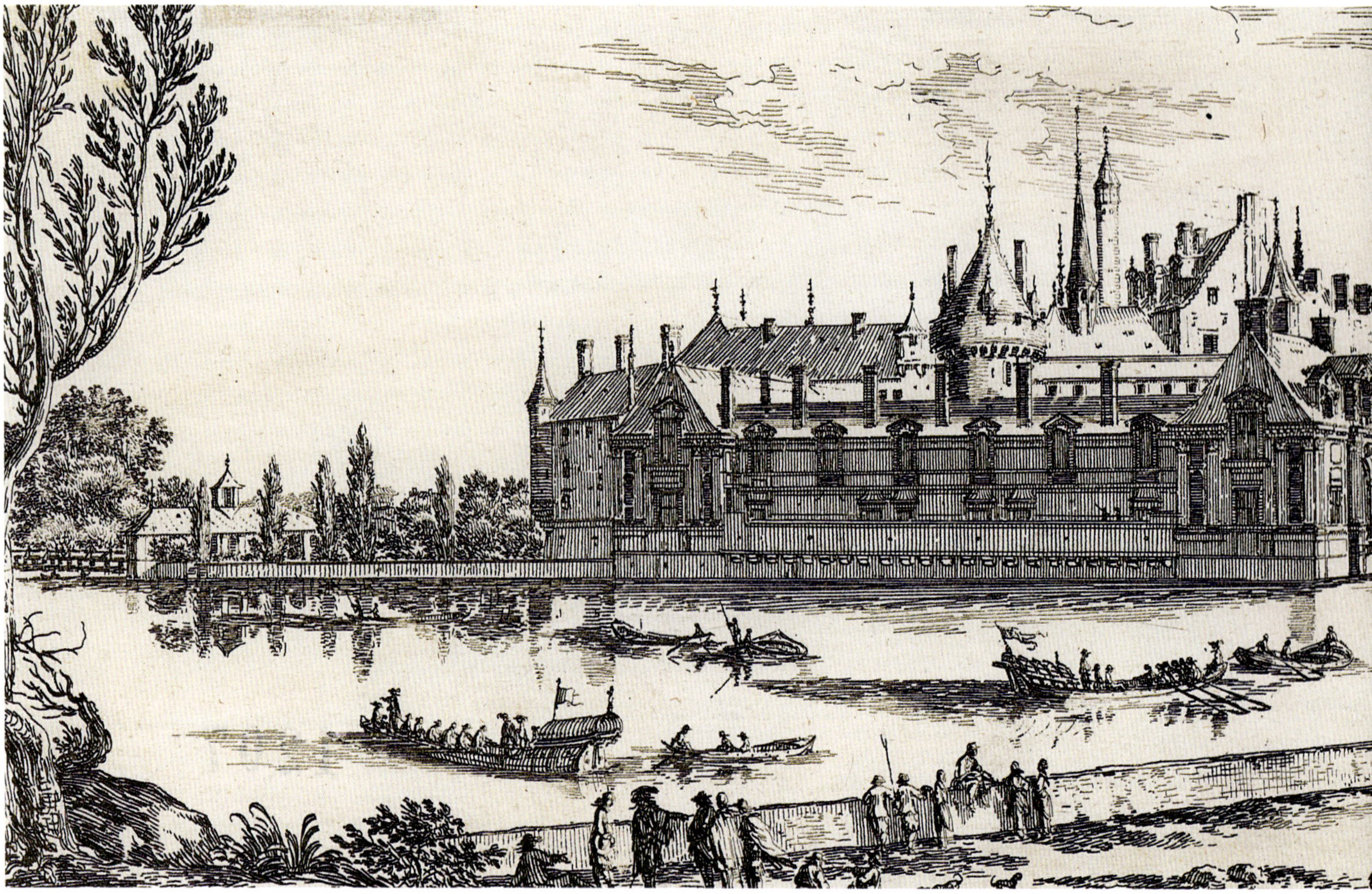

(and the poet Théophile) would embellish with a name charged with meaning: Sylvie, the nymph of the forest. The pond that lapped against the right side of the made-up causeway carrying the Paris road was fed at the east end by a gushing spring. The first Constable had already erected a building in this shady spot and a description dating from 1582 mentions a "fountain and a cool room" nearby. The second Constable had this "maison du parc" rebuilt and decorated in 1604-06. It now contained a complete set of rooms, suitable for a pleasant retreat, with a *parterre* and a "pheasantry" alongside.

Henri IV had developed a passion for the estate of his Constable, to whom he referred familiarly as "mon compère" or fellow-sponsor, as the king had held Montmorency's son at the baptismal font. The king sang the praises of "your house at Chantilly, your covered walks, your gardens, your forest and your stags" and did not omit to make frequent visits[30] of several days' duration, always in March (1602, 1607, 1608, 1609), even when the master of the house was not there. At these times he was received by the Constable's two

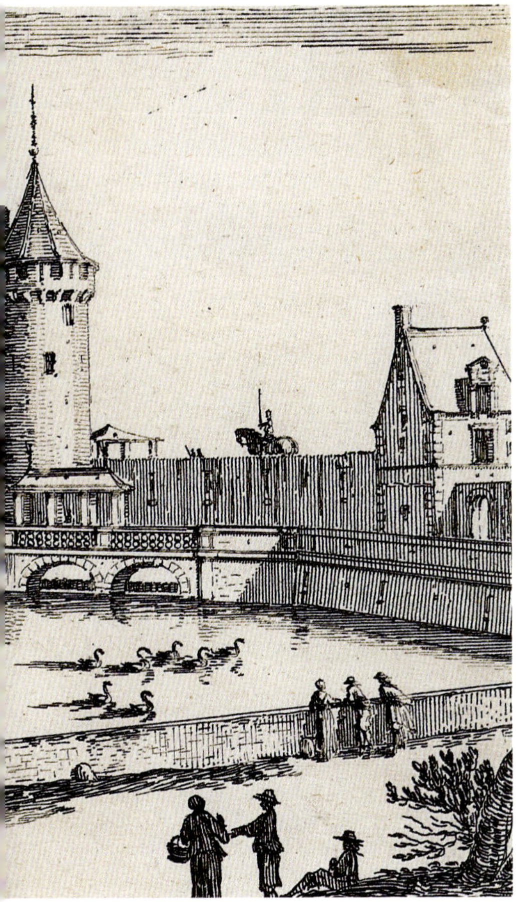

View of the Petit Château
Engraving by Israël Silvestre.
Beyond the pond with its many boats we see the Volière (aviary) and its garden on the left, and on the right the bridge to the Petit Château, the Capitainerie, the terrace and its statue.
In front of each of the drawbridges is a canopy supported by columns.

children, the son and daughter of his second marriage, who did the honours of the house and in whom he took a somewhat too close interest for their father's liking: Henri, whom the king wanted to marry off to Mademoiselle de Vendôme, his daughter by Gabrielle d'Estrées; and Charlotte-Marguerite, whose youthful beauty had suddenly aroused the old Don Juan. Between the two men there were only demonstrations of grudging friendship and numerous minor irritations throughout these years, but the king carried on inviting himself to the château – "His Majesty lodged in the Queen's bedroom to have greater convenience in climbing less" – to rooms that were splendidly equipped with hangings of silk and gold, statues and valuable pictures. He assessed the work in progress, gave his opinion on the livestock fed at Bucamp, admired the carp, pike and trout that filled the moats and canals and the swans swimming in the ponds, went out to visit the Maison de Sylvie – "your house near the fountain in the park" – and enthusiastically went hunting through mature forest and copse, "full of boar, stags, fallow deer and roe-deer". For Henri IV,

Chantilly was "the finest house in France, and finer than any of his own"; he even got round to suggesting to the Constable that he should exchange it for one of the royal châteaux, but his "compère" had an answer ready: "Sire, the house is yours; but let me be its keeper."[31] The king's tragic death in 1610 gave the Constable the last word. His son did not marry Henri IV's bastard daughter, but a young cousin of Marie de' Medici, Marie-Félice Orsini (des Ursins), and the young Prince de Condé to whom the king had married the beautiful Charlotte-Marguerite as a matter of convenience, a marriage celebrated and consummated at Chantilly on 17 May 1609, was able to return from his self-imposed exile in the Netherlands where he had immediately taken his wife to put her beyond the reach of the king's attentions. All that remained was for the Constable to set his signature on the site. As early as 1607 he had planned to erect a statue of himself on horseback at Écouen, using a bronze horse that was no doubt one of the works brought back from Italy by his father, just like Michelangelo's *Slaves* which were placed in the niches at Écouen. In the end the work was erected at Chantilly in 1612, in an exceptional position: on the terrace, opposite the château as if suspended in mid-air. The figure of the Constable, made up from an assemblage of pieces of beaten copper, was either the work of Pierre Biard, who died in 1609, or his son Pierre II. It remained gloriously in position until 1793, when it was transported to Paris to be melted down. The duc d'Aumale later had a statue of the first Constable erected on the same spot on the terrace. For Henri de Montmorency, that upright image was really his testament. After resigning his offices, he withdrew to Agde to the monastery he had founded, and on 2 April 1614 the old warrior died wearing the garb of the Capuchins, at the age of eighty.

The tragic end of the Montmorencys

For a long time the fate of Chantilly seemed to be tied up with the Montmorency family's brilliant destiny. The son of the last Constable, duc Henri II de Montmorency, the godson of the late King Henri, had all the qualities needed to make him popular: youth and good looks, gallantry and generosity. He distinguished himself when new wars against the Protestants broke out from 1621 to 1625, defeating Soubise's fleet before La Rochelle, and later on in the war in Piedmont he was victorious at Saluzzo and Casal. As Governor of Languedoc and Admiral of France, an office Cardinal de Richelieu forced

The fountain and the Étang de Sylvie
At the very beginning of the seventeenth century part of the woodland park of the château was landscaped to turn it into a recreational area with which the name of Sylvie or Sylvia, the nymph of the forest, was associated.

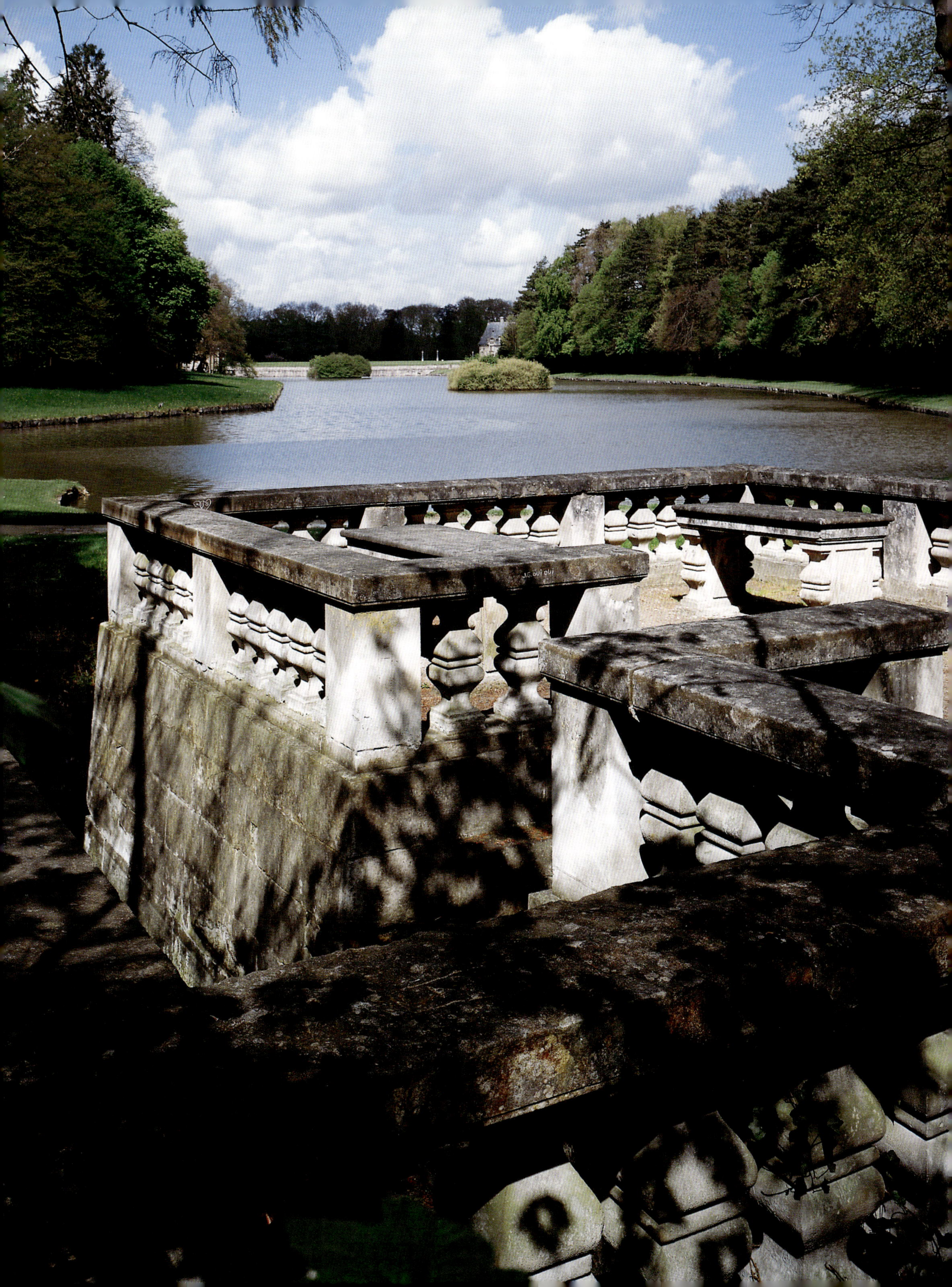

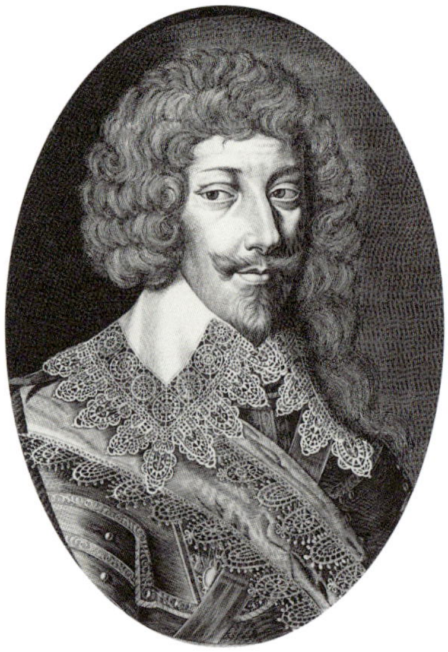

Henri II de Montmorency
Engraving by Jean Mariette.
Caught up in the plots of Gaston d'Orléans, the brilliant duc Henri II was condemned to death and executed, a victim of Richelieu's unrelenting harshness.

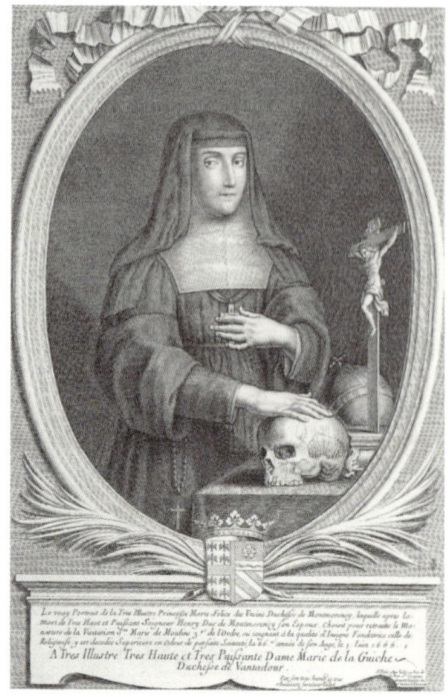

Marie-Félice des Ursins
Engraving by G. Valet.
Caught up in the plots of Gaston d'Orléans, the brilliant duc Henri II was condemned to death and executed, a victim of Richelieu's unrelenting harshness.

The pediment of the Caboutière
The arms of Louis XIII, king of France and Navarre, are stamped on the pediment of a pavilion built in the park of Chantilly during his reign. They were restored by the duc d'Aumale.

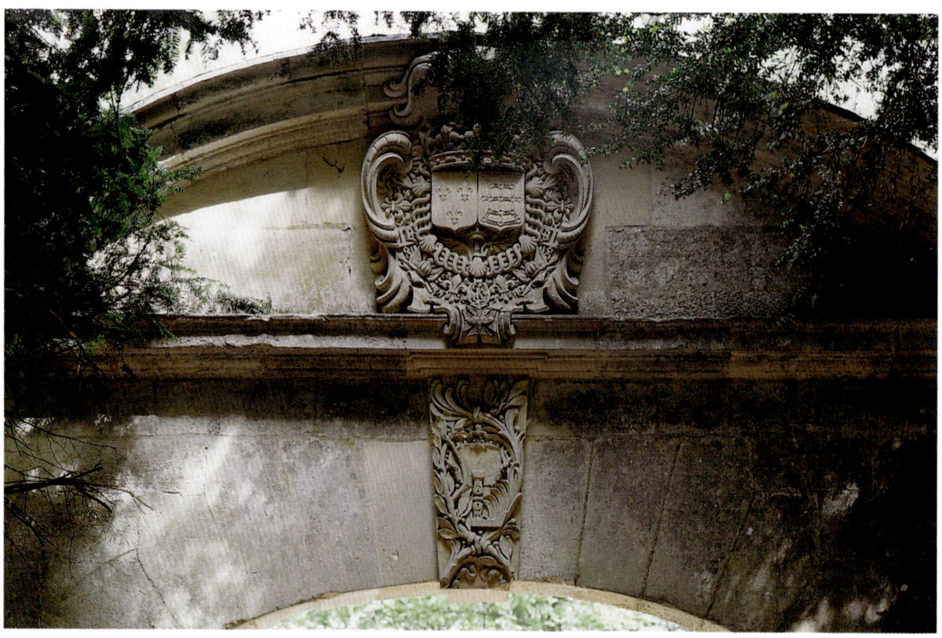

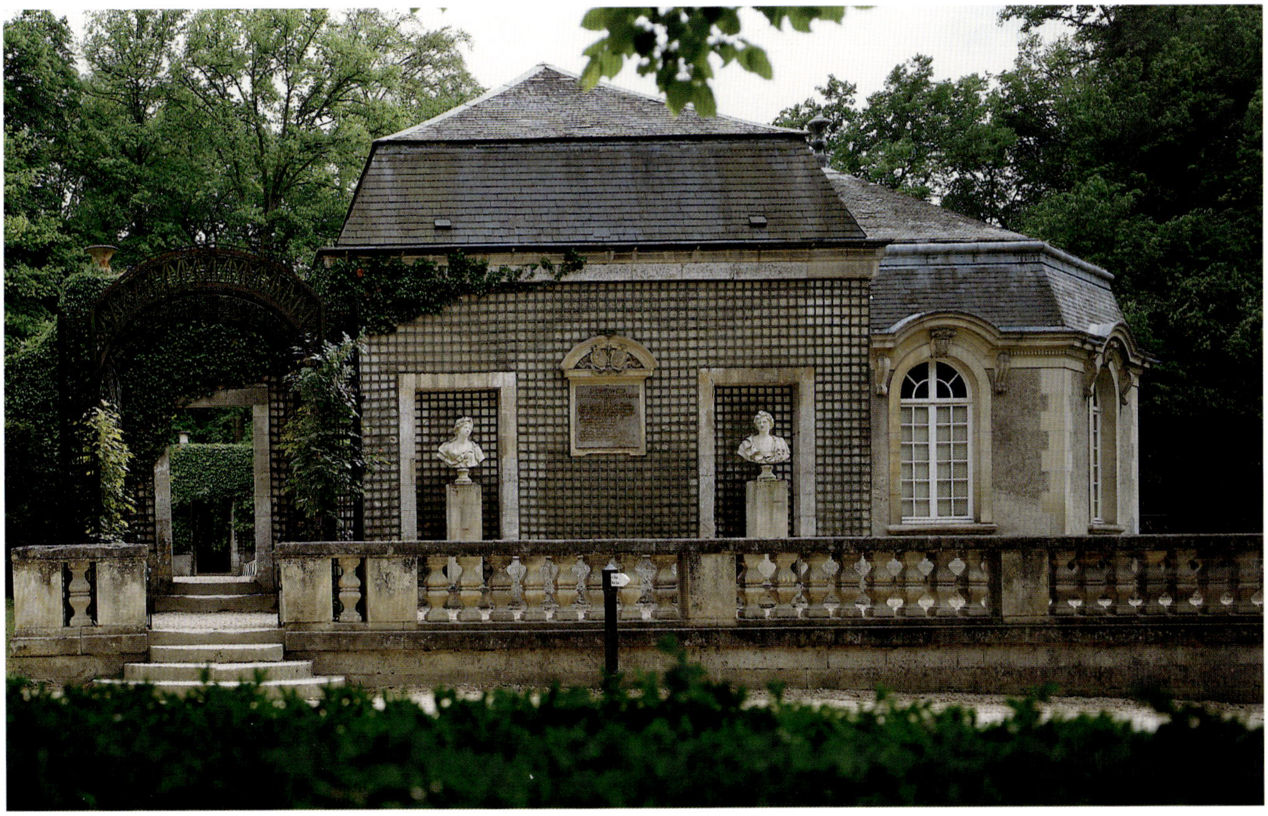

him to sell to him, and finally a Field-Marshal in 1630, everything pointed to his enjoying a long career in the king's service, and the tender love between him and his young Italian wife made him an even more interesting figure. A "rich, gallant, liberal" was the verdict of Tallemant des Réaux. The duke liked to be surrounded by men of intellect who wrote poetry for him, and around 1615 he included the poet Théophile de Viau, a libertine whose works and conduct were soon penalised by censorship, in his circle. Sent into exile in 1619, Théophile took refuge in Languedoc where he enjoyed the governor's protection. When another storm broke out over the obscenities in the *Parnasse satyrique* published in 1623, the duke had no hesitation in again hiding the literary rebel, but this time at his own home at Chantilly. The house in the park beside the fountain was used to lodge him, with the complicity of the duchess, who was fond of this secret spot and often went there to talk to the poet. This rustic idyll of 1623, so close to the amorous tales of mythology, was charmingly evoked by Théophile:

One evening as the sea waves
Were preparing their soft bed…

The Maison de Sylvie
The original building with a rectangular ground plan, the end of which can be seen in the centre, was built by Henri I de Montmorency.
This "house in the park" was rebuilt by the duc d'Enghien, the son of the Great Condé.
The duc d'Aumale added the rotunda that can be seen on the right.

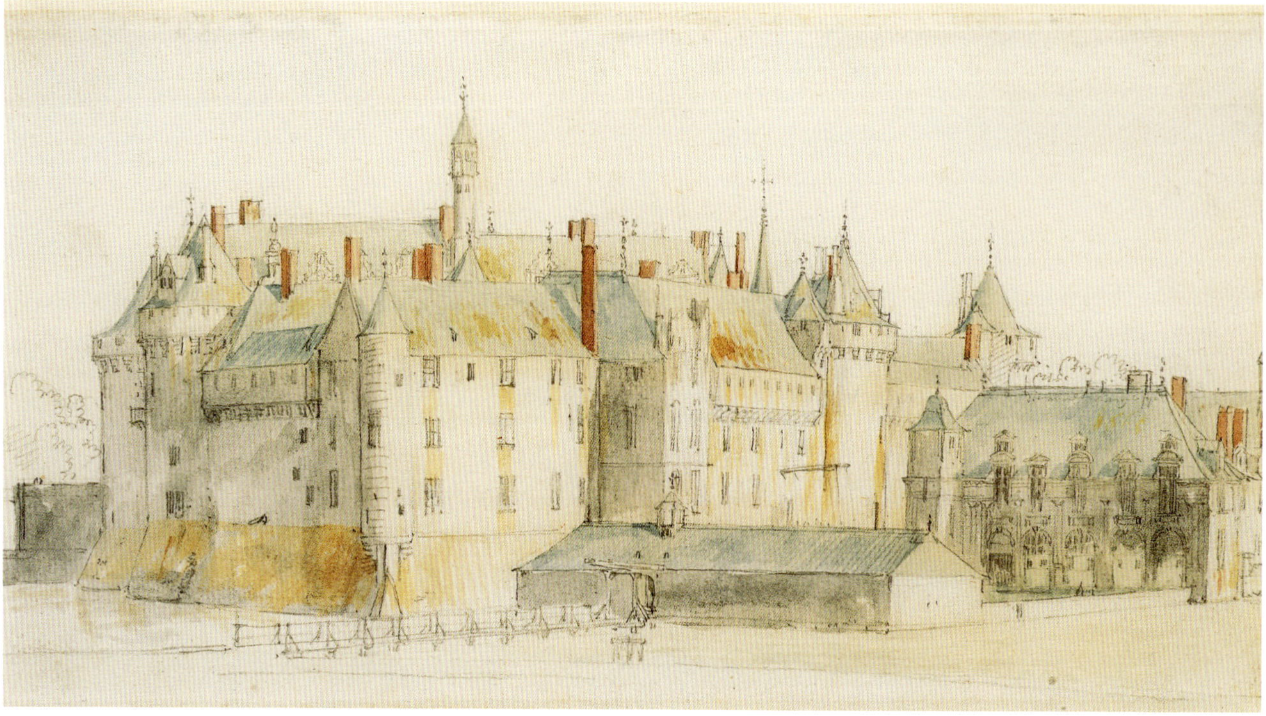

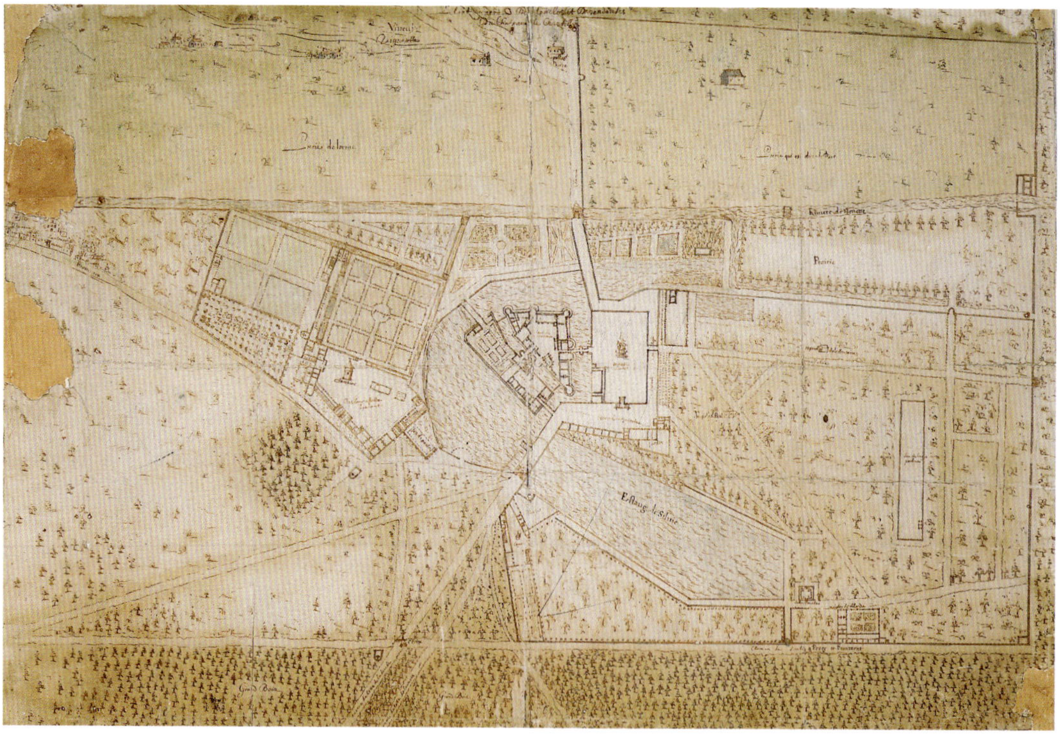

I inclined my eyes to the edge
Of a bed where the naiad sleeps,
And watching Sylvia fishing,
I saw the fish fighting
Over which would be first to give up its life
In honour of her fish-hooks.

And the name of Sylvia, or Sylvie, was retained for this house, this pond, this whole part of the park, in memory of Marie-Félice des Ursins. The fact that Théophile was condemned to death and executed in effigy did not deter the duke from protecting him; after being exiled, imprisoned then reinstated, the poet returned to Chantilly and finished his *Odes de la maison de Sylvie.* In 1629 his friend the poet Mairet, another protégé of the Montmorencys, gave the name *Sylvie* to a pastoral tragicomedy.

A man of independent spirit, head of the most illustrious family in the kingdom, and a natural enemy of Richelieu and his policies, Montmorency allowed himself to be dragged into an armed rebellion against the cardinal by the first prince of royal blood, the king's brother Gaston d'Orléans. Wounded and taken prisoner in fighting at Castelnaudary, he was immediately condemned to death as a rebel captured with his weapons in his hands, and executed in the Place de Toulouse on 30 October 1632. His widow was inconsolable and retired to the Visitandine convent at Moulins where she had an admirable mausoleum erected.

That was the end of the house of Montmorency; their property was confiscated, then shared among the Field-Marshal's three sisters, except for Chantilly whose attractions were such that Louis XIII kept the château and the estate for his own personal use.[32] On his very first visit to take possession of it, the king did not scruple to break up the treasures – manuscripts, medals and works of art – collected by Guillaume and Anne de Montmorency. His love of hunting brought him back to Chantilly every year, but his presence was also dictated by the need to defend the Picardy frontier against the Spanish in the year when Corbie was captured (1636), and it was to Chantilly that Queen Anne of Austria was summoned to explain her secret correspondence with Madrid, in a scenario reminiscent of *Ruy Blas.* "My health is good. I have taken three big wolves since I have been here": that is the tone of the correspondence addressed by Louis XIII to Richelieu on 31 January 1641. Both men would leave the stage within the next two years.

View of Chantilly
This fine watercolour by Adam Frans Van der Meulen, acquired by the Musée Condé in 2007, made before 1673 – the aviary is still there – offers us what was then the most flattering view of Chantilly. The buildings facing south opposite the Pelouse and the Bucamp gardens housed the princes' suites of rooms.

Plan of the Chantilly estate
The note "Orchard enclosure that the late princess had made" makes it possible to place this drawing to circa 1650, the year of the death of Charlotte-Marguerite, Princess de Condé.
We can see the two châteaux, the ponds and causeways for the Picardy road, the Bucamp farmyard and the Maison de Sylvie with its cool room.

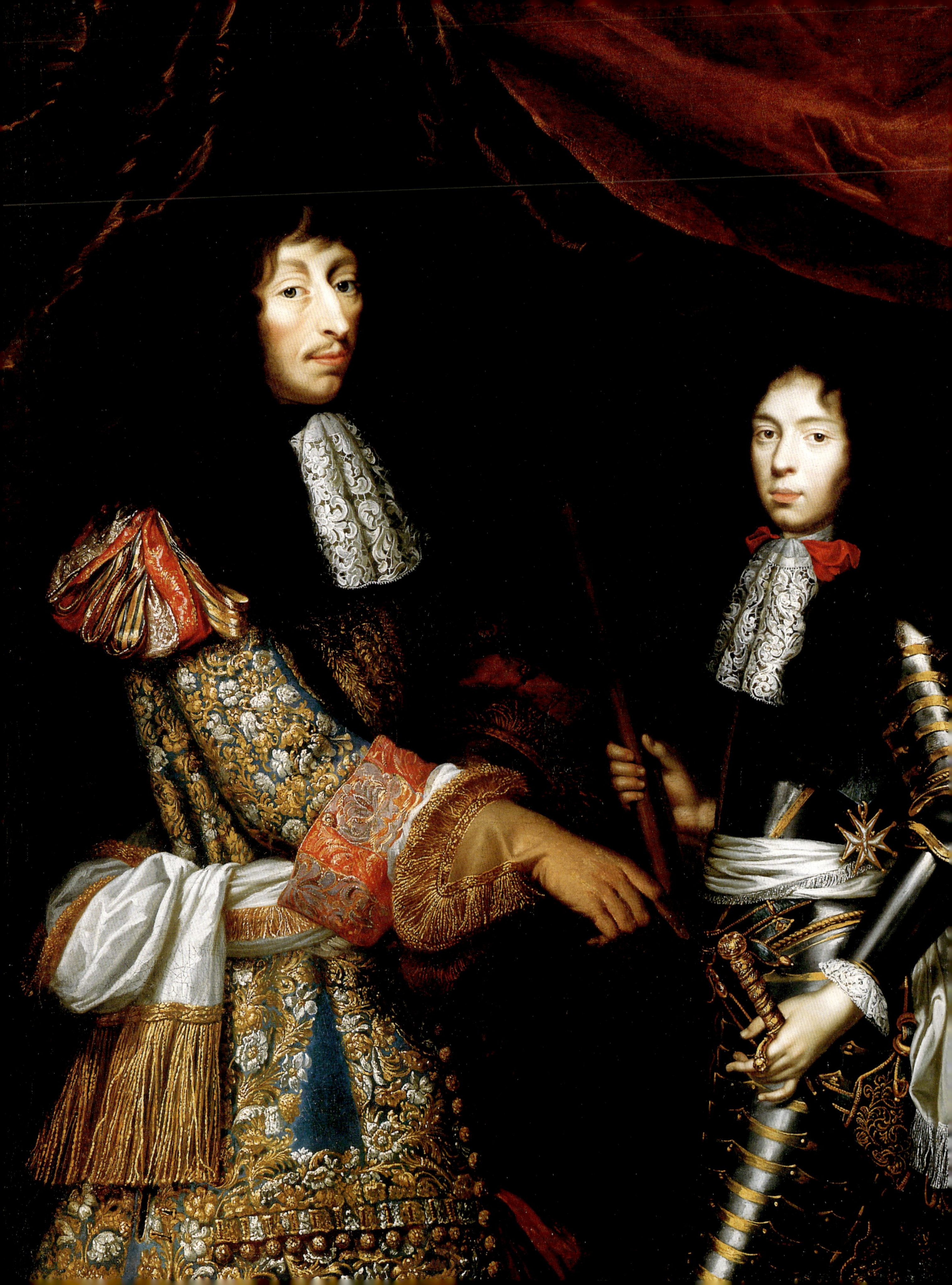

The Great Condé, rival to the Sun King

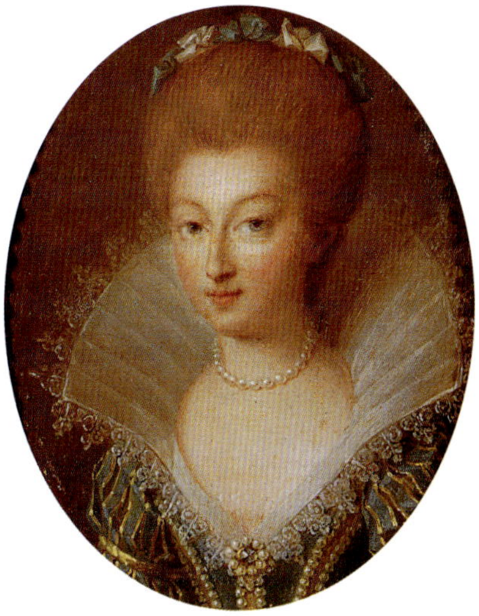

The Great Condé's mother
This portrait of Charlotte-Marguerite de Montmorency, wife of Henri II de Condé, was made by Jean-Marie Ribou (1744-1817) after her death.

The rebel pardoned

A new future opened up for Chantilly when the Regent, Anne of Austria, who took over as ruler of the kingdom on the death of Louis XIII, decided to return the splendid estate which the kings had always eyed enviously to its legitimate owners, in the person of Princess Charlotte, the sister of the last Montmorency who had been beheaded on Richelieu's orders. The princess had been the last love of Henri IV and wife of the first prince of royal blood, Henri II of Bourbon, Prince de Condé, a man who was as sad as his fate. Her family thus became the fourth dynasty to rule here, remaining at Chantilly for over two centuries until the last Condé, then continuing their residence by way of a nephew and godson on down to the duc d'Aumale, who died in 1897. Never had Chantilly been so close to the crown. It is true that in 1643 the Regent had good reason for wanting to placate the Prince and Princess de Condé: their son, the duc d'Enghien, in all the splendour of his twenty-one years, had just saved France and the throne of the young Louis XIV by repelling the Spanish invasion at Rocroi, on 19 May 1643.[1] The trumpets of fame thus made Chantilly part of the hero's destiny, but the troubled years ahead were to delay by twenty years the day when the king's cousin could really take possession of his estate. These were the years of the Fronde. At the start of the Regency, to be sure, there were once again festivities and poets along the banks of the Nonette where Queen Anne liked to come and join the two princesses, Charlotte who was widowed in 1646, and her daughter-in-law Claire-Clémence de Maillé-Brézé, a poor scatterbrain who had been married to the young Condé – who never loved her – on the orders of her uncle Richelieu, as well as a third lady, the splendid duchesse de Longueville, Condé's sister. But soon there were stirrings against absolute, centralist royal power in the form

The Great Condé and his son
In this picture attributed to Claude Lefebvre, the artist has ineptly juxtaposed the well-known figure of the father, with his authoritarian gesture of an army leader, and that of his son, the duc d'Enghien, proud of a cuirass that failed to ensure his military genius.

of the Fronde. The dissatisfied forces formed a coalition to overturn the new Minister, Cardinal Mazarin, the loathed favourite of the Queen Mother, and the most determined were those bearing the most prestigious names in France, the great feudal lords desperately eager to regain the rank and power of counsellors by virtue of birth at the side of the very young king to which they laid claim. On his father's death the Prince de Condé was rapidly appointed to the highest offices, Grand Master of France and Governor of Burgundy; after Rocroi Louis II de Bourbon continued to distinguish himself, leading the royal armies on the Low Countries front until the victory at Lens in August 1648, which led to a rapid peace settlement in Europe. As a victorious general at the head of his troops, he initially opposed the dissidents representing the *Parlement* and sided with the Queen Regent and the young king, opening the gates of Paris to them after a cruel blockade. But the prince of royal blood had not fought to put a man like Mazarin in power. The dynastic pride that was always heightened in the Condé lineage[2], traditionally tending to rebel against the senior branch of the Bourbons, reinforced by resentment at not having been thanked commensurately for the services he had rendered, prompted him to adopt a lofty, peremptory attitude towards royal power and to make contact with the rebellious princes and dukes. After being arrested in 1650, held prisoner at Vincennes along with his brother Conti and his brother-in-law Longueville, then freed a year later, he became more deeply implicated in the rebellion. The final threshold was soon crossed: he entered into negotiations with the king of Spain, then led the fight against the royal troops outside Paris, at the Porte Saint-Antoine. Condé had become a public enemy. Disowned by the *Parlement* and the people of Paris, he headed for the frontier and took refuge in the Netherlands, pursued by the armies of Turenne and La Ferté which sacked Chantilly on their way. His property was confiscated, and he was condemned to death on 27 March 1654. On the northern frontier Condé went back into service, but this time under the king of Spain's orders, and he led his armies in battles against his rival Turenne, some of which went badly, such as the Battle of the Dunes (14 June 1658). At Chantilly during his absence, the princesses associated with the Fronde inevitably felt the force of royal power, but once calm had been restored the French court gladly resumed its earlier outings there, with an increasing number of festivities being held in the banished prince's château; the Duke of Mantua and Queen Kristina of Sweden were received there. The war finally came to an end, thanks to French victories and Mazarin's astuteness. During negotiations leading to the Peace of the Pyrenees, King Philip IV did not prove ungrateful towards the prince, insisting on defending his interests. By showing contrition, Condé was able to recover his titles and property. On 29 December 1659 he left Brussels, and on 27 January he was at Aix-la-Chapelle (Aachen) where he threw himself at the feet of Louis XIV, who then handed him letters repealing his punishment. He could finally start with a clean sheet.

All the same, the king kept him on trial for ten years, but the prince carried out his duties assiduously, as a perfect courtier.[3] Then in December 1667 Condé at last received the military command to which he had long aspired in order to prove his loyalty; he was given command of the army of Germany and performed wonders. Glory again awaited him. Franche-Comté was conquered in a fortnight, and to his victories on the Rhine were added victories in the Low Countries (Seneffe, 1674) and finally in Alsace. But the following year the time came for him to retire from service at the age of fifty-four, suffering dreadfully from gout which had ravaged his emaciated body.

Le Nôtre at Chantilly - The gardener and his master

From the first year of his return to favour Condé demonstrated his interest in Chantilly. He fell in love with the site and had a presentiment of the great plans he could develop there. He also guessed that by making his principal residence at that distance from Paris he would have the opportunity to gather around him a true princely court, independent of but rivalling that of the king, because he could depend on the powerful links of patronage maintained by his family for the last century through all levels of society.

As usual the new master first tackled not the buildings but the gardens; to some extent they could be cleared, tamed and altered gradually at small expense, and his finances were still in a very sorry state. In 1662 he straight away called on the most famous of all "gardeners", André Le Nôtre – the man who could not be ignored – who had only recently created the marvels of Vaux-le-Vicomte for Superintendent Fouquet, in 1656-61.[4] It was again he that Louis XIV engaged for Versailles in 1661, and the transformations at Chantilly were thus implemented during the same years as the royal landscaping work, and certainly, on the prince's side, in a spirit of competition with his cousin, in spite of the obvious differences arising from history and the site.[5]

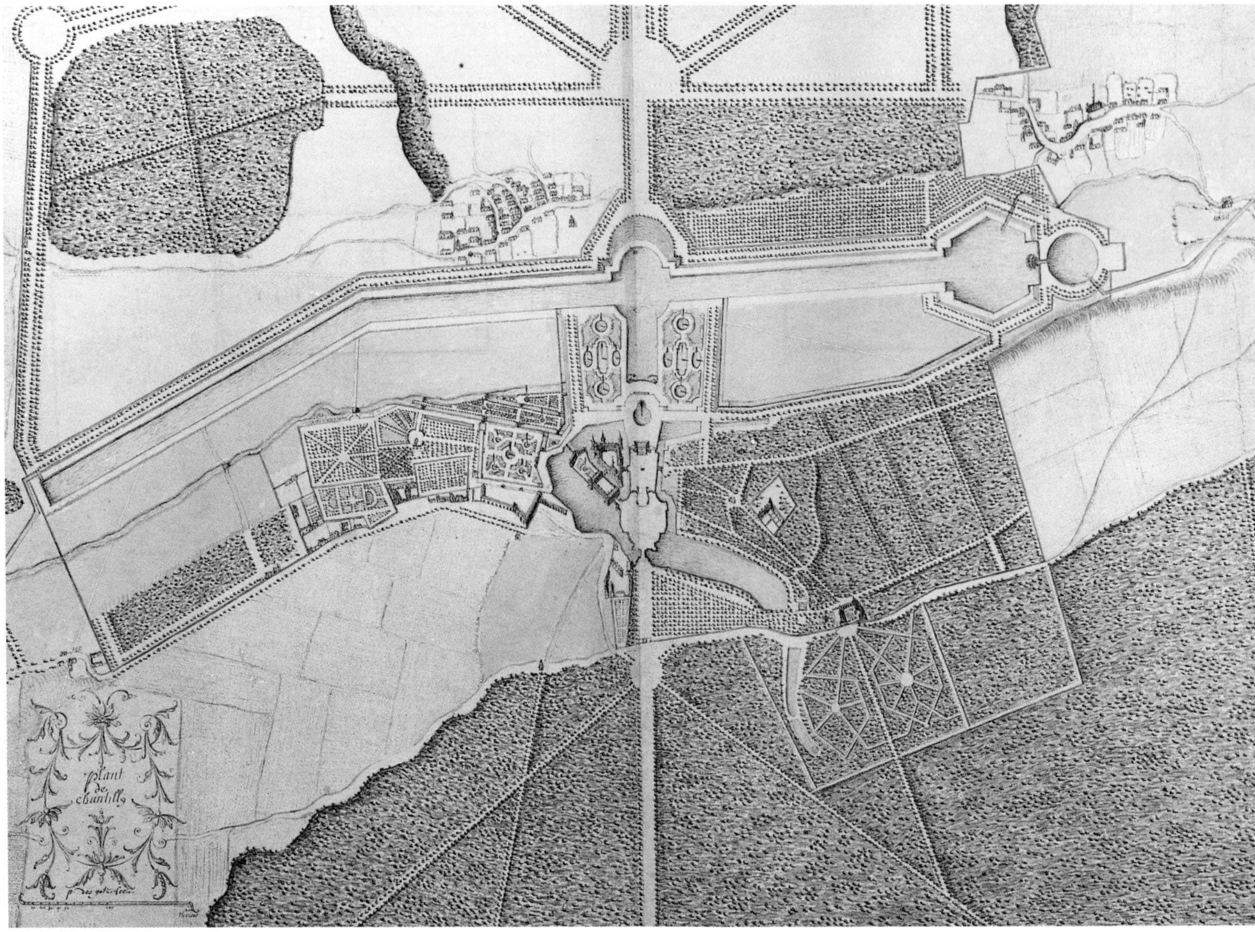

Plan of the gardens
Pierre II Desgots, a garden designer and the nephew and collaborator of Le Nôtre, drew up this plan in 1673. We can see the Grand Canal, the parterres and the gardens in the western sector.

At the age of forty-nine Le Nôtre was a man of great experience, and Chantilly was to derive immense benefit from his genius, capable of grasping the spirit of the place. At Chantilly he led a team of talented collaborators: his nephew Pierre II Desgots, Father Le Gendre, the curate of Hénonville, a specialist in fruit trees, later replaced by La Quintinye, Daniel Gittard, an architect who had worked on the site at Vaux before Le Nôtre and who later entered the service of the king's brother, Monsieur le Prince[6], and lastly at a later stage a financier clever at overseeing the hydraulic works, Jacques de Manse. Dom Louis Loppin, a Benedictine prior who must have had time on his hands, oversaw the work sites for six years.

Le Nôtre[7], looking with a new eye at the landscape as a whole and no longer just at the château and its immediate vicinity, gradually brought about a transformation of the site. Confronting nature in all its disparity, still no more than countryside, it was a hard task, but one that inspired his genius all the more:

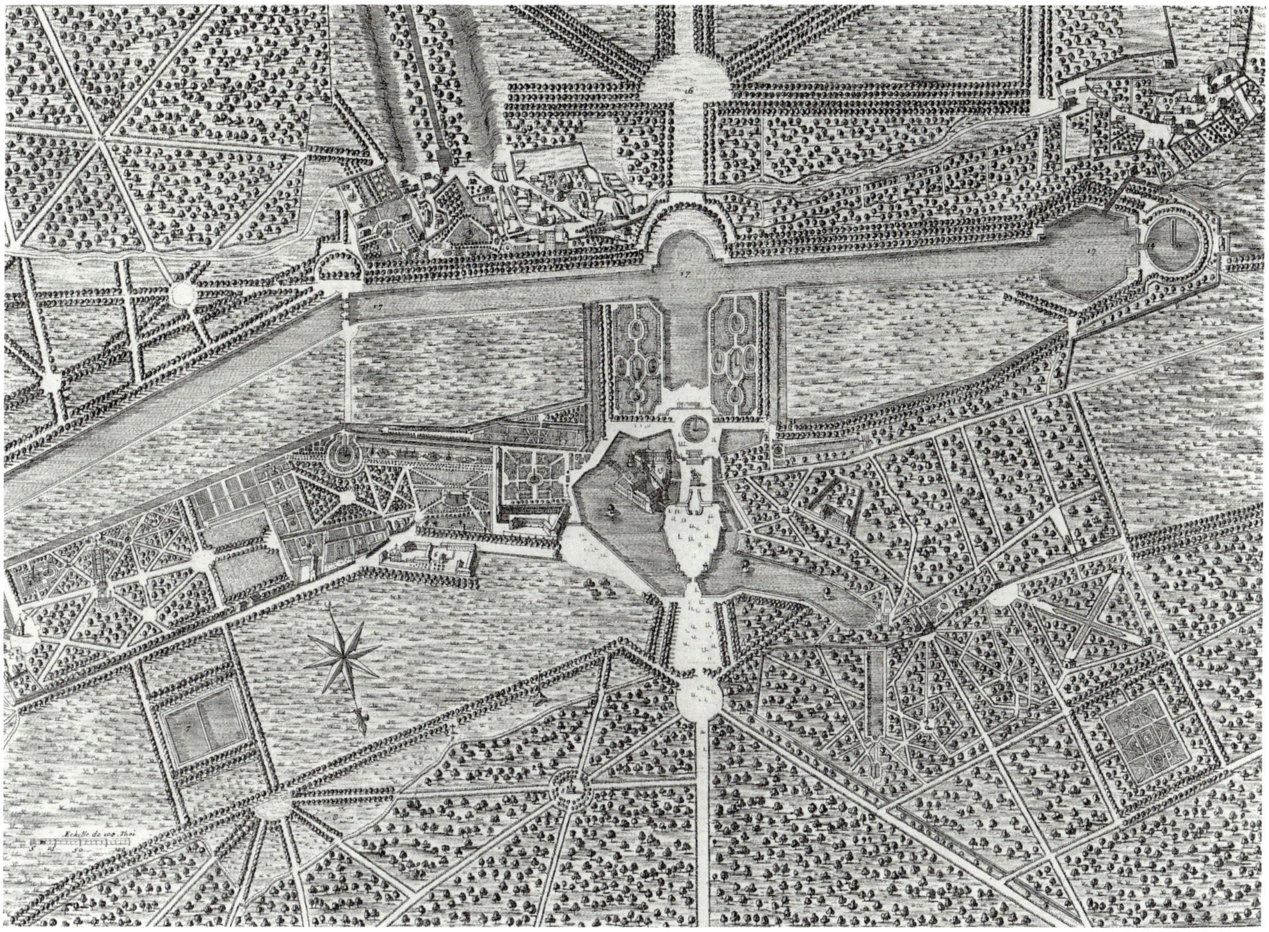

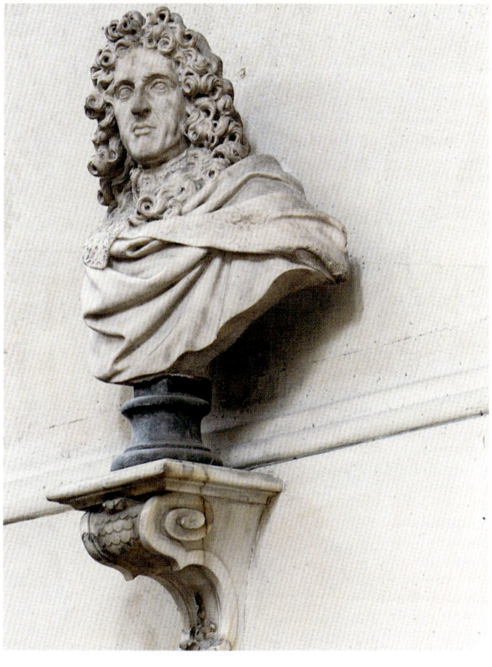

Plan of the gardens
This view engraved by Aveline after a drawing by a gardener at Chantilly called Breteuil is later than the plan by Desgots. The banks of the ponds surrounding the château have been straightened, the gardens on the west extended, and we can see the reservoirs on the Pelouse.

André Le Nôtre
This bust of the great gardener by Antoine Coysevox adorned his tomb, erected in his Paris parish church of Saint-Roch.

vistas had to be opened up, large masses balanced, and sky and water brought into harmony. There is an implied suggestion that Chantilly was one of his favourite creations in the letter he addressed in 1698 at the end of his life to the Duke of Portland, Ambassador Extraordinary to William III, who was then finishing his mission in France after negotiating the Peace of Ryswick: "Remember all you have seen by way of gardens in France – Versailles, Fontainebleau, Vaux-le-Vicomte and the Tuileries and above all Chantilly."[8]

In 1662, before embarking on new projects, it was necessary first to take stock of the estate and to set about enlarging it, a task the prince pursued with the zeal of an avid huntsman, setting off in conquest of the woodlands and nearby meadows between Vineuil, Saint-Firmin and Apremont.[9] He persuaded Cardinal de Retz, the abbot of Saint-Denis, to assign the lordship of Gouvieux and the woodlands of Saint-Denis to him (1663), and acquired still more woodland from the Priory of Saint-Leu-d'Esserent and the abbeys of Maubuisson, Royaumont and Chaalis (Commelles estate, 1666). The Great Park, is enlarged to over 2000 acres (900 hectares) and enclosed by walls. South towards La Chapelle en Serval, Le Nôtre could then design a magnificent network of straight roads cutting through the heart of the forest, twelve of them converging radially at the Rond-point de la Table. Further west, the Allée du Connétable, six *toises* (12 m) wide and one league (4 km) long, led to the château. That was the first job done.

It was then time to move on to the implementation of a twenty-year plan aimed at profoundly altering the design of the gardens. These were divided into three large sectors which we find recurring regularly at each stage of the history of Chantilly: the west behind the château in the direction of the town, the north opposite the terrace towards Vineuil, and the forested east in the Sylvie area towards Avilly. The old sixteenth-century gardens to the west were the first to be altered, for a crucial reason: they were in the princes' field of vision from the windows of their suites of rooms in the Old Château. Just as on the south *parterre* at Versailles and at the same time, Le Nôtre first planted a *bois vert* or green wood, a copse of coniferous trees, pines and cypresses which formed a sharp contrast with the foliage of deciduous leaves; this was a fashionable course of action, updated from the Jardin des Pins created for Francis I at Fontainebleau. The *parterres* near Bucamp and in front of the Galerie des Cerfs were reorganised along new lines, with new beds being created, like the Parterre des Grenouilles, at the end of the Pont de la Volière alongside the pond. They were embellished by ornamental ponds, one decorated with a lead hydra made by the sculptor Blanchard. Further north, a canal lapped the shores of two islands in the triangular network created by its arms.

It was in 1665 that Le Nôtre began to deal with the northern sector, the valley of the Nonette, an area of marshy meadows, as yet completely untouched, which provided the landscape architect with favourable opportunities for opening up the main axis of his composition to the north. After filling in half of the pond known as the Étang du Serrurier[10] and taking care of the preparatory work for the construction of a large staircase leading down from the Terrasse du Connétable, he had the circular Bassin de la Gerbe dug out on the main axis, and its water effects were tried out in 1666: "Tell M. Le Nôtre," the prince wrote to his secretary in December, "that I would like him to come here. We have tried the Gerbe water spray; but it does not produce quite the effect I had hoped for; his opinion is needed to set it to rights." The following year he designed the two large *parterres* on the right and the left, with ten ornamental ponds that act like ten mirrors lighting them up, but soon there was no money left to carry on, and patience had to be exercised while waiting for the steward Hérauld de Gourville to re-establish order in his master's finances.

By 1670 this had been done, and work could be resumed, with an eagerness rendered feverish by the announcement that the king would be coming. Louis XIV's visit to Chantilly on 23 and 24 April 1671 has been chronicled many times[11], in particular in a frequently quoted letter from Madame de Sévigné who took part in the festivities, a famous visit like the one the king had paid to Vaux ten years earlier, and while it did not prove fatal to the owner, it was fatal for the unfortunate major-domo of the prince's household, François Vatel, formerly employed by Fouquet, whose honour was put at stake: on the first day there was no roast meat at a few tables, and the belief that the fish had been delayed led him to take the irreparable step of killing himself. It may be surmised that journeys by the court were a terrifying burden to those organising them, who had to lodge, feed and entertain thousands of people, but for Louis XIV in 1671 it was the ideal opportunity to demonstrate ostentatiously the esteem and affection he felt towards his cousin. Moreover, he was unstinting in his praise, approving the new work carried out and the future plans as a connoisseur, and admiring the parterres where Condé who had a great knowledge of botany had given free rein to his passion for flowers.

Following pages

Le Nôtre's *parterres*
The Bassin de la Gerbe, the Manche, the Grand Canal and in the background on the right the Vertugadin.

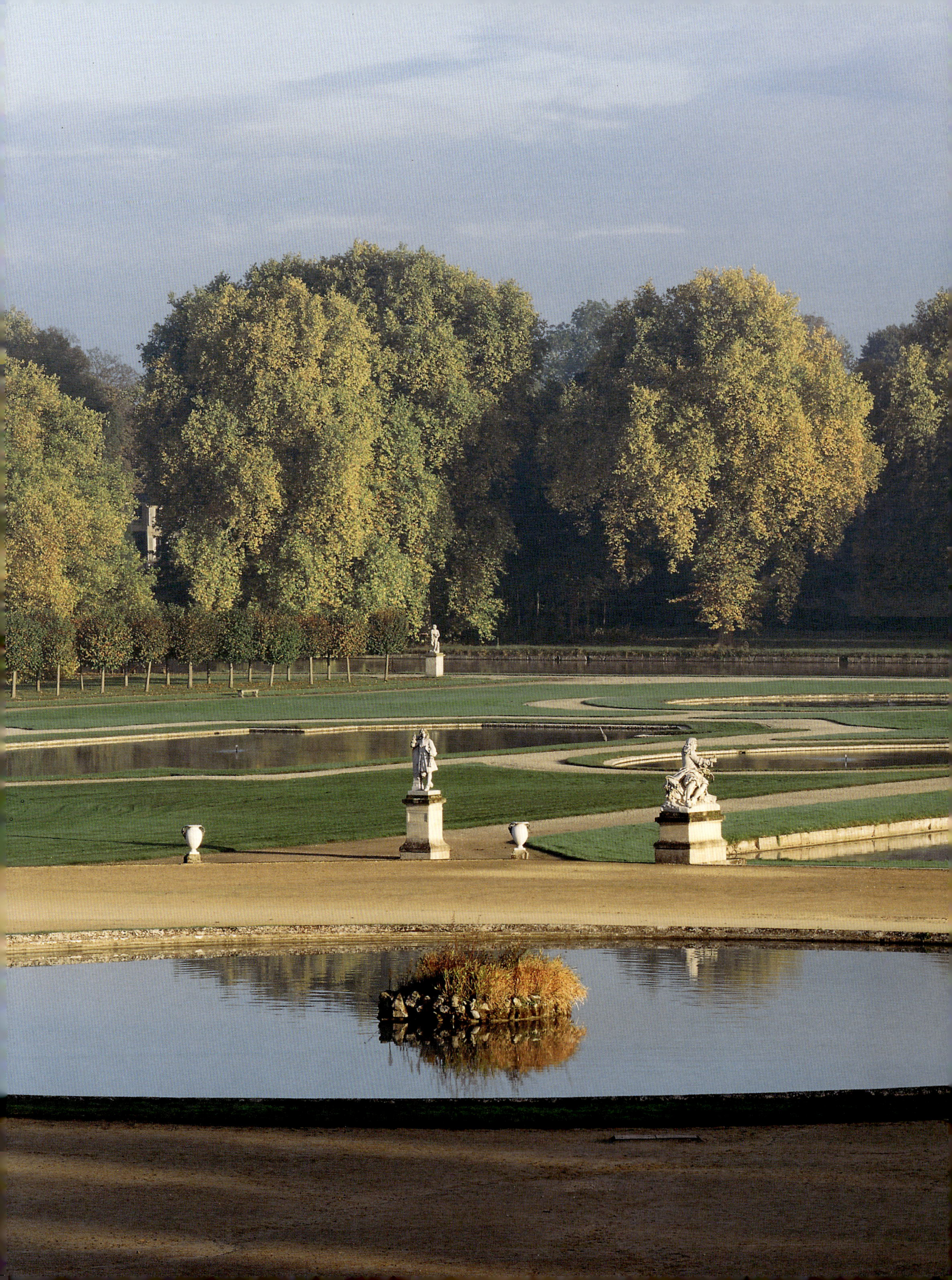

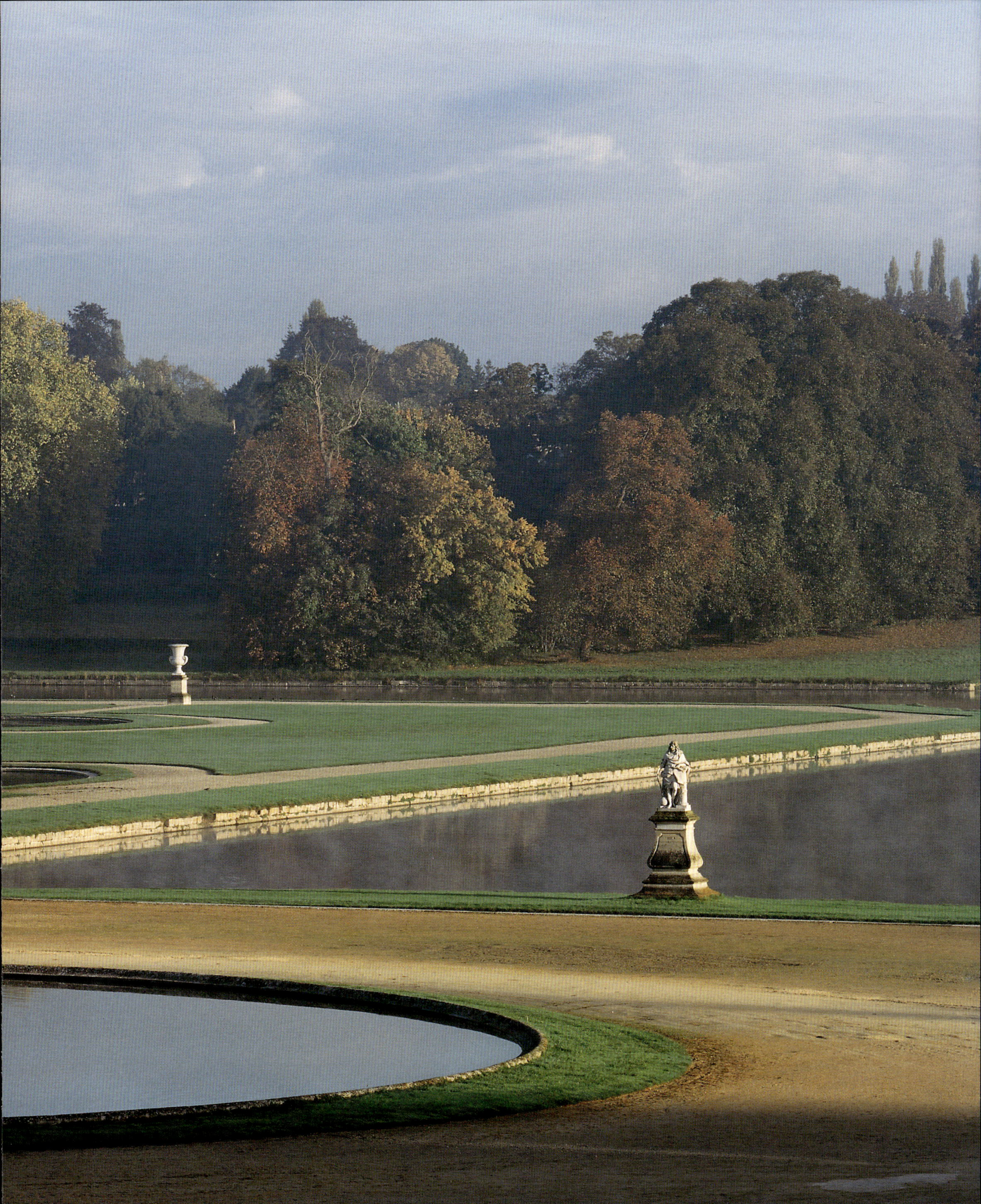

In the course of the next two years, in 1672-73, the meadows were drained and the Nonette diverted. Captured to the east, it fed a round ornamental pond, which emptied as a waterfall into an octagon that formed the head of the Grand Canal, a huge expanse of water of a size never previously known in France[12] since it was 2,500 m long and 30 m wide. This artificial river crossed the entire site, with a change of axis at the Trois Ponts du Coude, where it met the road to Veneuil and Senlis. On the north side it was edged with avenues of tall trees, and on the main axis enhanced by being widened at one point to form a semi-circle enclosed by grassy slopes in the shape of an amphitheatre. This is the "Vertugadin" (literally, "farthingale") which ends with a large perpendicular opening towards the horizon. This is the backdrop of the setting on the Vineuil side. On the Chantilly side, the canal washed the banks of the two parterres laid out on the low ground below the Terrasse du Connétable, and between them it received a tributary, the Manche, a wide perpendicular arm that could be used as a landing stage by lovers of boating. Le Nôtre here used the idea of the large transversal canal he had laid out at Vaux while grafting on an arm of the Versailles canal longitudinally. When faced with the horizon, he was never short of ideas. The unanimous verdict was one of admiration – La Rochefoucauld, Colbert and Dangeau all lauded the superb arrangement of the waterways round which they were shown by the steward, Gourville, while his master was serving his king in Holland. "Of all the places the sun shines on," Madame de La Fayette wrote to Madame de Sévigné, "there is none that can be compared with this." Further west Le Nôtre started work on a new site, the scope of which we can no longer appreciate since a whole district of the town has been built over the far end of these gardens whilst the remainder, after the havoc wrought by the Revolution, was transformed into an English garden. So the few traces of the former terracing have to be searched for on the ground, and to picture this superb ensemble that could rival the gardens of the Grand Trianon we have to resort to the many, invaluable seventeenth-century prints which depict it systematically, in particular those engraved by Adam Pérelle, who worked to order here because the prince had chosen him as drawing master for his son, the duc d'Enghien. The invaluable river Nonette supplied water to a second canal on this side, the Canal Saint-Jean, almost parallel to the Grand Canal, from which it was separated by vast meadows left as grass; it went to the former hamlet of Quinquenpoit, the houses of which were demolished at this time. The new

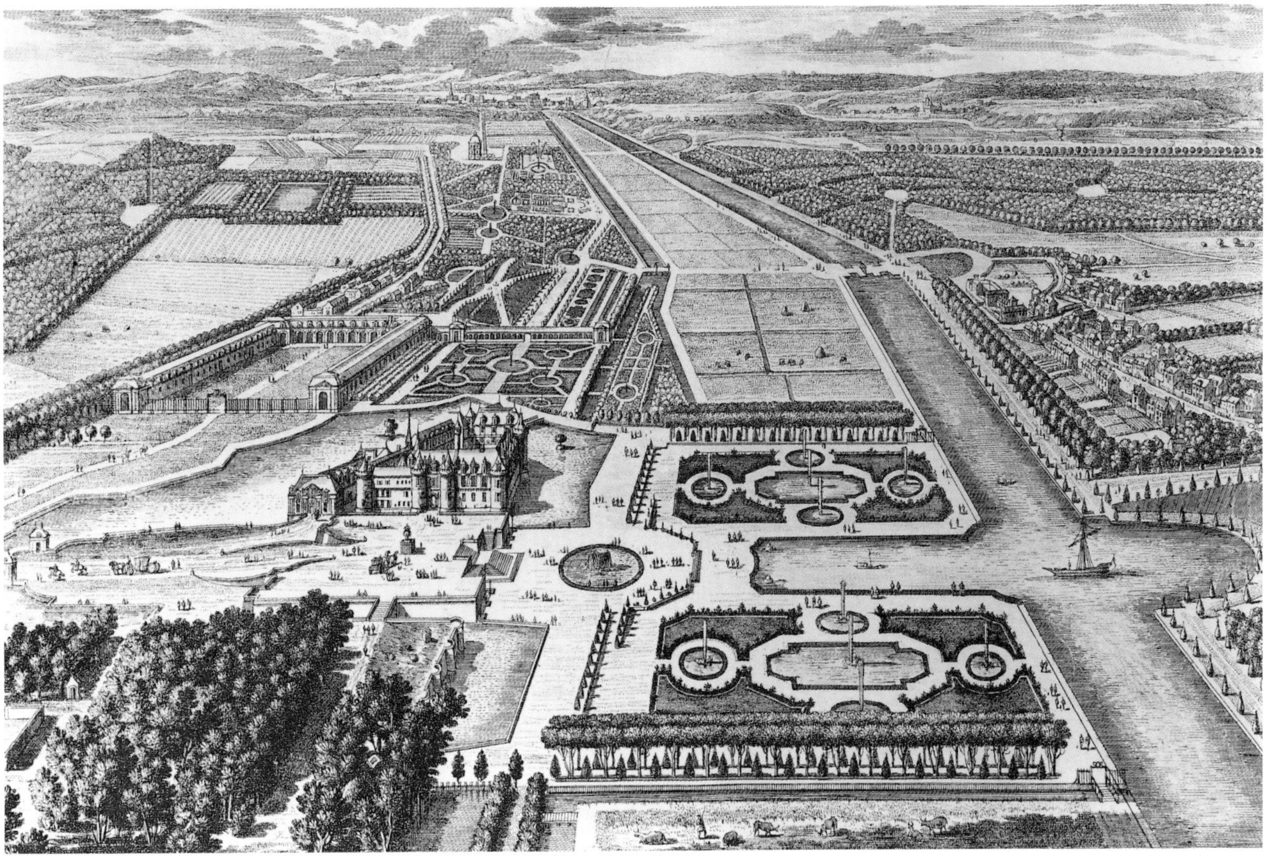

Bird's eye view
Engraved by Adam Pérelle, this view behind the château shows the Orangerie by Jules Hardouin-Mansart, between its main court (a project never carried out) and its square *parterre*, then the Galerie des Cerfs and the gardens beyond to the west.

gardens designed by Le Nôtre occupied the gentle ups and downs of the valley adjoining the south bank of the Canal Saint-Jean, and were arranged following the lines of the longitudinal pathways that kept to the different levels, or perpendicular ones descending the slope. At the foot of the large square Parterre de l'Orangerie, there was first the Île du Bois Vert, embellished with small cascades, vases, and above all a series of trelliswork arbours and porches, in one of which two bronze dragons faced one another with their jets of water. As craftsmen were being sought to assemble these light structures, the Great Condé who was then campaigning in the Low Countries realised that the Dutch were very skilled at building small wooden houses for themselves, and he recruited three joiners who settled at Chantilly and became established there; their descendants worked as the boatmen on the Grand Canal.

Further west on the lower part was an elongated *parterre de broderies* (knot garden), and halfway down the slope were fountains and groves. The Bassin de Beauvais is very fortunately still in place, the only remaining trace we can admire, a long stretch of water that fed the Petites Cascades, decorated with basins and

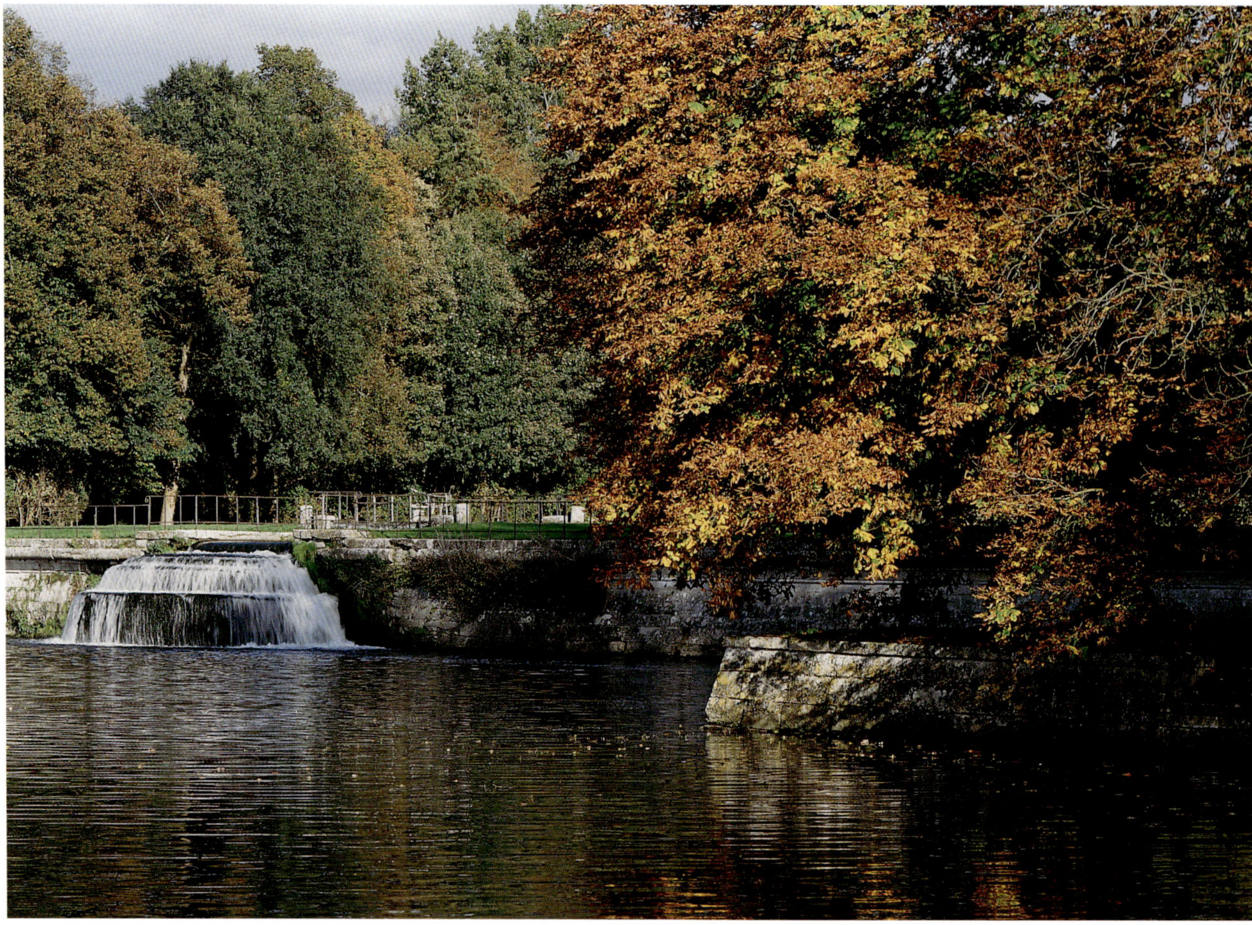

Waterfalls at the head of the Grand Canal
The water supplied by the Nonette falls from the round ornamental pond known as the Bassin des Sources into "the octagon", which is more of a hexagon.

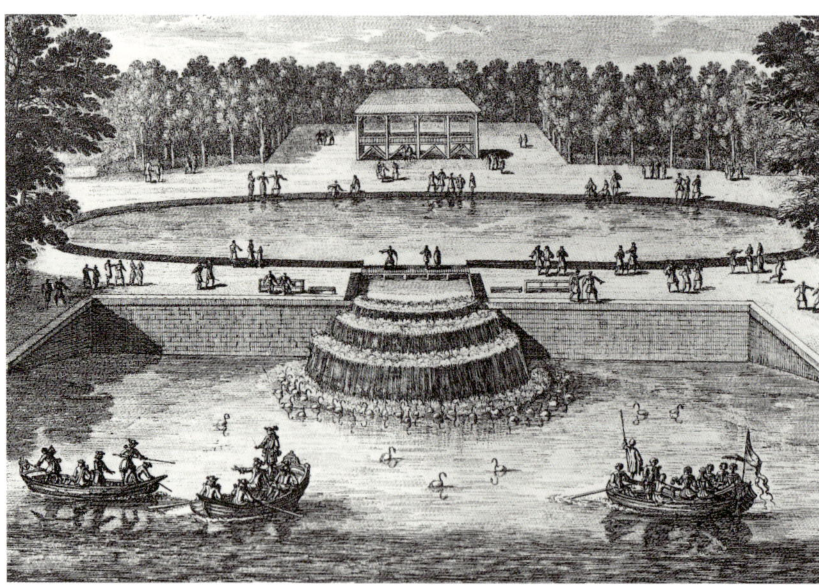

The Grand Rond and waterfall at the head of the canal at Chantilly
Adam Pérelle made this engraving in 1680.

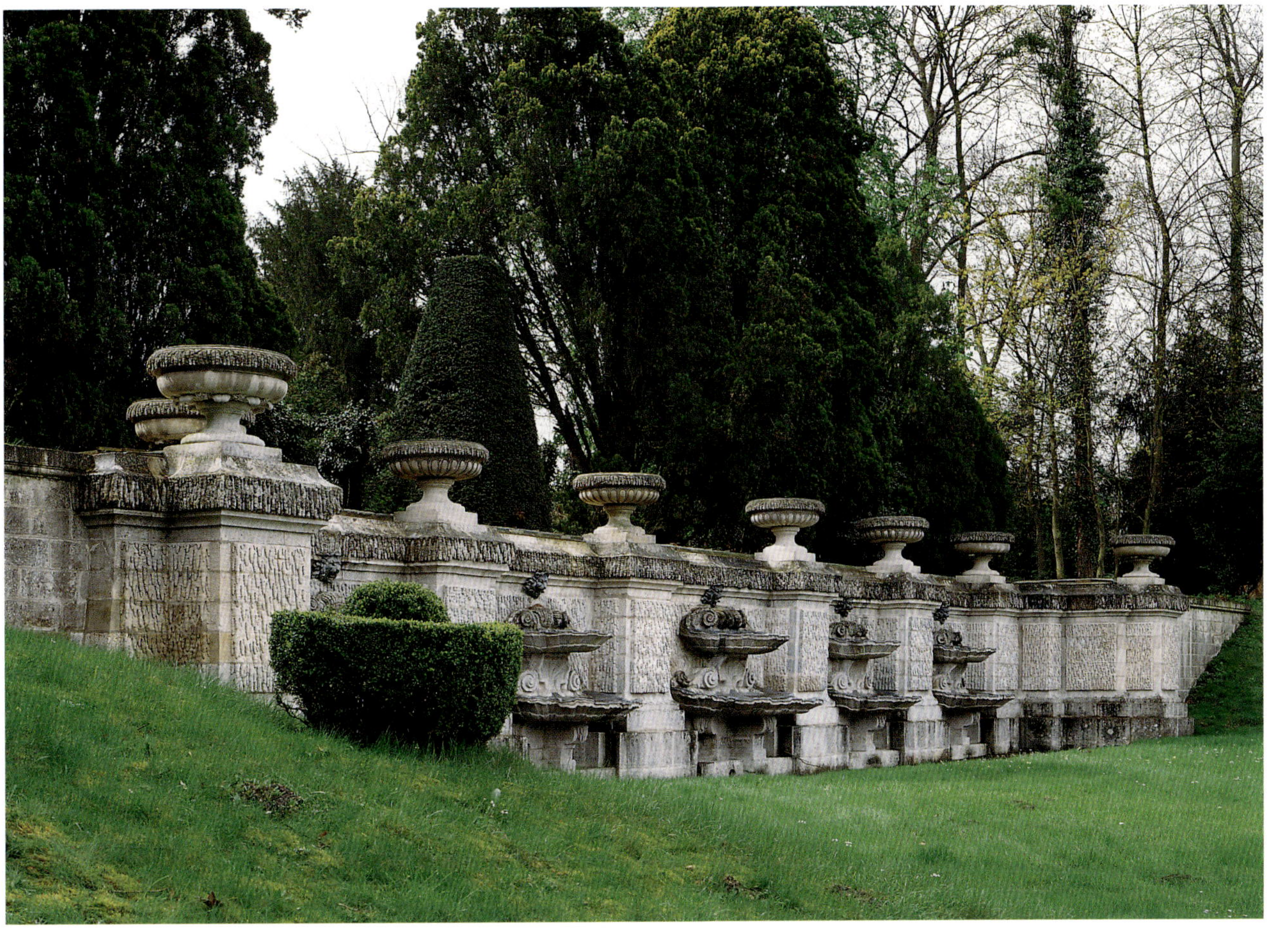

The Cascades de Beauvais
The magnificent array of water with its vases, basins and stalactited ornamentation is all that remains of the western gardens laid out by Le Nôtre.

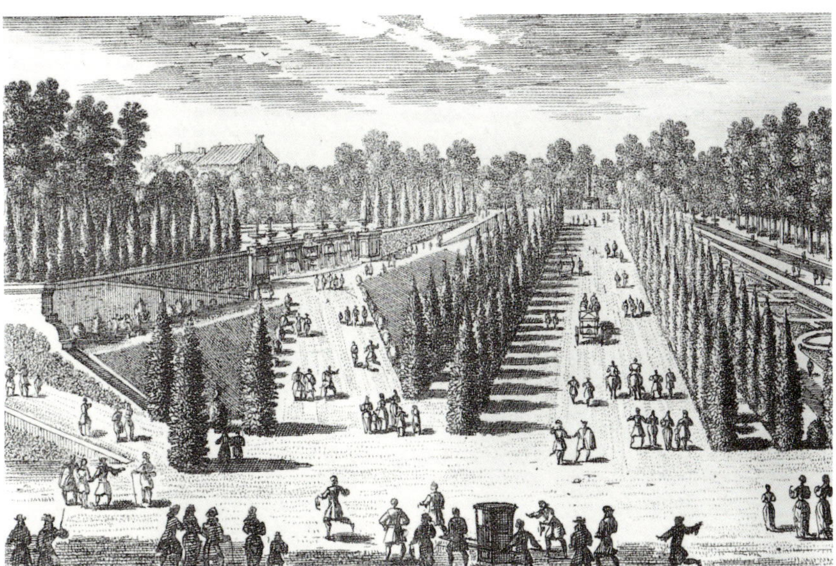

The Boulingrin (lawn) and the Cascades de Beauvais
This engraving by Adam Pérelle makes it possible to pinpoint the position of the Cascades de Beauvais, placed halfway up the slope on the left above the avenues and parterres beside the Canal Saint-Jean.

The Pavillon de Manse
This strange, handsome structure now encircled by the development of the town was the nub of the hydraulic arrangements at Chantilly.
The water was sent to the reservoirs on the Pelouse and then distributed to the ornamental pools and fountains.

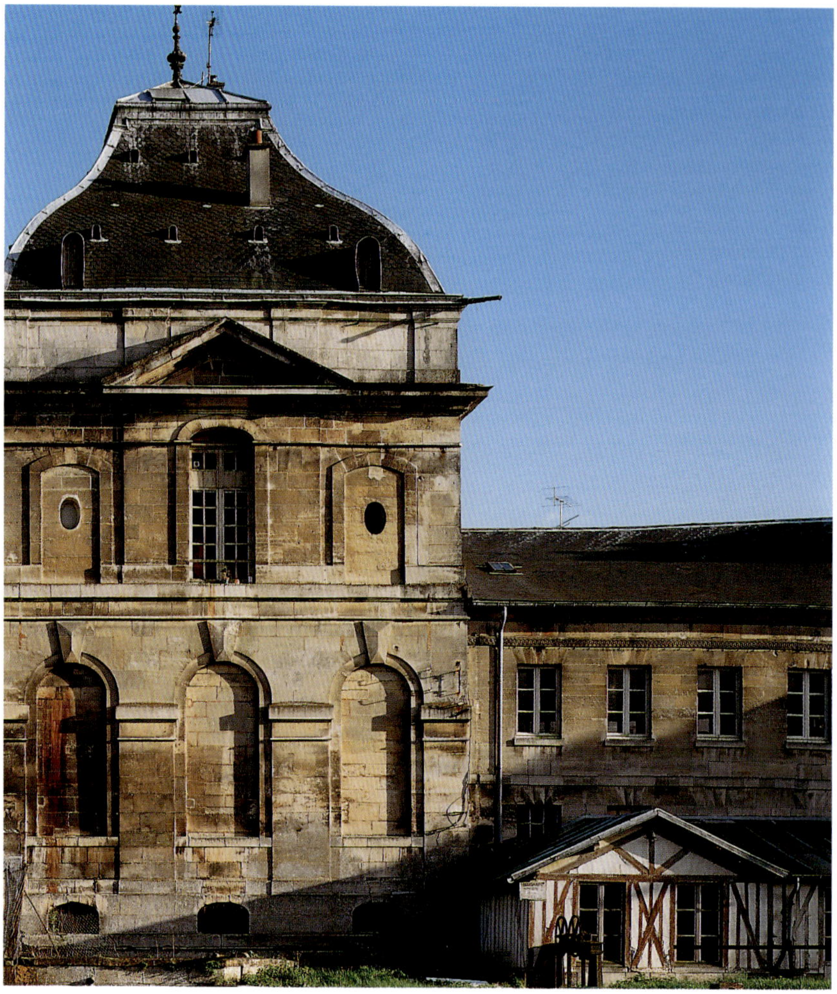

The Grande Écluse and the Pavillon de Manse
Engraving by Adam Pérelle.
The side canal and its lock rejoined the Grand Canal well after the bend where the road to Senlis now crosses.

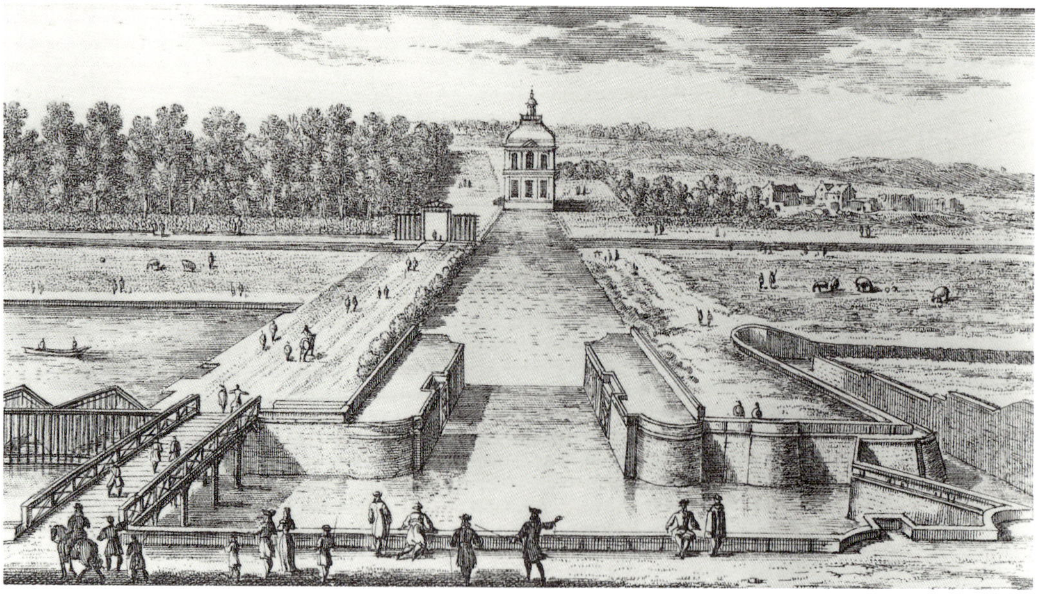

shells modelled by the sculptor Jacques Houzeau in 1682. The next feature was the Bosquet de la Tenaille, a grove enclosing a circular ornamental pond, then the pheasantry, the kitchen garden and the Grandes Cascades, the masterly effect of which was reminiscent of the waterfalls at Saint-Cloud. The roads in the town of Chantilly later laid out on those sites were given the same names. Finally the ultimate effect was produced by the Bassin du Grand Jet. Still further on the Pavillon de Manse remains like a marker, now isolated in the middle of the town with its canal and lock. This extremely original building, topped by a two-storey roof, used to house the engine of the hydraulic system, the machinery that made the water play throughout the park.[13] As far back as 1627, duc Henri II de Montmorency had taken care to capture springs at Saint-Léonard – four kilometres away – and lead them via an aqueduct to a spot under the terrace where the château of Enghien now stands. In the time of the Great Condé, these precious resources were stored in a reservoir dug out beneath the Pelouse, and in 1677 Jacques de Manse[14] had the lifting machinery constructed in the pavilion that bears his name. The water was distributed towards the ornamental ponds and fountains along wooden conduits made from hollowed-out tree trunks; it was only from 1719 on that they were gradually replaced by metal pipes supplied by Pollard, the contractor for the king's fountains, who allowed Chantilly to benefit from the stocks left unused since the death of Louis XIV. Finally to the east, the Maison de Sylvie was rebuilt on the orders of the young duc d'Enghien, who

The Fontaine de Sylvie
Engraving by Adam Pérelle.
The terrace arranged above the springs that feed the Étang de Sylvie provided a pleasant area for relaxation.

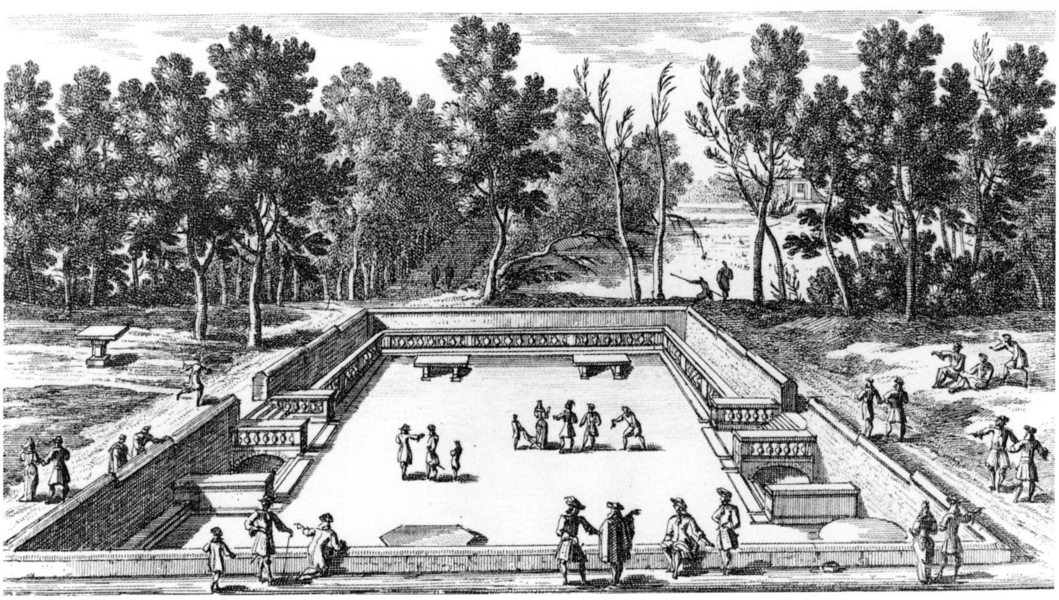

ably assisted his father at Chantilly. The new pleasure pavilion had the honour of a visit from Louis XIV in 1671, and it was surrounded by a new park cut out from the forest, with a half-moon, groves and lastly a maze, designed by Desgots in 1679. Lower down, above the pond, the Fontaine de Sylvie was arranged as a resting place and picnic area, edged by balustrades and equipped with tables, conducive to conversation or to reverie.

The main challenge, however, was still the approach to Chantilly, which was hardly a source of satisfaction to the master of the house since it was necessary to follow an awkward zigzag roundabout route before reaching either of the two châteaux, and their links with the gardens and the park still followed a somewhat labyrinthine course. In short, it was the entire system of an earlier age that had to be rethought, derived from military history that had now moved on: the Picardy road crossing the ponds and overlooked by a castle on its rock. Condé and Le Nôtre felt it was right to break free of these constraints and clear an open thoroughfare along the approach axis, and since the configuration of the site meant it was not possible to lead up to the château as its culminating point, as at Versailles, the focal point had to be in mid-air, directed towards the statue of the Constable, and the terrace nobly linked to the arrival court on the one side and the gardens on the other. This bold, long and expensive programme did not deter the prince, and today forms the main beauty of Chantilly, and its profound originality.

The new plan of action consisted first of bringing a straight avenue – the Allée du Connétable – in from the forest along the edge of the Pelouse as far as the new point chosen for crossing the Étang de Sylvie, and filling in part of the pond to create an oblong esplanade on its site, with its edges cut out with curves and stepped shapes like the compartments of a *parterre.* Instead of the narrow causeway that travelled at an oblique angle[15] across the water to the lower court of the château, it was now the earth that advanced towards the visitor, as if to welcome him. All that remained was to cross the short span of a drawbridge from the south bank, where a harmonious intersection was designed. At that point, a railing and two stone look-out towers topped with accolade mouldings bring us back into the reassuring world of classicism. In 1673, the building work on the forecourt was completed by Gittard from Le Nôtre's drawings.[16]

On the left, still on the low level of the esplanade, an oblique avenue led to the bridge of the Petit Château; the old Capitainerie buildings in front of it were

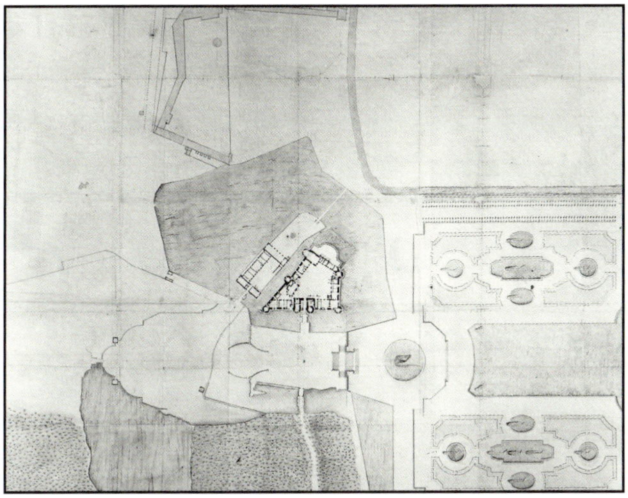

The Château and the *parterres* circa 1683
This drawing made by Jules Hardouin-Mansart's office shows the initial arrangement of the forecourt, still linked to the land on the west side, as well as the asymmetrical plan of the terrace.

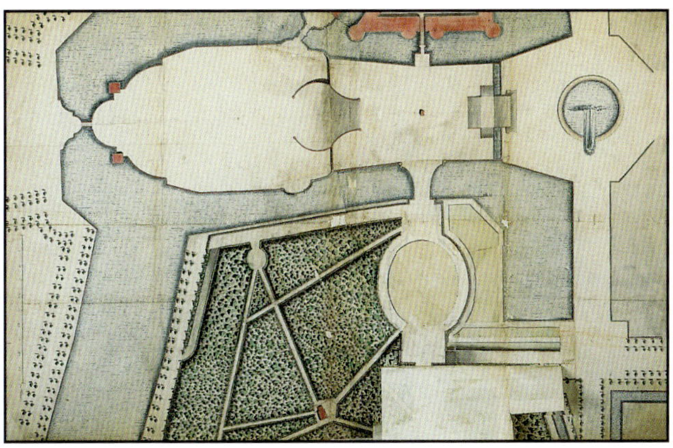

Scheme for the forecourt and terrace
The forecourt is finished and the terrace straightened out, but a branch of water was intended to pass under the Pont du Roi and join the Étang du Serrurier, and would have led to an oval green room – octagonal on the variant drawing – at the edge of the wooded park.

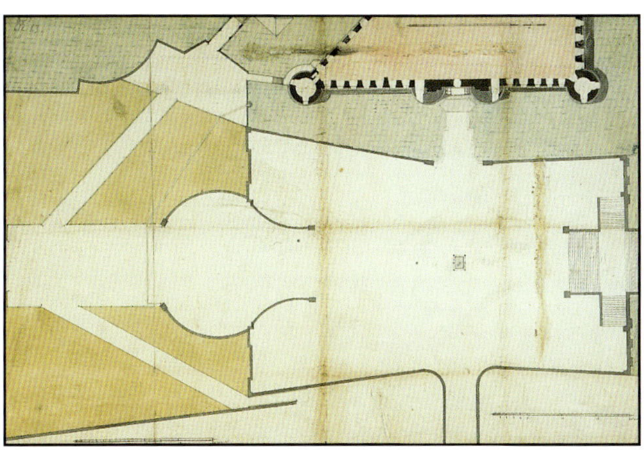

Plan of the forecourt and terrace
This ink drawing corresponds to the work as it was carried out.

razed to the ground. On the approach axis, on the other hand, it was necessary to climb up one level to reach the statue of the Constable, using the staircase built in 1538. The old terrace which followed an irregular rectangular plan was bordered along the sides by a parapet, broken along the east-west axis by the drawbridges leading on one side to the Old Château, and on the other to the road to Senlis and the park. The retaining walls surrounding it were faced with dressed stone on the sides that were visible, but probably not on the north, or on the east either, where the cut into the rock remained obvious on both sides of the dry moat (i.e. in front of what is now the château of Enghien), as can be convincingly seen from studying the engravings. Le Nôtre kept the level of the terrace and improved the openings in the parapet leading to the bridges to the château and the park, the latter also known as the Pont du Roi;[17] he had masonry work carried out on the east wall after making it symmetrical with the west side by means of a slightly concave curve harmoniously complementing the design of the terrace. Detailed study of some plan drawings suggests that Le Nôtre had intended to cover the east side of the terrace with water, by digging out an arm that would have joined the stretch of water known as the Étang du Serrurier by passing under the Pont du Roi, in order to make the layout completely symmetrical. For reasons unknown to us, the area was left as a lawn.[18] To the south and north, on the other hand, major terracing work completely changed the previous configuration of the site: the approach had to be given a monumental character and the platform turned into a true view-point, while at the same time becoming the hub of the whole arrangement. On the south side, Le Nôtre replaced the staircase with a wide ramp following the shape of a lyre, that led at a gentle gradient from the forecourt to the statue of the Constable. On the north side, where the difference in level had to be overcome more quickly while an outstanding view of the parterres and the Grand Canal could be enjoyed, he and Gittard produced designs for a monumental staircase. The opinion of Jules Hardouin-Mansart, then at the outset of his brilliant career,[19] was sought regarding these designs; it was no doubt Le Nôtre who requested this consultation for such a critical project, and who introduced the architect to the duc d'Enghien – his presence at Chantilly is documented in May 1674.[20] Mansart probably had a hand in several projects that are reminiscent of his manner, such as the vaulted galleries dug out under the terrace to the left of the ramp[21] and some aspects of the design of the staircase which we

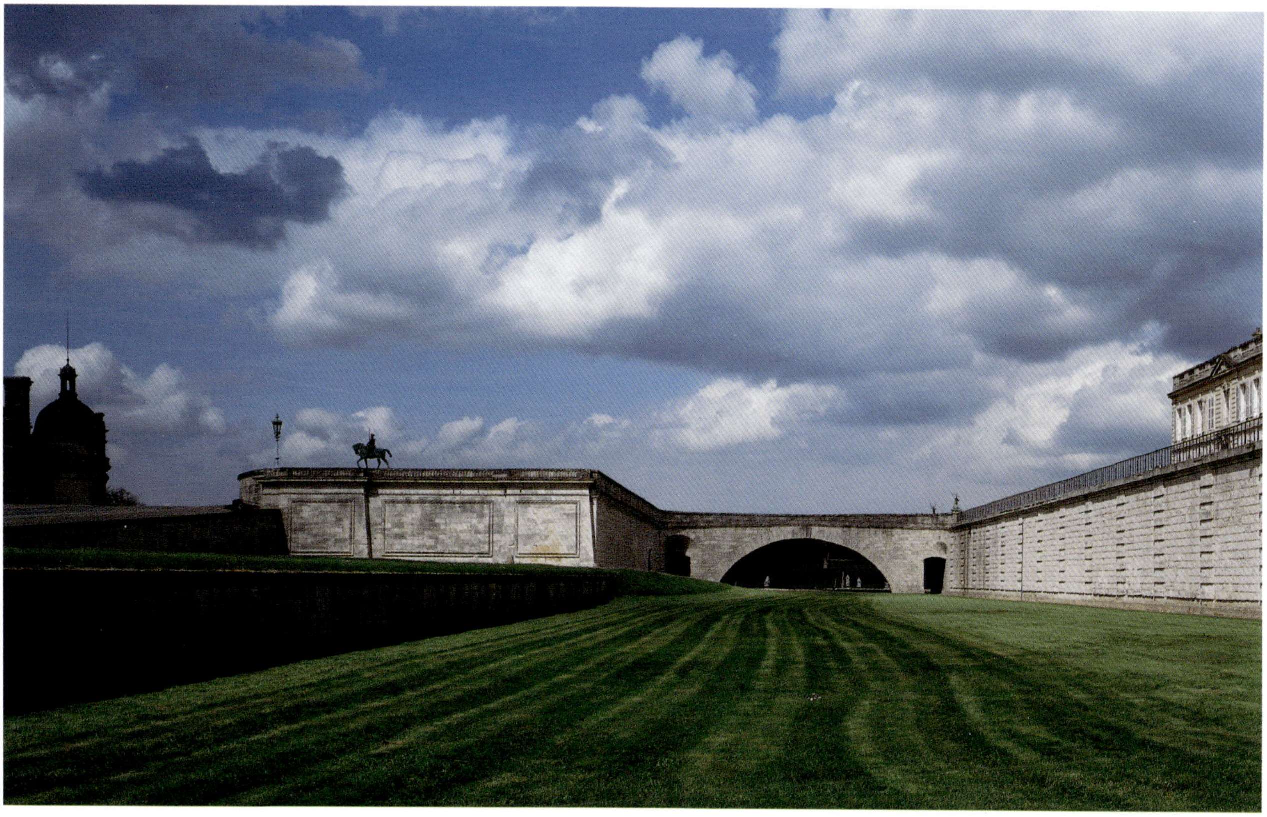

will discuss. The Grand Degré was undertaken in 1681, a crucial project linking the terrace and the parterres, thanks to its three upper arms – an axial and two lateral ones – harmoniously brought together by a shared landing from which the single lower flight starts. Gittard was its designer, while Le Nôtre devoted all his attention to the grottoes created under the two inclines. The steps and grottoes bring to mind the similar structures built by the two men at the far end of the great vista at Vaux-le-Vicomte. On the other hand the projecting side parts with niches framed by pairs of sturdy Tuscan columns with rustication differ from the rustic Mannerism of the projecting structures at Vaux in their classical monumentality, which is closer to the Orangerie at Versailles, its central projecting part in particular, which Mansart was to build in 1684. Le Nôtre attached great importance to the ornamentation of this piece fit for a king. On 21 September 1683 he wrote to the Great Condé: "This is all I can do to adorn the bottom of your grand staircase; I wish you may like it as much as I do. The river will be made of stucco, and so will the rest. Bertier will make the roof entirely of rock. The urn will throw up as much water as you want to give

The Pont du Roi

Constable de Montmorency had made the old road to Picardy pass under a bridge located at this spot, a road that the Great Condé finally had re-routed outside his park. The arm of water Le Nôtre certainly intended to have here was never dug. The new bridge, known as the Pont du Roi, was constructed by Prince Henri-Jules shortly after 1700.

Following pages

Le Grand Degré

This great staircase was the work of Le Nôtre and Gittard.

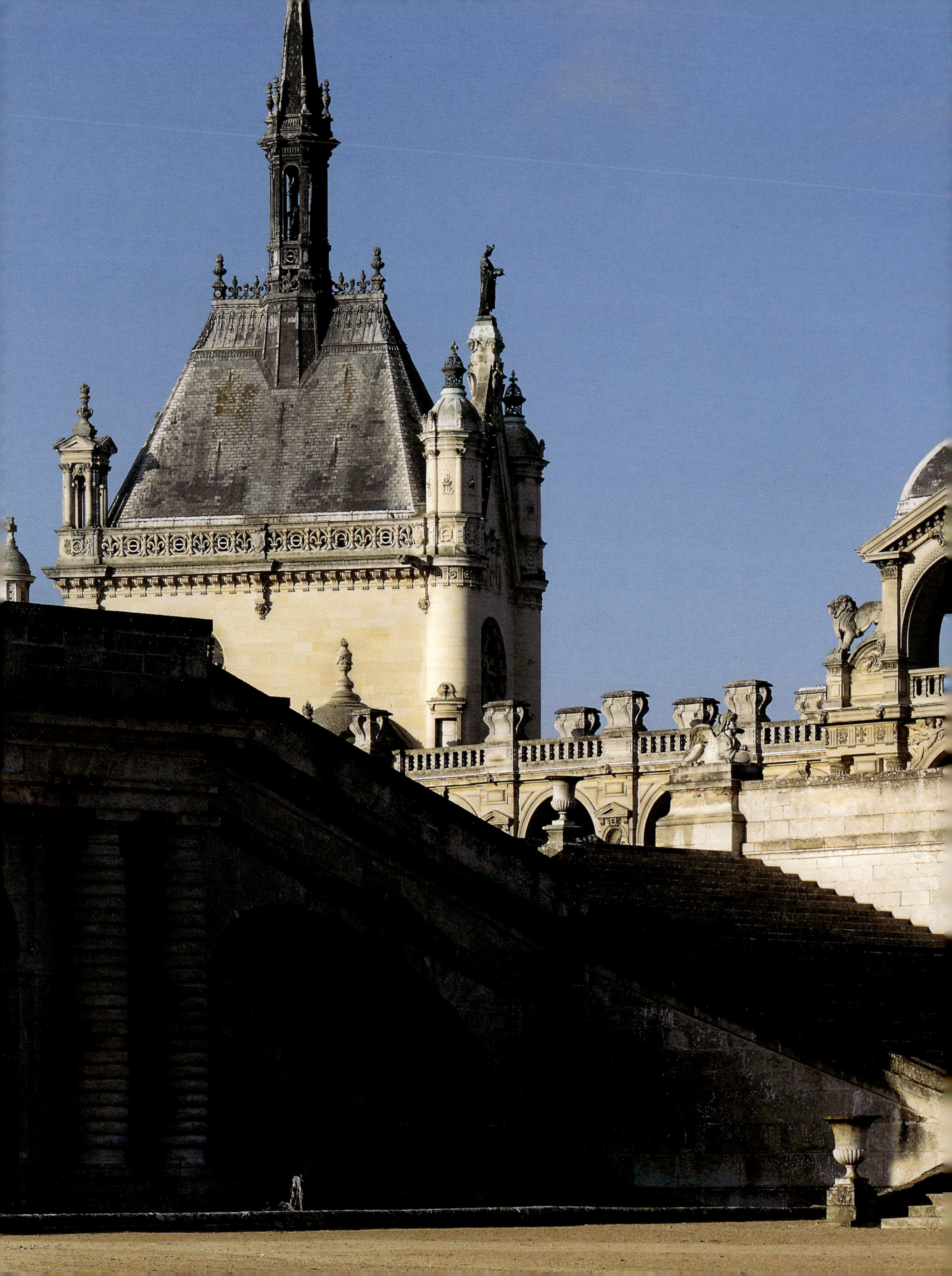

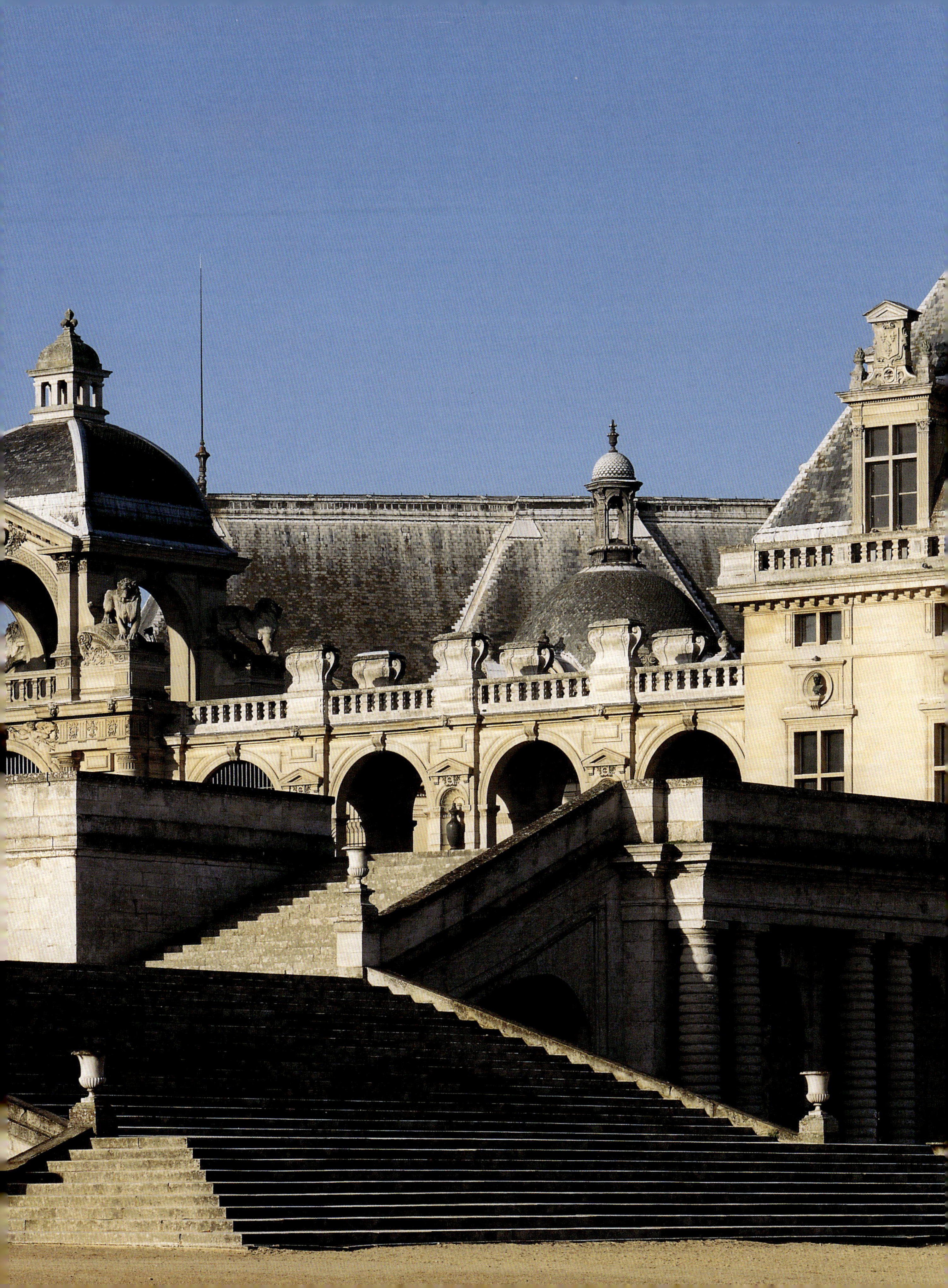

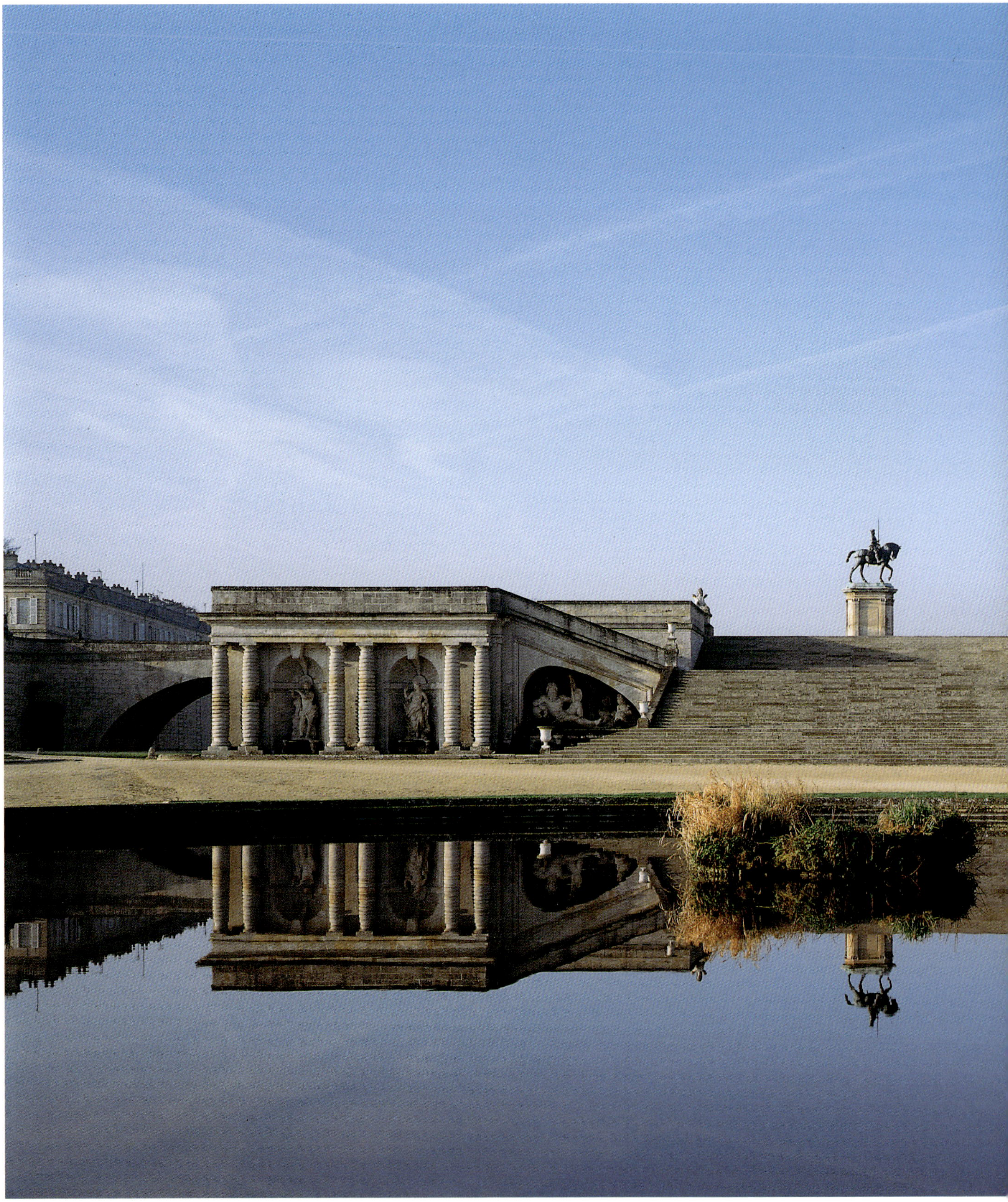

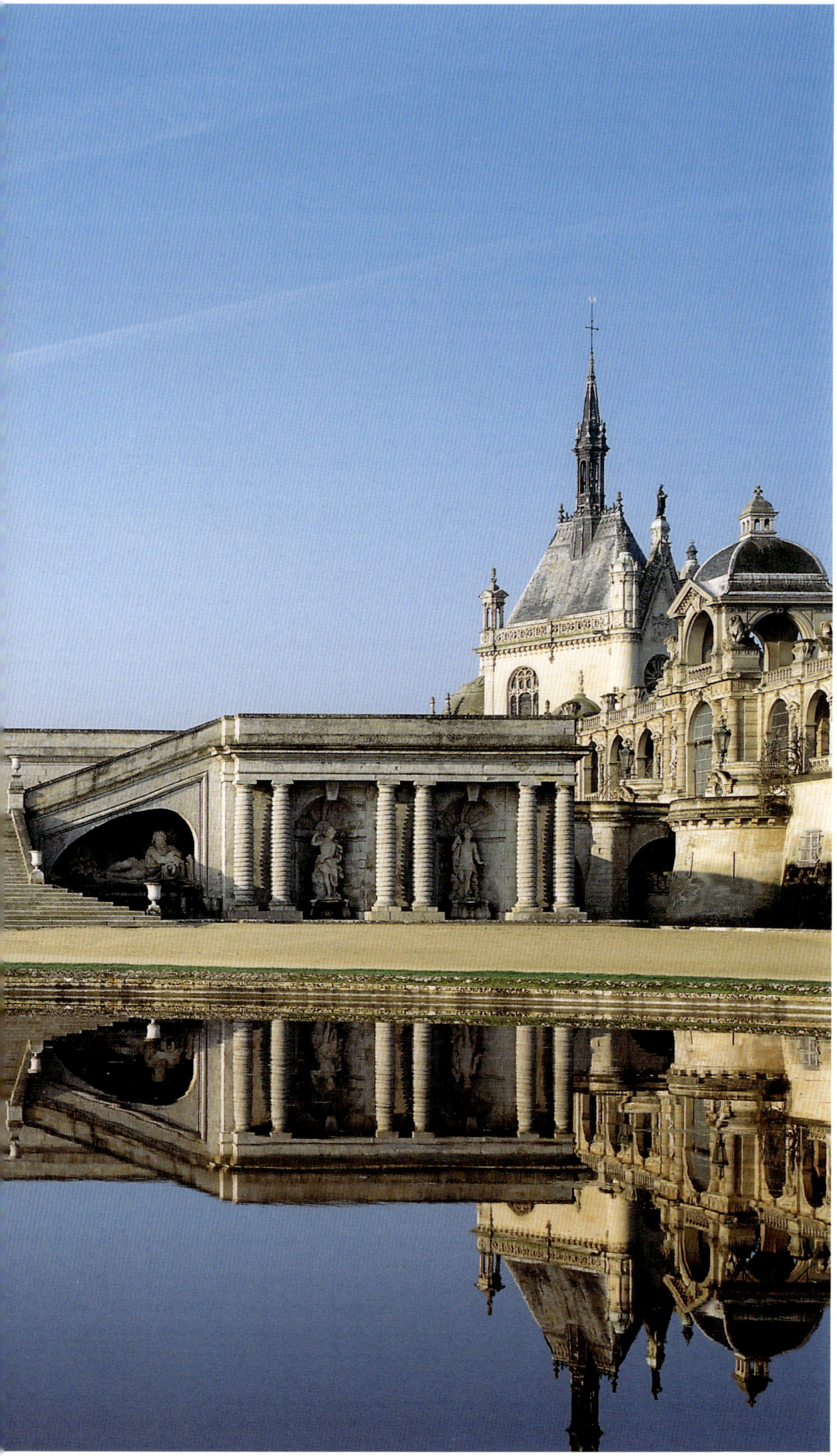

The Grand Degré
In this axial view, the statue of the Constable is silhouetted against the sky above the brilliantly designed flights of steps between the parterres and the terrace.

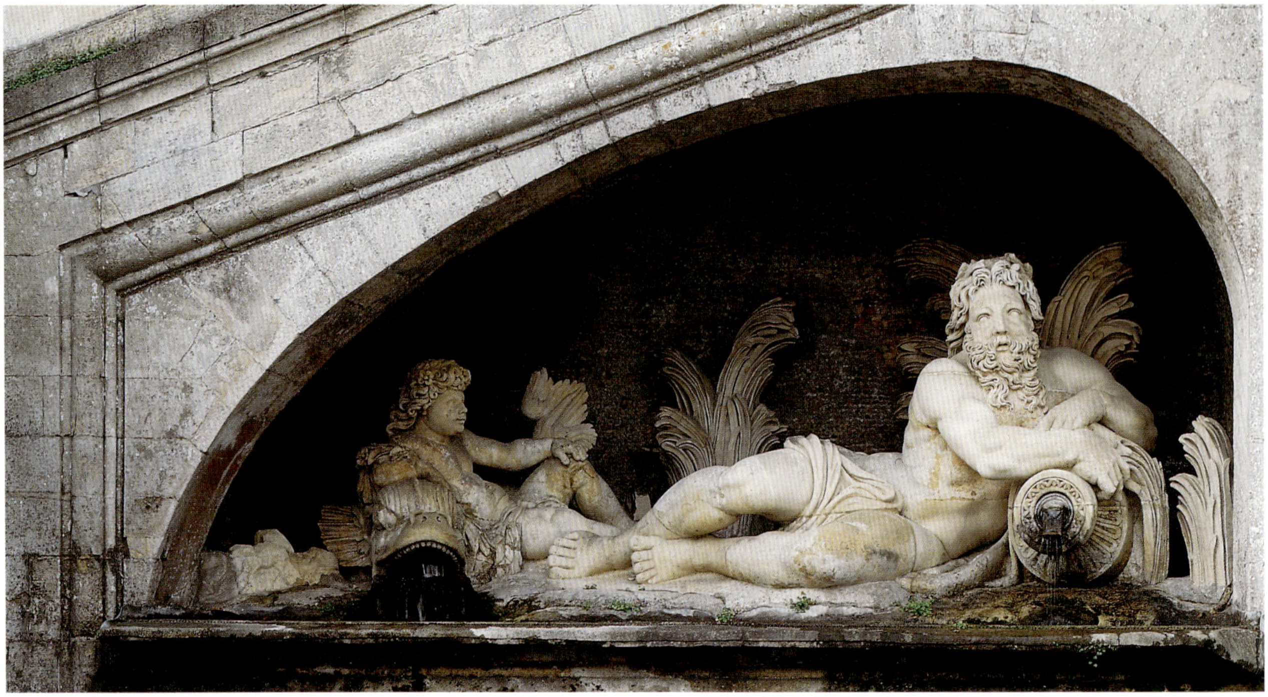

The sculptures on the Grand Degré
Jean Hardy completed the figure of the river god reclining in the grotto and those of Acis and Galatea in the niches in 1684.

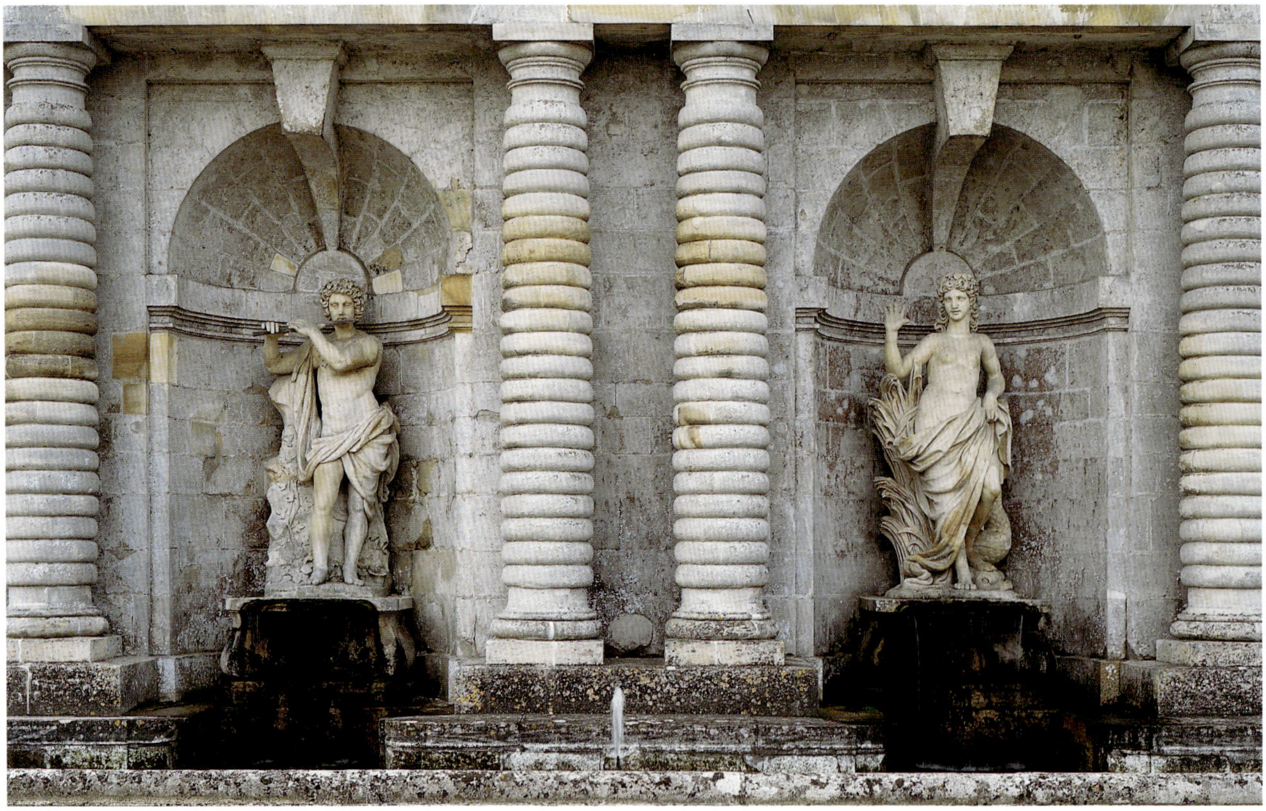

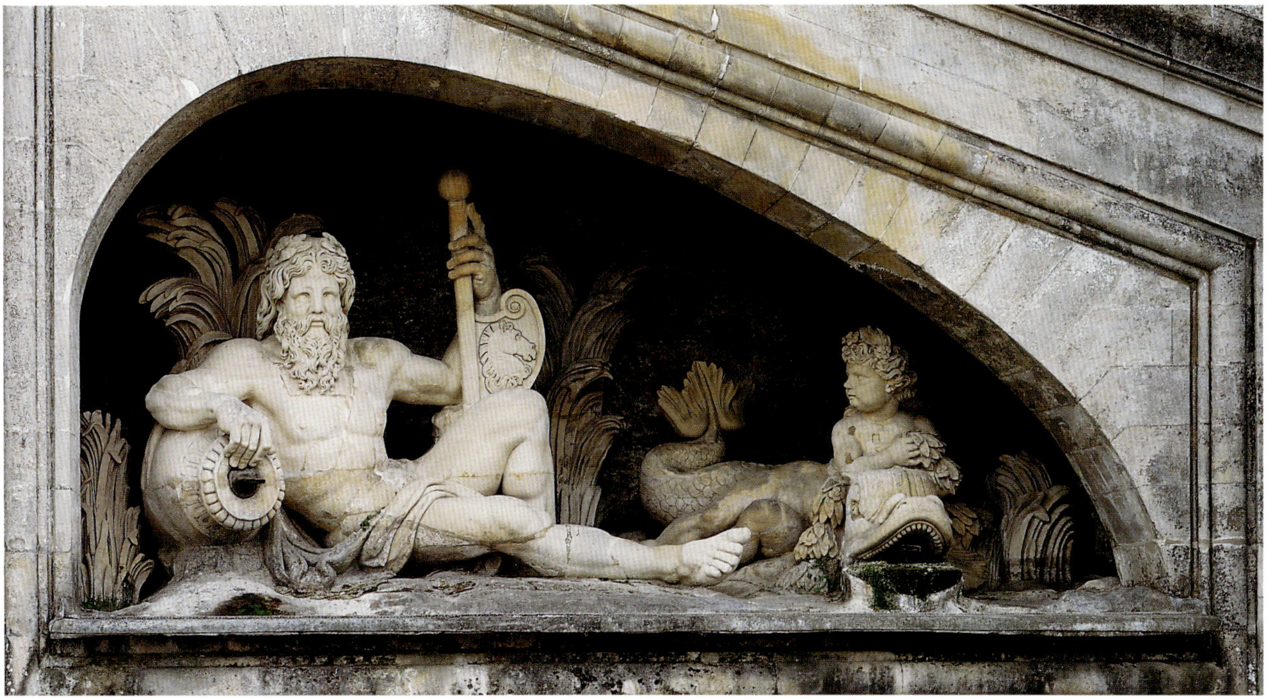

The sculptures on the Grand Degré
Below another figure of the river god in the grotto stand the figures of Arethusa and Alpheus, likewise completed by Jean Hardy in 1684.

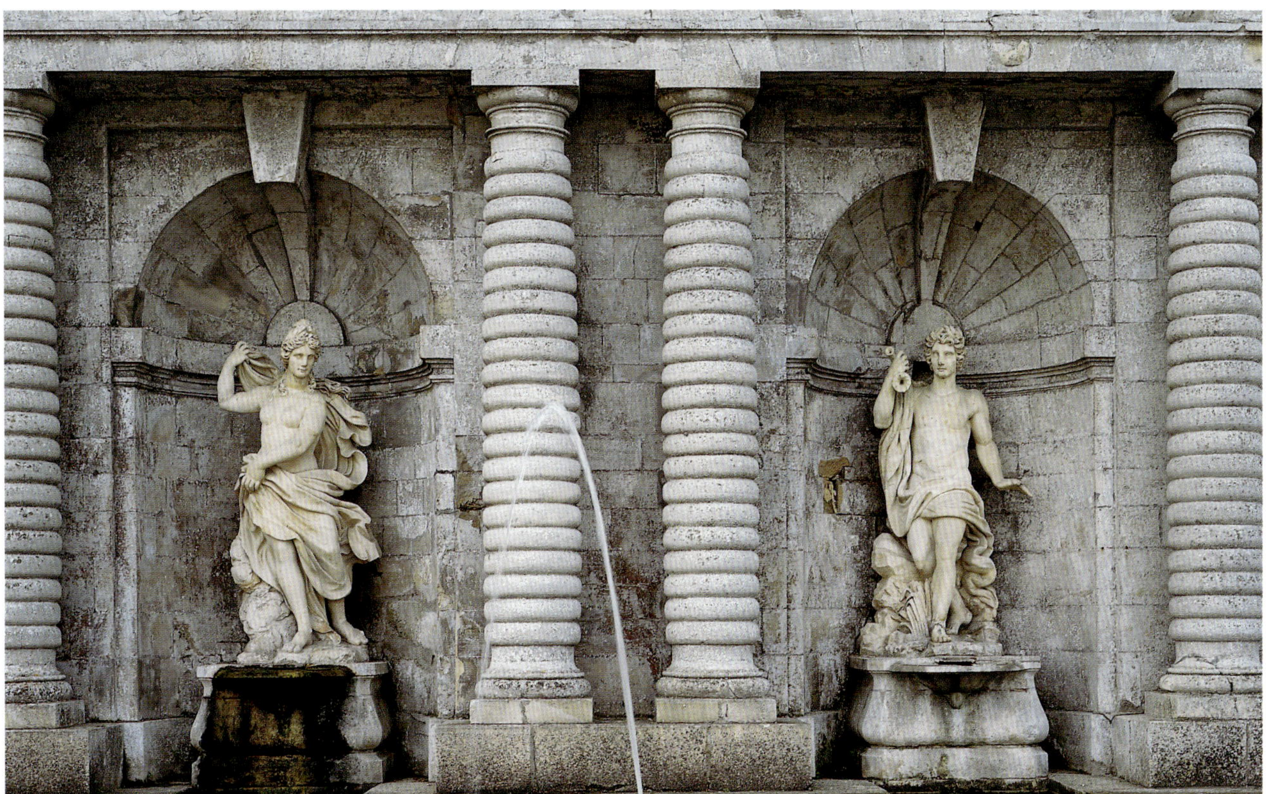

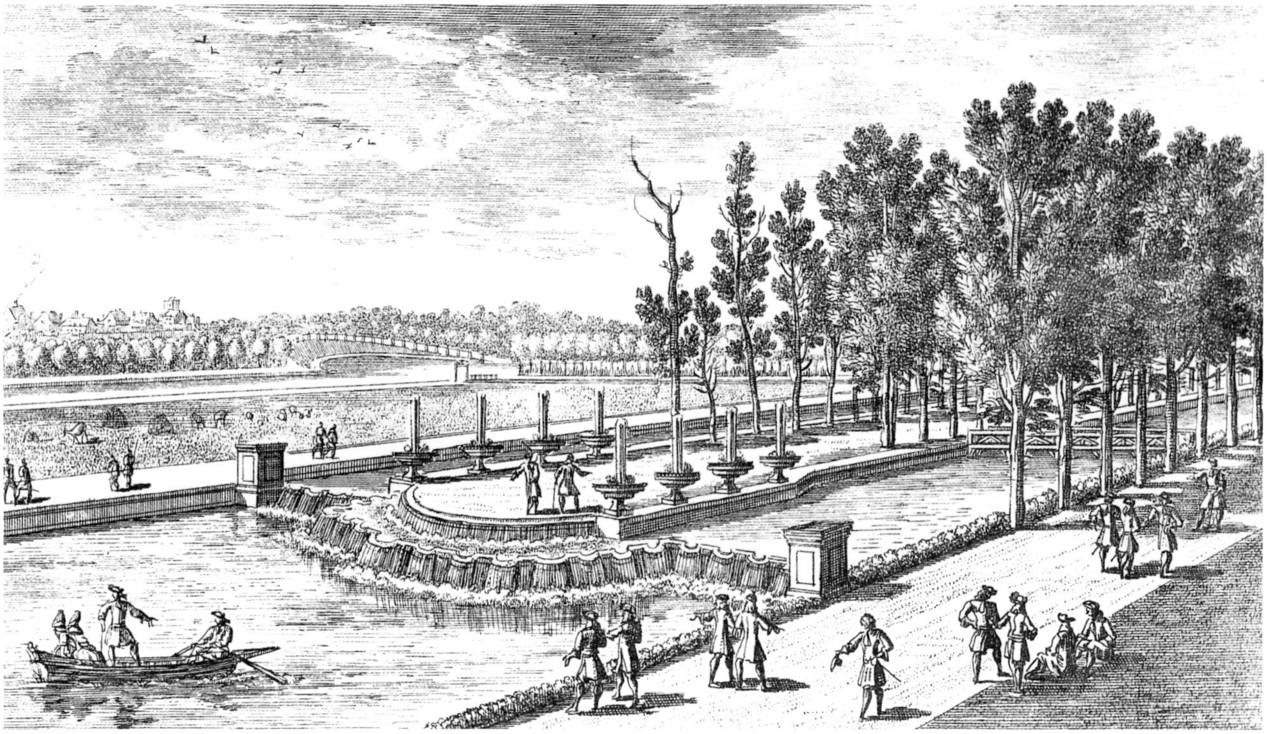

The Cascade at the head of the Petit Bois
Engraving by Adam Pérelle.
Bathed by the Canal Saint-Jean, the Île du Petit Bois, formed by a strip of earth protruding from a triangle, was located alongside the meadows that bordered the Grand Canal. In the background the Vertugadin can be glimpsed.

it; the feet of the figures will do the same. This structure can be made quickly and at little expense; the sculptor very much wants to make it." The sculptor was Jean Hardy, who in 1684 completed the figures of the river gods reclining in the grottoes, as well as the pairs of lovers that bring life to the niches on either side, Alpheus and Arethusa, Acis and Galatea.

We again encounter Mansart for the last major scheme carried out in the gardens in the prince's lifetime, the new Orangerie. Although Gittard continued to be in charge of the site work, this time it really was the first architect to the king who very officially provided the plans and came to the site to discuss them with the duc d'Enghien. By juxtaposing the correspondence exchanged and such of Mansart's drawings as have been identified[22], we can follow the gestation of the scheme step by step from 1682 to 1684. The idea was to demolish the Bucamp farm buildings and replace them with a large square courtyard, open to the east and framed on the other three sides by long wings, but in the end only the north wing was built, which was to have separated the planned courtyard from the Parterre of the Galerie des Cerfs. The long vaulted building was intended to house the Orangerie, lit by large south-facing windows. The Orangerie was linked to the west with the Galerie des Cerfs (which would be altered in the same style to suit the taste of the day in 1704) by a pavilion and a small building with three openings inserted in it, making it possible to circulate freely between it and the gardens. The whole structure topped by a long gambrel roof displayed a sober arrangement of arches enlivened by a few projecting bays with a striped pattern created by the margins of the building stones being set below the rest of the face, topped by pediments, just like the orangery Mansart built for Colbert at the same date. This can still be viewed at Sceaux, whereas the orangery at Chantilly was lost at the time of the Revolution.

Mansart had visited the site repeatedly, altering his plans while at the same time paying court to the prince as was his custom: "I think this is all Your Most Serene Highness has done me the honour of instructing me to do," he wrote on 6 February 1683. "If by any chance there should be any difficulty regarding the drawings I have provided, the contractors only have to let me know, I will resolve it for them immediately, and go to Chantilly if it is necessary, making it my complete pleasure that my services may be pleasing to Y.M.S.H., of whom I am with the deepest respect, Monseigneur, the very humble and very obedient servant of Y.M.S.H."

The pleasures of court

Forced into retirement by the state of his health, the Great Condé took ever-greater pleasure in his visits to Chantilly where he liked to entertain princes – the ex-king of Poland John Casimir as early as 1669 – and the cream of the nobility, artists, men of letters, scholars and ambassadors from far-off countries such as Siam or China. Transforming a princely duty into an art of living, he exercised his patronage here with real enjoyment. Racine and Boileau, Madame de Sévigné and La Fontaine, Bossuet, Malebranche and Fénelon joined him to practise the art of conversation he had learnt in his youth at the Hôtel de Rambouillet, arguing with complete freedom of mind and tone. The subjects discussed included poetry, theatre, theology and botany, and in his funeral oration Bossuet was later able to write: "Without envy, without disguise, without ostentation, always great in action, he appeared at Chantilly as he did leading his troops. Whether embellishing this magnificent, delightful house, or conducting his friends along these superb pathways, to the sound of the innumerable jets of water that are never silent day or night, he was always the same man, and his glory followed him wherever he went." La Bruyère was chosen as tutor to the grandson of the house, and Abbé Jean de Santeul, canon of

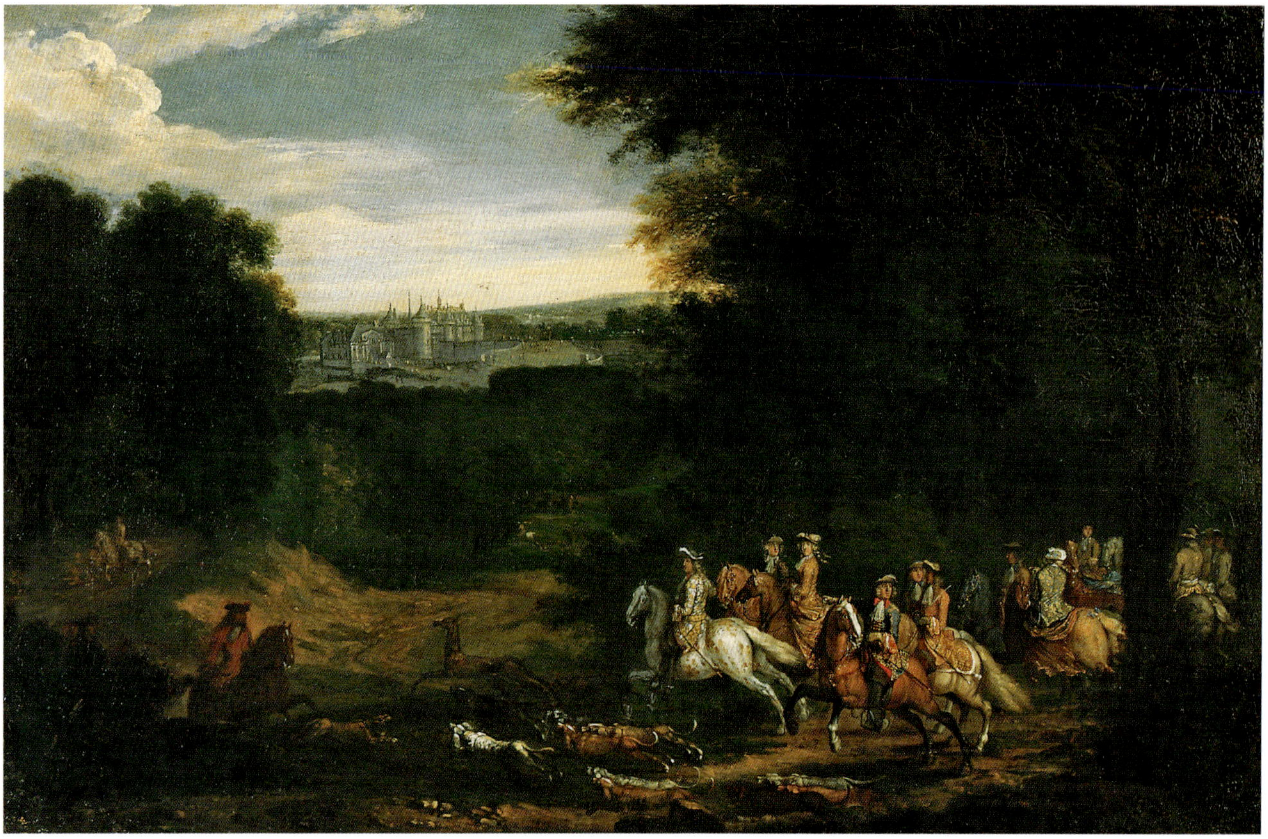

Louis XIV hunting at Chantilly
This painting by Adam Frans van der Meulen shows the king hunting a stag near the Carrefour de la Table.

Saint-Victor, exercised his talents as a poet writing in Latin – perhaps the last to do so – by exalting the beauties of Chantilly in the hexameters of his *Cantiliaca* (1684). A great theatre lover like all those he invited to his house, the prince brought Molière and his players to Chantilly on several occasions. In 1663 they performed *L'École des femmes*, and in 1668 *Le Tartuffe*, a play Condé personally defended against the fanatical religious faction and which was performed here in the presence of the duc and duchesse d'Orléans. To make sure of permanent entertainment in the summer season, he then called on a troop of actors who performed there for two months every year, but the regular presence of the actors quickly led to complaints about the absence of a permanent theatre. A visit by the Grand Dauphin in 1688 precipitated the decision: there had to be a theatre at Chantilly, and drawings were requested from Jean-Louis Berain, the famous decorative artist, for converting the square pavilion linking the Orangerie and the Galerie des Cerfs for this purpose. It kept the name *Oronthée*, from the title of the tragedy set to music by Le Clerc and Lorenzani which was the first play performed there.

Finally, hunting continued to be the prime justification for Chantilly's existence. Answering the innate vocation of the forested, well-watered site, it attracted the flower of the nobility and formed the main attraction of their visits. Condé's packs of hounds were as good as the king's for hunting and shooting, and clearly better when it came to hawking, a difficult art going back to the great mediaeval tradition which the prince became particularly fond of when pain made it impossible for him to mount a horse, and he had to leave feats of prowess to his beloved falcons.

Mansart's renovation of the Petit Château

The two châteaux of the Montmorencys could hardly cope with entertaining such brilliant company comfortably, as was realised when the king and the court came there in 1671. At the time when he was working on the Orangerie, Mansart had doubtless suggested an overall scheme to Condé for renovating both the Old Château where the prince and his family had their quarters and the Petit Château used as a service area, but the decision was made first of all to transform the latter; since the aviary had been destroyed it had the advantage of overlooking the Parterre de l'Orangerie, which could be reached directly via the footbridge. It was there that the great man now wanted to take up residence and Mansart handed him his drawings in December 1684.[23] Everything pointed to the use of the gallery wing to accommodate the prince's suite of rooms, but its depth did not match the requirements of a modern layout, in particular for fitting out a large bedchamber with an alcove, and the architect was forced to double its depth, eating into the court, where a new façade was constructed in the style of Bullant.

The building work engaged the attention of the duc d'Enghien who altered the proposals to improve the layout of the rooms intended for his father's use, pencilling over and annotating Mansart's drawings, especially concerning the proposed improvements to the connection between the two châteaux.

Communication was already established, as may be remembered, via a bridge crossing the moat at the level of the first floor of the Petit Château. Mansart's plan was to make this point of juncture between the two buildings monumental by means of a structure in some way grafted on to the bridge, an oval vestibule, an incongruous form of room at that period, but one that had a great future; it would have been a kind of visual echo of the nearby tower. This too innovative

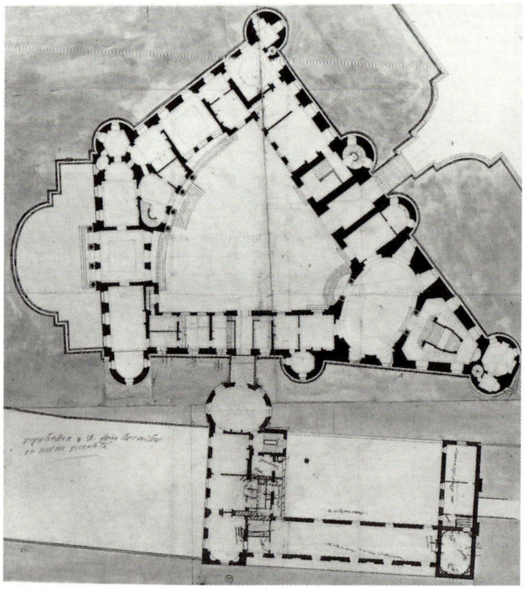

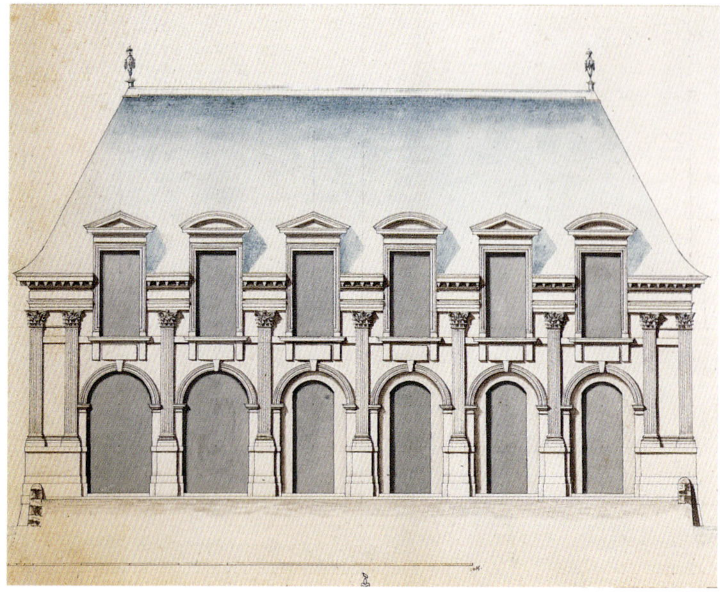

Scheme for the Grand Château
This drawings by Hardouin-Mansart's office show the architect's plans for the reconstruction of the Grand Château and the new layout of the Petit Château, with annotations in the duc d'Enghien's handwriting (1684).

Elevations of the Petit Château
Above: The façade overlooking the garden has been altered, and has six bays rather than five, and the small staircase tower has disappeared. Opposite: Altered elevation of the façade overlooking the court. The wing on the right has been doubled in depth, with a new façade and balcony.

View of the château and *parterres*
This coloured gouache by the seventeenth-century French School (previously attributed to the Flemish Lieven Cruyl, v. 1640-1720) shows the château around 1680, before Hardouin-Mansart's alterations, from the Grand Canal which is full of graceful boats.

idea was abandoned, and the link left in the open. But the old gallery was then extended by one bay in the direction of the bridge, the spiral staircase turret being sacrificed. Facing the Jardin de la Volière, Bullant's façade was slightly altered with regard to the openings of the partial dormers, to take account of the fact that that floor was higher internally, while the two end façades – north and south – were rebuilt. On the ground floor the former gallery, then known as the Galerie des Canons, made way for vestibules communicating on the courtyard side with a new staircase designed to allow the prince's sedan chair to be carried up. On the first floor was his suite of rooms: an antechamber, a large bedchamber with an alcove and a large corner study on the water side, and parallel with them a small study, a small bedchamber and two wardrobe closets. Mansart worked wonders in the way he brought these new volumes together. While respecting – and even pastiching – Bullant's architecture, at the same time he could not refrain from making the openings more regular, so erasing their Mannerist oddity. In the south wing, beside the water, the servants' quarters were replaced on the ground floor by two symmetrical suites of rooms, and the upper floor was converted to accommodate a gallery framed by two small rooms, following the model of Versailles. The building work was completed in November 1686, but it was too late for the Great Condé to be able to benefit

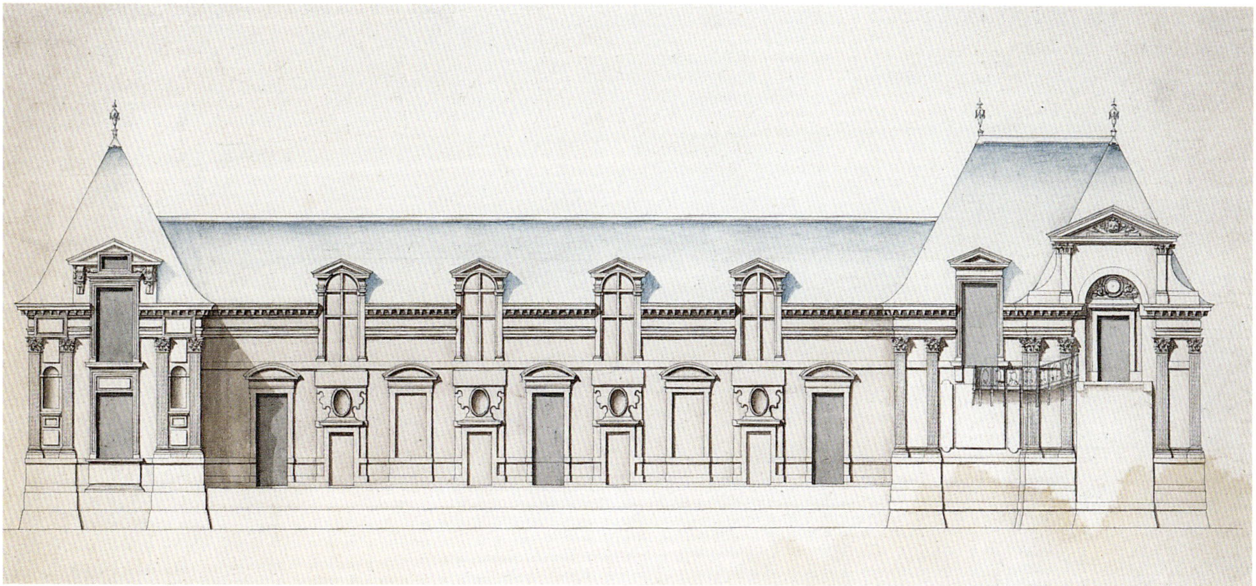

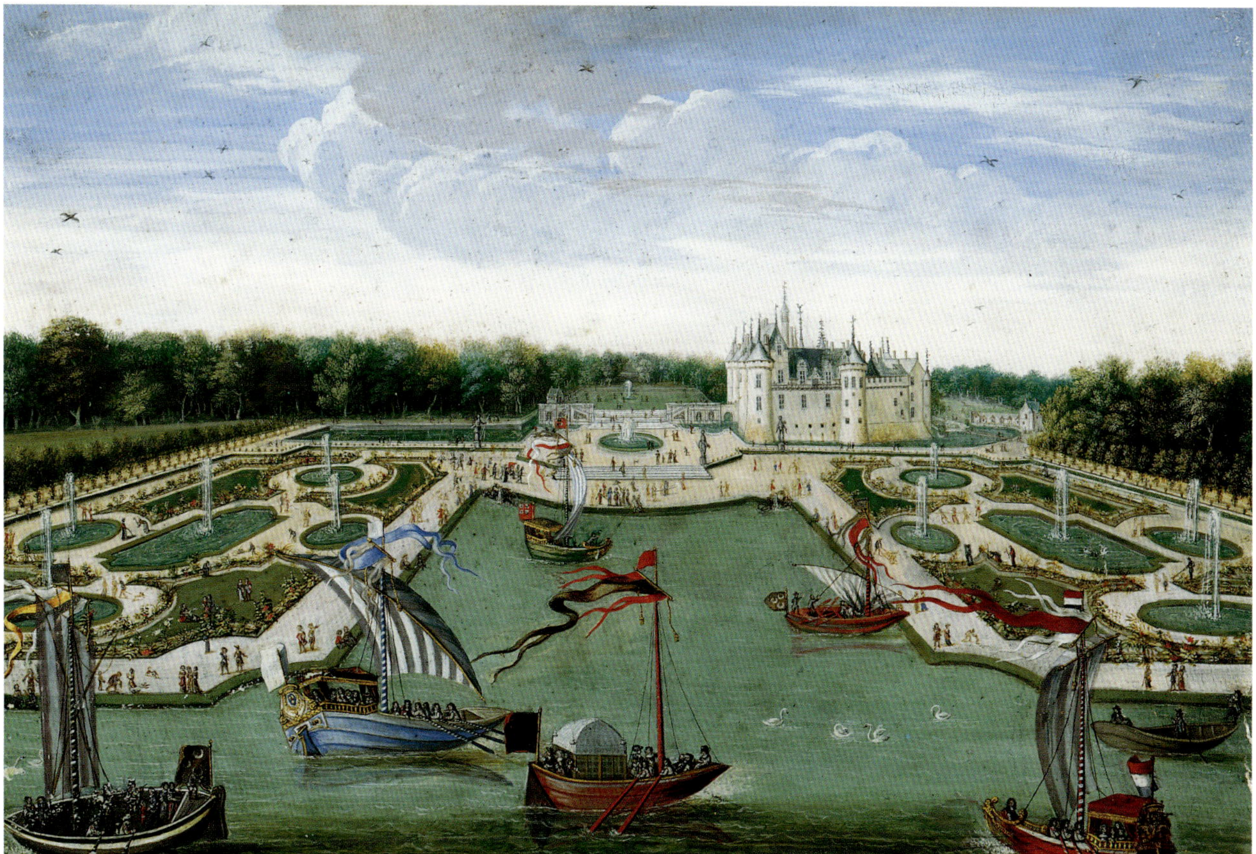

Scheme for a gallery
Even if this scheme was no doubt drawn not for Chantilly but for another of the Great Condé's residences – it bears his written approval – it is of great interest as regards the layout of the paintings in a gallery.

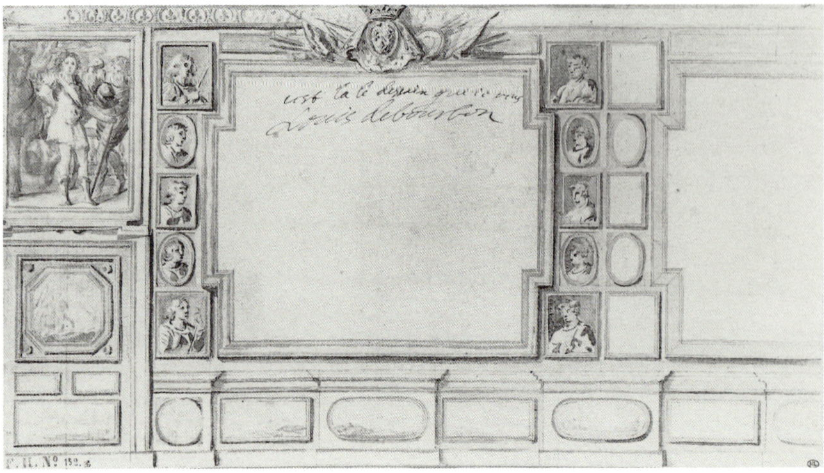

The Great Condé's Repentance
Michel Corneille painted this extraordinary composition in 1691, after the hero's death and at his son's request, to adorn the gallery at Chantilly.

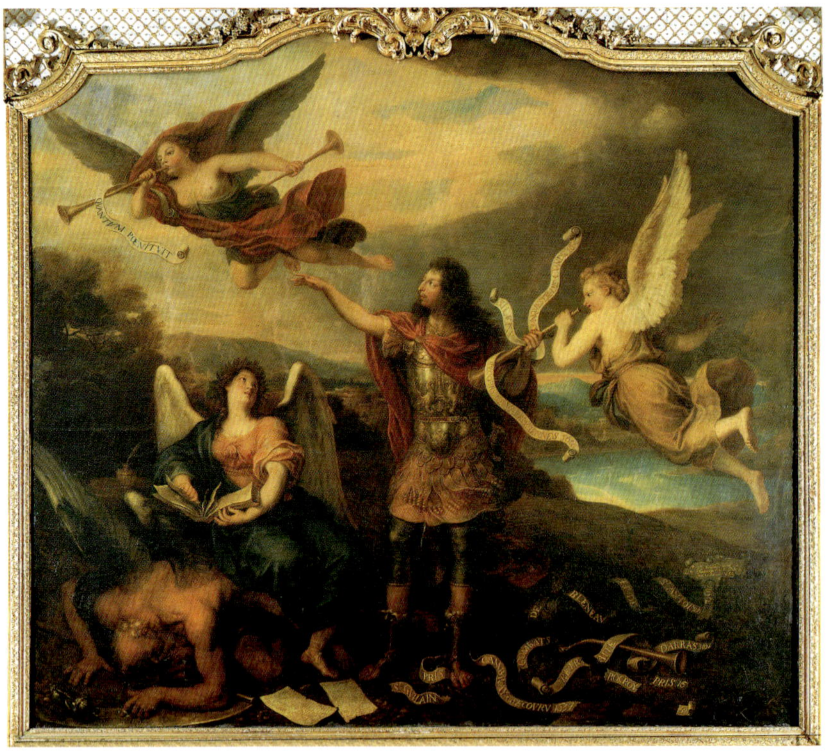

Opposite
The Battle of Nördlingen
This picture is one of the battle scenes painted by Sauveur Le Comte for the Galerie des Actions de Monsieur le Prince.

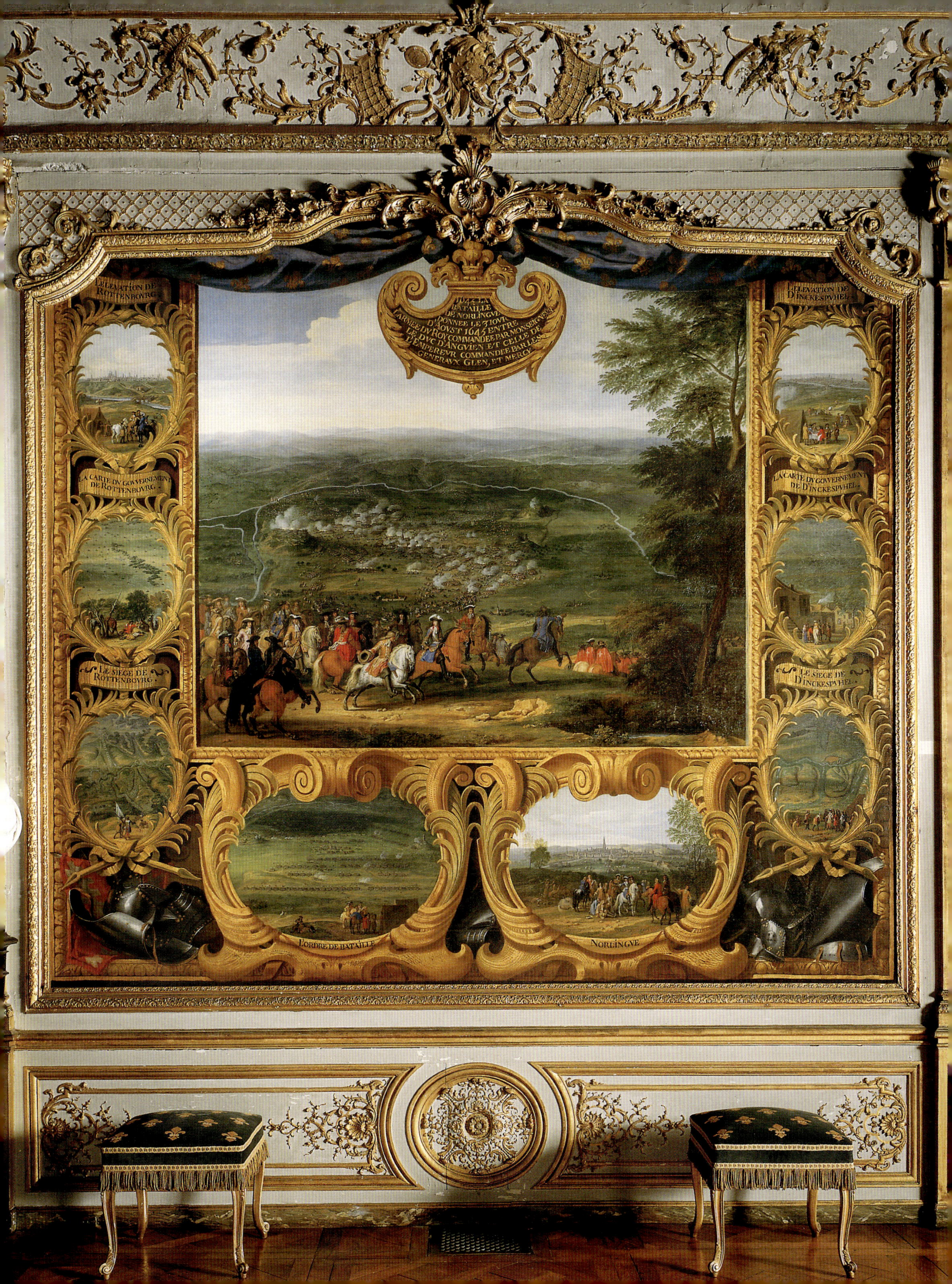
BATAILLE
DE NORLINGVE
DONNEE LE 3 IOVR
D'AOVST 1645 ENTRE
L'ARMEE DV ROY COMMANDEE PAR MONSEIGNEVR
LE DVC D'ANGVIEN ET CELLE DE
L'EMPEREVR COMMANDEE PAR LES
GENERAVX GLEN, ET MERCY
L'ELEVATION DE ROTTENBOVRG
LA CARTE DV GOVVERNEMENT DE ROTTENBOVRG
LE SIEGE DE ROTTENBOVRG
L'ELEVATION DE DINCKESPVHEL
LA CARTE DV GOVVERNEMENT DE DINCKESPVHEL
LE SIEGE DE DINCKESPVHEL
L'ORDRE DE BATAILLE
NORLINGVE

from it, as he died at Fontainebleau the following 11 December, after making his peace with the Church. "I have just lost the greatest man in my realm," Louis XIV declared. The decoration of the gallery, a project particularly close to his heart[24], had been decided upon during his lifetime, no doubt based on Mansart's instructions. Again as at Versailles, Meudon, or in the refectories of the Hôtel des Invalides where Louis XIV's victories were celebrated, Condé wanted a gallery to be devoted to the memory of his feats of arms for the edification of future generations. The windows on the north wall were sealed, and twelve spaces were provided along the two long sides, above low wainscoting and between woodwork pilasters that were painted white and yellow, to receive representations of battles – he himself had decided on the list – alternating with mirrored piers assembled with beadings of gilt bronze. A painter was chosen for these compositions: Sauveur Le Comte[25], a pupil of Van der Meulen, the famous painter of the battles of Louis XIV. Condé did not see them carried out.

We now see the "Galerie des Actions de Monsieur le Prince" in its 1722 condition, not as it was seen by the Grand Dauphin, who came to visit Chantilly with his half-sisters in August 1688. He was accommodated on the first floor of the Petit Château in the rooms designed for the dead prince, while the duchesse de Bourbon and the Princess de Conti were in the ground-floor suites overlooking the water, decorated with pictures illustrating the story of Venus and Diana, Flora, Bacchus and Momus.[26] By that date, four of Le Comte's paintings had been installed, those covering the prince's youthful campaigns: Rocroi (1643), Freiburg (1644), Nordlingen (1645) and Dunkirk (1646).[27] The episodes are integrated into huge compositions reminiscent in their pedagogical emphasis of old portrait galleries or pages from contemporary almanacs: the main action, which unfolds behind theatre curtains, fills the middle of the picture, and other actions are painted round it in cartouches, with accompanying commentaries. The other canvases were painted from 1688 to 1693: Arras, Aire and Perpignan (1640-42), the Catalonian campaign (1647), Lens (1648), the blockade of Paris (1649), Besançon (1668), the crossing of the Rhine (1672), Seneffe and Oudenaarde (1674).[28] As early as 1643-45, a full-length portrait of the hero had been commissioned from Juste d'Egmont with scenes from Rocroi, but we do not know whether it was integrated into the decoration of the gallery from the start; its presence there is first mentioned in 1688. As for the amazing allegorical figure of the prince as a rebel subsequently pardoned, it was commissioned from Michel Corneille in 1691. Was it possible to fail to mention the victories won by his father against the royal armies, and if not, how should they be treated? Prince Henri-Jules pondered over that question. There were the battles of Bléneau and of the Faubourg Saint-Antoine, the retreat from Arras, the relief of Valenciennes and Cambrai. Only allegory made it possible to get round the difficulty. We see the repentant prince holding back the trumpet of Fame which is about to celebrate those double-edged successes while Clio pulls out the pages in the book of History where she had unwisely recorded them.

Chantilly IV - Reconstruction of the Old Château by the Great Condé's son

As we have seen, Mansart had put forward designs in 1682-84 for reconstructing the Grand Château of the Montmorencys, where the royal apartments and the prince's suites of rooms in particular were located, but Condé died before giving instructions for them to be carried out. His son Henri-Jules, who had held the title of duc d'Enghien during his father's lifetime, succeeded him in 1686. He was married to Anne of Bavaria whose mother, Anne of Gonzaga, the witty Princess Palatine, had played the role of mistress of the house at Chantilly during the absences of the Princess de Condé, who showed some signs of mental illness. The young prince had been well loved by his father, accompanying him on his campaigns on several occasions, admittedly without showing any great talent for military matters. He was first and foremost a great connoisseur of architecture and his father had often allowed him *carte blanche* at Chantilly; he gave free rein to his passion as soon as he was sole master there. "Chantilly was his delight," Saint-Simon wrote; "he walked around always followed by several secretaries, with their writing desks and paper, who noted down as he spoke whatever passed through his mind to repair and embellish it; he spent prodigious amounts on it."

Piety and duty meant that first of all he had to carry out his father's wishes in the burgeoning town of Chantilly. Condé had granted plots of land between Bucamp and the Maison de Beauvais for the building of the houses and hostelries required by the local activity engendered by his presence at the château, just as the King had done at Versailles; but the small centre still lacked a place of worship, and in his will the prince had given instructions for the building of a parish church. It was constructed between 1687 and 1688 to Mansart's design.[29]

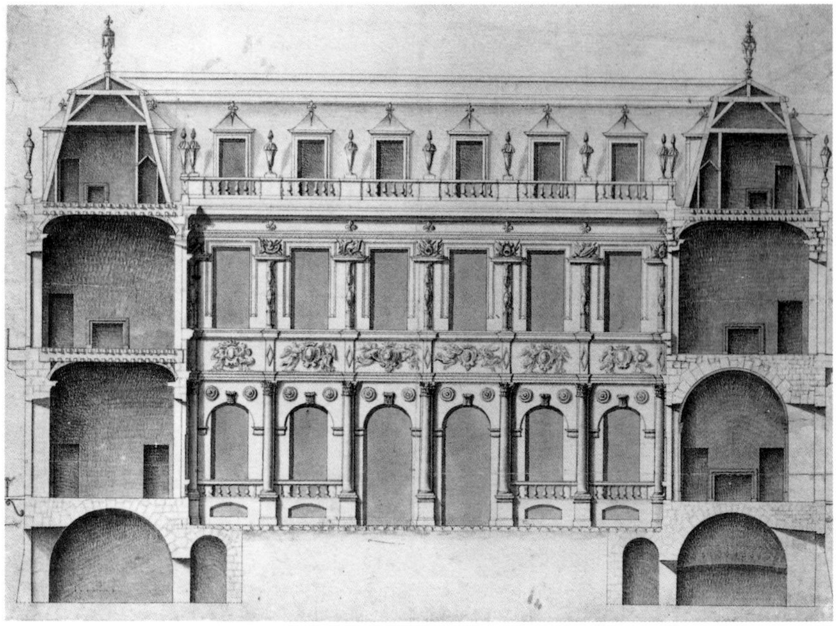

Elevation of the north-west wing
In this wing which rises above the court, Hardouin-Mansart has pastiched the style of Pierre Chambiges.

Next, for his personal pleasure, Henri-Jules had the new menagerie of Vineuil enlarged; it had been built in his father's time on the other side of the canal to replace the one on the south bank of the pond demolished by Le Nôtre to open up the approach to the forecourt. This building by Daniel and Pierre Gittard after drawings by Mansart was in response to the Great Condé's encyclopaedic curiosity, and even included an aquarium.[30] In 1687-88 two wings were added to it, one intended to house an apartment that could be used as a quiet retreat, with a sitting-room decorated as if it was the temple of Isis, while the other contained a dairy[31] decorated with paintings depicting La Fontaine's *Fables*, a fashionable theme which also inspired the subjects of the lead groups in the nearby ornamental ponds and waterfalls, just as at the Bosquet du Labyrinthe at Versailles. In one of the courts, the figure of the shepherd Narcissus was reflected in an ornamental pond;[32] a house in Vineuil adjacent to the park has kept the name "Narcisse". In the same direction, other graceful white houses are still in existence, which can be glimpsed among the foliage that closes the horizon to the side, above the north bank of the Grand Canal: the Maison Saint-Pierre at Vineuil, and further on near the head of the canal, the Château Saint-Firmin.

The new prince then made up his mind to reopen the question of reconstructing

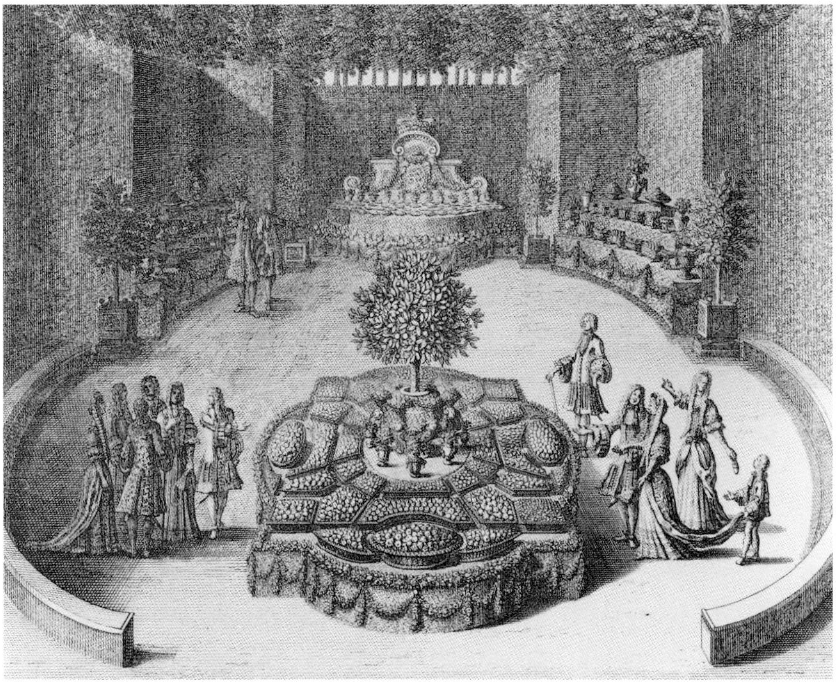

The refreshments offered to the Grand Dauphin
The 1688 festivities orchestrated by Jean Berain were among the finest ever seen at Chantilly. The tables for the refreshments were set up in the centre of the maze.

the Old Château, the brain-teaser that had constantly been shelved. From studying the successive drawings by Mansart that have been identified by Bertrand Jestaz, it becomes clear that the architect had set himself two objectives in order to give a regular appearance to the buildings with their out-of-date construction, framing an internal courtyard where breaks in alignment left over from the Middle Ages exercised a tyrannical influence: on the one hand it was necessary to replace the old buildings on the west point which enclosed a minuscule triangular court that could not be used, and on the other to build at the south-east point the wide, open staircase which the old castle lacked. Henri-Jules took a personal interest in the plans, the development of which then took a more ambitious turn. If it was accepted that Chambiges's loggia and the 1507 chapel could be destroyed, it would become possible to arrange two regular, symmetrical wings occupying the sides of the acute angle. The point of the angle, softened on the courtyard side by quarter rounds, would house a vestibule with an oval ground plan – Mansart reverted here to his abortive project for the Petit Château – leading to a grand two-level staircase inserted at the end of the triangle, backing on to the south-west tower, known as the Tour de Paris. There was no better way of dealing with that infernal acute angle. On the

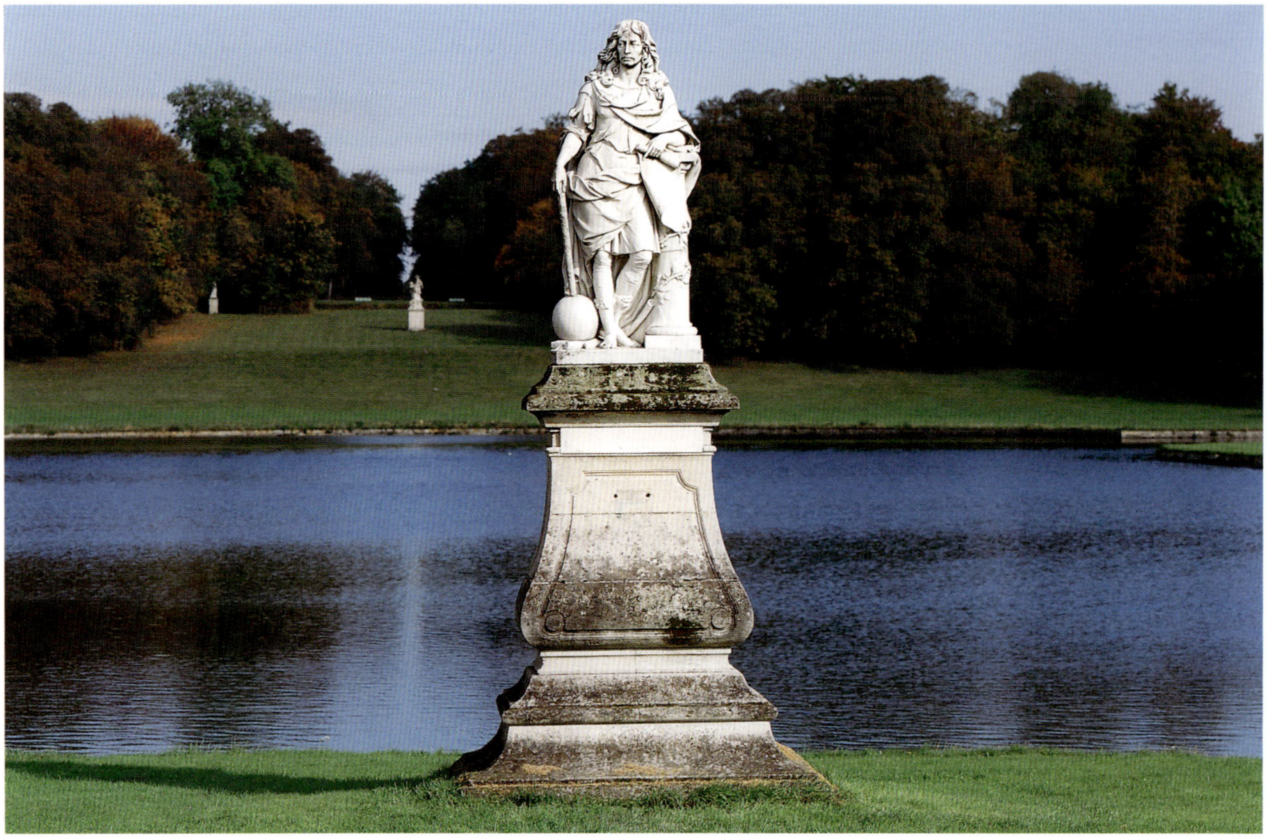

The Great Condé
Sculpted by Antoine Coysevox, 1690.
The statue of the master of the house was returned to its place in the middle of the parterres in the duc d'Aumale's time. It stands out against the background of the Vertugadin, where Frémin's statue of *Hercules abducting Deianira* can be glimpsed.

west side, Mansart had set all the resources of his fertile imagination in motion to design convenient suites of rooms, accessed from round or oval rooms serving as hinges, the only means of using such an irregular layout. All this would have cost a great deal of money, and the prince, now able to avail himself of the renovated Petit Château, scaled down his ambitions.

The programme of building work embarked on at the end of 1687 consisted firstly of demolishing the buildings on the west point, the oldest ones in Chantilly, and replacing them with imbricated buildings with a triangular layout, served on the courtyard side by a central staircase in a rectangular stairwell. A gallery with a view of the gardens was arranged between the tower known as the Tour de Vineuil and the former small Tour des Prisons, replaced by a round tower, the Tour du Trésor. Of this work, the vaulted ground-floor rooms of the building facing the Jardin de la Volière are still in existence; a new bridge was thrown over the moat – the Fossé des Carpes – leading to the garden. Next, the north wing housing the old sixteenth-century gallery where Henri-Jules still had his suite of rooms was altered, to give a regular elevation to the two façades facing

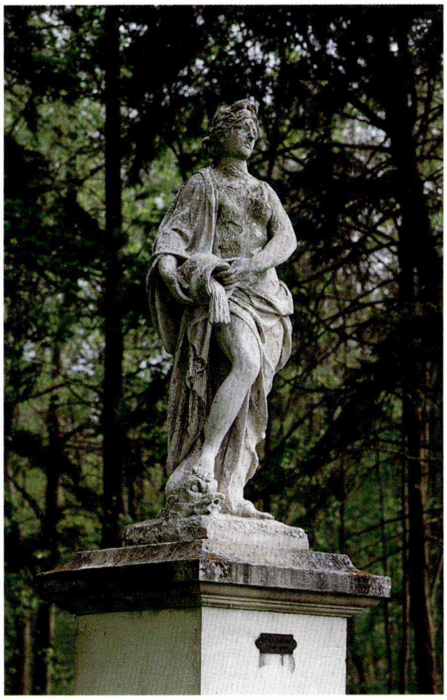

Water, by Antoine Poissant, 1700

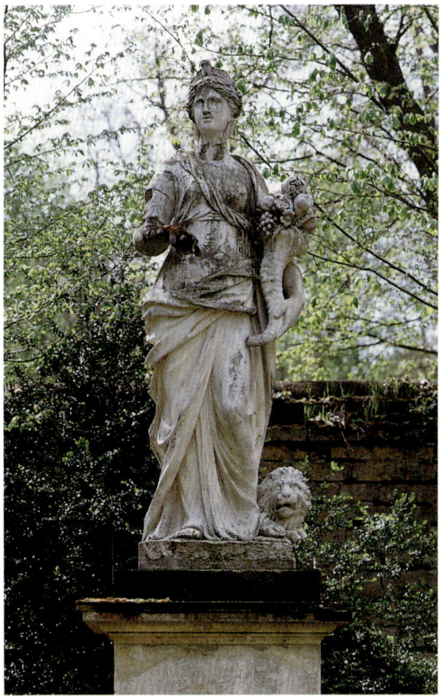

La Terre, par Antoine Poissant, 1700 *Earth*, by Antoine Poissant, 1700

Air, by Henri Legrand, 1700

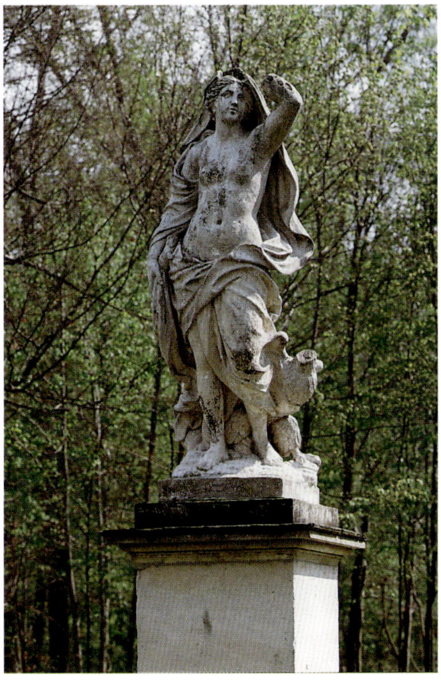

Fire, by Henri Legrand, 1700

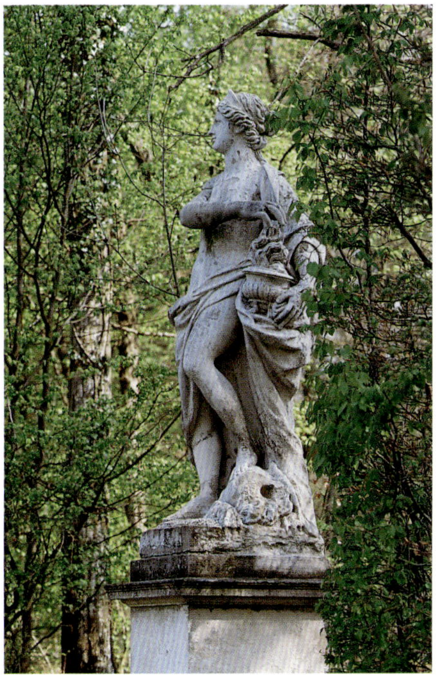

The Maison Saint-Pierre
This house in the village of Vineuil looking on to the Grand Canal takes its name from the chapel of Saint-Pierre built by the Constable and incorporated into its outbuildings. Beside it the Maison Narcisse serves as a reminder of the Great Condé's Menagerie and the Bassin de Narcisse.

The château Saint-Firmin
In the duc d'Aumale's day this fine house located in front of the head of the Grand Canal was occupied by his nephew, Robert d'Orléans, the duc de Chartres. The Princesse de Salerne lived in the neighbouring Maison de la Nonette.

the court and connecting the sides of the obtuse angle. For the ornamentation of his new wing, Mansart, as was his wont, drew his inspiration from the sixteenth-century decoration, taking over its columns, pilasters decorated with candelabra, medallions and angels bearing coats of arms, as a drawing held in the Musée Condé attests. Viewed externally, however, the great off-putting towers were still there, and the buildings along the curtain walls had been very little changed, except for rows of windows being inserted in them, continuous balconies being affixed and the roofs being made uniform. The halting of the building work in 1690[33] after only two sides of the old castle had been completed left the bitter taste of a job unfinished, and ultimately of failure. Throughout this time the new prince had carried on with the embellishment of the gardens, where he continued to organise splendid festivities which delighted his visitors: the Grand Dauphin in 1688, the reception for whom cost three hundred thousand *livres*, then Louis XIV himself who came at frequent intervals, in 1692, 1693 and 1695, as well as other members of the royal family, not to mention the Elector of Cologne, the pretender to the English throne.... It was during this period that the stone arch of the Pont du Roi was built, the bridge leading from the Terrasse du Connétable towards the park on the right, and the parterres, fountains and forest paths were furnished with statues. Filial piety led his son to commission a statue of the Great Condé in white marble from Antoine Coysevox (1690) to be placed in the middle of the parterres,[34] and another in stone from Nicolas Coustou (1700) to be placed in the park near the Grand Jet, though the latter did not survive the Revolution. The same artist supplied a figure of Diana, two lions and two sphinxes for the terrace, and two mastiffs for the bottom of the ramp.[35] A dealer called Louis Alvarez who had copies of antiques made in Rome received an order for busts of the four seasons, other busts of Roman emperors (on the façade of the Petit Château), a Bacchus and a Silenus (the Allées des Philosophes beside the Canal) and the Medici Venus (for the Île d'Amour), while competent French sculptor's assistants like Legrand or Poissant sculpted the figures of the four elements: Air and Fire copied from Versailles (on the Vertugadin) and Earth and Water (for the Parc de la Caboutière). Finally other sculptors made the statues for the Parc de Sylvie: Ariadne, Theseus and the Minotaur.

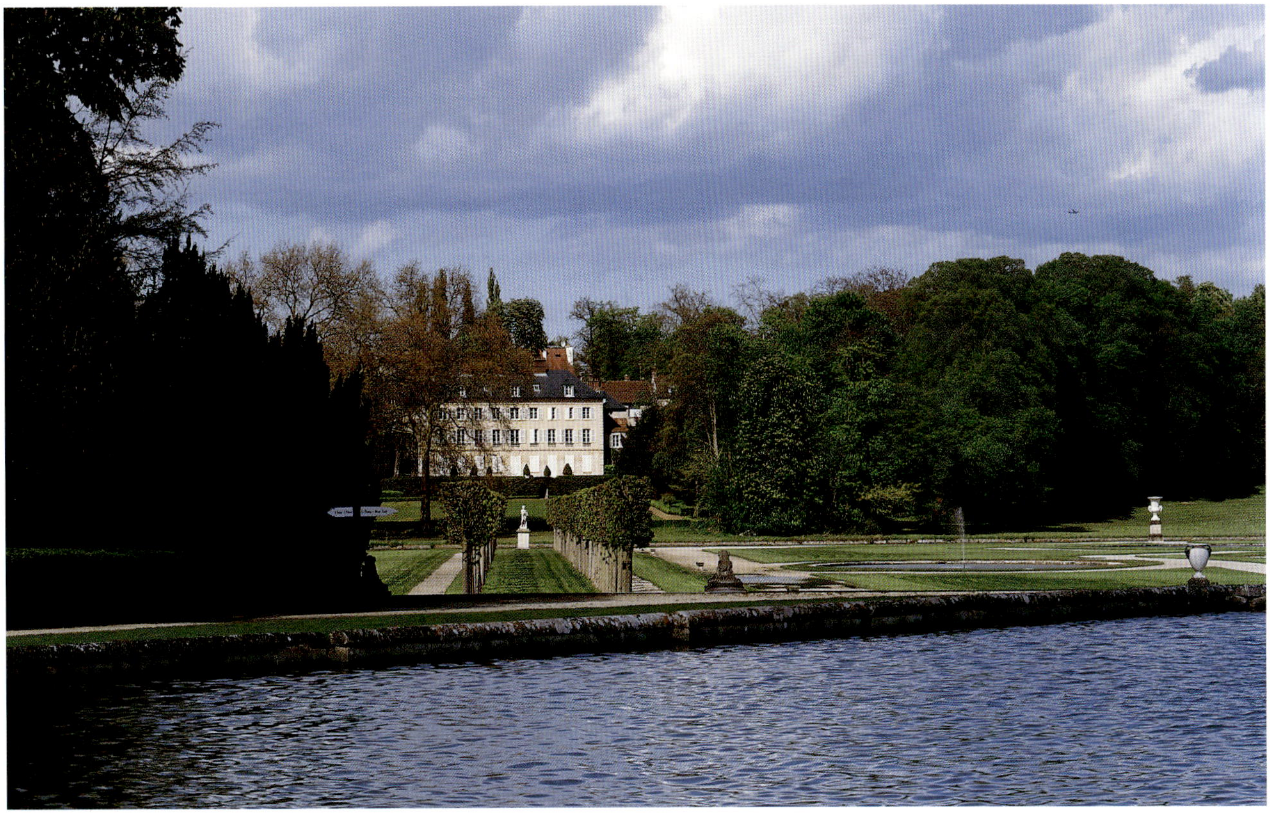

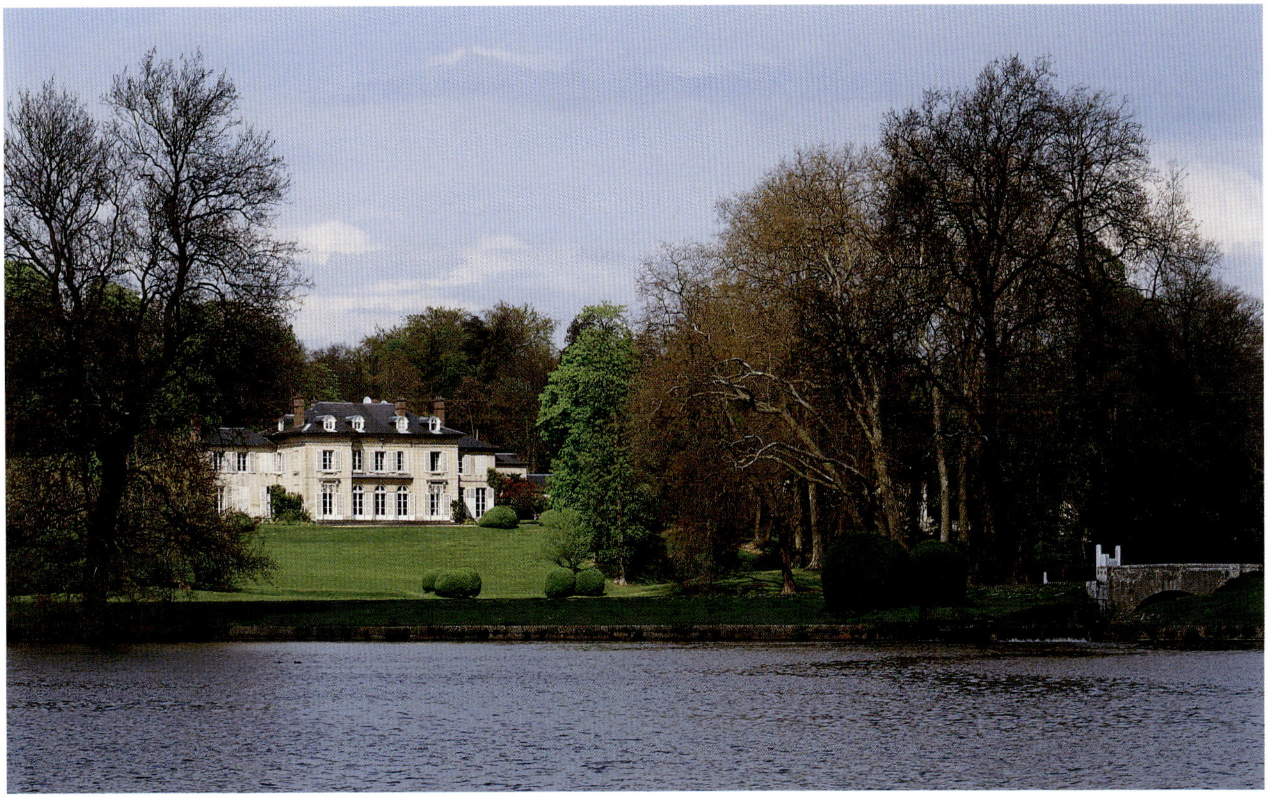

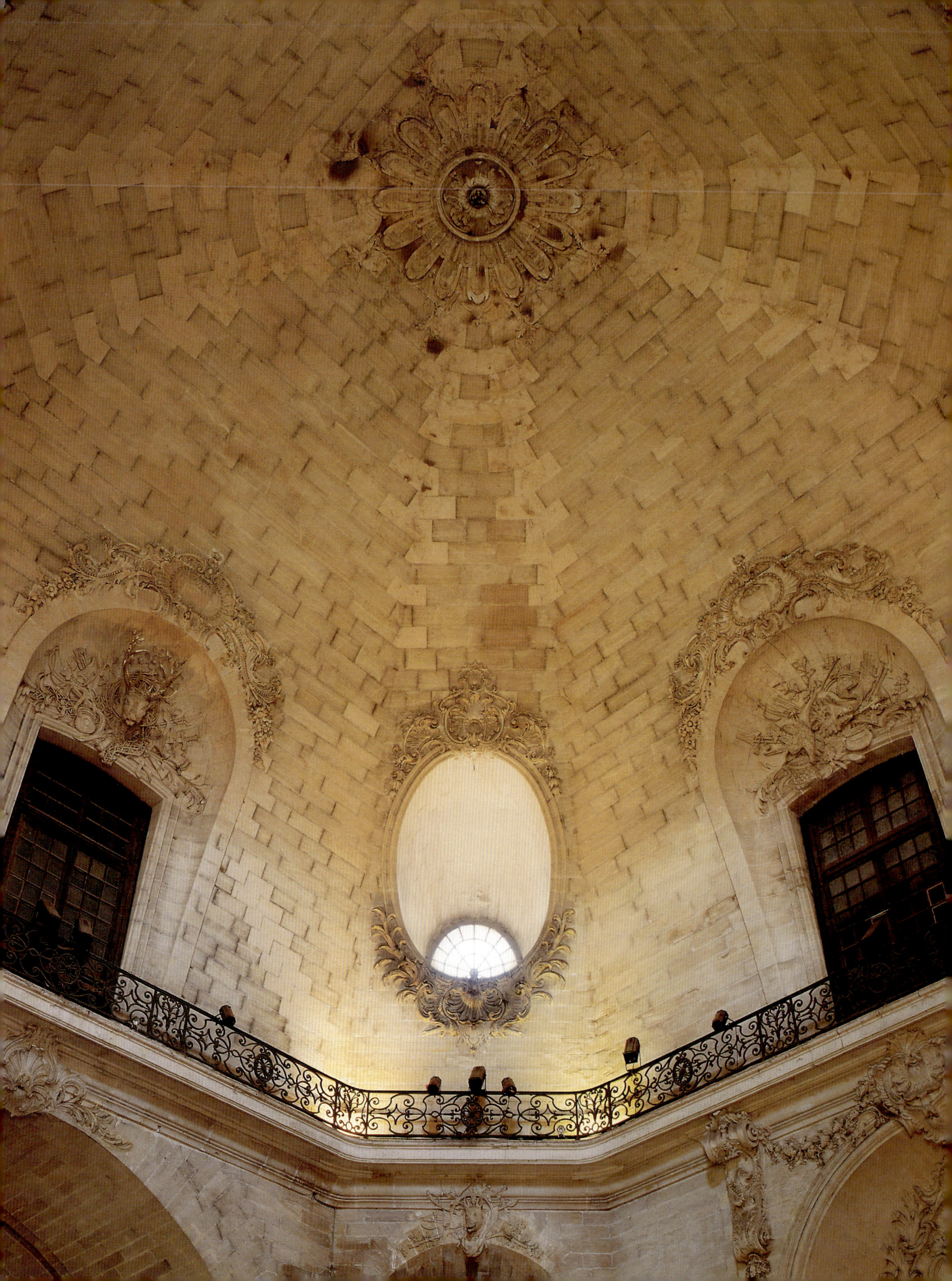

The Bourbon-Condés in the age of Enlightenment

Monsieur le Duc, Prime Minister

Henri-Jules, the son of the Great Condé, was still a man of the seventeenth century – known in France as the Grand Siècle – and high in the favour of the old king; he had been very quick to agree to the marriage of his own legitimate children to the king's "legitimised" children, his daughter Louise-Bénédicte marrying the duc du Maine, and his son Louis, Mademoiselle de Nantes.

When he died on 1 April 1709, he was succeeded by Louis III, a poor "epileptic dwarf"[1] who outlived him by just one year, and left no great impression. In 1710 a sudden jump of two generations abruptly put Chantilly in the hands of a man who belonged to the new society, the society of the Enlightenment. It is significant that Louis-Henri retained the title of duc de Bourbon which he received on his father's death and never took the title of Prince de Condé, as if it was too heavy a burden to bear in this new century. He became a widower in 1720 on the death of his wife, his cousin Marie-Anne de Bourbon-Conti, and took the ambitious Agnès Berthelot de Pléneuf, marquise de Prie, as his mistress; he had met her two years earlier.[2]

We know that Louis XIV was reluctant to give his cousins, the princes of the blood, the slightest share in the decisions of his Council, but after his death times changed and the Orléans branch, the closest to the throne, claimed and obtained the Regency of the kingdom in the name of the young Louis XV, to the detriment of the "legitimised" sons, in whose hands the old king had seemed to want to place power. After the death of the Regent in December 1723, why should a Condé – and a grandson of Louis XIV on the wrong side of the blanket to boot – not seize the reins of government in his turn? The duc de Bourbon, brought into the Council by the Regent and often appearing

The dome of the Grandes Écuries.

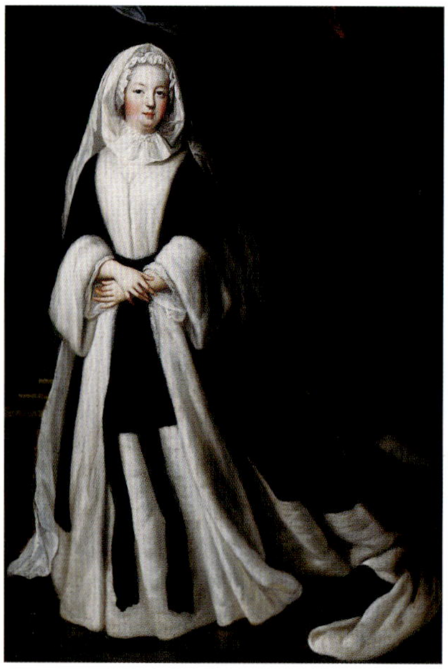

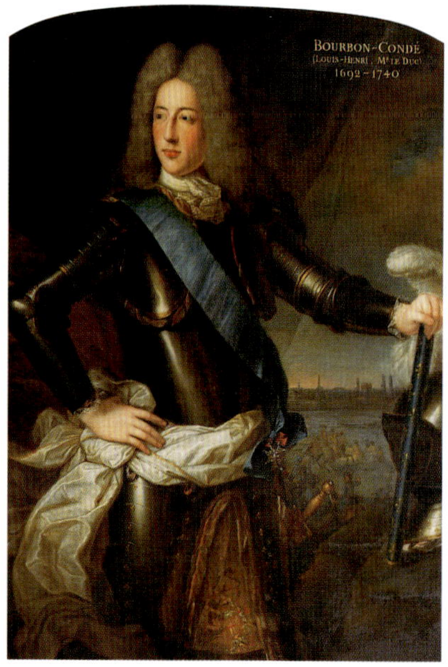

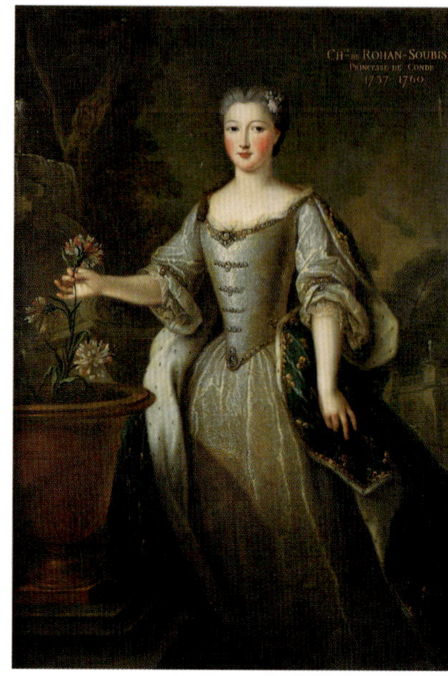

Mademoiselle de Nantes
Portrait of the wife of
Louis III de Bourbon Condé, by Pierre Gobert.

Louis Henri duc de Bourbon
Portrait of Louis XV's Minister,
by Pierre Gobert.

Caroline de Hesse-Rheinfels
Portrait (wrongly inscribed) of the
second wife of Louis-Henri, duc de Bourbon,
by Pierre Gobert.

to be his right arm, claimed succession and obtained the title of Prime Minister, almost by surprise. For three years he directed the policy of France, with Madame de Prie at his side taking care of the distribution of favours. Then as Louis XV became more independent he tired of a Minister who decided everything without consulting him, and replaced his cousin with his old tutor, Cardinal de Fleury, for whom he had retained his childhood affection. So in 1726 Bourbon was exiled to Chantilly and his mistress to Normandy where she died shortly after. Although he was able to reinstate himself in the king's good graces at the end of 1727, Louis-Henri never regained any political influence and was free to devote himself passionately to the embellishment of Chantilly, after contracting a second marriage to a German princess, Caroline of Hesse-Rheinfels, in 1728.

Completion of the reconstruction of the Old Château

When as early as 1718 the duke decided to carry on with the modernisation of the Old Château embarked on by his grandfather, Mansart had been dead for ten years. But the architect had left drawings reflecting with subtle variations the various projects he had dreamt up[3], probably with the help of Jean Aubert[4], a draughtsman in his office who had become one of his collaborators.

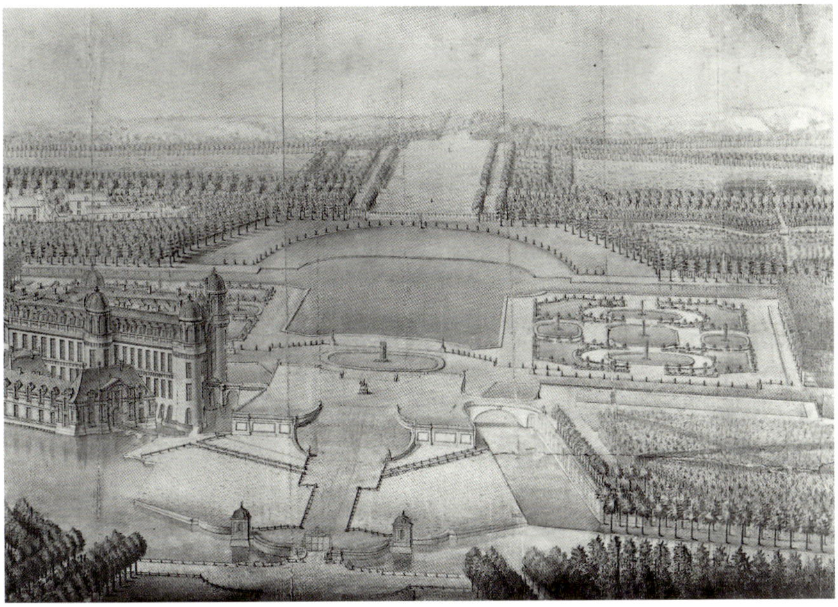

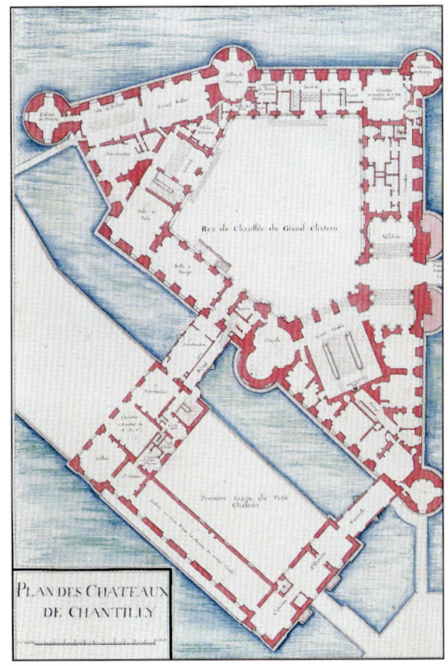

Bird's eye view of Chantilly in 1738
Detail of a drawing by Claude Dubourg. The Grand Château bears the marks of the work carried out by Mansart and de Aubert, with its ungainly towers and their lantern tops.

The château after the building work carried out by Jean Aubert
Plan taken from the *Album du comte du Nord* by Chambé, 1784. The square grand staircase and the oval chapel are of particular note.

Aubert left the king's service on the death of his master Mansart, and devoted his talents to the duc de Bourbon's building projects, first the château of Saint-Maur from 1709-10, then the Palais-Bourbon in Paris and the château of Chantilly, and finally the Grandes Écuries, his masterpiece.

The resources mobilised were enormous, commensurate with – or proportionate to the lack of moderation of – the crazy prodigality of the new master of the place who had managed to do well out of the collapse of the Law banking system.[5] After the building work carried out by Henri-Jules, the two sides of the acute angle pointing towards the east still had to be transformed, or rather rebuilt, destroying the chapel, the loggia and the staircase by Chambiges. "H.M.S.H. had three sides of the court of the château knocked down and rebuilt, namely the side through which you enter, that containing the main staircase, and that facing the Petit Château," we read in a booklet recapitulating the building work in 1760.[6] The principle defined by Mansart was therefore maintained, finally managing to create a regular pentagonal court integrating the obtuse angle and the acute angle, but this was achieved with less subtlety. So a grand staircase, built on two levels with three straight flights, was inserted abruptly, as if by forceps, into the group of buildings at the acute angle, without passing through the graceful transition of a vestibule, which was taken back to the entrance into the old keep, while a chapel with an oval ground plan and a projecting apse was fitted into the tower facing the Petit Château. On the outside, Aubert retained the towers but raised their height above the parapet walk, modernised by the addition of a balustrade, by means of small lantern turrets lit by arched openings and with domed roofs. Only the towers of the old entrance keep were razed to the level of the bridge to allow room for a gate "rebuilt in the modern style and decorated with sculptures", as Piganiol de La Force[7] put it. This was a projecting structure, its columns decorated with trophies supporting a wide pediment with the king's arms borne by two angels, framed by two large trophies of arms, all carved by the sculptor Remy-François Bridault. This was normal practice in the palace architecture of the time, a court dress thrust on to an old fortress to bring it up to date, and to improve the entrance they could do no less than replace the bascule bridge with a masonry structure with two arches. Work was completed in 1721, but the result was extremely disappointing, as can be seen from pictures and engravings.[8] The triangular ground plan which accentuated the lines of perspective gave the architecture – which was setting out to be classical – a contorted, bastard appearance, oddly emphasised by the verticals of the lantern-towers.

Suites of rooms in the new fashion

As a well-informed lover of art, the duke immediately proceeded with the decoration of the suites of rooms in the Old Château, the finest on the first floor being intended for the king and queen,[9] with the queen's rooms facing the Jardin de la Volière. On the ground floor there were rooms and galleries known by the names of Tasso (scenes from *Jerusalem delivered*), *Georgics* (by Virgil) or the *Fables* of La Fontaine, and everywhere there was a profusion of pictures by old and modern masters and magnificent tapestries, some of which had come down from the Montmorencys. Nothing remains of these rooms since the château of the Bourbon-Condés failed to survive the Revolution.

On the other hand, in the Petit Château which the duke had reserved for his own use we can form an opinion of the talent deployed by Jean Aubert in 1718-20 in bringing the former rooms of the Great Condé up to date in the taste of the day. The style that became fashionable during the Regency is triumphantly illustrated, thanks to the talent of the ornamental sculptors and

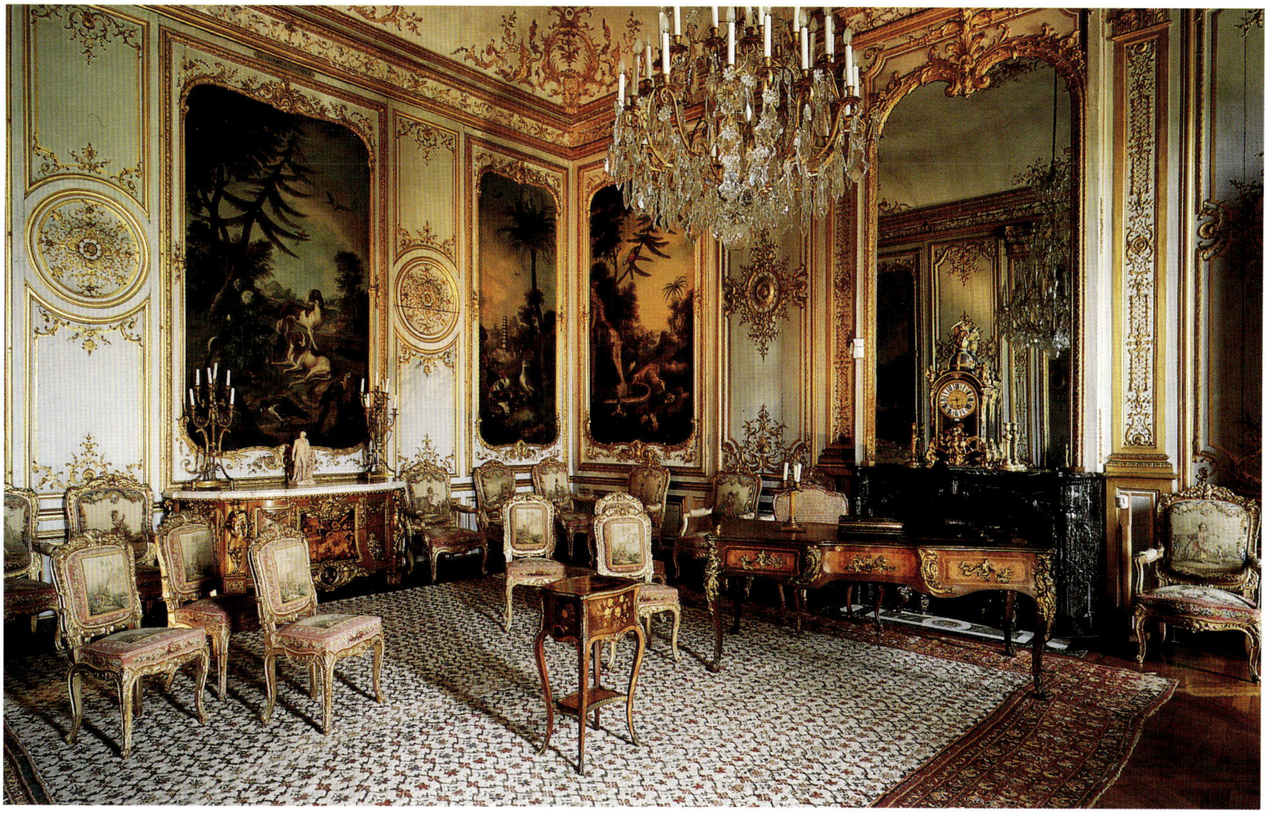

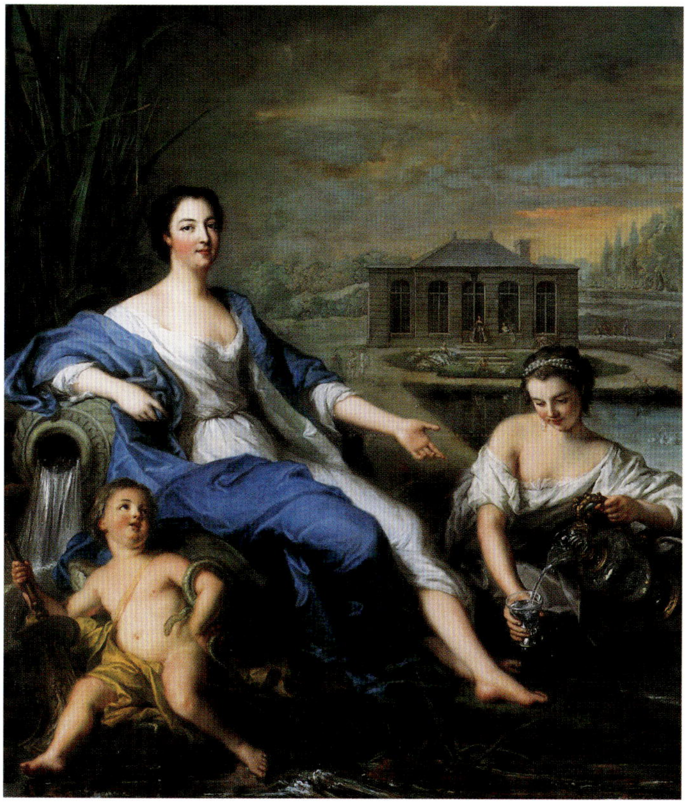

The Bedchamber of Monsieur le Prince
Before the alterations made at the time of the French Restoration, an alcove occupied the left part of the room. A chest of drawers by Riesener stands in the place for the bed; it was delivered in 1775 for Louis XVI's bedroom at Versailles.

Mademoiselle de Clermont with the waters of Chantilly
This fine portrait of Marie-Anne de Bourbon by Nattier (1729) used to hang in the alcove of the bedchamber.

craftsmen who had worked at Versailles until 1715, then found new young, wealthy patrons to replace their lost royal custom.[10] Charles-Louis Maurisan with the skilled gilders Autin and Dezauziers was the main creator of the decorative schemes at Chantilly, schemes that are very close to the most splendid contemporary interiors in Paris at the Hôtels de Parabère, Peyrenc de Moras and Angran de Fonspertuis on the Place Vendôme, and the Hôtels de Lassay and Biron in the Faubourg Saint-Germain; the last two were built or altered by Aubert himself, which is more than just chance.

Two suites of rooms at the Petit Château still bear the mark of the combined talents of Aubert and Maurisan. The first is the large suite on the first floor reached from the courtyard of the Old Château, formerly via a vaulted passage followed by a bridge, today directly through the *vestibule d'honneur*. On the walls in the antechamber, added later by the duc d'Aumale above the former moat, are paintings by Desportes of hounds from the duke's pack and two hunt scenes by Oudry which were commissioned in 1725 for the Salle des Gardes in the king's suite in the Old Château.[11] After the Salle des Gardes, formerly an antechamber, comes the bedchamber, fitted with white and gold wainscoting above which are a cornice and a wide cove in gilded stucco. The alcove which was originally lined with silk hangings was decorated with a portrait of Mademoiselle de Clermont painted by Nattier, and portraits in pastel of Monsieur le duc and Mademoiselle de Bourbon by Lenoir. This room was turned into a billiard room at the time of the French Restoration and the former alcove was used to display a series of paintings depicting animals, dogs, monkeys and exotic birds in landscapes, recessed in new wainscoting panels. These pictures had been commissioned in 1735 from the ornamental and animal painter Christophe Huet for a different purpose.[12] The large corner study which comes next is again decorated with magnificent white and gold wainscoting; the large arched panels that frame the window affording a splendid view of the Pelouse and the Écuries are particularly to be admired.

The small square study that follows round the corner leads into the gallery. This is called the Grande Singerie (big monkey-house) since the wainscoting, of the same date as that in the bedchamber and large study, is decorated with paintings, convincingly attributed to Christophe Huet. The date 1737, legible on the door opposite the windows, leaves no doubt as to the intervention of a decorative painter fifteen years or so after the installation of the panelling.

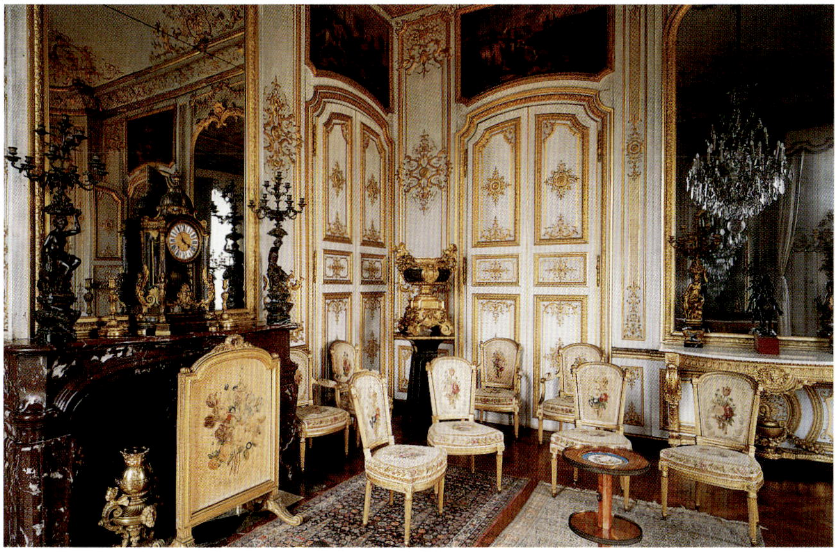

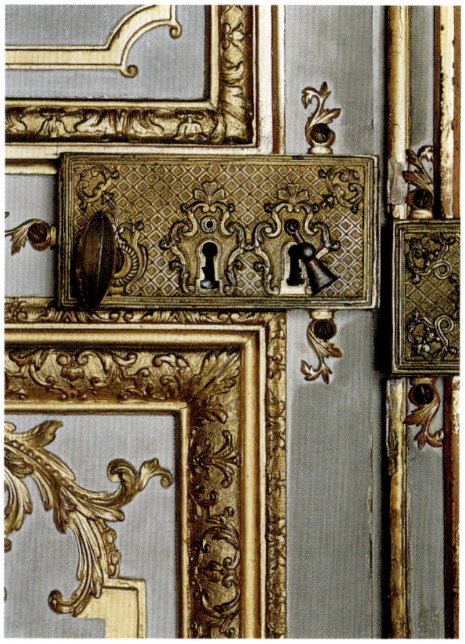

The large corner study
Jean Aubert designed the magnificent white and gold wainscoting for this room in 1718-20.

Lock on the study door

Huet was a pupil of Claude Gillot, a successor to Berain and d'Audran in a decorative genre that combined figures, landscapes and arabesques in a dreamlike world bathed in the poetry of Watteau – a genre that was applied to panelling, fireplace screens and sedan chairs alike; he had made a speciality of these pleasing compositions in which monkeys took the place of humans, while a few story-book Chinamen looked on.[13] We also know of other "female monkeys" painted by him at the Hôtel de Rohan-Strasbourg in Paris (1750) and the château of Champs (1755), but they are later than these. So the duc de Bourbon had launched the fashion, unless he had followed the example of his friend the banker Pâris-Duverney in his château of Plaisance at Nogent-sur-Marne, or his cousin the Regent at the château of Bagnolet, residences that are no longer in existence.

In fact the duke was personally responsive to the exoticism of the Far East which he cultivated as a true connoisseur. At Chantilly there was a laboratory for making Chinese-style lacquer, a workshop producing cloth painted in the Indian manner, and there would soon be the famous porcelain factory. In the *Livre de dessins chinois* dedicated to him in 1735 by the painter and graphic artist Jean-Antoine Fraisse, the artist goes into raptures regarding the treasures from India, China and Japan held in the château. Therefore in the Grande Singerie Christophe Huet, if it was in fact him, satisfied the particular taste of the prince. His programme of allegories spread over the six large panels in the room – with themes that are eminently suitable for the study of a great prince,

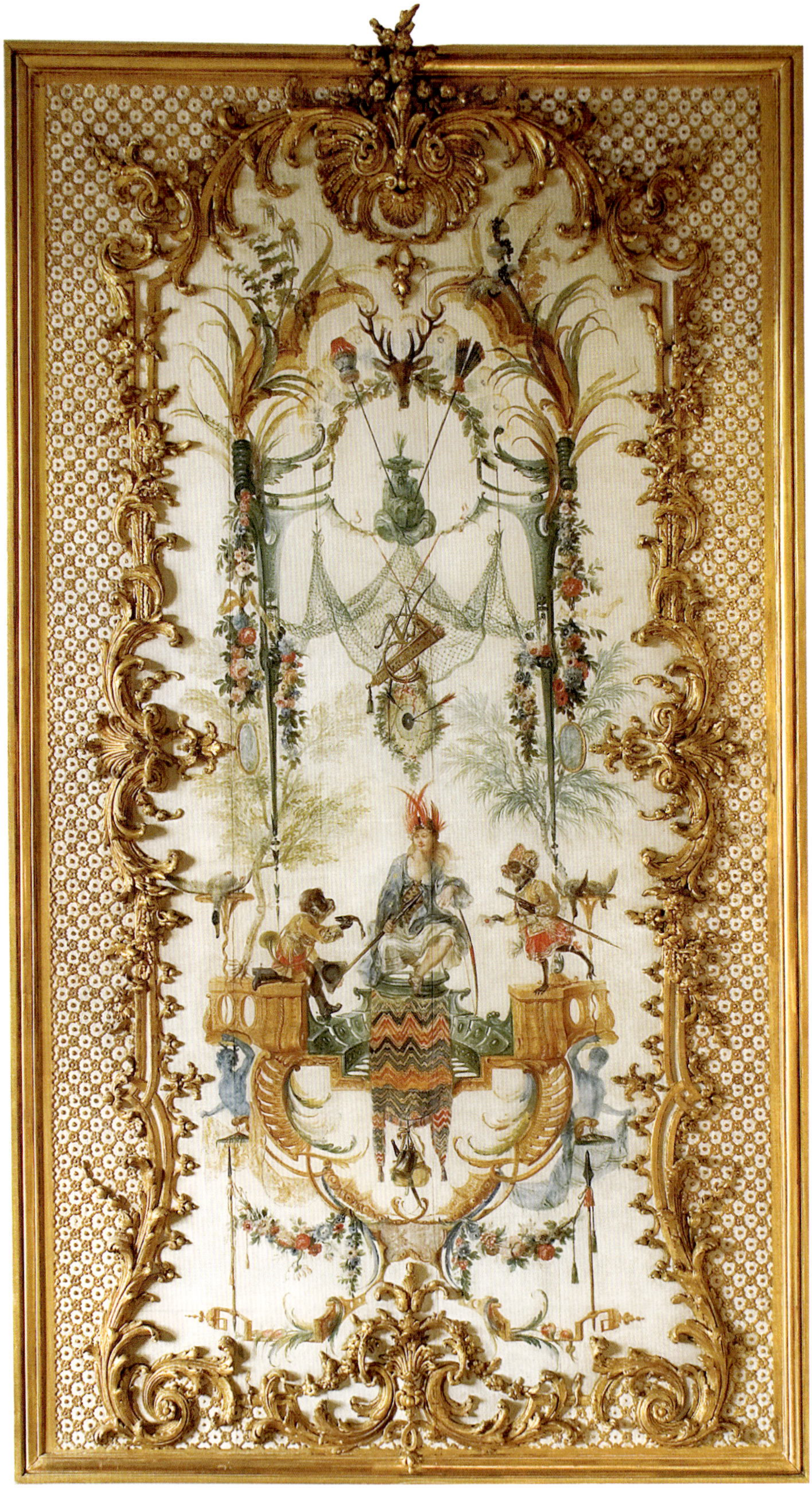

A panel in the Grande Singerie
This panel from the wainscoting was probably painted by Christophe Huet in 1737. America with a feather hairstyle or Touch; a whipper-in wearing the yellow and red hunting livery of the Condés is awarding
him the foot and the courier hands him a letter.

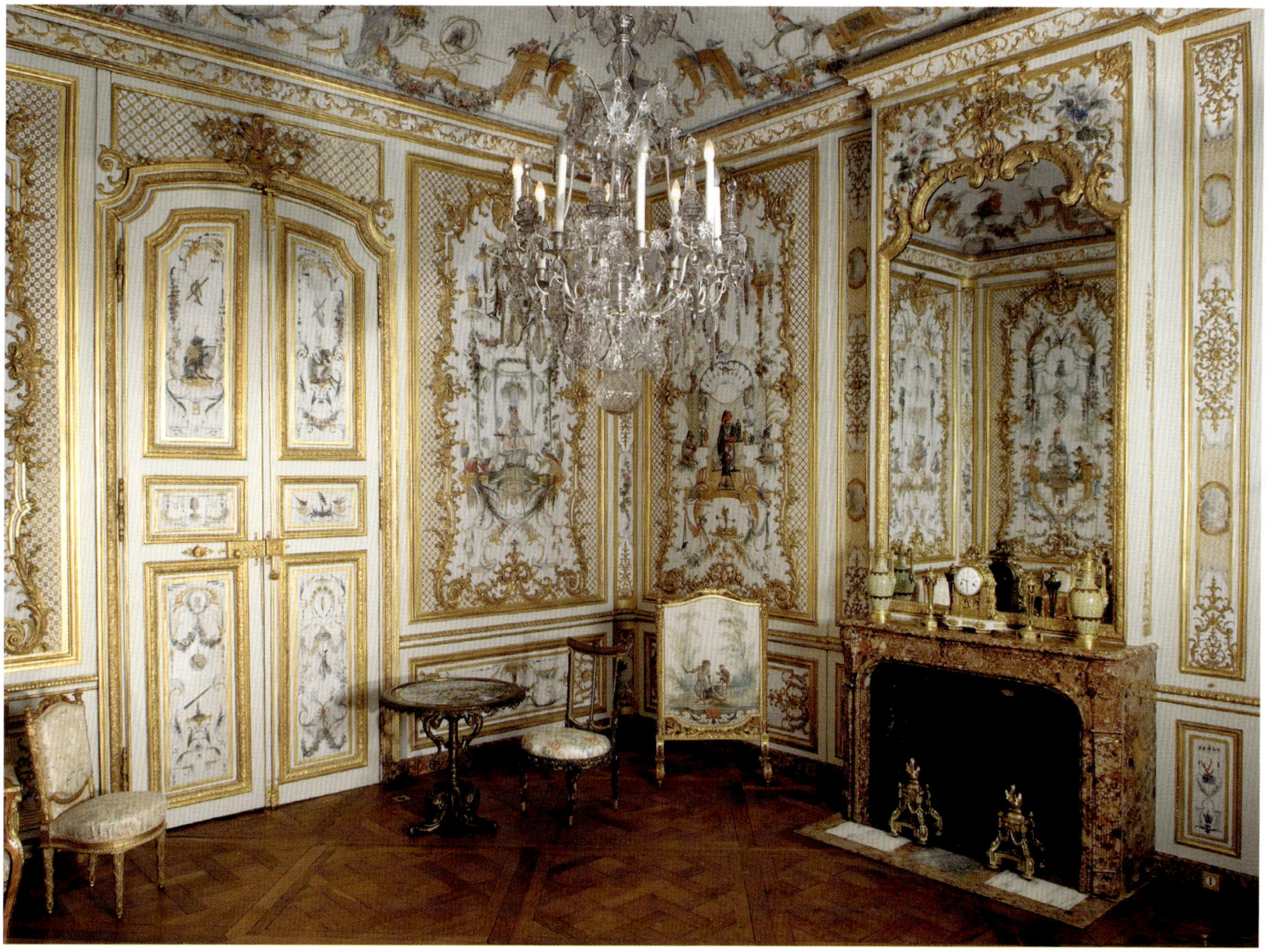

The Grande Singerie
General view of the room decorated by Christophe Huet, with its ceiling and high and low wainscot panels.

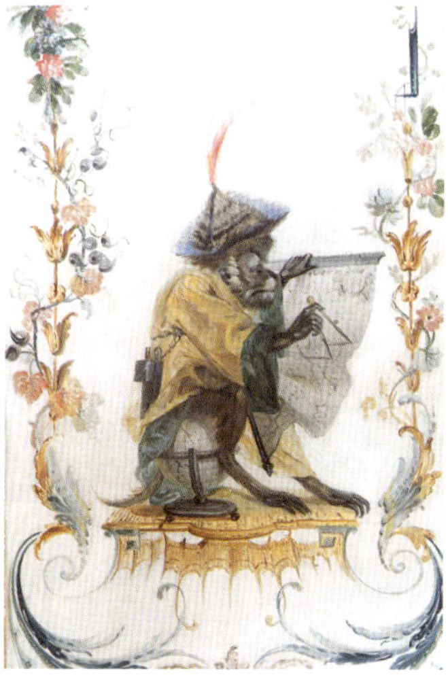

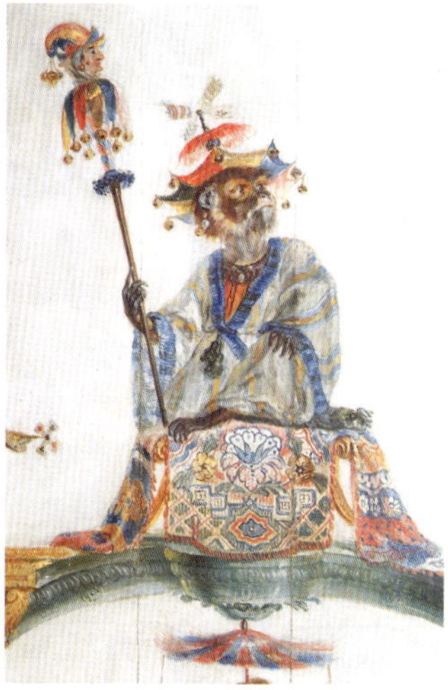

Details from a panel in the Grande Singerie
Left: a geographer monkey is sitting on a globe.
Right: a monkey plays with bells and rattles.

Following pages

The Galerie des Actions
Here we see the new layout of Monsieur le Prince's gallery celebrating his military exploits.

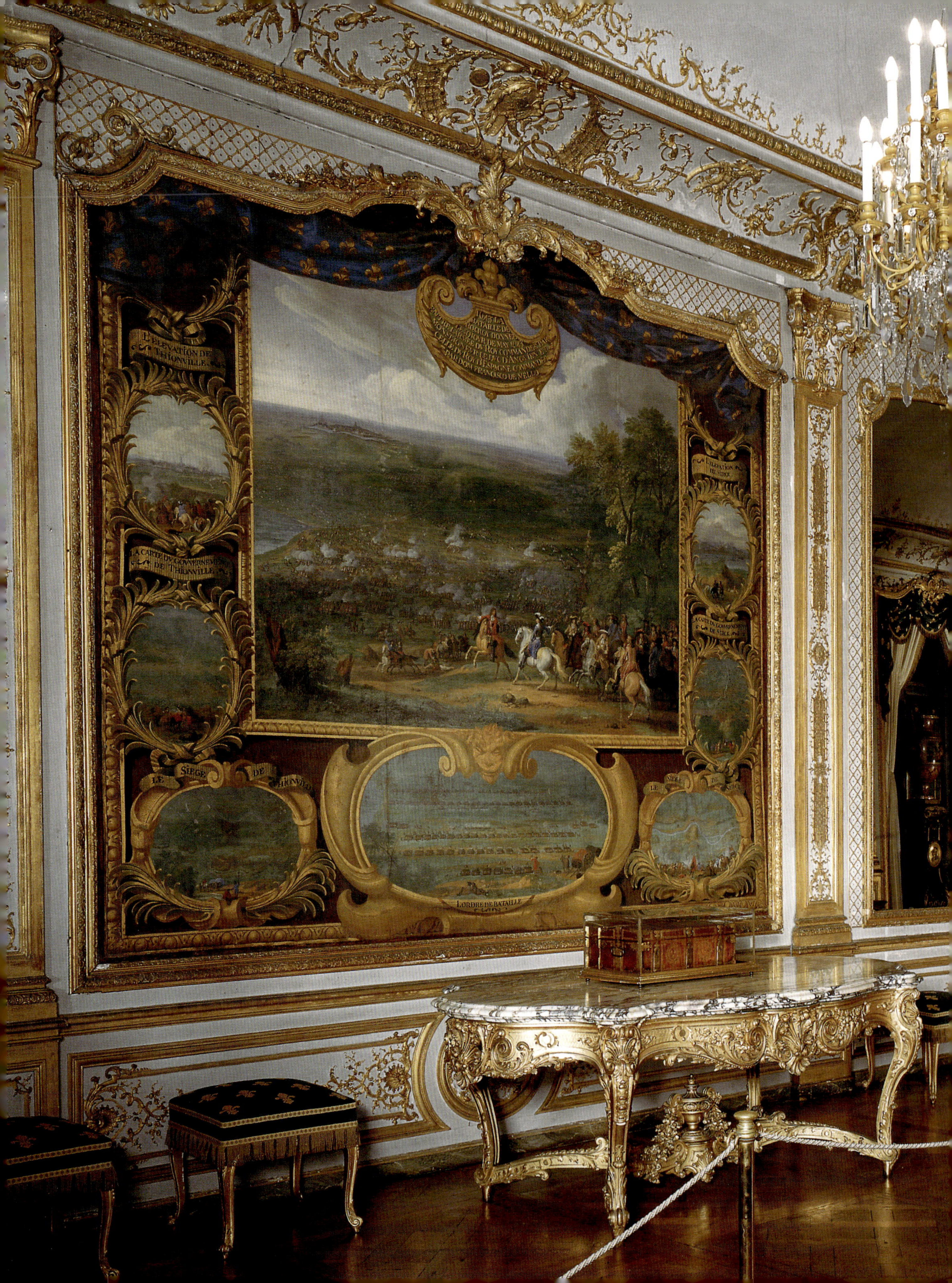
L'ELEVATION DE THIONVILLE.
LE SIEGE DE
L'ORDRE DE BATAILLE

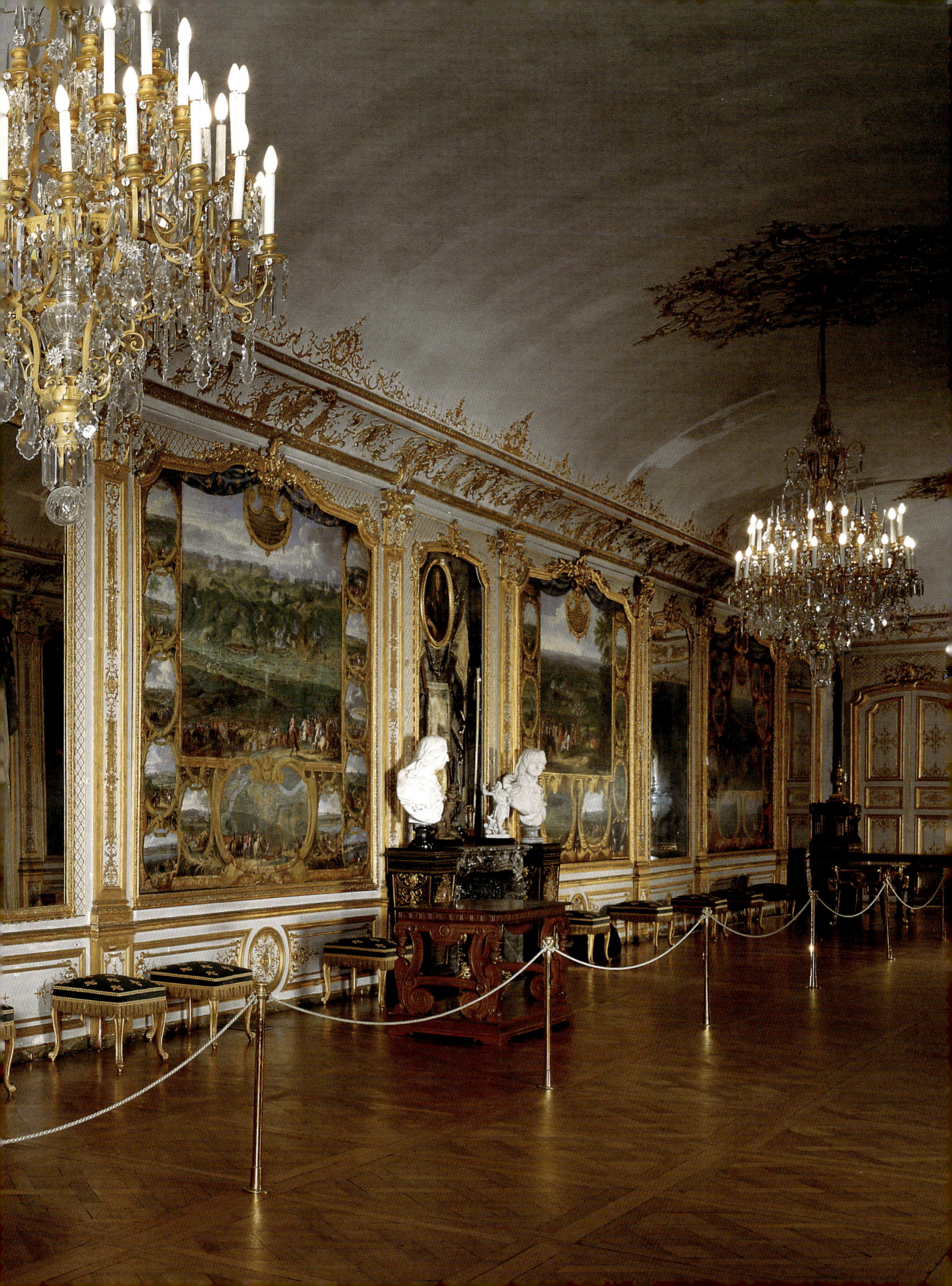

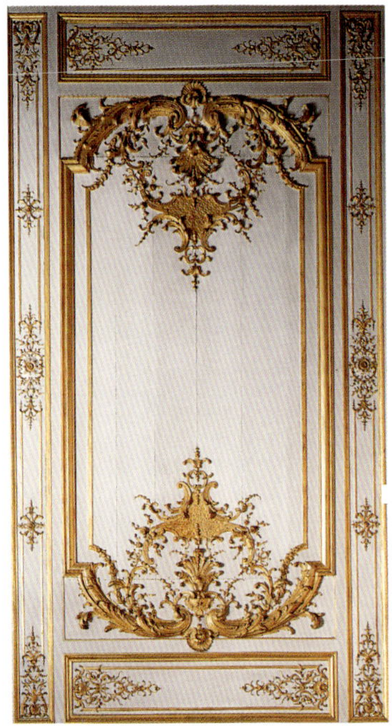

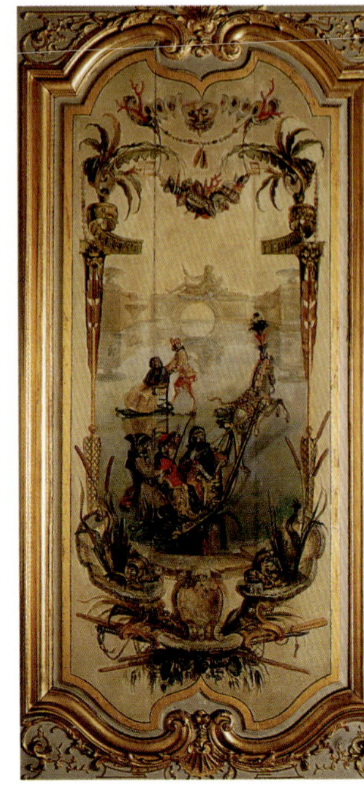

Wainscoting in the Music Room

The sledge ride
Christophe Huet is probably also behind the paintings in the Petite Singerie where men and women are replaced by monkeys and she-monkeys. Here we see a scene from life at Chantilly symbolising winter.

War, Hunting, Painting, Sculpture, Geometry and Chemistry – is handled with the lightness, fantasy and scepticism that characterise the spirit of the time, and there are transparent allusions that do not spare the master of the house himself.[14] The ceiling is painted with the same masterly skill.

The Galerie des Actions de Monsieur le Prince was also altered to suit the taste of the day in 1718-20: ornately shaped frames, pilasters with unpainted motifs on a painted ground, the frames of the mirror piers against a mosaic-style background, doors with slightly arched openings, decorated cornices and coves standing out in gold against a white background. The same style can be recognised in the graceful wainscoting in the music room that ends the enfilade of rooms.

On the ground floor of the same wing, "level with the water of the great moat", as Piganiol de La Force nicely puts it, two suites of rooms had been fitted out for the duke and duchess, linked as was then fashionable[15] by a shared large or small room. Again according to Piganiol, this was decorated "with pictures depicting the finest houses in the neighbourhood of Paris". His evidence notwithstanding, there is a temptation to identify the communicating room with the boudoir adjoining the duchess's former bedroom (replaced in the time of the duc d'Aumale by the Salon Violet, or purple room). This little room with a flat ceiling still has its original decoration: it is the Petite Singerie. The

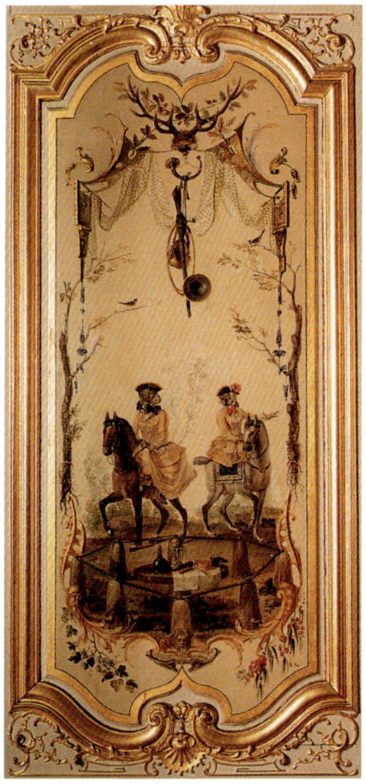

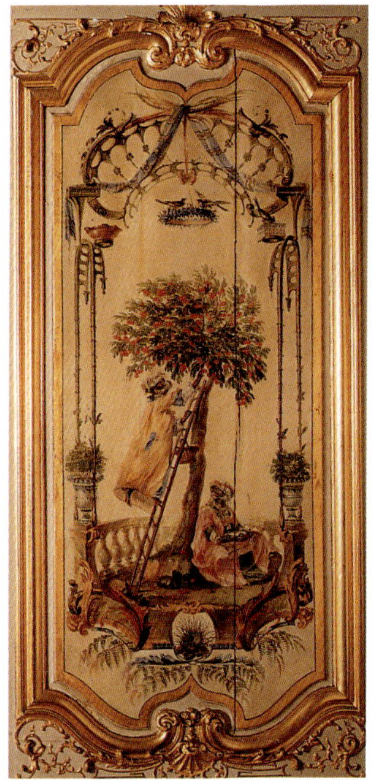

Refreshments during the hunt
This scene symbolises autumn.

Picking cherries
This scene symbolises spring.

date 1735 which can be read on the back of the right shutter does not apply to the gilded wainscoting, no doubt also earlier, but to the paintings covering it, most probably again attributable to the talent of Christophe Huet. The motifs decorating the six tall panels are composed like scenes from a play framed with curtains and arabesques, brimming over with unflagging imagination. There are monkeys and she-monkeys going about all the everyday activities of court life at Chantilly throughout the four seasons of the year, hunting, picking flowers, playing games, plus scenes of dressing and bathing, very fashionable in genre painting.[16]

Except for Huet's paintings, the suites of rooms were certainly finished in 1722 in time for the visit by Louis XV. The whirlwind of festivities had got under way again, starting with the visit in September 1718 of the duchesse de Berry, the beloved daughter of the Regent, which was remembered because a tiger escaped from the Menagerie in the course of the day, but was recaptured without doing any harm. The 1722 festivities were intended to surpass all those that had gone before. It was an opportunity to offer the young king returning from his coronation at Rheims a new, more brilliant and more entertaining visit after a two-day break staying with the Regent at Villers-Cotterets – longer too, five days full enough to provide material for a printed booklet. Fairy-tale scenes with a mythological theme on the Grand Canal, a ballet at the Orangerie, stag-

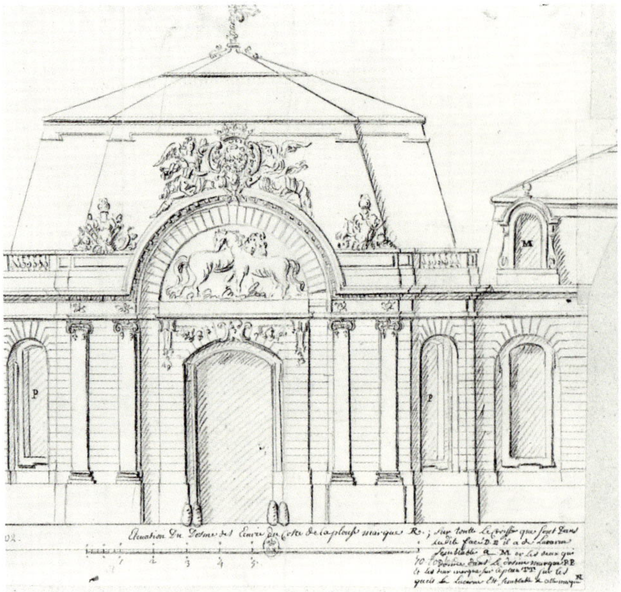

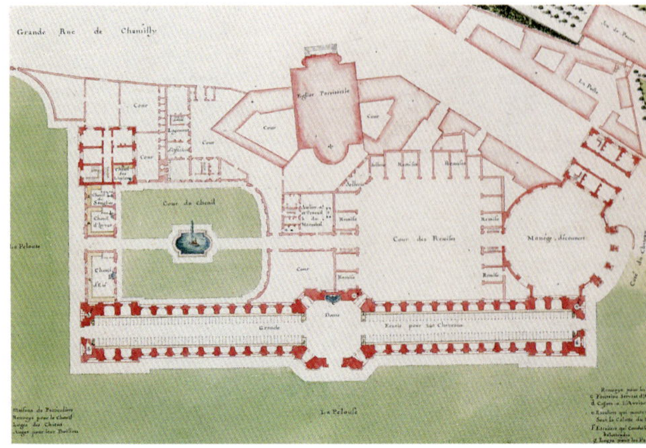

The central pavilion of the Écuries
Drawing by the architect Jean Aubert, 1719.

Ground plan of the Écuries
In this plan from the *Album du Comte du Nord* by Chambé (1784) we see the kennels courtyard on the left, and on the right the courtyard for the carriages with the manège and the Porte Saint-Denis.

hunting, gaming, a concert, a play, and night-time festivities with a naval battle and fireworks with all the buildings highlighted by pyrotechnics delighted the court and the king who took a liking to Chantilly, "the most beautiful place in the world" as Field Marshal de Villeroy wrote. He returned there for the month of July in 1724, and for June and July in 1725 – at the time when the duke/Minister was still in favour.

A palace for horses, the Grandes Écuries

His passion for hunting, and no doubt his desire to show off to the whole court horses and packs of hounds that rivalled those of the king, led the duc de Bourbon to construct a colossal building, a real secular cathedral that has never ceased to elicit surprise and admiration. Chantilly is still one of the capitals of the horse, and has preserved the passionate tradition of the princes in general and Monsieur le Duc in particular as a permanent feature up to the present day, so that his inordinate investments have to some extent proved justified. The Grandes Écuries have thus kept their vocation as stables up to the present by housing the Musée Vivant du Cheval, and their façade provides a splendid setting for the races held on the Pelouse. Quite apart from their usefulness, they remain a major eighteenth-century building, demonstrating the monumental

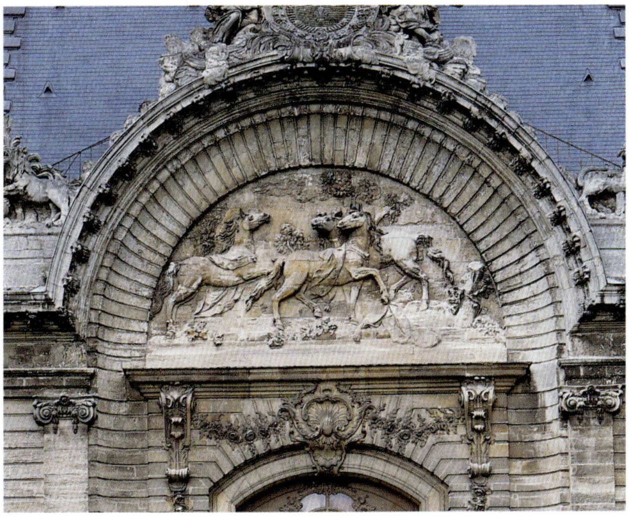

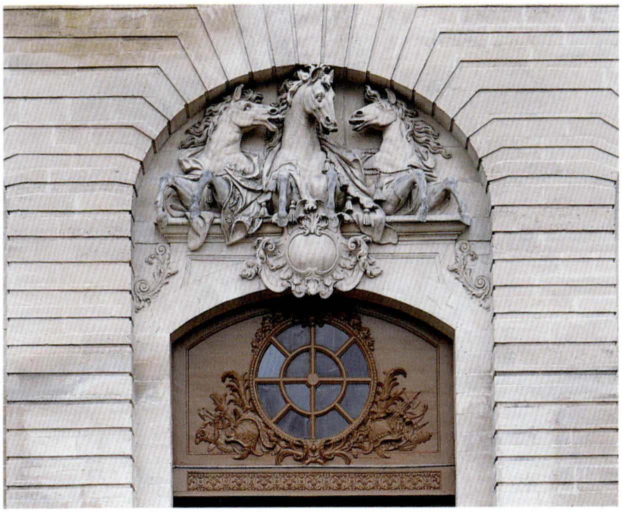

qualities of the Louis XV style at its best. The duc de Bourbon is entitled to our gratitude for having erected this major work. Because of the site he had chosen, the project was closely integrated with the development of the town of Chantilly;[17] this was the personal wish of the prince who wanted to demonstrate his care for those living there, following the tradition of his predecessors. The old road to Gouvieux, straightened out, became the main street, ending at the Hospice Condé, originally founded by Charlotte de Montmorency, Princess de Condé; it was rebuilt in 1723 and a regularly shaped public square was introduced in front of it. The church was enlarged in 1724, and the plots along the Pelouse were conceded between 1722 and 1730 for the building of uniform houses, the designs for which were provided by the duke's architect. In 1730 the prince bought the old Ferme de Normandie in what used to be the hamlet of Les Fontaines, now part of the town, to set up a porcelain factory the output of which was one of the glories of Chantilly: "M. le Duc has established a factory where they make pieces of porcelain which perfectly imitate those of Japan, so much so that there are pieces that cannot be distinguished from the real thing. It works for the public."[18] Because of this the adjacent street was for some time known as the Rue du Japon. To replace the indifferent stables of his predecessors, installed in the wings of Bucamp, the duc de Bourbon had

The horses on the pediments of the Écuries
On the left, the decoration above the door of the central pavilion; on the right that above the door of the north pavilion, the work of the sculptor Bridault.

Following pages
The Écuries and the Porte Saint-Denis seen from the forecourt

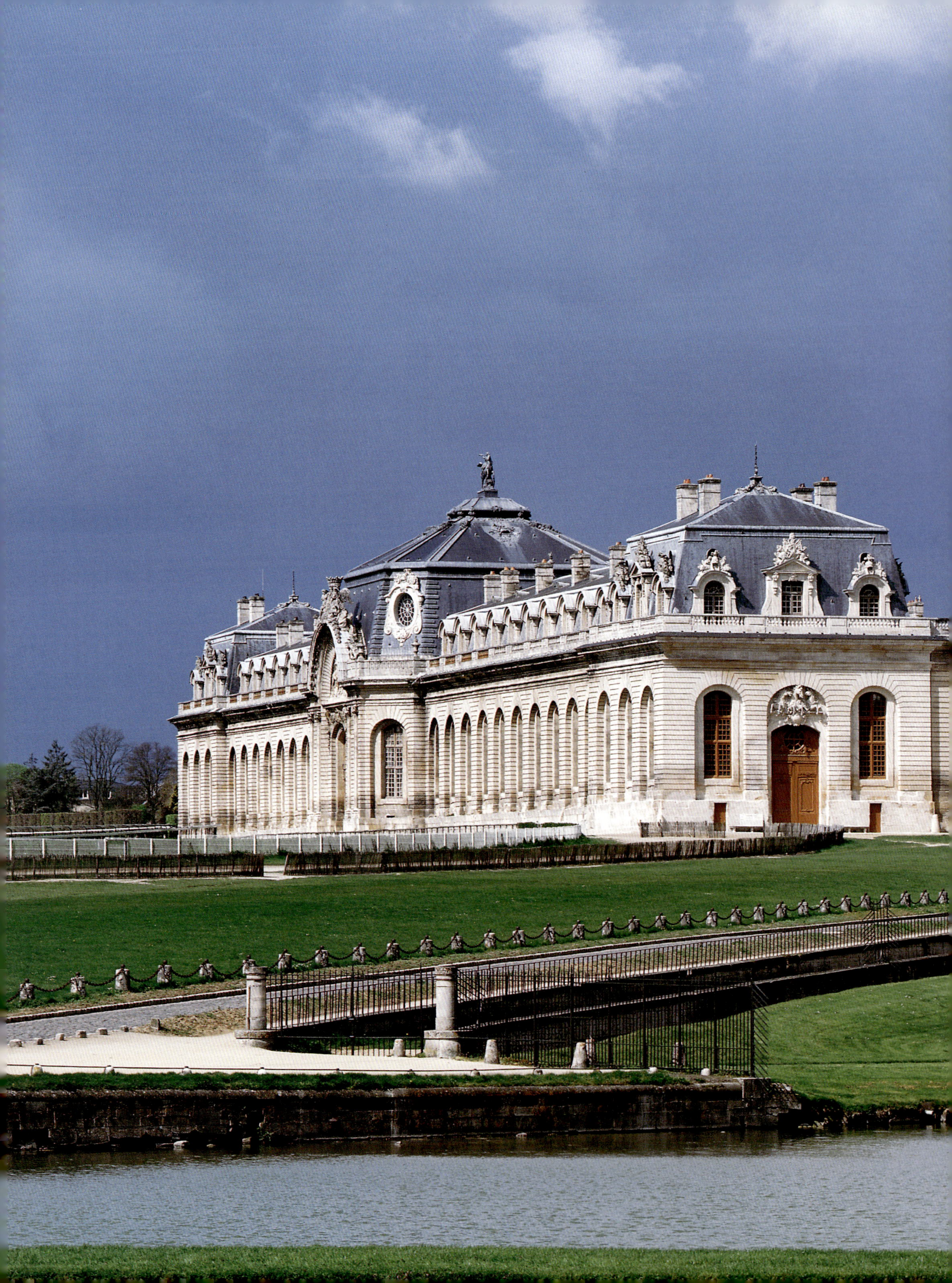

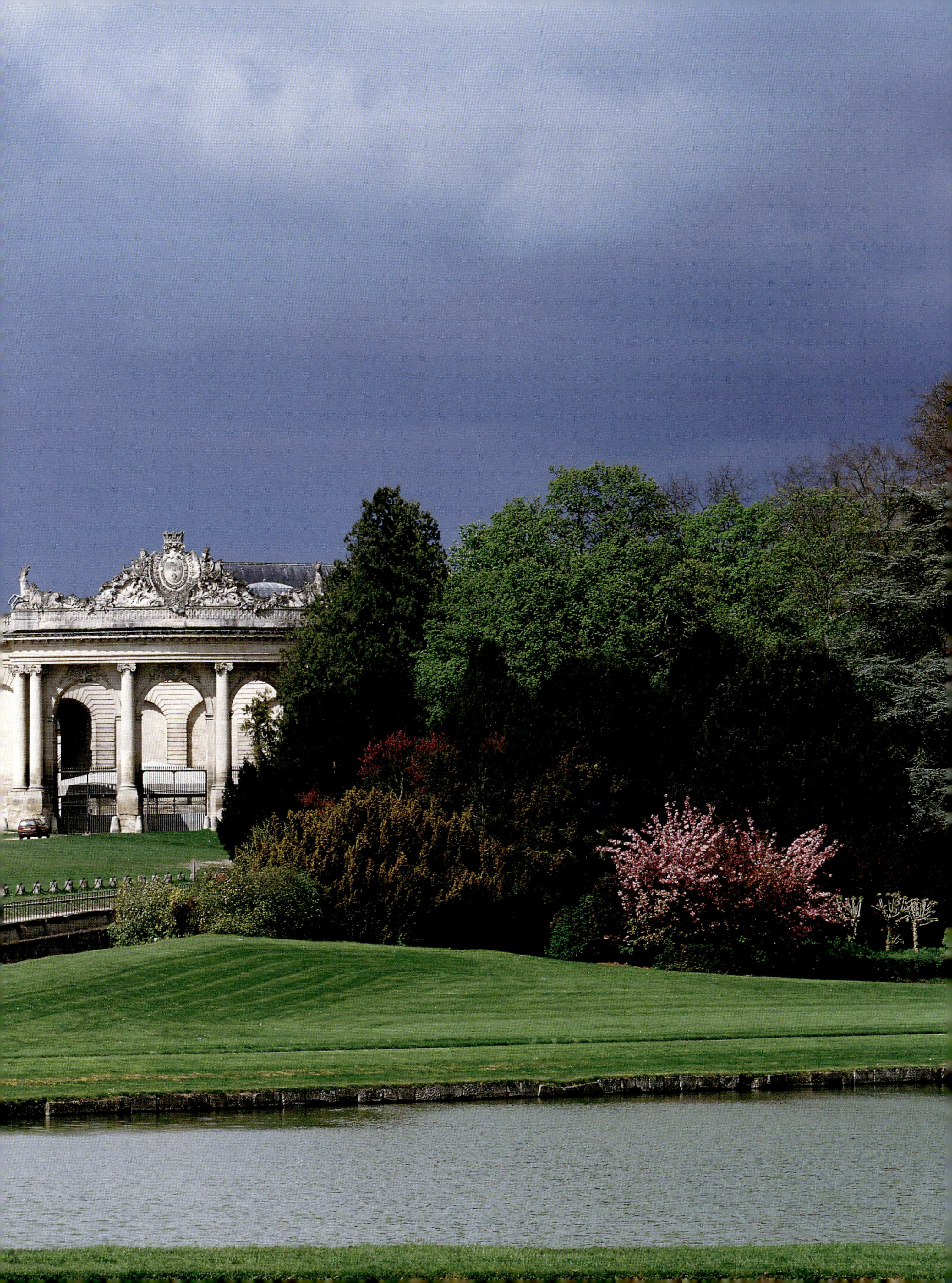

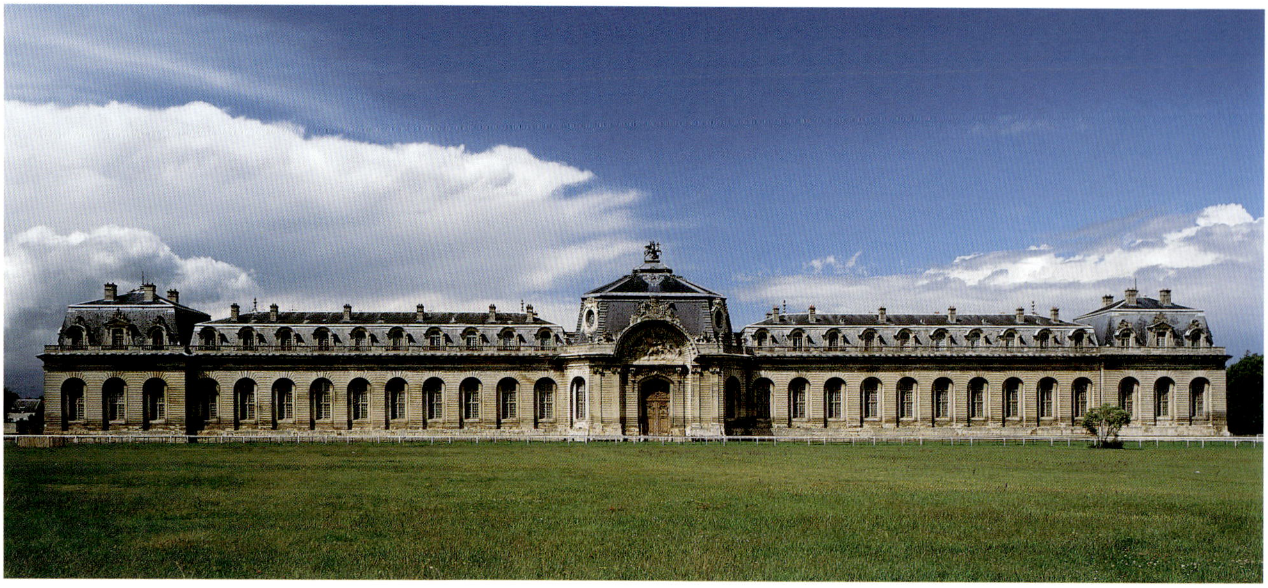

The Écuries seen from the Pelouse

The colonnade of the Manège

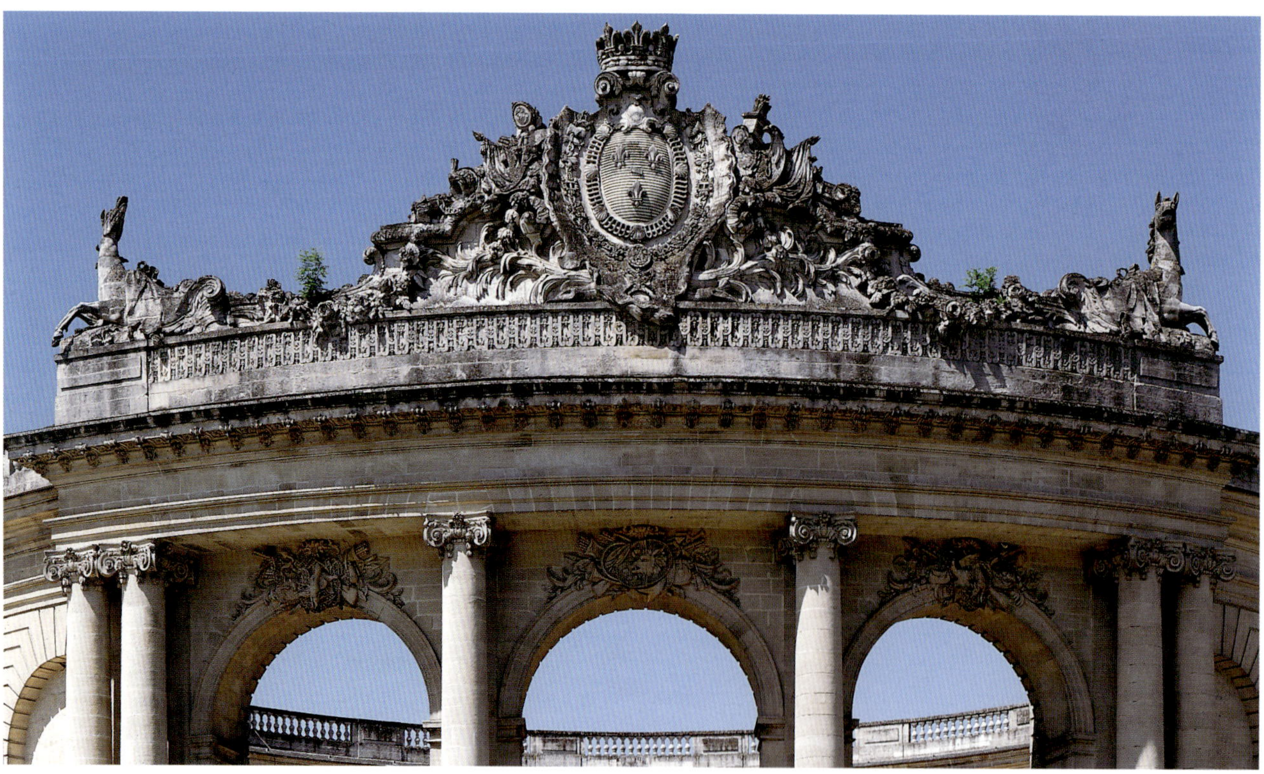

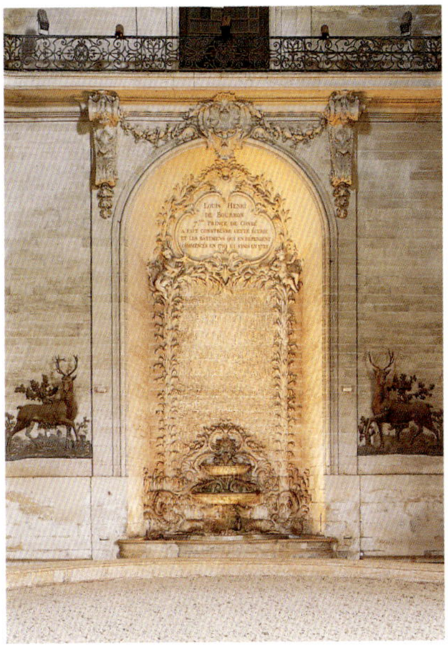

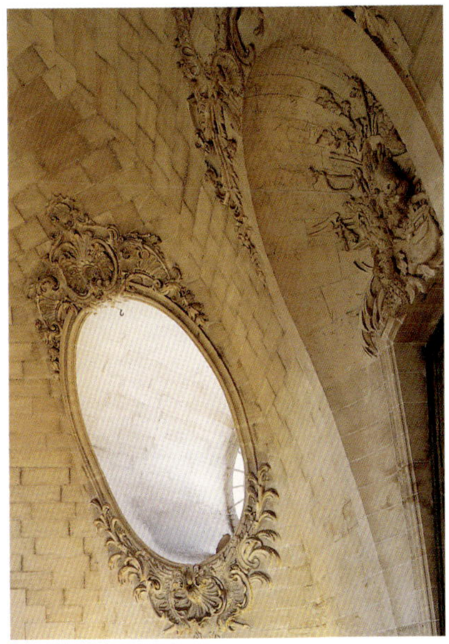

The drinking trough
Under the central dome, the old drinking through still has a few remnants of its superb decoration, with an inscription in honour of the duc de Bourbon.

An *œil-de-bœuf* window in the dome

The main body of the stables
The Musée Vivant du Cheval perpetuates the memory of the famous stables of the Condés.

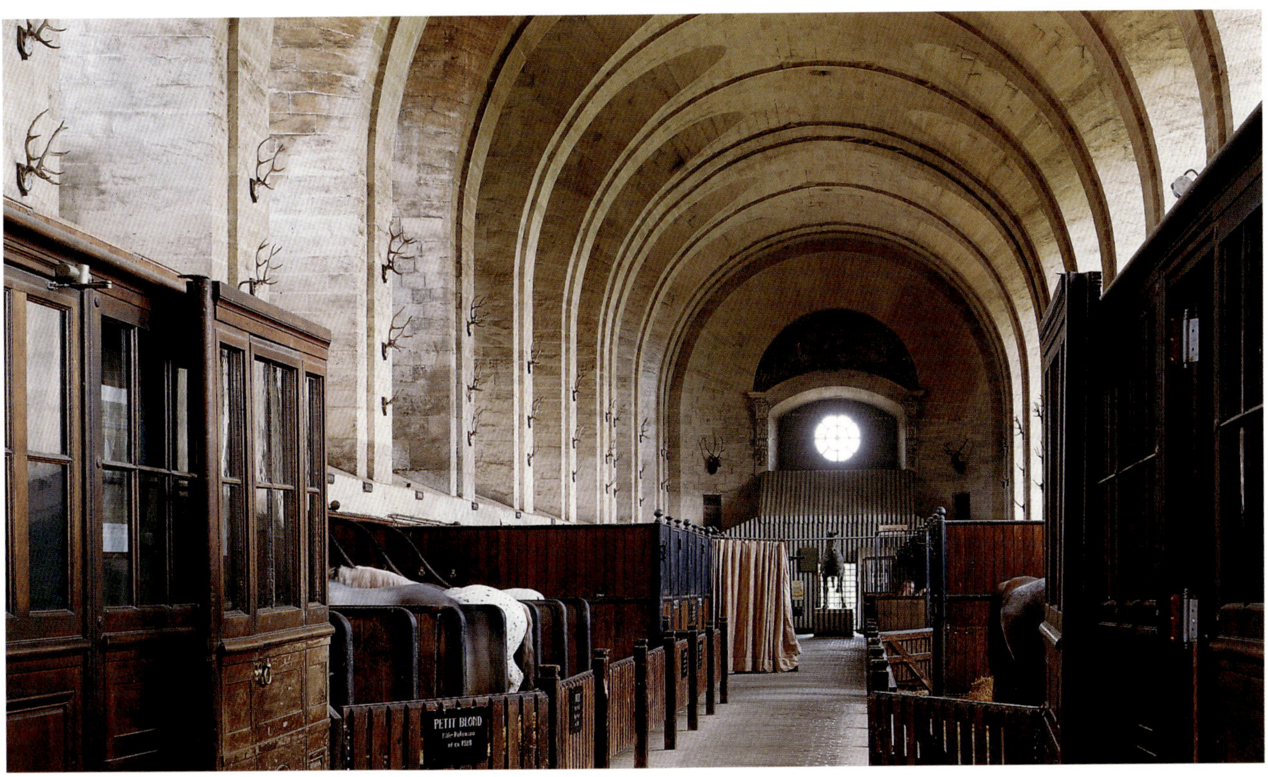

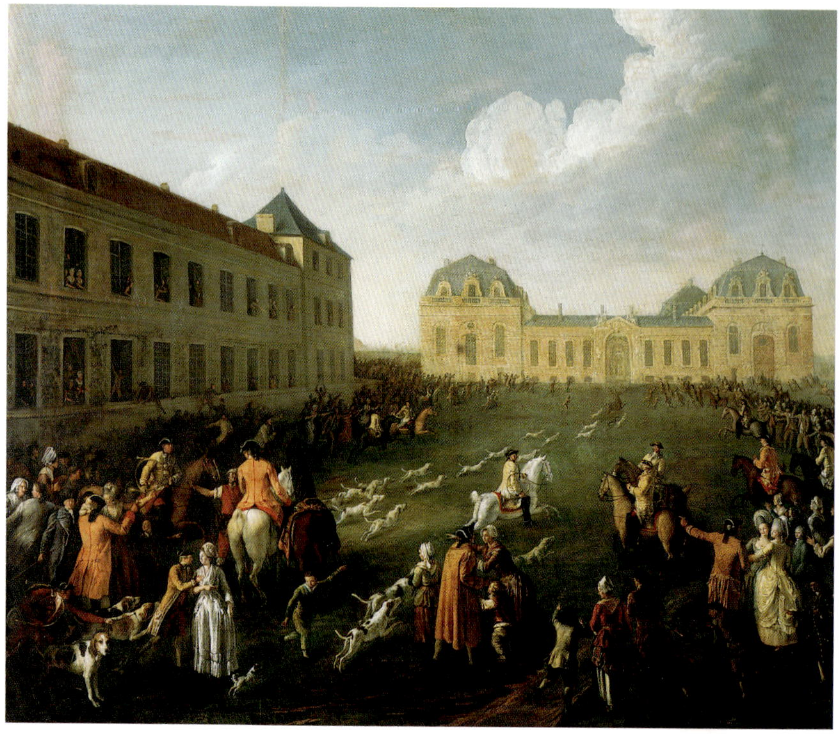

Mort of the stag at the Grandes Écuries
Nicolas Dubois's picture (1780) preserves the memory of a hunt held on 13 September 1776. On the left we see the line of houses of the town of Chantilly, and at the back the façade of the kennels of the Écuries.

decided to put up an independent and very imposing building backing on to the burgeoning town. The idea of building palaces for horses was not a new one in those centuries when horse-riding was regarded as one of the major arts and horsemanship was a factor in all the activities of daily life, from transport and travel of every kind to war and of course hunting. At Versailles, Hardouin-Mansart had laid out the twin complexes forming the Grande and the Petite Écurie symmetrically on the curve of the Place d'Armes, opposite the château, and they are considered to be among his finest works. Elsewhere a single rectangular building was erected along a forecourt with architecture that was as decorated at that of the château: for instance Henriette de La Guiche at the château of Chaumont-La Guiche in Burgundy in 1650, or a few years later the president of the *Parlement* at his château of Maisons-sur-Seine, thanks to the genius of François Mansart.[19] At Chantilly, the exceptionally clear view from the entrance towards the château and towards the gardens ruled out building on the forecourt or even in front of the main gate, sacrosanct spaces that could not be spoilt. Yet again, as in Le Nôtre's day, the natural site was safeguarded, more than that it was extended, at the cost of the inconvenience imposed by

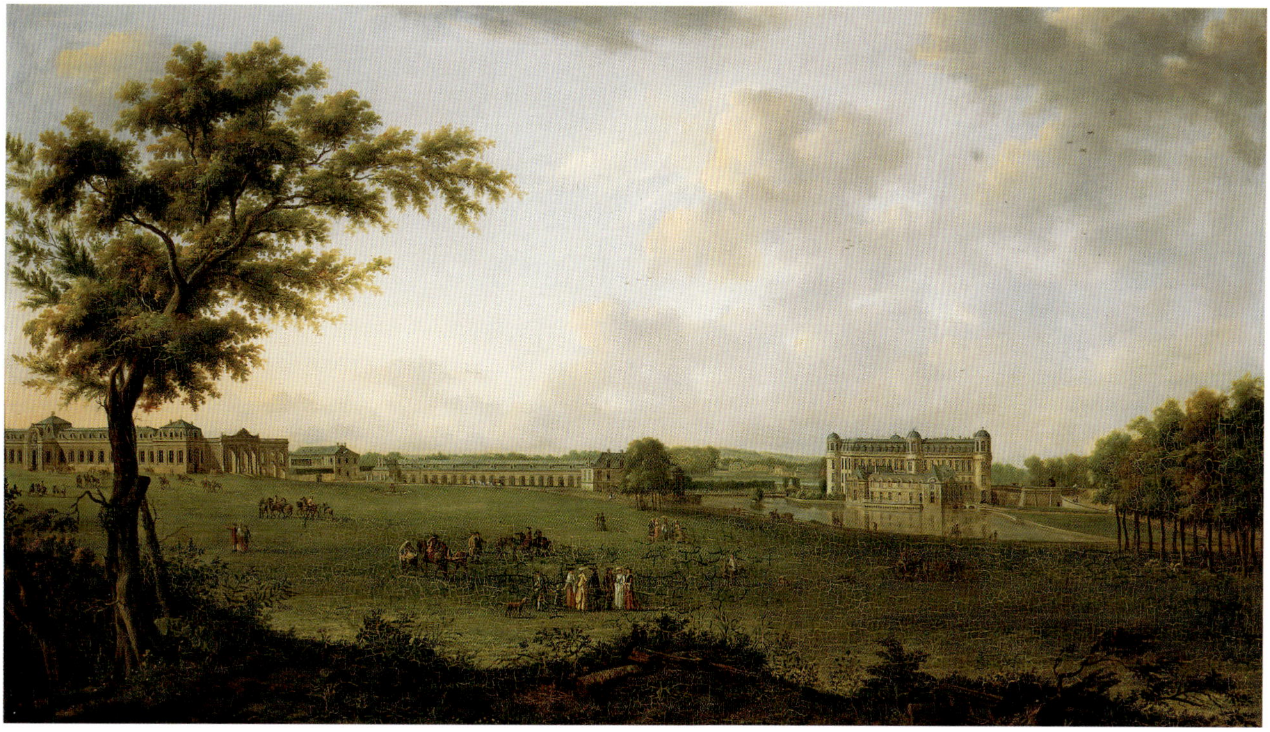

The Écuries and the château of Chantilly seen from the Pelouse
This painting by Hendrik Frans De Cort (1781) shows the new Jeu de Paume built in 1756-58 and the château as it was after the work carried out by Hardouin-Mansart and Aubert.

the remoteness of the stables. Thus in balancing the large masses, the forest that lines the axial thoroughfare – the Allée du Connétable – was respected, as was the Pelouse, a huge grass-covered space the sight of which from the suites of rooms in the Petit Château represents their main attraction, and a site bordering the Pelouse to the north, at the junction of the road that leads to the town after skirting the pond, was chosen for building the stables. The excavations required for the large foundations of the projected building started in 1719, and under the Pelouse they were fortunate enough to find the quarries needed for the construction. This is the Oise after all, the paradise of stone; the first of these stones was laid by Monsieur le Duc on 16 May 1721. The buildings were completed in 1735 and from 1734 to 1736 the excellent sculptor Remy-François Bridault whom we have already met at the château carried out the major sculpted decoration with the help of his fellow-workmen Bernard, Coutelet, Brault, Lefèvre and Buret.

The architect Aubert had thought big.[20] The actual stables which are opposite the Pelouse and the forest form a parallelepiped 186 metres long by 18 metres wide, rising to 13.8 metres at the entablature, constructed entirely from bonded stone. Three pavilions with a square ground plan lend rhythm to this immense volume: those at the ends are only slightly stepped, whereas the central pavilion, with chamfered corners, projects from the alignment by five metres. The building is structured uniformly by large rounded arches with a striped pattern created by the margins of the building stones being set below the rest of the face, at the back of which are the window apertures. On the entablature, a balustrade runs along at the starting-point of the gambrel roof which is broken by stone dormers; the pavilion roofs are topped with hunting trophies and various ornaments. Above the doors of the side pavilions which open on the return sides are horses springing straight ahead, prancing and with their manes swept by the wind. These high reliefs by Bridault bear comparison with the similar groups at the Versailles stables which are earlier, or those at the stables of Cardinal de Rohan in Paris, sculpted by Robert Le Lorrain around 1735.

The central pavilion is handled in the triumphal manner; this is expressed in particular by its amazing roof, a dome with flat slopes the lower of which, constructed very vertically like some roofs by François Mansart, has large *œil-de-bœuf* apertures, while the very flat upper slope is topped by a small overhanging apex roof intended to be used as the base for a statue. The equestrian figure of Fame made of lead, melted down at the time of the Revolution and recently reinstated, was a copy of one of the groups sculpted by Coysevox for the drinking trough at Marly, which it has been possible to admire in the Tuileries gardens since 1719. Pairs of Ionic pilasters frame a large arch topped by an archivolt which is somewhat reminiscent of the one at the Hôtel des Invalides by Jules Hardouin-Mansart. Above the monumental doorway is a tympanum where three horses are caracoling in profile. The decoration is extremely rich: the brackets and hasp of the door are decorated with garlands of flowers, and there is a large cartouche at the apex of the arch with the coat of arms of the Bourbon-Condés borne by two angels, with groups of lions on the sides.

Inside, the domed pavilion houses a large vertical space vaulted in eight sections, 28 metres high and 20.5 metres across. Its five-metre-thick walls have arched openings the lunettes of which are ornamented with hunting trophies. The drinking trough occupies the arch facing the entrance: it is a fountain surrounded by palm trees and stalactites, and its water is spread in cascades by two shells in the basin of the drinking trough. Unfortunately the sculpted figures that went with it were lost at the time of the Revolution: the lead dolphins which supported one of the shells and the two life-size lead horses which stood in the basin, one accompanied by a huntsman sounding the horn, the other drinking out of a marine conch presented by a child. On the sides are four figures of stags made of stone and lead, painted in lifelike colours.

On either side of the dome, the stable extends in two huge aisles the impressive proportions of which are more suggestive of religious than secular architecture; these are yet another reference to the work of the master Mansart at the Orangerie at Versailles. The stable could accommodate 240 horses, in four rows of sixty stalls separated by a central aisle. We know that in July 1772 it housed 125 riding horses and 102 carriage horses, which reflects a style of living of great opulence: the prince had a choice of ten mounts.[21] Above the vault there were 24 lodgings, and others were distributed round the courtyards, for the grooms, coachmen and postilions, and farriers.

Behind the main building, Aubert laid out huge outbuildings backing on to the town, among which the parish church is stuck like a wedge in a tree-trunk. They were distributed round the two courts for the carriages and kennels, and were very lavish in the allocation of space. In the buildings round the first courtyard dozens of carriages, berlins, barouches and post chaises were kept, not forgetting the sledges that were used for outings on the canals when they were frozen over. The kennels could accommodate 150 pack hounds, a main kennel, a winter kennel for the stag hunt, and a kennel for wild boar hunts. Their west-facing façade is flanked by two symmetrical pavilions and the large arched doorway is framed by pilasters adorned with hunting trophies beneath a pediment sculpted with six dogs and bitches attacking wild boar, with the figures of Diana with the doe and the shepherd Cyparis with his stag on the sloping parts. In 1778 the Prince de Condé embellished the pond laid out at the centre of the court for the pack to quench their thirst with a lead stag commissioned from the sculptor Jean-Baptiste Stouf as a reminder of the kill that had taken place at that very spot two years earlier, but it did not survive the Revolution.

At the other end, nearer the château, the composition is more ambitious still, and one of the most beautiful ever conceived to link a palace and a town using the art of the hinge, which makes the greatest feats of skill possible. Behind the east pavilion, with the richly decorated façade we have described,

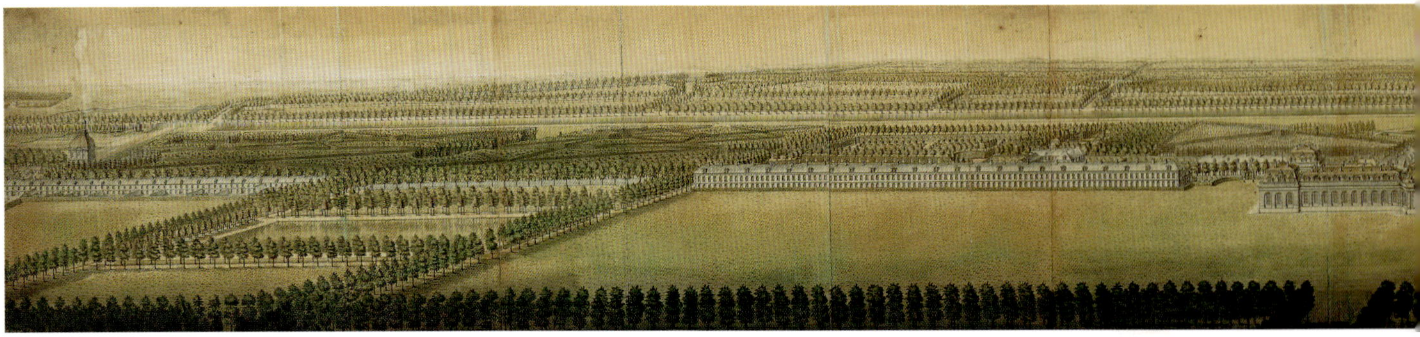

Panorama of Chantilly in 1738
Claude Dubourg's huge drawing gives some concept of the size of the site, the dimensions of the Pelouse and the length of the Grand Canal.

Aubert designed a riding-school courtyard for *haute école* exercises: it is round, 40 metres in diameter, and surrounded by large blind arches with a striped pattern created by the margins of the building stones being set below the rest of the face. On the outside a monumental portico of three bays of Ionic columns rests on the open arches, its balustrade topped by a large sculpted cartouche presenting yet again the arms of the Condés. Long garlands of flowers – the symbolism is eloquent – join the cartouche to figures of whinnying horses, their heads raised towards the sky. The rotunda was to have been articulated at an obtuse angle with a square pavilion symmetrical to the previous one, to be passed through by people wanting to enter the town, on the axis of the main street. The death of the duc de Bourbon in 1740 interrupted the building work, but we still have the east façade of that pavilion, an unfinished façade with toothing stones, like the remains of an ancient triumphal arch. This is the Porte Saint-Denis. The Chantilly stables, which were used on several occasions for princely festivities, stupefied the duc's contemporaries. Some, like the Prince de Ligne, expressed the opinion that the building was "superior to the palaces of several kings", while others like the duc de Croy considered their magnificence overdone. Piganiol de La Force[22] devotes an enthusiastic 24-page description to them and draws attention to one of the unsuspected effects of the design: from the window of his study in the Petit Château, when the doors of the stables were open, the duke could look right through the building and see an axial avenue 226 *toises* (450 metres) away. The building kept its reputation: as one of the finest buildings of the eighteenth century, it was remembered later in the repertory of historical styles for its façades, its decoration and its so unusual roofs, as an examination of certain structures dating from the end of the following century such as the Petit Palais in Paris will prove.[23]

In the gardens, the duke had "considerable embellishments"[24] carried out

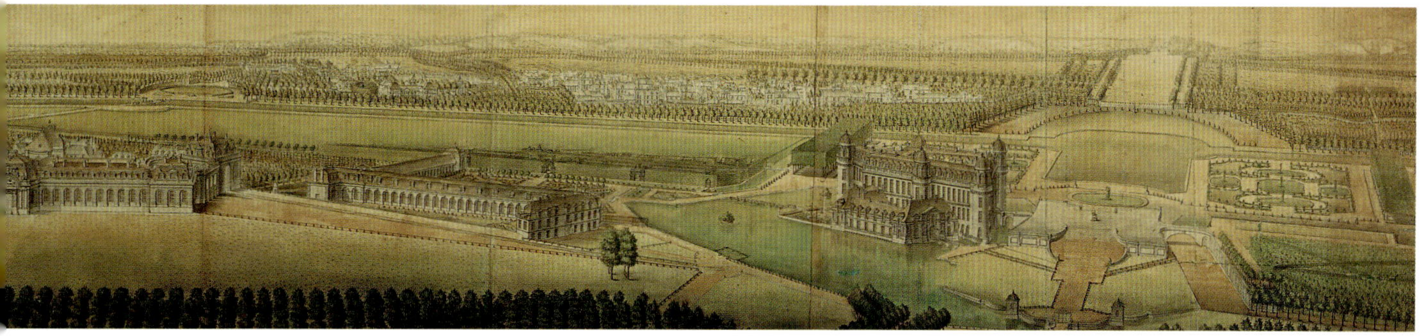

which have left very little trace: new paths including the Allée du Pont du Roi, on the axis of the Terrasse du Connétable, new green arbours and clumps of trees in the gardens of the Jeu de Mail (game of pall-mall), the Parc de la Caboutière and the Parc de Sylvie, arranged by Nicolas Breteuil, "gardener to Monsieur le Duc at Sylvie". On the north-west side he had the mineral-water fountain installed, with a pavilion and a *parterre*, the Îles du Bois Vert were transformed, and the Allée des Soupirs was laid out behind the Galerie des Cerfs. Let us remember above all the installation of some fashionable attractions for the entertainment of the aristocratic society, the Jeu de l'Oie (game of goose) for example, a few elements of which, a bridge and stone plinths, are still standing near the fork on the Chemin d'Avilly. Marie Lesczinska enjoyed playing when she stayed here in August 1739, the duc de Luynes tells us: "The queen went to the Jeu d'Oie, which is a grove made a year or two ago, where there is a race for rings, seated on chairs or mounted on geese; the queen sat in one of the chairs and even took a good many rings."[25]

The work carried out by the last Prince de Condé, 1740-89

The death of Louis-Henri, duc de Bourbon, in 1740 interrupted the lavish building work at Chantilly for some time. He left behind him a four-year-old son, Louis-Joseph, who was orphaned of his mother one year later. The child again took the name of Prince de Condé, which he was to distinguish leading the royal armies during the Seven Years War, where he was one of the few French generals to be victorious, then later against the Republic at the head of the *armée des Émigrés* (émigré army). For some years his uncle the comte de Charolais acted as guardian to the little prince, managing his property meticulously and ensuring the proper upkeep of the estate, then on 3 September 1748 he took possession of Chantilly personally, welcomed by the local population

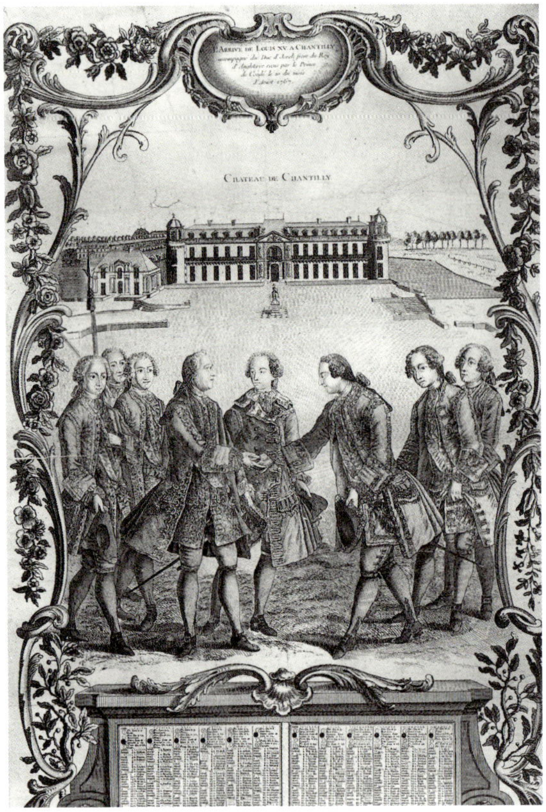

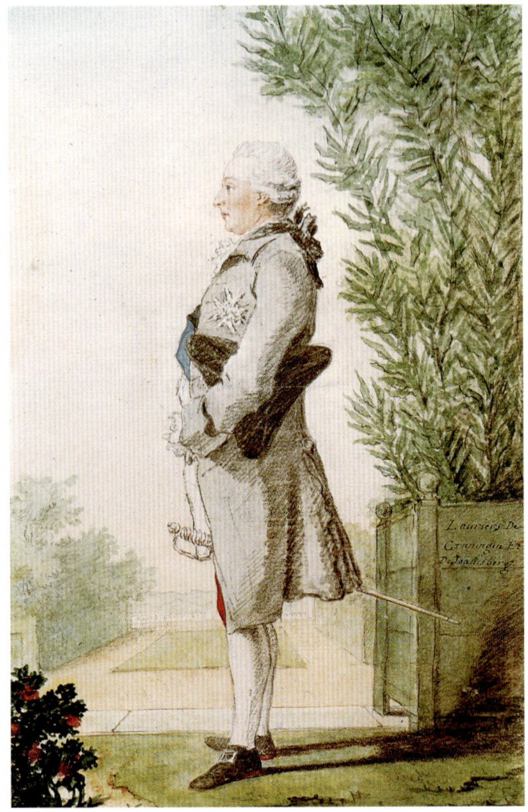

Louis XV at Chantilly in 1767
The Almanac of 1768 takes the king's visit on 10 August 1767 with the Duke of York, the brother of the king of England, as its theme. He is received by the Prince de Condé.

Louis-Joseph de Bourbon, Prince de Condé
One of the 484 witty portraits by Carmontelle held at Chantilly. On the box round the laurels the names of the prince's victories, Grüningen and Johanisberg, can be read.

with transports of joy. These first days were of course given over to outings and hunting, but also to celebrations to which the local people had been freely invited, a ball, a puppet show, shooting and archery contests, festivities that would be renewed every year on a fixed date until the Revolution. In 1753 at the age of seventeen Condé married, making a love match with the daughter of the Prince de Soubise, Charlotte-Élisabeth-Godefride de Rohan.

The very young couple then embarked on a new round of gaiety at Chantilly, in an exuberant, unbridled *dolce vita* atmosphere: day followed night without any break in outings, hunting, fishing, dancing, and one morning at dawn they piled into a "gondola" drawn by eight horses to go and see the sea at Dieppe, and eat fish, which they failed to find.... The princess's death in 1760 put an end to these happy meetings. A widower at the age of twenty-three and the father of two children, Condé did not remarry, but five years later embarked on a long, steady relationship with Marie-Catherine de Brignole, Princess of Monaco; he finally married her while an émigré, in 1808. Like his ancestors the new prince had a passion for buildings, which he assuaged ostentatiously in the alterations to the Palais-Bourbon carried out

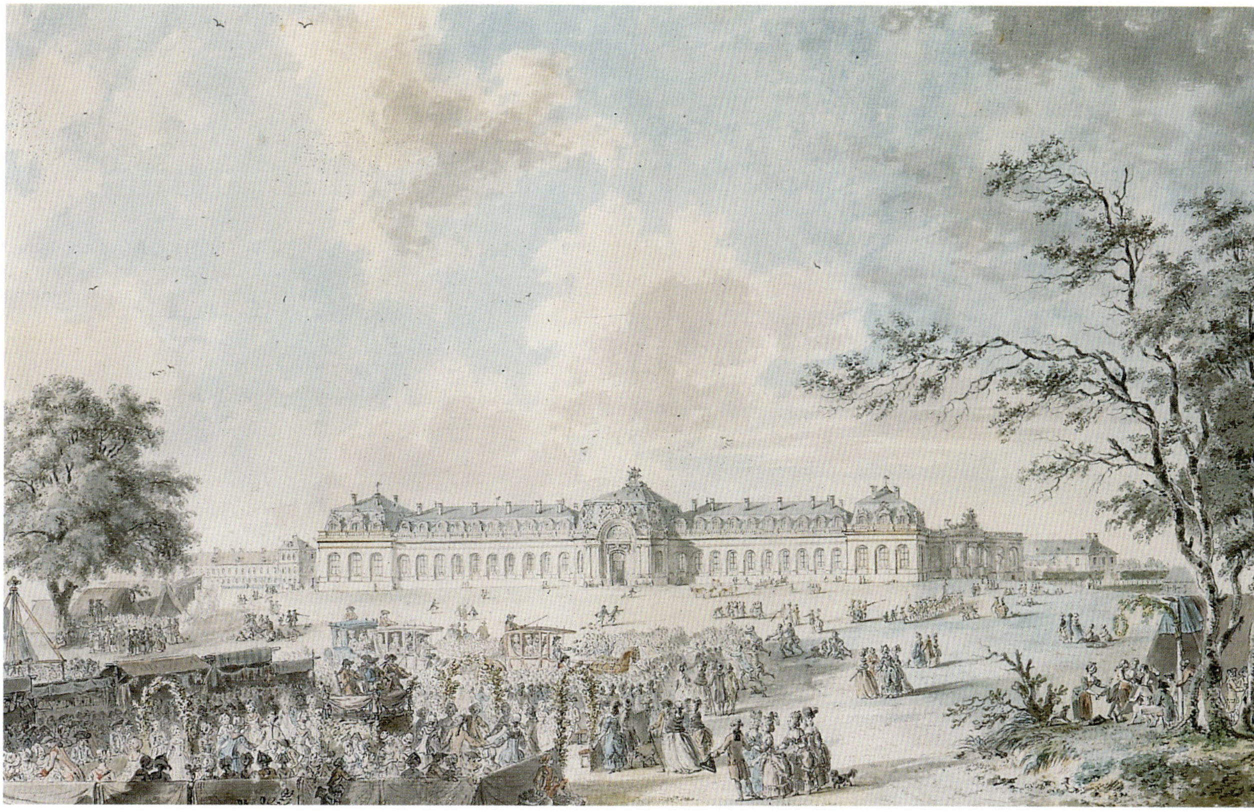

The Pelouse and the Écuries on the open day at Chantilly in 1785
The unknown author of this watercolour successfully conveys the atmosphere of the popular celebration which brought together courtiers and the inhabitants of Chantilly,
four years before the fall of the Bastille.

by his new architect Claude Billard de Bélisard, Aubert having died in 1741. At Chantilly, his attentions turned first to the gardens which were to be marked by the new sensitivities of the day, Rousseau's love of nature and the simple world of the peasants. But the first thing was for him to satisfy his tastes as a young sportsman by building a new close tennis court or Jeu de Paume, the one built by the Montmorencys having long since disappeared. Erected in 1756-58 behind the Orangerie and near to the town, the building is still standing.

Later, on his return from the Seven Years War where he won victories in command of the royal armies at Grüningen and Johannisberg (1762), the prince had changes characteristic of the new spirit implemented in his gardens. To the west, the islands cut like small tongues of earth between the arms of the canals were transformed into a park of attractions to meet the latest fashion in entertainment. At the tip of the Île d'Amour, the Pavillon de Vénus was erected in 1765, a light structure enhanced with columns and balustrades made of trelliswork, in which a cool room, very richly decorated with scenes depicting lovers and pastoral games, received the company for refreshments. At the centre of each window a jet of water spurted up, looking like a candle.

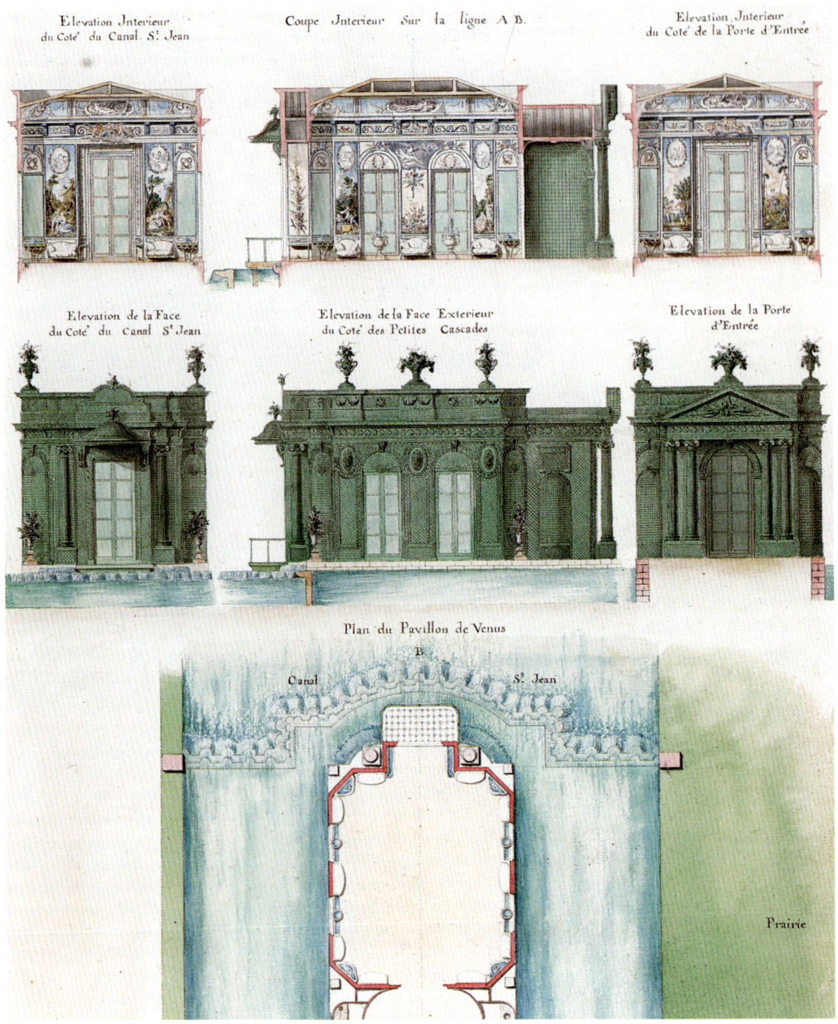

The Pavillon de Vénus
This attractive pavilion stood in the gardens to the west, at the end of the Île d'Amour. Drawings by Chambé in the *Album du Comte du Nord*, 1784.

Other small resting places made this island attractive, such as an open-air suite of rooms – the room of service trees, the circular room, and the room of Love – a few invaluable watercolours painted by Delagardette are all that is left to preserve their memory. Parallel with the Île d'Amour, the former Île du Bois Vert, rechristened the Île des Jeux, assembled the amusements expected by society: tilting at the ring, the game of *château*, *portique*, English skittles, swings, *cochonnet*, *rossignol*, *passe-dix*, a tombola, troll-madam, bowls, seesaws. Next you moved on to the dance hall, and then into the old rooms built in the seventeenth century (decorated with the battle of the Dragons) before reaching the terrace above the water where you could daydream at your leisure, seated on a double-backed bench. Beyond that the former pheasantry of the Great Condé was replaced by yet another pavilion for refreshments, the Pavillon Romain, surrounded by gardens containing flowers, fruit and vegetables.[26] Laid out as

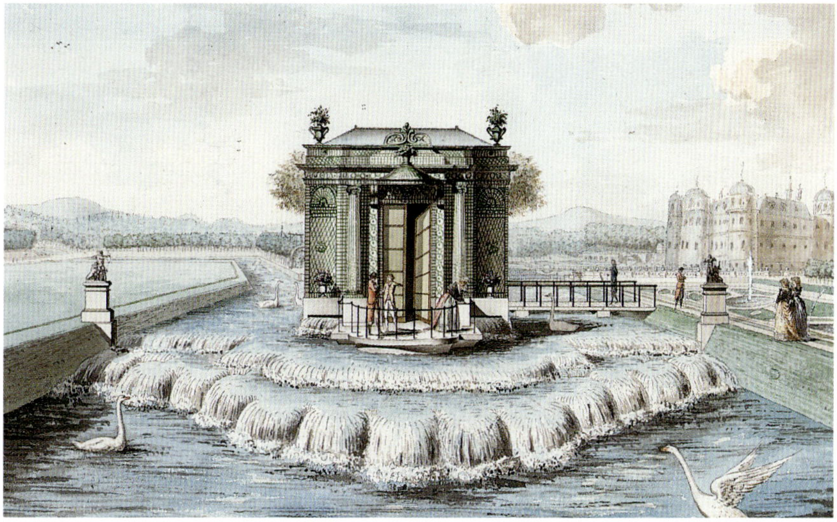

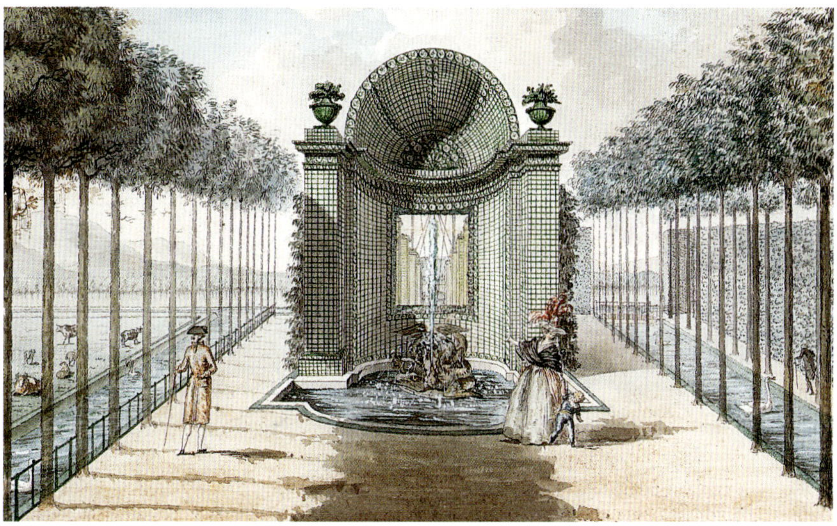

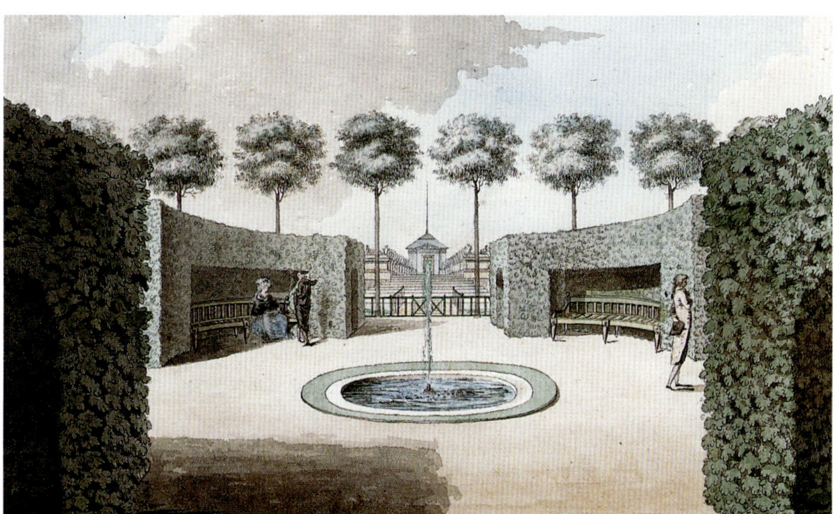

The new decorative features of the islands
These three watercolours by Delagardette dated 1787 form part of a set of fifteen. They depict the new arrangements made by the Prince de Condé on the islands in the Canal Saint-Jean. Above, the Pavillon de Vénus seen from the direction of the Cascade (cf. figure on p. 92); in the middle the Fight of the Dragons, a legacy from the gardens by Le Nôtre; below, the Salle Circulaire opposite the Orangerie terrace.

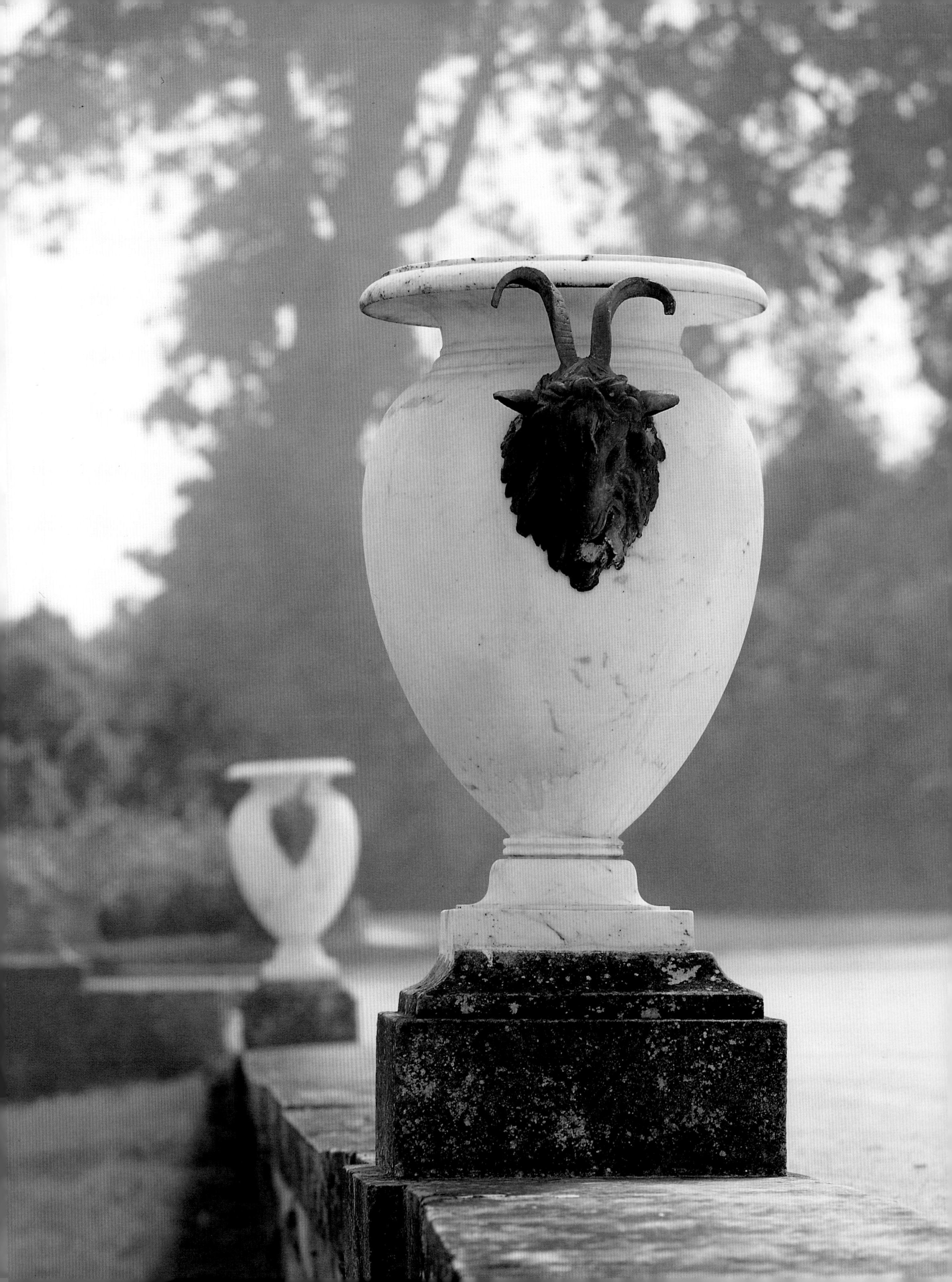

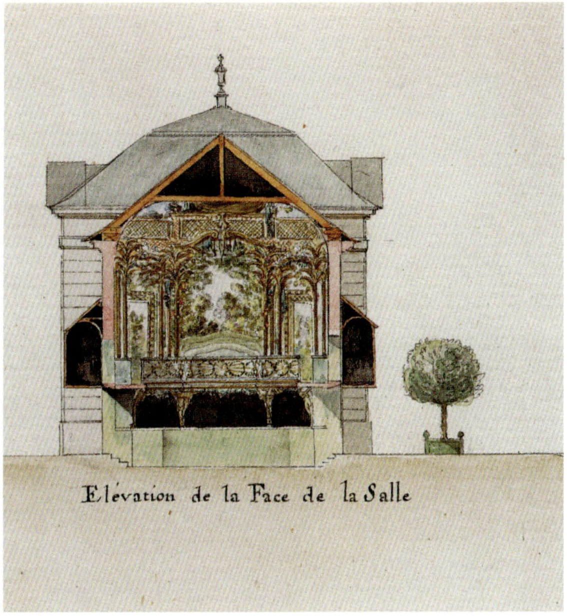

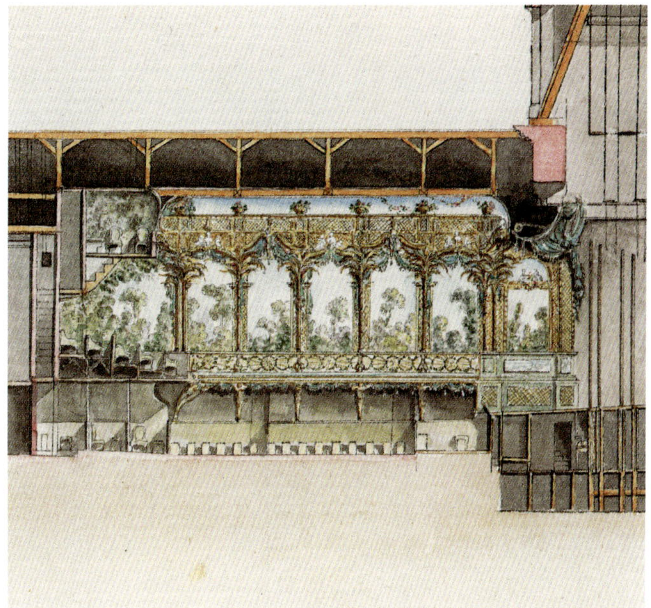

The new theatre
These two drawings by Chambé from the *Album du Comte du Nord*, 1784, show the decoration of the theatre. This was built for the Prince de Condé by Jean-François Leroy to designs by Bélisart, beside the Orangerie by Hardouin-Mansart.

a modest annexe of the Orangerie, the little Salle d'Oronthée seemed quite inadequate to a prince smitten with the theatre; like the aristocratic society of his generation, he felt a real passion for plays put on by professional actors or amateur performances in which he took part, along with his family. So in 1767-68 a new theatre was made to replace the pavilion, designed by Bélisart and built by Jean-François Leroy, who was now in charge of building work at Chantilly: it cost more than 200,000 *livres*, and the decoration painted by the ornamental designer Pierre Sauvage was not completed until 1786. The previous year, to clear more space for the theatre, it has been decided to knock down the old Galerie des Cerfs built by Guillaume de Montmorency, and replace it with a terrace edged with balustrades; the pilasters on these were fitted with mascarons spewing out water, and supported white marble vases ordered from Italy, their handles formed from ram's heads made of lead.

Known as the Galerie des Vases, the new terrace gave access to the Salon d'Apollon, a square pavilion guarded by statues of Ceres and Bacchus which formed the vestibule of the theatre. On its walls, paintings in *trompe-l'œil* depicted the Apollo Belvedere and opposite it the great men of the French theatre, Molière, Racine, Regnard, Crébillon, Corneille, Piron, Voltaire and Destouches, with medallions painted *en camaïeu* depicting a scene taken from their most famous plays. Staircases with gilded wooden banisters painted a mahogany colour led to the auditorium decorated with palm-tree trunks;

Vase from the former Galerie des Vases

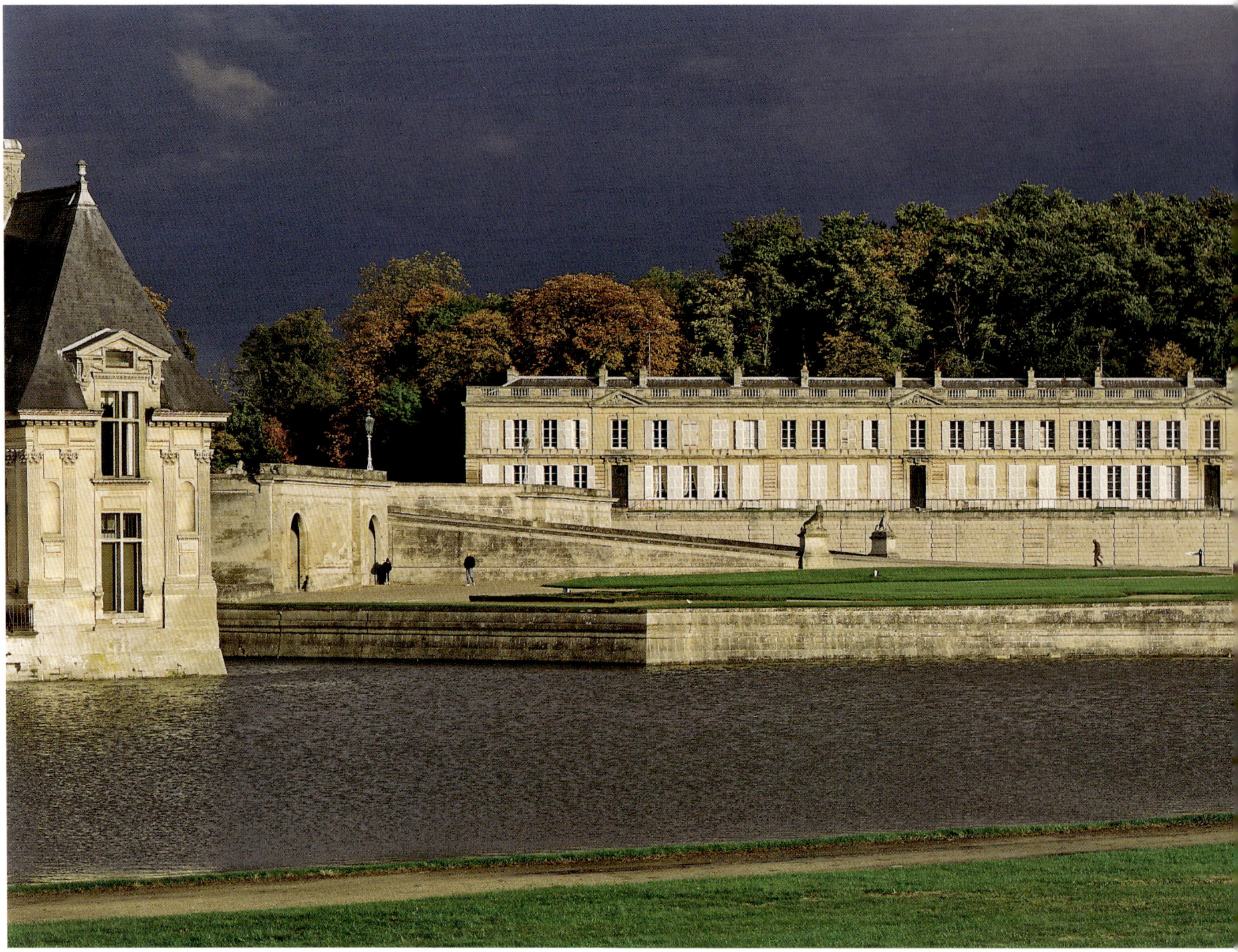

The château of Enghien
This long wing with its minimalist decoration was erected by the architect Jean-François Leroy beyond the Pont du Roi opposite the Petit Château to provide serviceable accommodation.

it could accommodate around 300 people. The back of the stage held a surprise: machinery made it possible to spirit away the wall, and from the hall you could see a vista of a niche hollowed out in an adjacent wall, below the road, where a statue of Thetis stood, surrounded by water which fell in cascades into an ornamental pond.[27] To the left of the Salon d'Apollon, the stairs going down towards the Île d'Amour were decorated with reclining marble statues of Bacchus and a bacchante. There is nothing left of these splendours.

In 1770, the marriage of his son, the duc de Bourbon, to Princess Bathilde d'Orléans, the sister of the man who came to be known as Philippe-Égalité, was an opportunity for new celebrations, during which the whole royal family came to stay at Chantilly. There was not enough space to house the princes and their

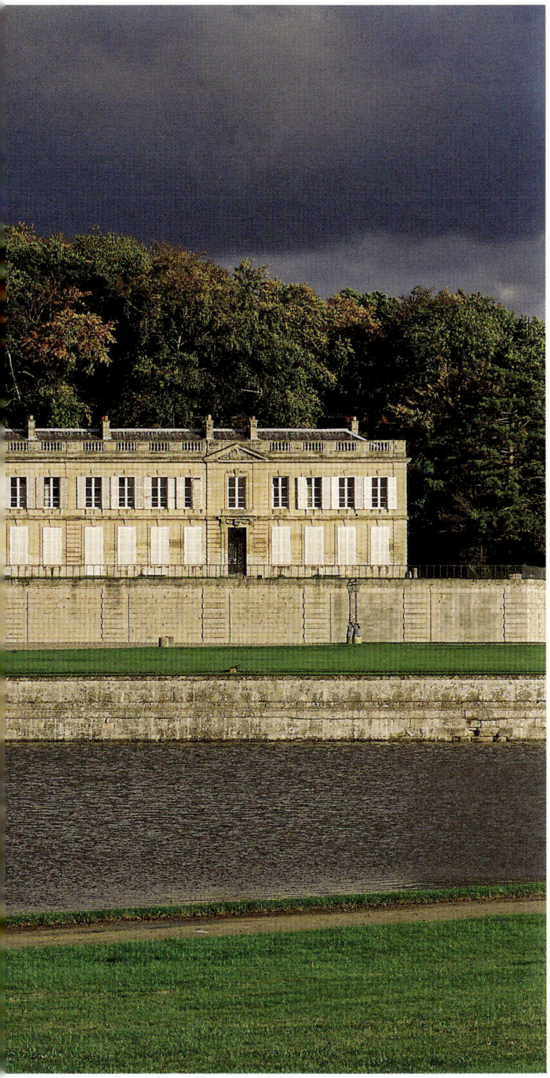

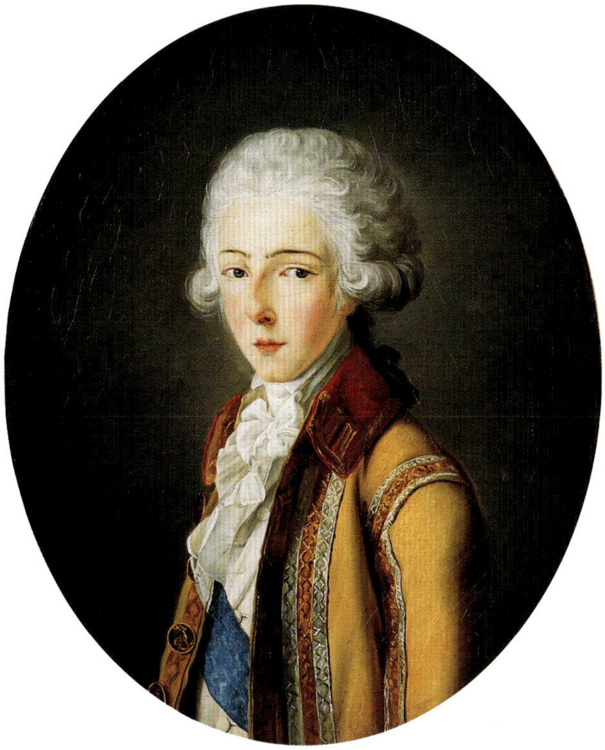

servants, so Condé decided to erect a new building, the first stone of which was laid on 24 October 1769. The spot chosen respected the site since it stood to the right of the esplanade, on the other side of the moat opposite the château. The architect was Jean-François Leroy who had been in the prince's service at Chantilly since 1768.[28] It is a long single-storey block, constructed in the Italian style, with a low roof concealed by a balustrade. The decoration is minimalist – four narrow projections topped by pediments – and its purpose was virtually that of a hotel: sixteen suites of rooms on two levels, uniformly composed of a vestibule, a large bedroom and a small bedroom. Its first occupant was the little duc d'Enghien, to whom the young duchess had given birth in her suite of rooms at the Petit Château on 2 August 1772 – his father was

The duc d'Enghien
This portrait by Nanine Vallain (circa 1789) shows the young prince who gave his name to the château of Enghien. He perished by the bullet in the moats of Vincennes on the orders of the First Consul.

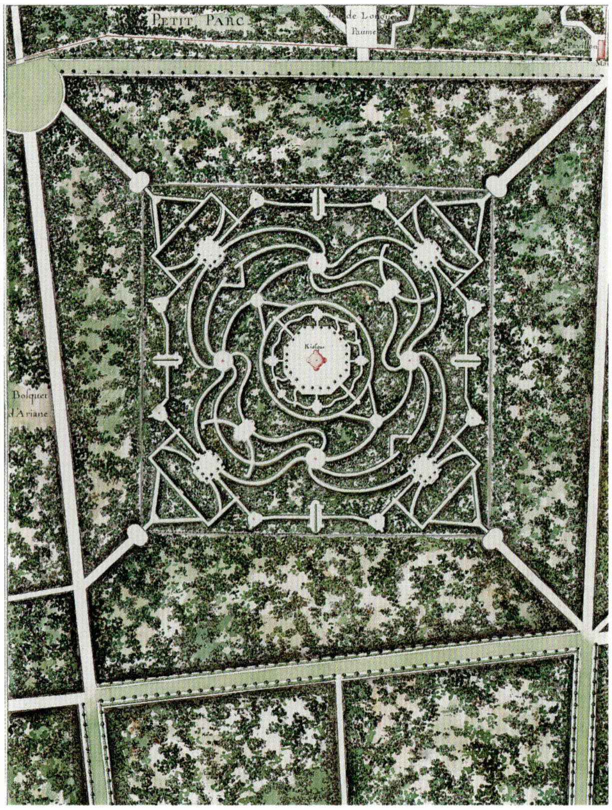

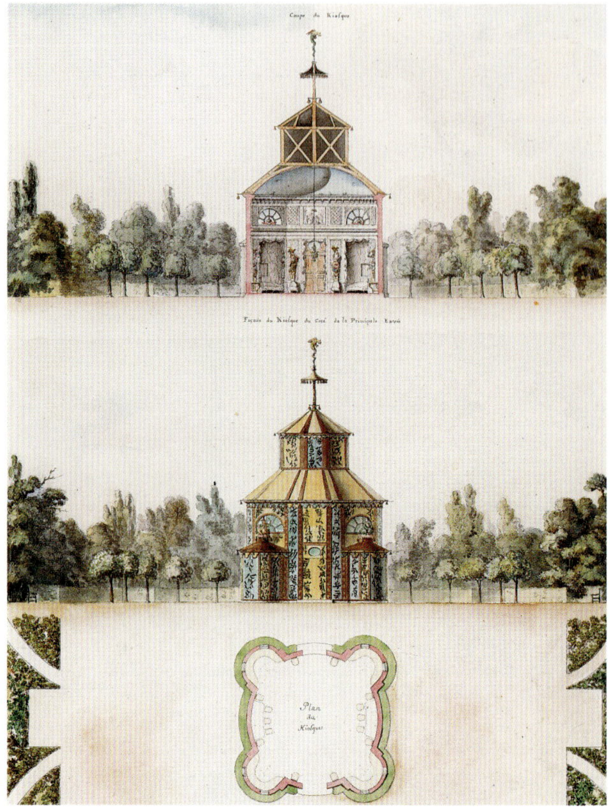

The maze and the Chinese bandstand
A new maze was created in the Parc de Sylvie in 1771 and a Chinese bandstand erected at the centre. Drawings by Chambé, *Album du Comte du Nord*, 1784.

sixteen years old, his grandfather thirty-six – but he had to be taken as an emergency, completely blue from a deficiency of oxygen, to the "new building". It was therefore given the name "château of Enghien", which it has kept.

The Hameau at Chantilly

To the east, Condé embarked on other projects, again on a considerable scale, first of all in the Parc de Sylvie; after Desgots' maze had been destroyed, another one was laid out in the Carré de l'Arquebuse. At its centre the Kiosque or Pavillon Chinois was constructed, opened in 1771; its lantern turret was fitted out to accommodate musicians. Other changes were made to the Parc de la Caboutière, where the Jeu de l'Oie was done away with and the Allée du Quinconce extended as far as the Salles du Sphinx. All this led imperceptibly but inexorably to the creation of an English garden that would be a counterpart on the east to the landscaping transformations carried out in the previous years, more discreetly, on the west side. Building work got under way in the winter of 1772-73. For the prince and his family, it was an opportunity to travel in a dug-out canoe through the undergrowth

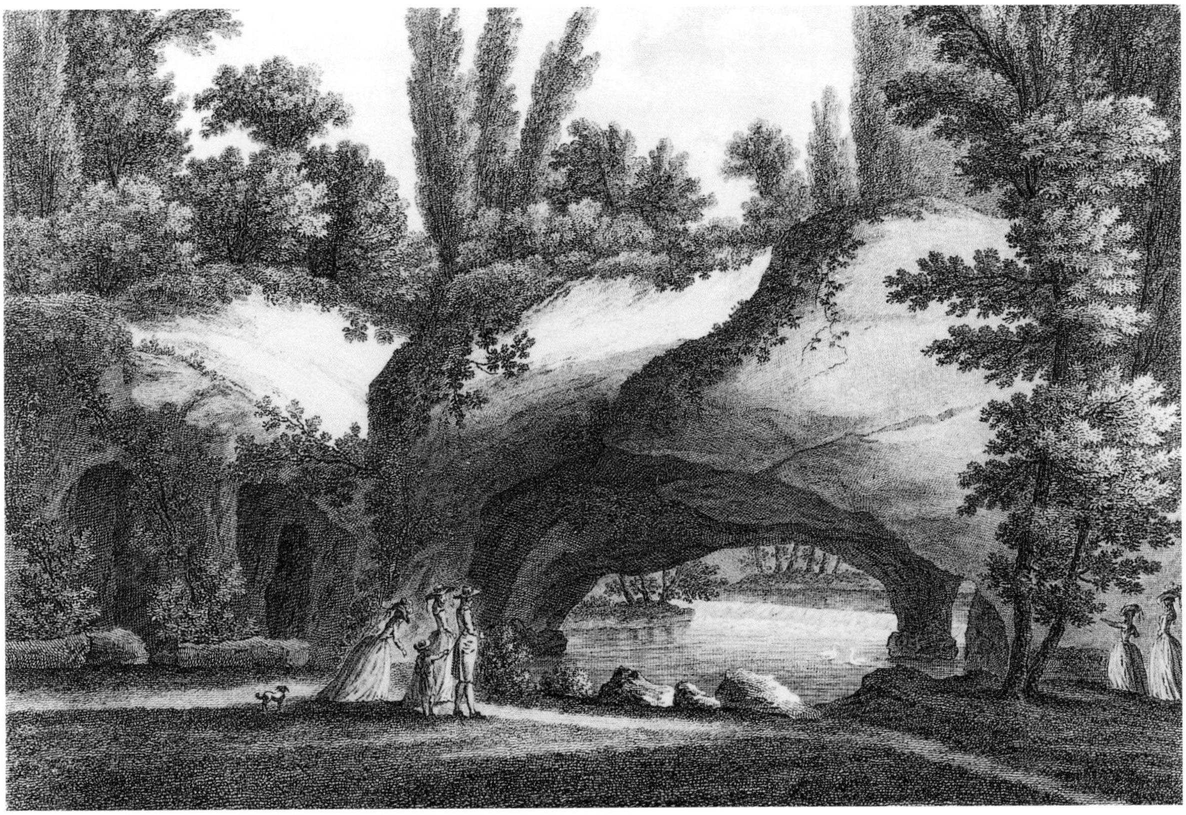

The grotto in the Jardin Anglais
The new landscaping of the gardens to the east matched the taste for untamed nature.

that extended beyond the Sylvie area and discover amidst the pasture land and turf many discreet improvements that could be made with an eye to the future: a rock which served as a vista for a small canal laid out earlier by Le Nôtre, a cove for the boats, a *cave* where the water rumbled (a grotto, of which only a few stones are still standing, in the direction of the Canal des Morfondus), a cottage where they could slake their thirst, all in all a wild harmony that had to be exploited for the further new pleasures which they took for granted, and would above all be expensive.

The time was ripe for building the Hameau[29], a decisive step, implemented at an accelerated pace by Leroy. After the painter Watelet who had had a rustic dwelling known as the Moulin joli built on an island in the Seine in 1754, the Orléans family had led the way with pseudo-rural constructions, the duke at Le Raincy and the duc de Chartres, the brother-in-law of the duc de Bourbon, at Monceaux. At Chantilly, the Hameau was opened during the celebrations for Easter in 1775. The prince then regularly took his family and visitors there for dinner or supper, for boating and to listen to music. In a clearing, village houses were laid out round a small green shaded by an elm tree. They were

The Hameau at Chantilly

On this plan drawn by Chambé for the *Album du Comte du Nord*, 1784, we see the village square with the houses grouped around it as well as the little canal left over from Le Nôtre's landscaping.

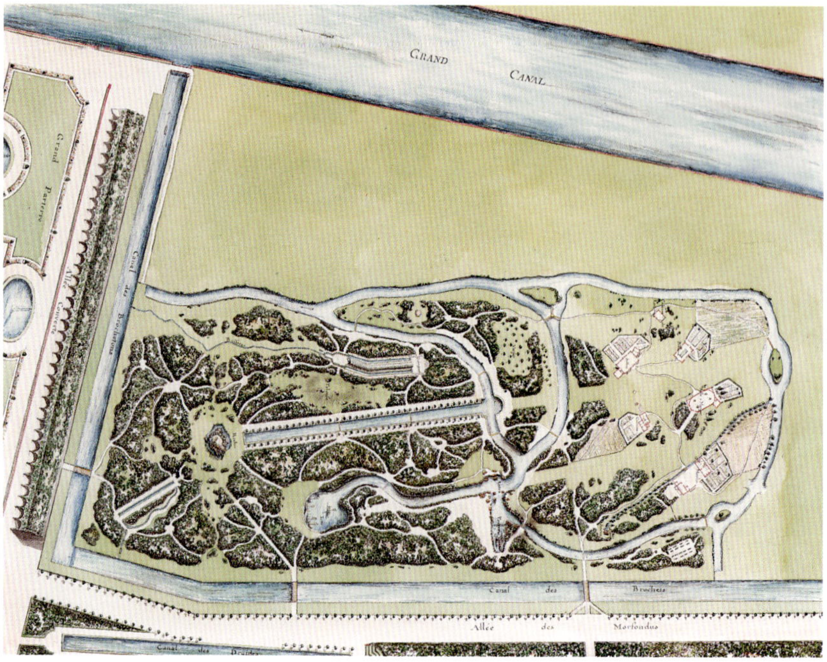

The attractions of the Hameau

On this card from the *Jeu de cavagnole* pack which had 32 cards (24 preserved at the Musée Condé), we see watercolour pictures of the Guinguette (inn), the Antre (cave), the Moulin (mill), the Port (harbour) and the Rocher (rock) all from 1780.

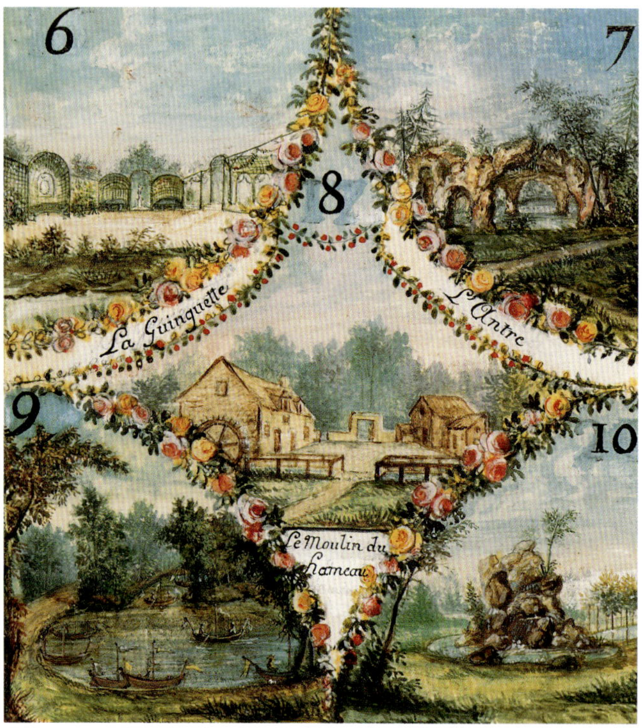

The Laiterie or dairy

Drawing by Chambé from the *Album du Comte du Nord*, 1784. It was near the Vineuil Menagerie.

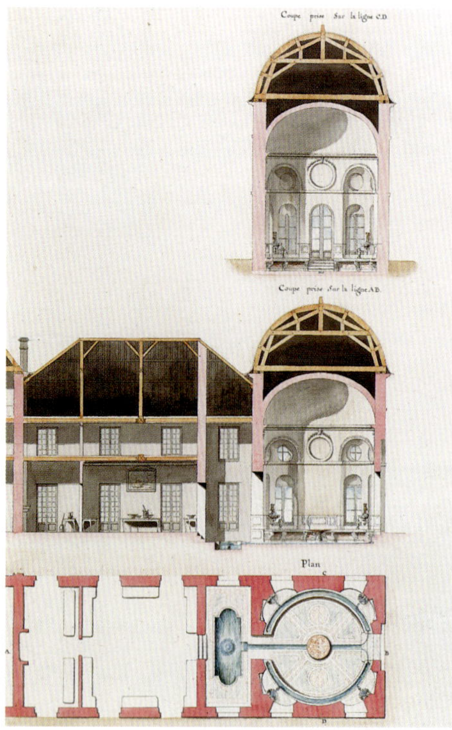

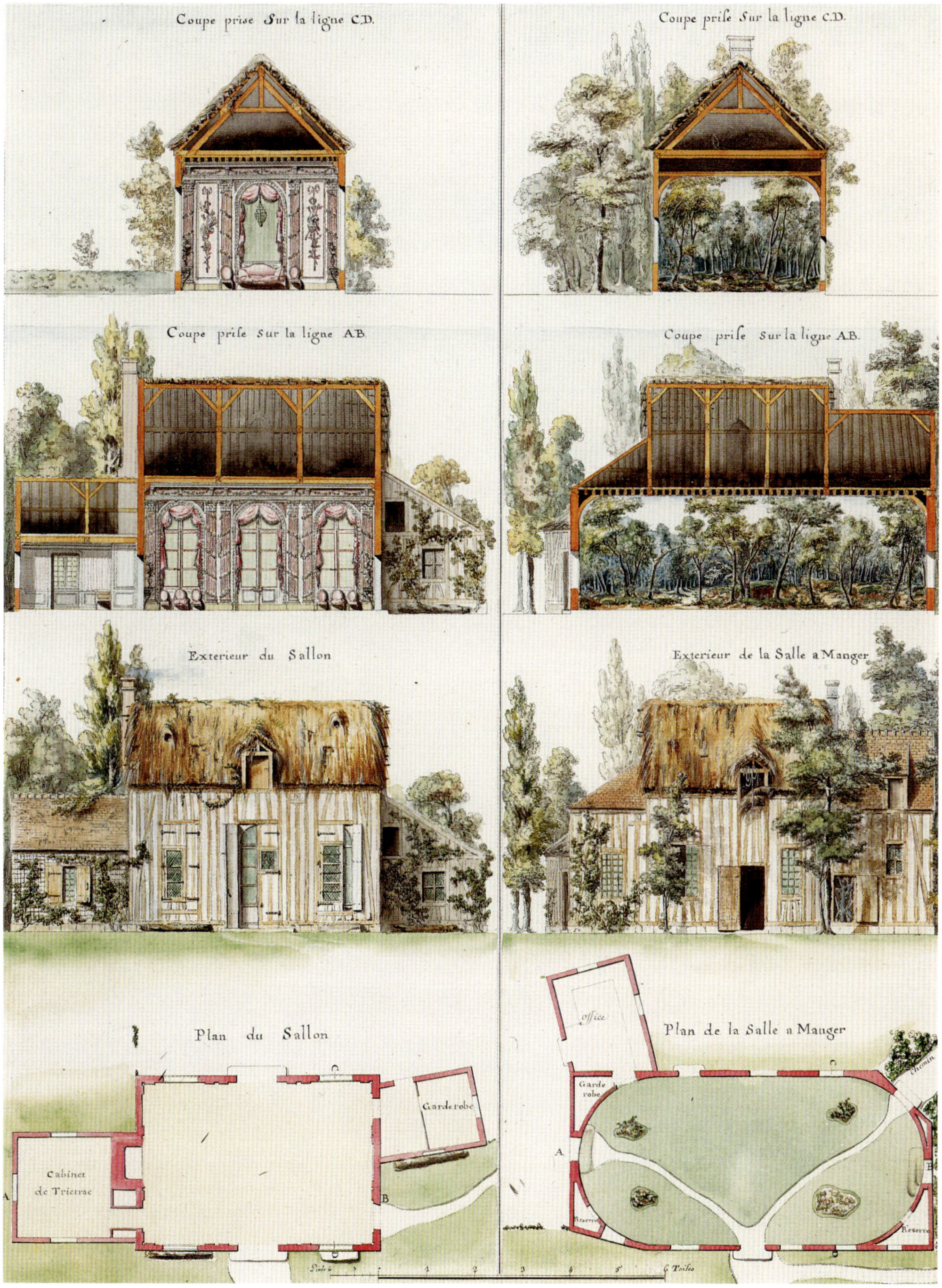

The sitting-room and dining-room at the Hameau

Officially opened during the Easter celebrations in 1775, the Hameau received the prince and his friends for lunch, dinner or to listen to music. Drawings by Chambé from the *Album du Comte du Nord,* 1784.

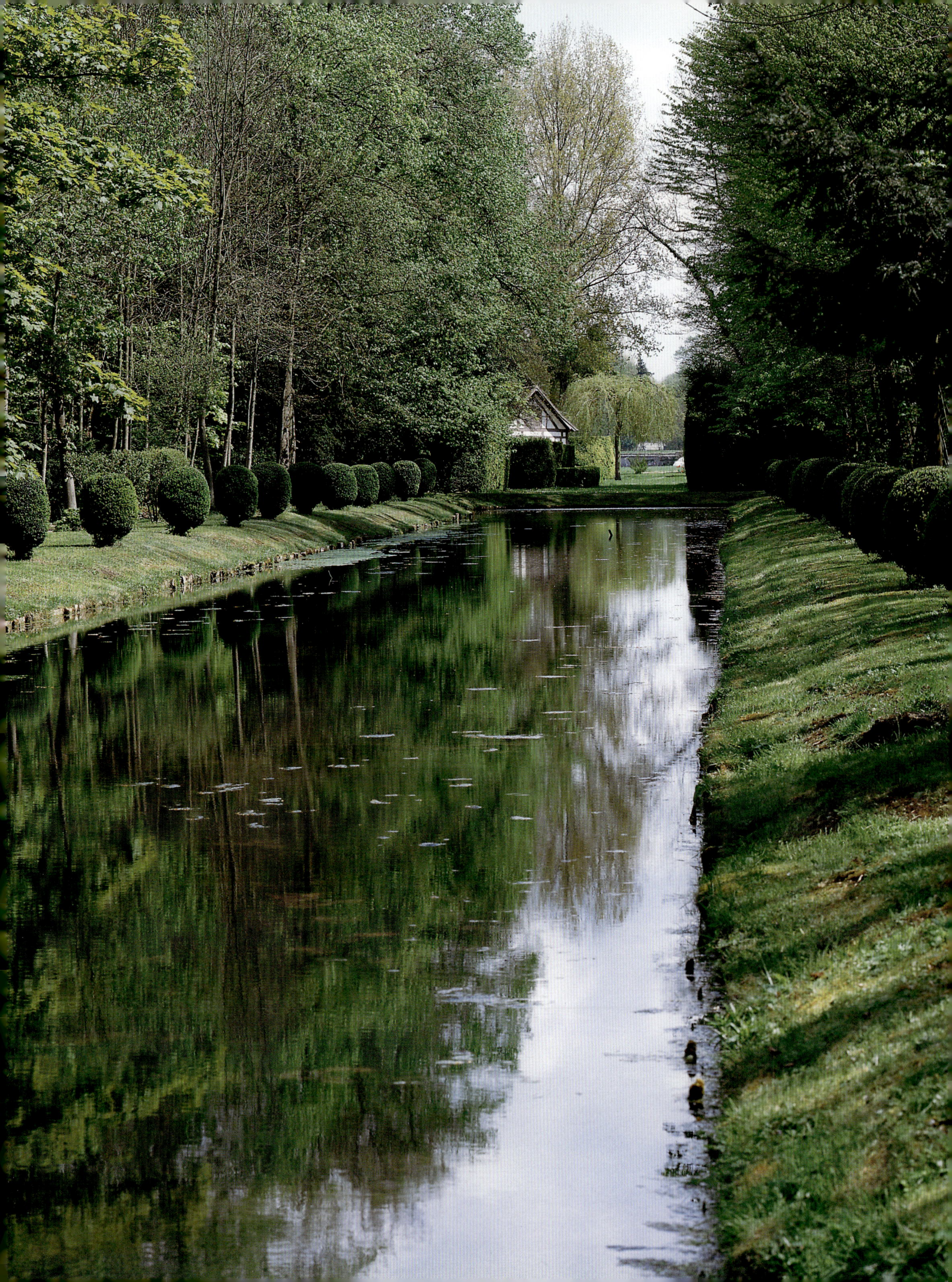

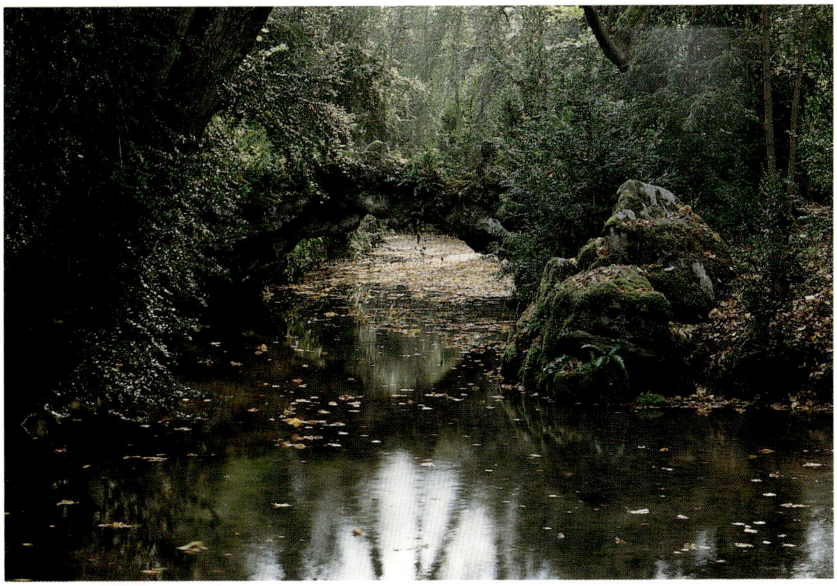

The Canal des Brochets or des Morfondus

This view is in the direction of the Hameau.

The rocks in the Antre (cave)

The houses in the Hameau

The village houses were timber-framed with thatched roofs. Behind them were little gardens surrounded by fences.

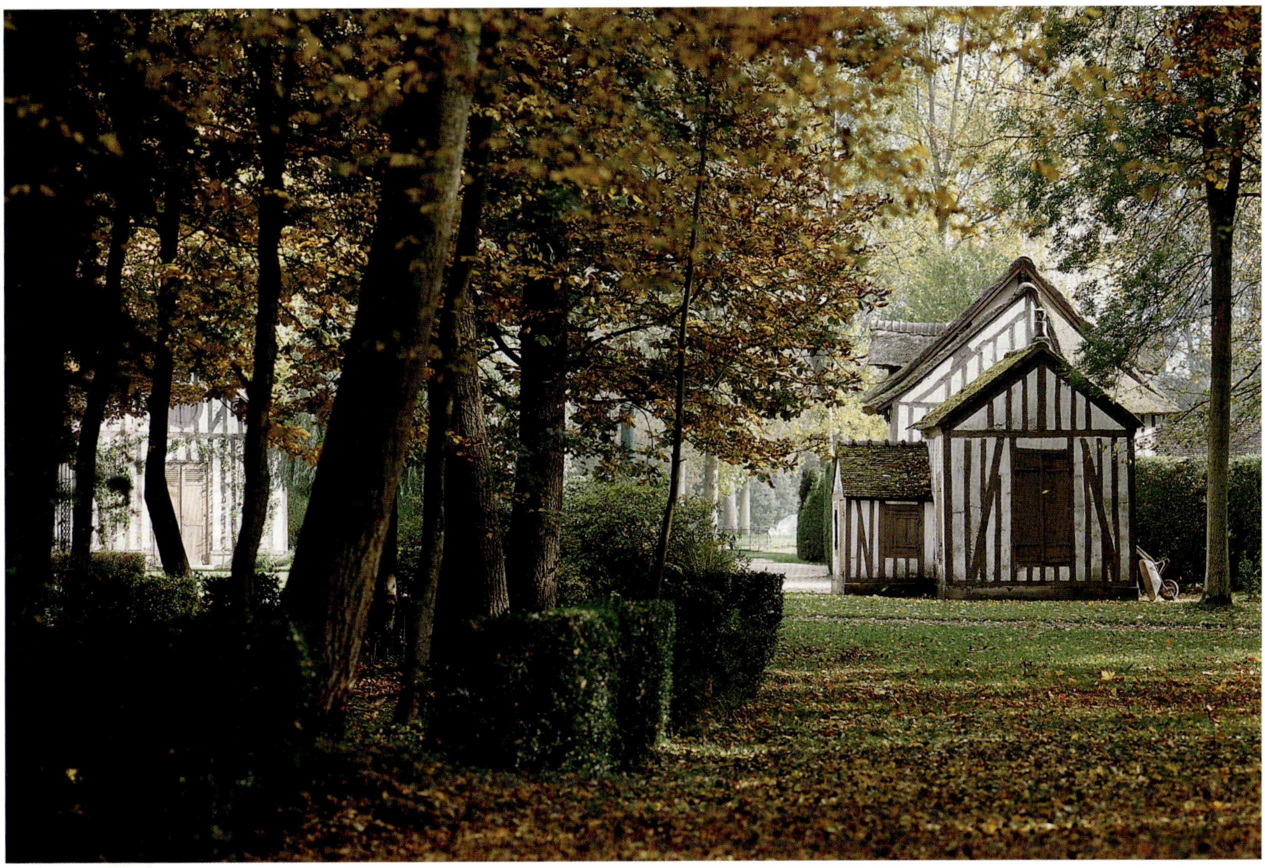

timber-frame buildings with thatched roofs, and at the back they had little gardens enclosed by fences with vegetables and fruit trees growing in them. The cow-shed, dairy and mill fulfilled their true functions, and the tavern with its arbour and well provided the kitchen required for meals. Surprises started with the barn which actually housed a huge dining-room, its walls painted with thick foliage and its seats made from tree-trunks. There were even greater surprises in store in two peasants' cottages that housed a billiard table and a reading-room, culminating finally with a third cottage that contained a paradoxically and incongruously luxurious salon: geminated Corinthian pilasters, a frieze enhanced with garlands, a ceiling painted with cupids, mirrors, and pink taffeta drapery and furnishings.

Everyone wanted to come and admire the Hameau at Chantilly, which so perfectly matched the new taste for artificial effects that the Prince de Ligne made this subtle comment with regard to it: "I do not think that it looks sufficiently like a quotation. By dint of being natural, it first makes one regret that it has not been knocked down." In May 1777, Emperor Joseph II of Austria, the brother of Marie-Antoinette, who came to Chantilly incognito took care not to miss the Hameau on his visit. Then it was the turn of Princess Louise de Bourbon-Condé, the prince's daughter, who was leaving her convent and for whom a rustic party was organised. Mesdames, the daughters of Louis XV, and Grand-Duke Paul of Russia also hurried to see it. A clever entertainer called Laujon, who wrote ballets, impromptus and pretend peasant songs, was the indispensable factotum who organised the spectacles that went with these visits, either at the Hameau or the Laiterie of the Ménagerie de Vineuil which the prince had again enlarged, adding a farm and a pheasantry of Chinese pheasants.

In each of the new fields into which Condé ventured, he seemed to know how to create the perfect model, with the lavishness made possible by his freedom from any financial constraints. In these final carefree years, the young generation of princes, the comte d'Artois and the duc d'Orléans, led the way where modernity was concerned in architecture, the decoration of suites of rooms, furniture and gardens, but it could be said that the Prince de Condé had a head start on them. Marie-Antoinette had come to Chantilly in 1770 while she was still Dauphine, but she does not appear to have gone back subsequently; yet the buildings she had erected by her architect, Mique, on her Le Petit Trianon estate seem to make reference, closely or obliquely, to the creations of the Prince de

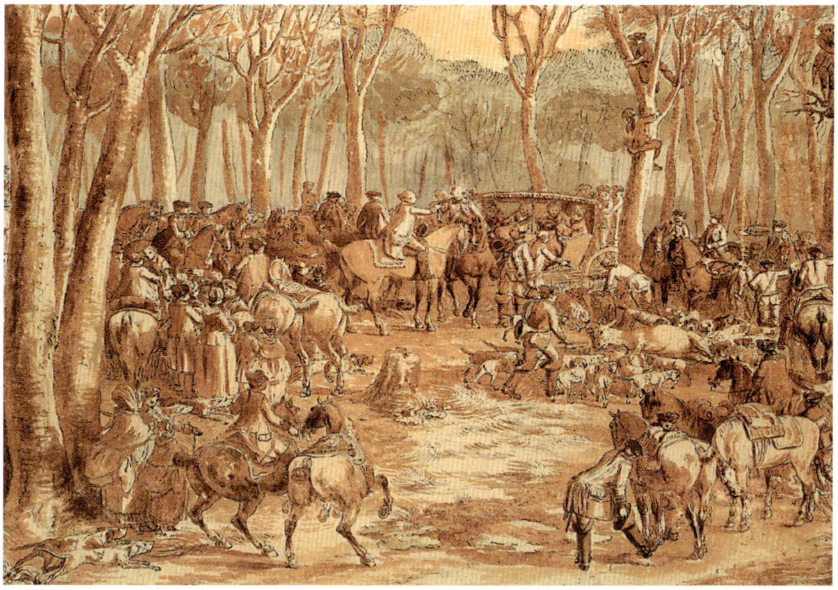

Mort of a stag in the forest
This drawing by Jean-Baptiste Le Paon and the one on the right-hand page were executed to commemorate the stag hunt staged for the Comte du Nord (Count of the North) on 12 June 1782. The heir to the throne of Russia travelled under this assumed name.

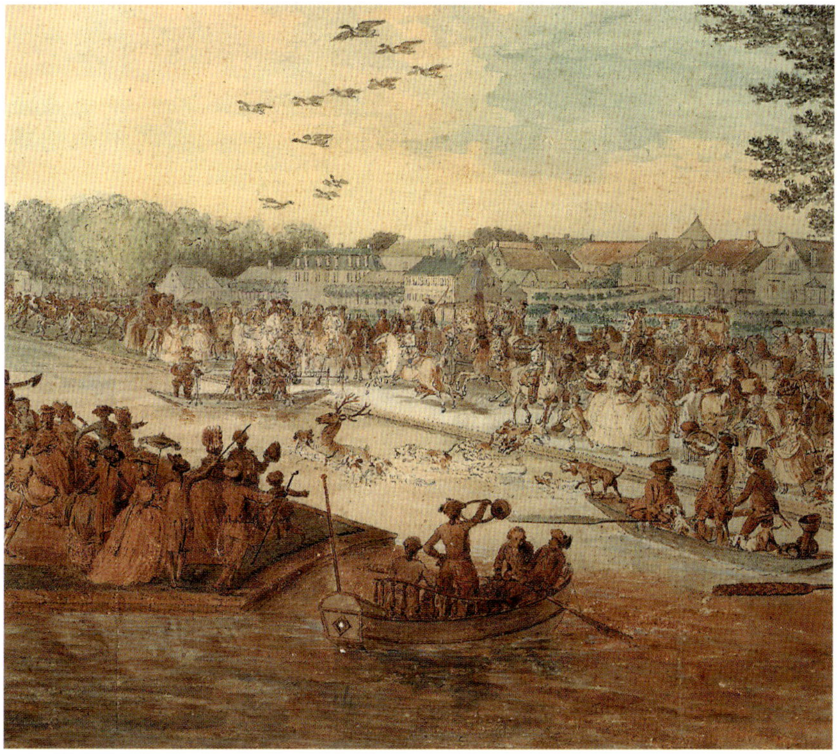

***Mort in the Grand Canal,* detail**
These two drawings were made as preparatory drawings for paintings that were sent to the tsar and are still in Gatchina Palace. A copie of this drawing is exhibited in the Musée Condé.

Condé: the Temple de l'Amour on an island (1778), the little Theatre (1782) and even more the Hameau (1783). The wonders of Chantilly had conquered the French court and those of Austria, Russia and Sweden. Everyone could subscribe to the opinion of Abbé Delille in his poem on the gardens (1782):

Admire Chantilli in its elegant pomp,
Embellished from one hero and one age to the next.

In these final years of the Ancien Régime, festivities carried on with the same thirst for pleasures – the pleasure of the theatre, the pleasure of hunting. In 1780, a visit from the heir to the throne of Russia and his wife, travelling under pseudonyms as the Count and Countess of the North, was the occasion of memorable hunts, and the painter Le Paon was charged with commemorating the episodes. Condé further added to his forest by acquiring the Bertinval woods in 1784. The Carrefour de Pilâtre in the forest of Coye is a reminder of the descent that same year of Pilâtre de Rozier's hot-air balloon, which had set out from Versailles. At the château the duc de Bourbon had separated from his wife, and it was his sister, the beautiful and devout Louise de Condé, who took care of the education of the little duc d'Enghien and shared the management of the house with the Princess of Monaco, her father's mistress. The first symptoms of the spirit of protest were shown during 1788 amidst the forests rich in game: the common people went hunting, in spite of the prohibitions. But the real events did not take place at Chantilly, where the local people were still very attached to the Condés, but in Paris and at Versailles. For the princes, the taking of the Bastille was the advance notice of a rebellion the king did not intend to repress as they would have wished. Their reaction was immediate: emigration, the very first example of it. The prince went to Versailles on 15 July, but he was deeply disappointed by the king's attitude. On 17 July he left Versailles for Chantilly at four o'clock in the morning, and at half past two in the afternoon of the very same day he got into a carriage with his son and grandson and set out for Flanders – Brussels, then Turin, later Worms – temporarily turning his back on a country which in his view had broken the implicit contract that was the foundation of the monarchical state.[30] The gesture, extremely unwise politically, left the inhabitants of Chantilly in no doubt regarding the Prince de Condé's profound, categorical hostility towards the new ideas, and after a few days of stupefaction it provoked the first reprisals. A new story had begun.

The Prince de Condé's mineralogical cabinet
The last Prince de Condé took a very keen interest in science and owned well-stocked collections relating to physics and natural history. King Gustav III of Sweden who had been his guest at Chantilly had this splendid piece of furniture which contained a rare mineralogical collection made for him in 1774 by the cabinet-maker Haupt.

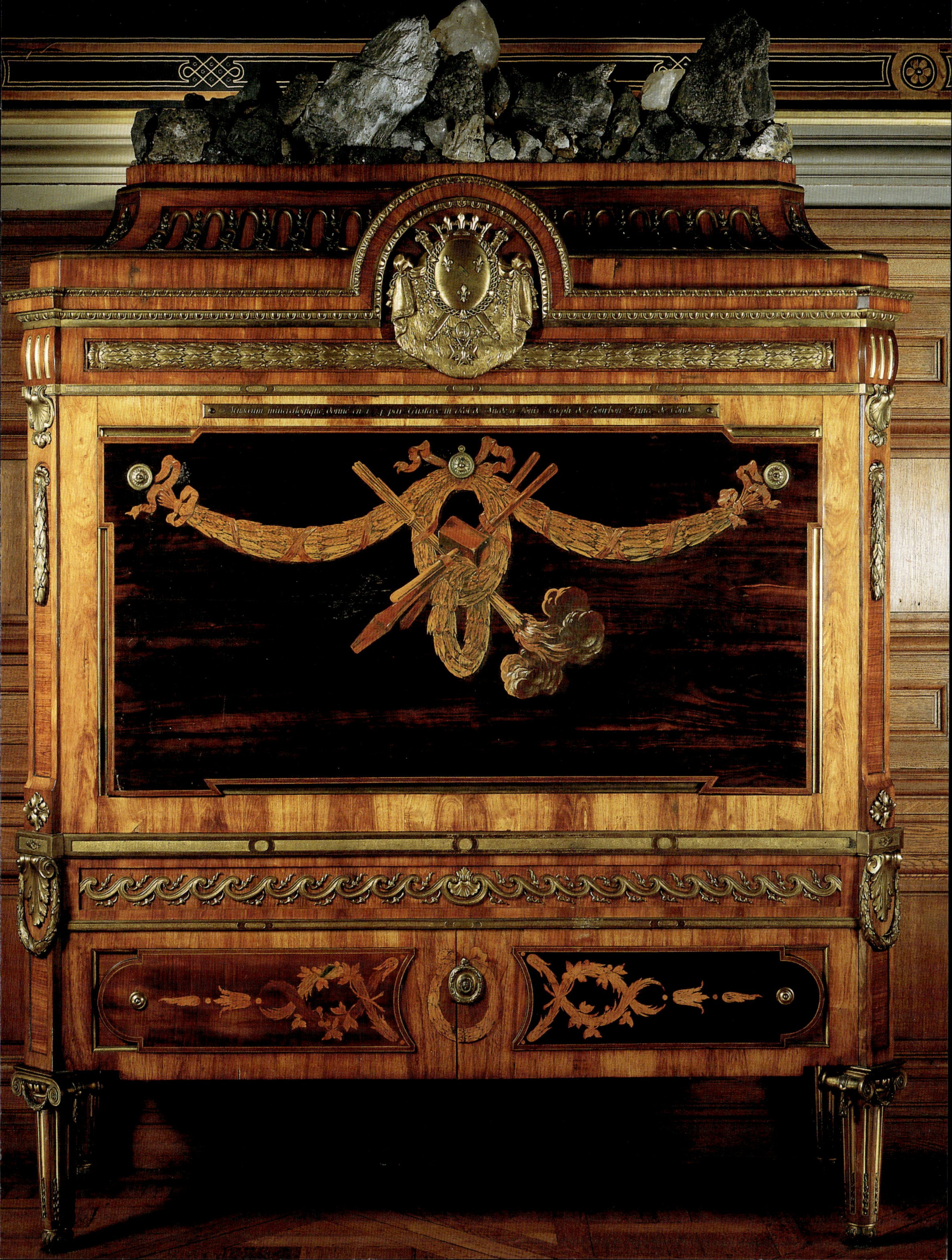

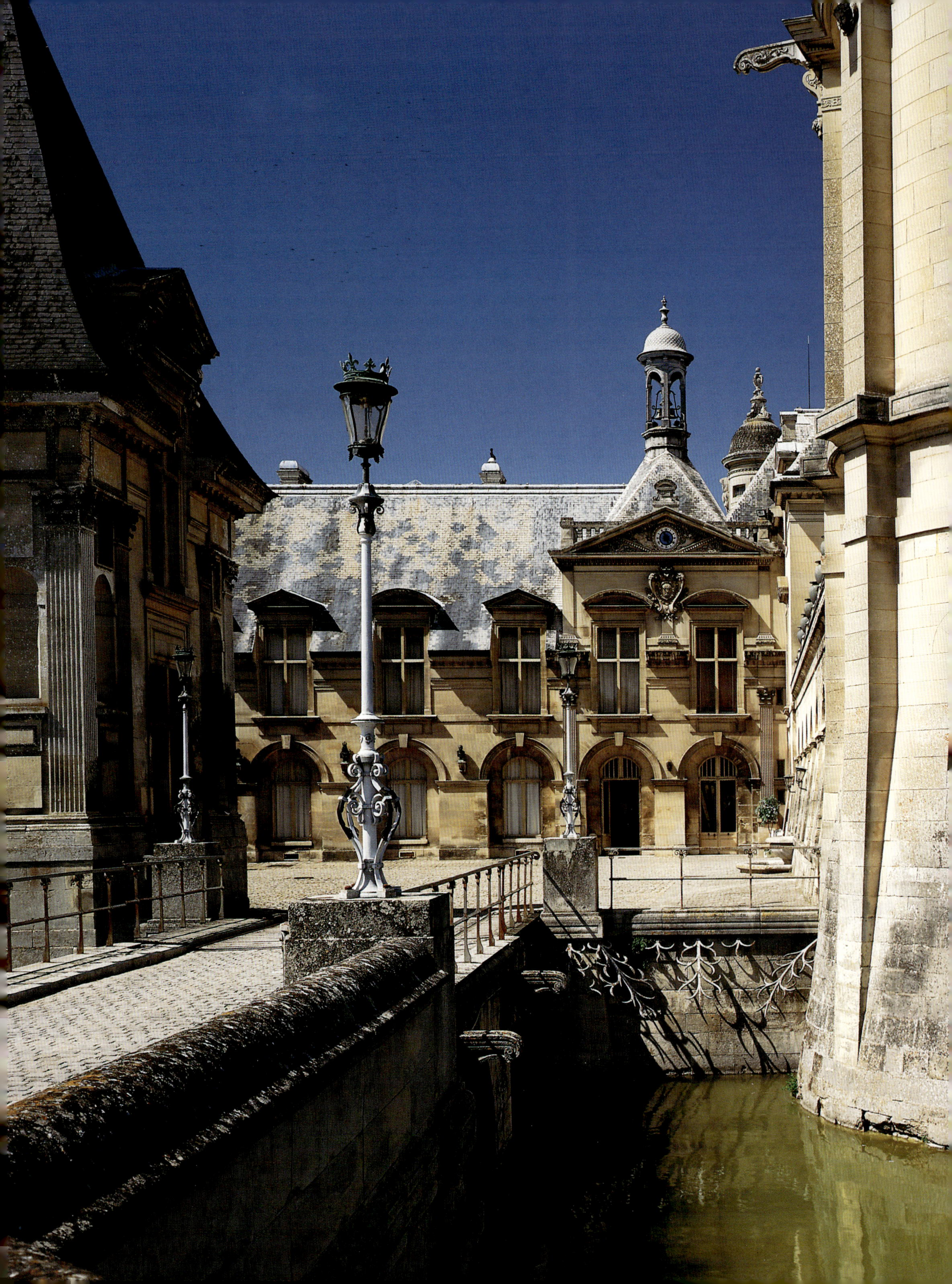

The twilight of the princes: the end of the Bourbon-Condés

Chantilly through the trials and tribulations of the Revolution

The princes' departure left the château and its outlying buildings vacant, abandoned the park to anonymous depredations and ruined the town which had always lived in step with its overlords. For some time, the prince's agents who were still on the spot, the captain of the hunt and the factor Antheaume de Surval, opportunely appointed mayor of Chantilly, managed to ensure minimum maintenance of the Condés' estate in the face of Revolutionary violence. But the forces of destruction finally got the upper hand after 10 August 1792.

The first target had been the artillery kept in the château, the firearms used during festivities to fire peaceful salvoes, which included the pieces taken from the enemy during the Seven Years War, placed at the foot of the statue of the Constable: thirty canons in all which the Parisians came in search of, in the exaltation following the taking of the Bastille, in August 1789. Then the Cabinet d'Armes – weapons room – was raided and the Menagerie was stripped of its exotic animals. Finally the property of the man who had become the abhorred leader of the *armée des Émigrés* was confiscated in its entirety and sequestered[1], and while the signs of feudalism and religion were being eliminated, the statue of the Constable was knocked down, the château pillaged, the furniture sold, and the bronze and lead fittings pulled out of the fountains to be melted down at the Mint.

The government at the time of the Reign of Terror decided to shut up suspects arrested in the department of Oise in the empty château, and a first convoy of prisoners was consigned to it on 28 August 1793. More than a thousand people were held there, aristocrats, inhabitants of Chantilly, and Abbé Jean-Marie Daniel, who illustrated his memories of captivity with invaluable drawings.

The court of the Petit Château enlarged
It was in 1821 that the duc de Bourbon had the moat separating the two châteaux filled in. The bridge was moved and the west wing lengthened at the end of the nineteenth century by Daumet.

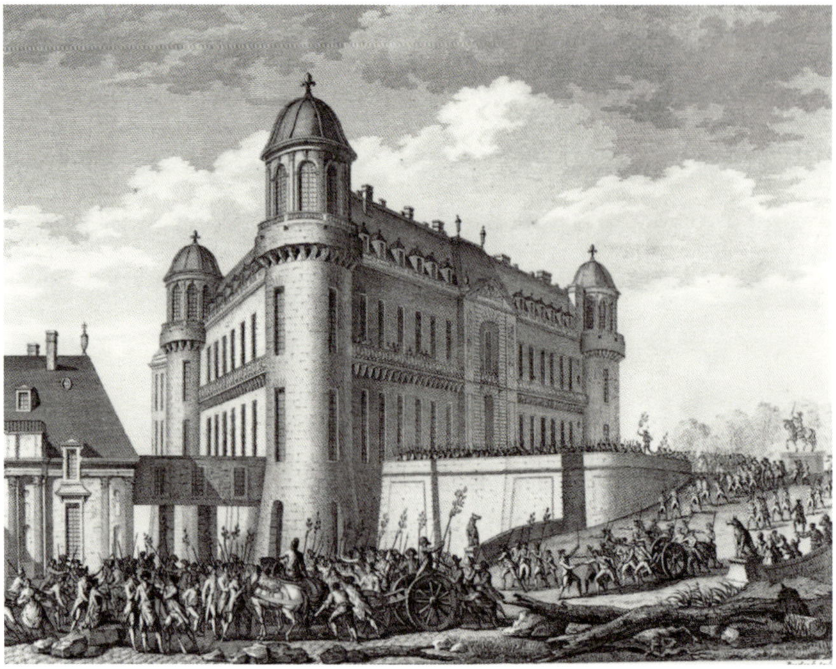

Parisians at Chantilly
Engraving by P.G. Berthault.
On 9 August 1789, three weeks after the fall of the Bastille, a group sent from Paris invaded the château of the Condés, who had emigrated, to take possession of the cannons that were kept there.

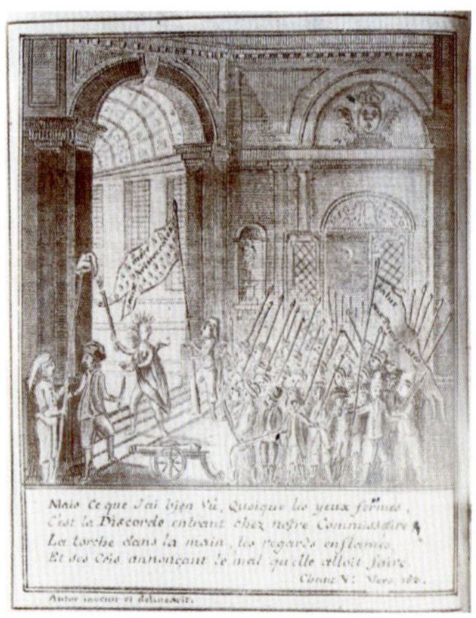

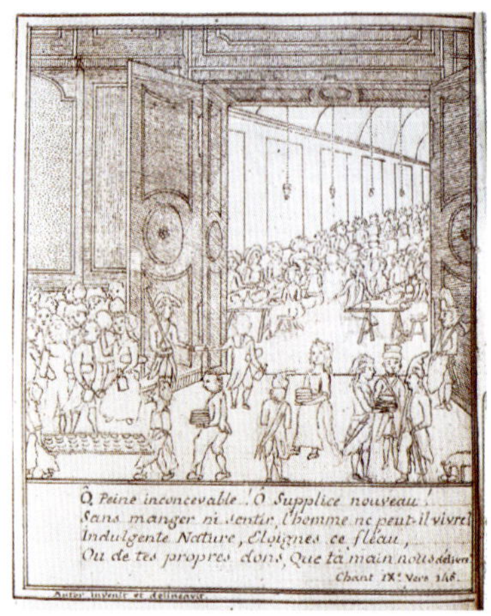

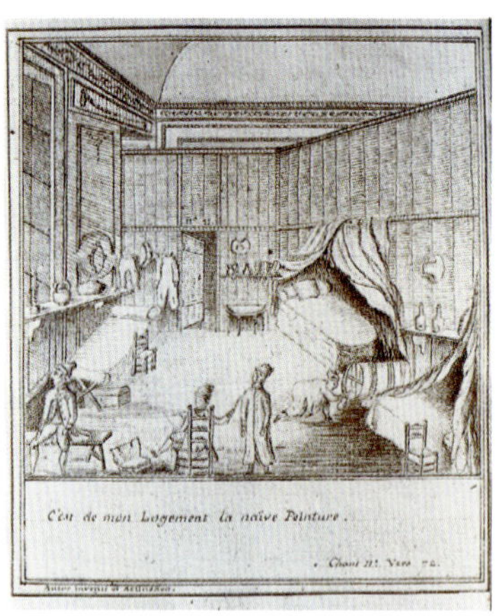

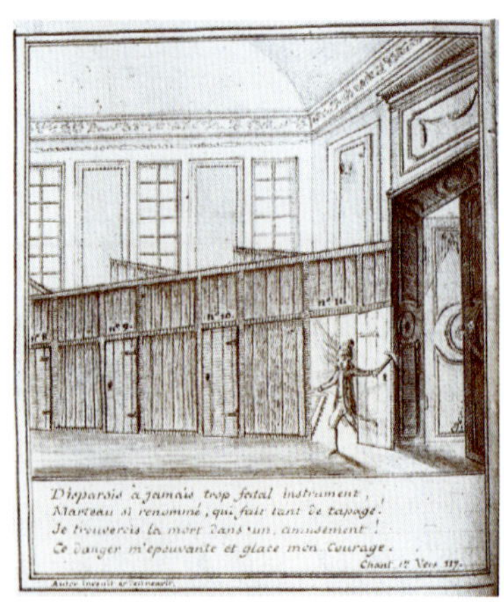

The sketches by Abbé Daniel
The handwritten diary of the Abbé, who during the Terror was imprisoned in the château which had been turned into a prison, was illustrated with invaluable vignettes of which only photographs have been preserved. They show the princely rooms in an unexpected light.

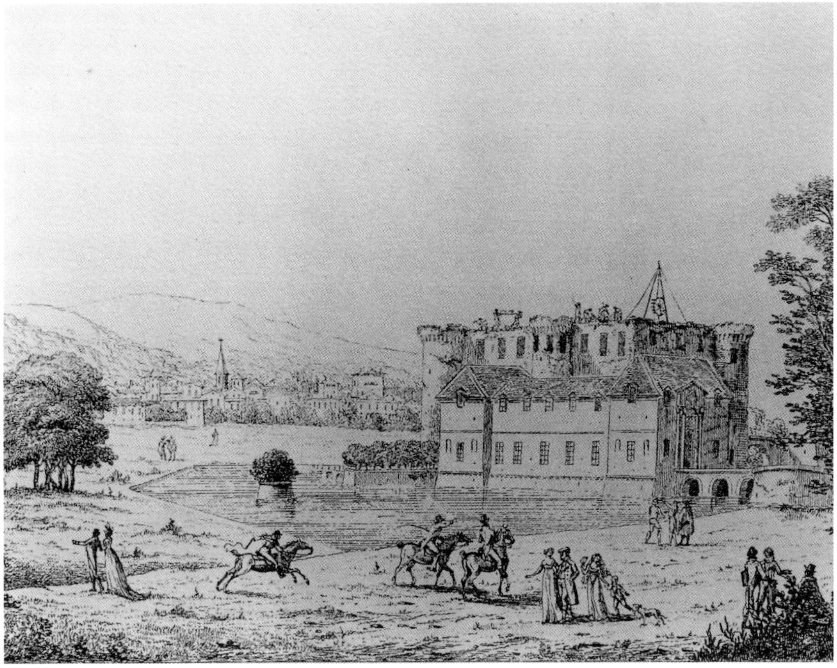

Demolition of the château of Chantilly
Engraving by Thomas Naudet.
Two contractors who had purchased the château in 1799 had the Grand Château demolished to recover the building materials. All that was left was an earth platform.

They are among the few pictorial records we possess regarding the suites of rooms and the inner court of the Grand Château built by Mansart and Aubert.[2]
The break-up of the estate had started in 1793, either through assignment to the state or through sale to individuals. As for the château, which for several years was left abandoned, the Estates administration which did not know what to do with so many princely residences finally knocked it down on 17 July 1799 through two infamous contractors, Damoye and Boulée. To recover the building materials, they demolished Bucamp, the Orangerie, the Theatre, the temple of Venus, the Menagerie, and finally the Grand Château itself, which was razed to the level corresponding to that of the Terrasse du Connétable and so transformed into a platform of earth following the shape of the original triangle with its round towers. The Petit Château fortunately escaped destruction. As for the Jardin Anglais and the Hameau, which so very well matched the taste of the day for a rural and hence necessarily virtuous world, they were rented out to a manufacturer who according to legend received the beautiful Térésa Cabarrus, Madame Tallien, there. Other buildings that escaped being destroyed or sold were the château of Enghien, the Maison de Sylvie, the Caboutière and the Écuries, which had been assigned to a regiment of dragoons as barracks. During the Empire, in 1811, Napoleon included Chantilly in the appanage of his stepdaughter,

Queen Hortense, but that situation did not last long. As soon as the first Restoration began, Louis-Joseph de Bourbon, the last Prince de Condé, came back.

The Prince de Condé on his return from emigration

In spite of long years of exile, devoted initially to fighting the armies of the Republic and then saddened by cruel family losses – his grandson the duc d'Enghien was shot in 1804 in the moat at Vincennes after being abducted in Baden by the police of the First Consul (Napoleon), then his second wife the Princess of Monaco died in 1813 – the seventy-eight-year-old prince had retained an ineradicable attachment for his beloved Chantilly.

"Yes, gentlemen, I will go to Chantilly as soon as possible, should I have to sleep in the cellars, so great is my love for the place and its inhabitants," he declared on his arrival to a delegation of notables who had come to Compiègne to entreat him to do so on 14 April 1814. But the Hundred Days obliged him to accompany Louis XVIII into a second exile, this time of short duration. After Waterloo, the Bourbon monarchy moved back into its palaces and Condé resumed his title of Grand Master to the king. His daughter, Princess Louise, had become a Benedictine nun and was elected prioress of the Convent of the Temple in Paris, from which she never emerged. His son, the duc de Bourbon, who had spent many years in London, kept there by the charms of his mistress Sophie Dawes, also returned to France in July 1815.

At Chantilly, in the stricken estate, the gardens assigned to others, the Petit Château stripped bare, the Grand Château reduced to the bases of its walls, the Prince de Condé set enthusiastically to work, helped by his son. First of all an architect had to be chosen.[3]

Jacques-François Leroy, who had succeeded his father Jean-François, the architect of the Hameau and the château of Enghien, had looked after the upkeep of the buildings and gardens until the Revolution, but after that he had had to live on his wits and in the end he was guilty of lapses of tact. After taking up residence at Chantilly on 17 March 1817 the duc de Bourbon decided to dispense with his services and the following 12 September appointed Victor Dubois, a nephew of J.-D. Antoine, the architect of the Mint in Paris, in his place. The newcomer was immediately commissioned to draw up plans for rebuilding the destroyed château, in which he by and large followed the awkward layout of the vanished building, without showing much imagination. In particular

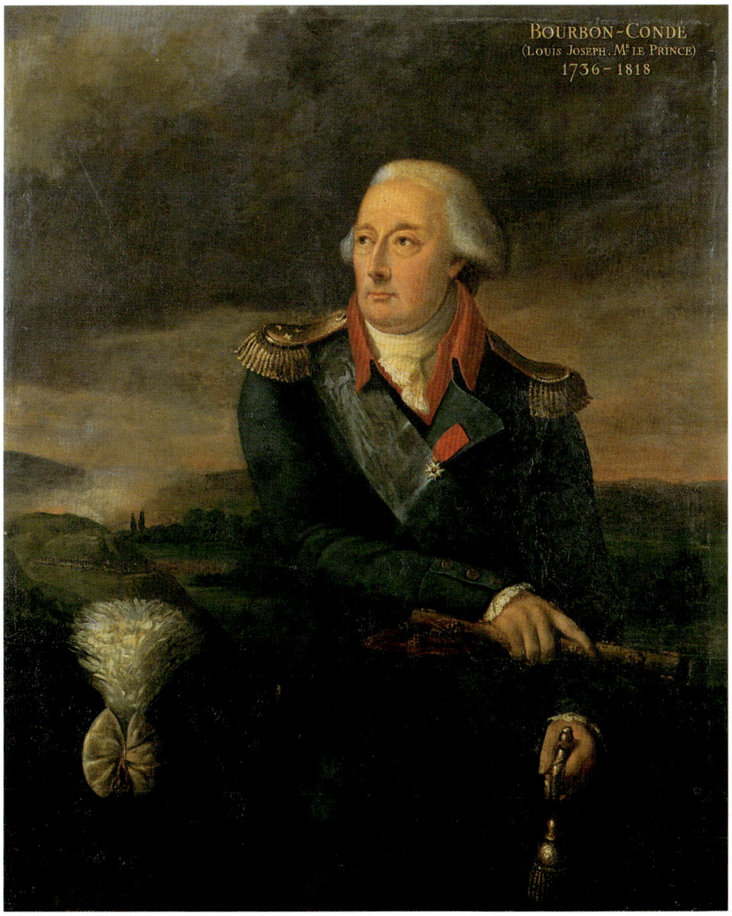

Louis-Joseph de Bourbon
This portrait of the last Prince de Condé by Sophie-Ernestine de Tott was made while he was an émigré in 1802.

he proposed to fit out two large suites of rooms, a virtually royal suite for the prince, the other for his son, but this expensive scheme was not followed up, and Dubois was asked initially to accommodate the princes in two suites of rooms at the Petit Château.

Around the disfigured château – to mitigate the wound, a garden surrounded by a balustrade had been planted on the platform of earth – there was one imperative and indispensable task, the need to regain the vital space assigned to other owners during the Revolution. In 1817 the Prince de Condé managed to buy back the immediate surroundings of his abode: the Bucamp and Orangerie lands, the islands, and the meadow stretching as far as the Grand Canal. The treatment of the recovered areas had to obey the new taste for natural gardens, with winding paths in the Romantic spirit enhanced by pavilions in a variety of styles to provide a resting place during outings and to nurture reflection, and there was no question of reinstating the gardens aligned by Le Nôtre. So Victor Dubois drew up plans for the new gardens at Chantilly. To the west, he levelled

Following pages

Arial view of the castle and French gardens of Chantilly
The large perspective from the main gate to the French style parterres was designed by André le Nôtre for the Grand Condé at the end of the XVIIth century; This perspective crosses the Grand Canal which is formed by the waters of the river Nonette and runs to the North (at the top of the photograph) beyond the lawn of the Vertugadin.

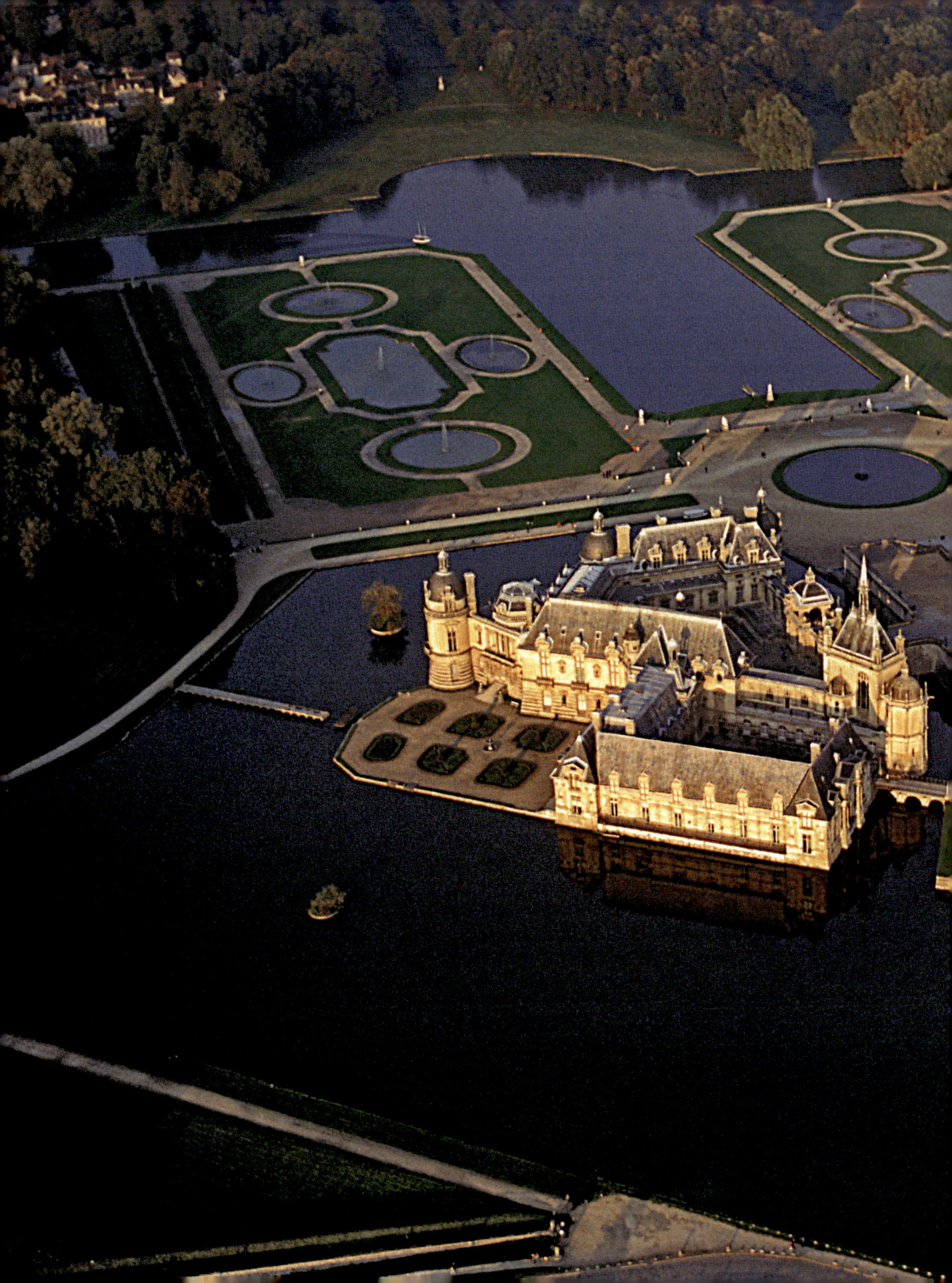

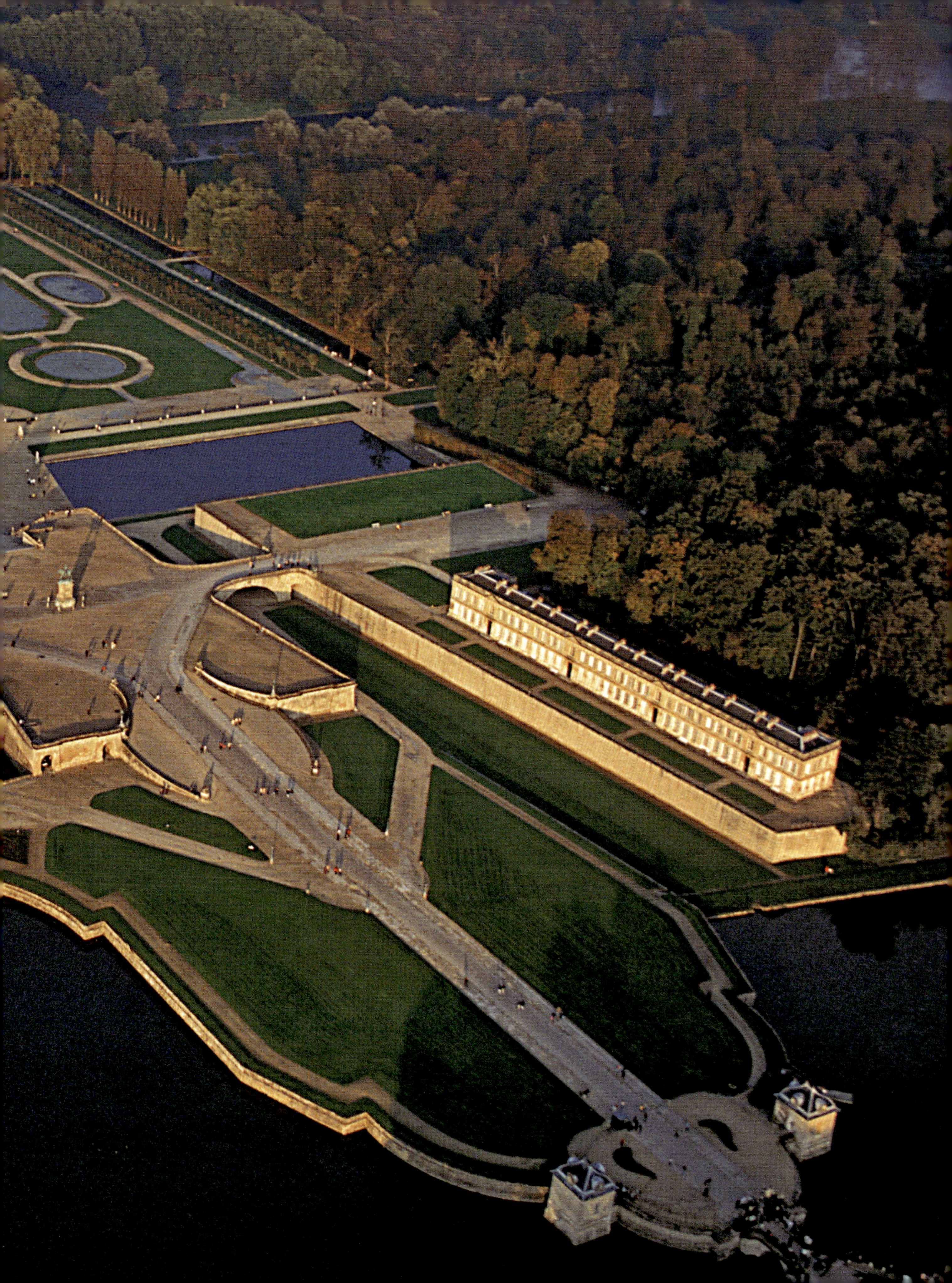

Scheme for reconstructing the Grand Château
The duc de Bourbon dispensed with the services of Jean-François Leroy in 1817 and instructed the architect Victor Dubois to come up with new designs for reconstruction.

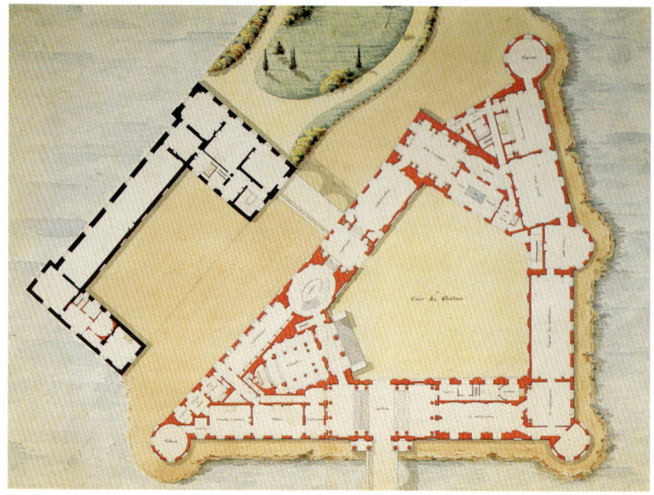

Plan of the new gardens
The new gardens designed by Victor Dubois were implemented in 1819 and 1820.
On the right, three of the medallions that go with this plan depict the Petit Château, the neo-Gothic chapel and the Pavillon de Vénus.

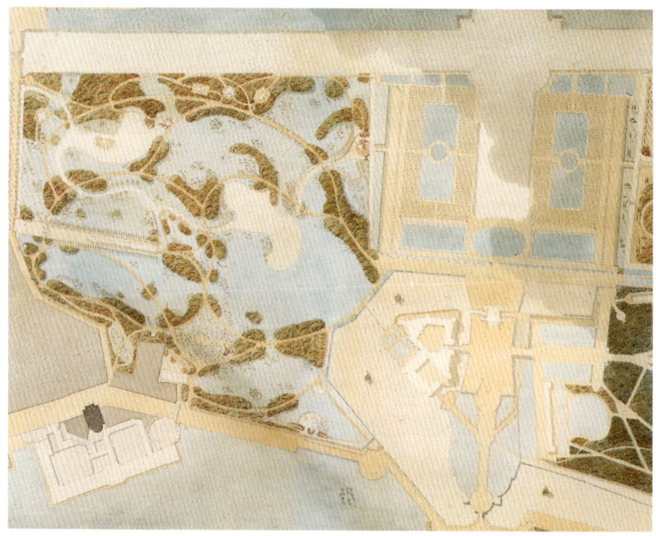

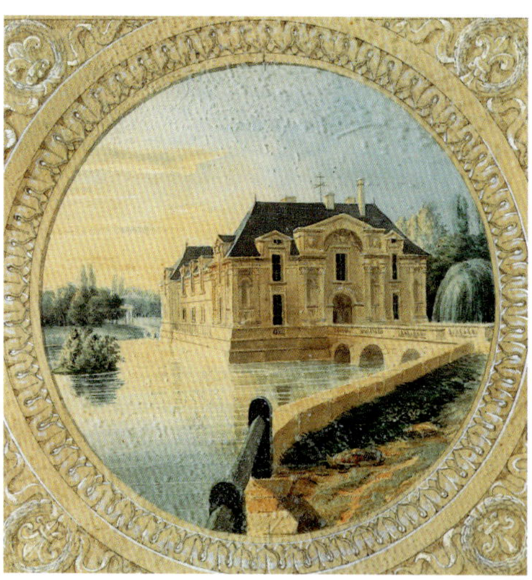

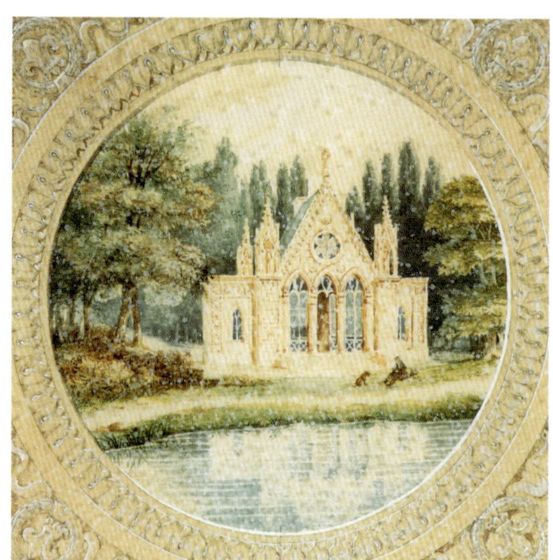

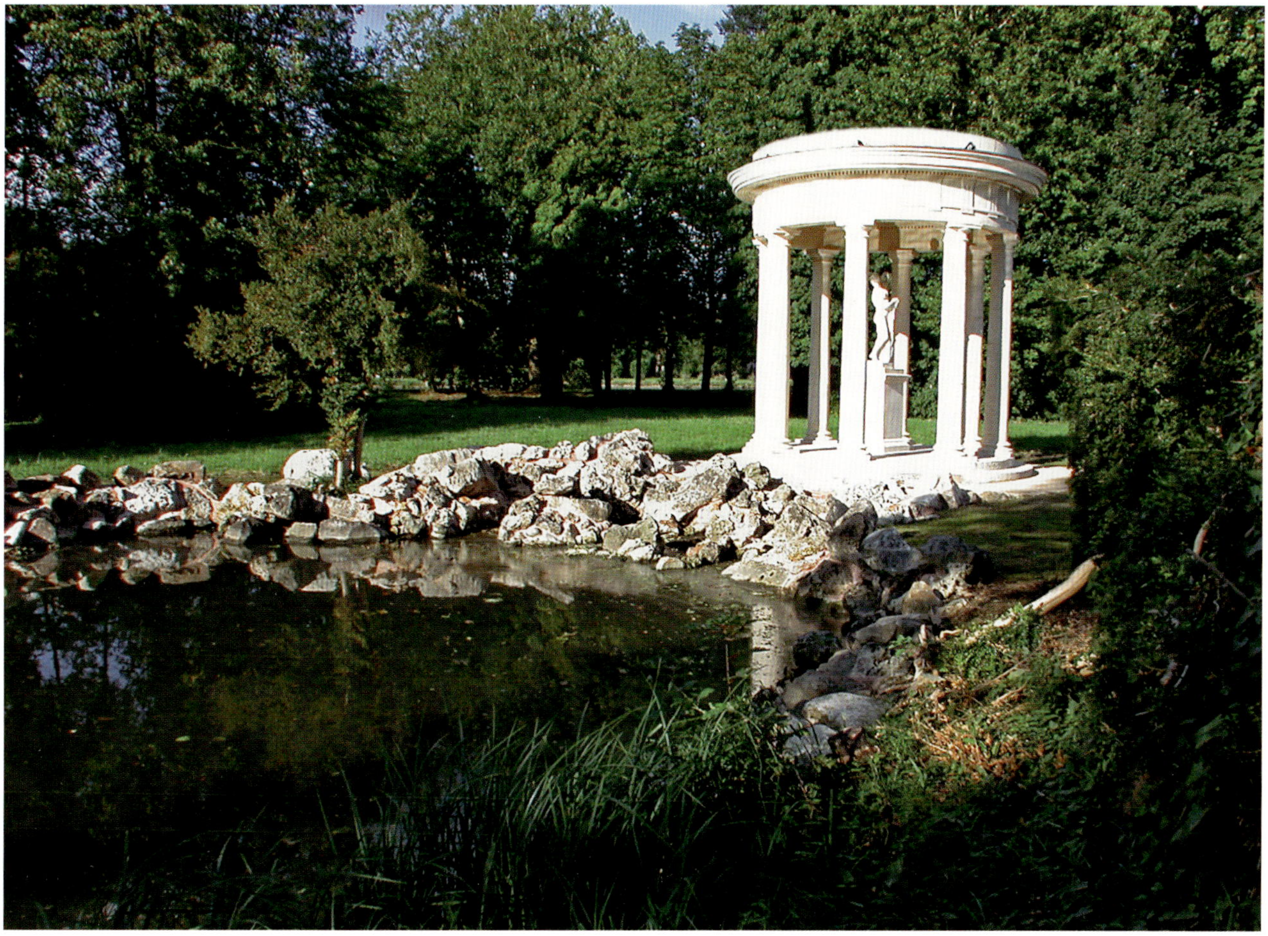

The temple of Venus in the Jardin Anglais
The area regained had to obey the liking for nature and be in keeping with the Romantic spirit. The temple of Venus, which has been restored in 2002, was part of the wish to make excursions more attractive by installing various pavilions.

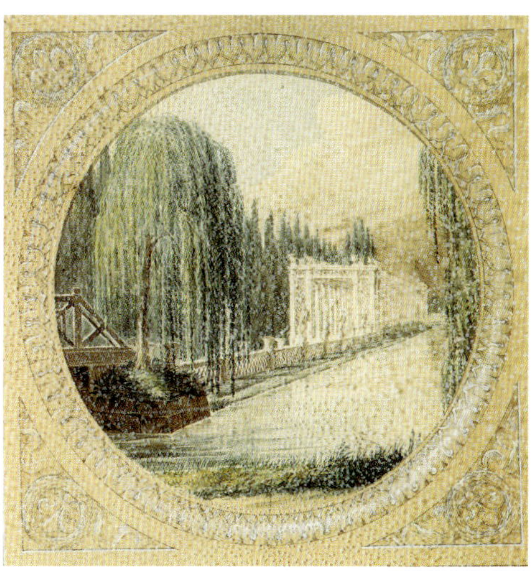

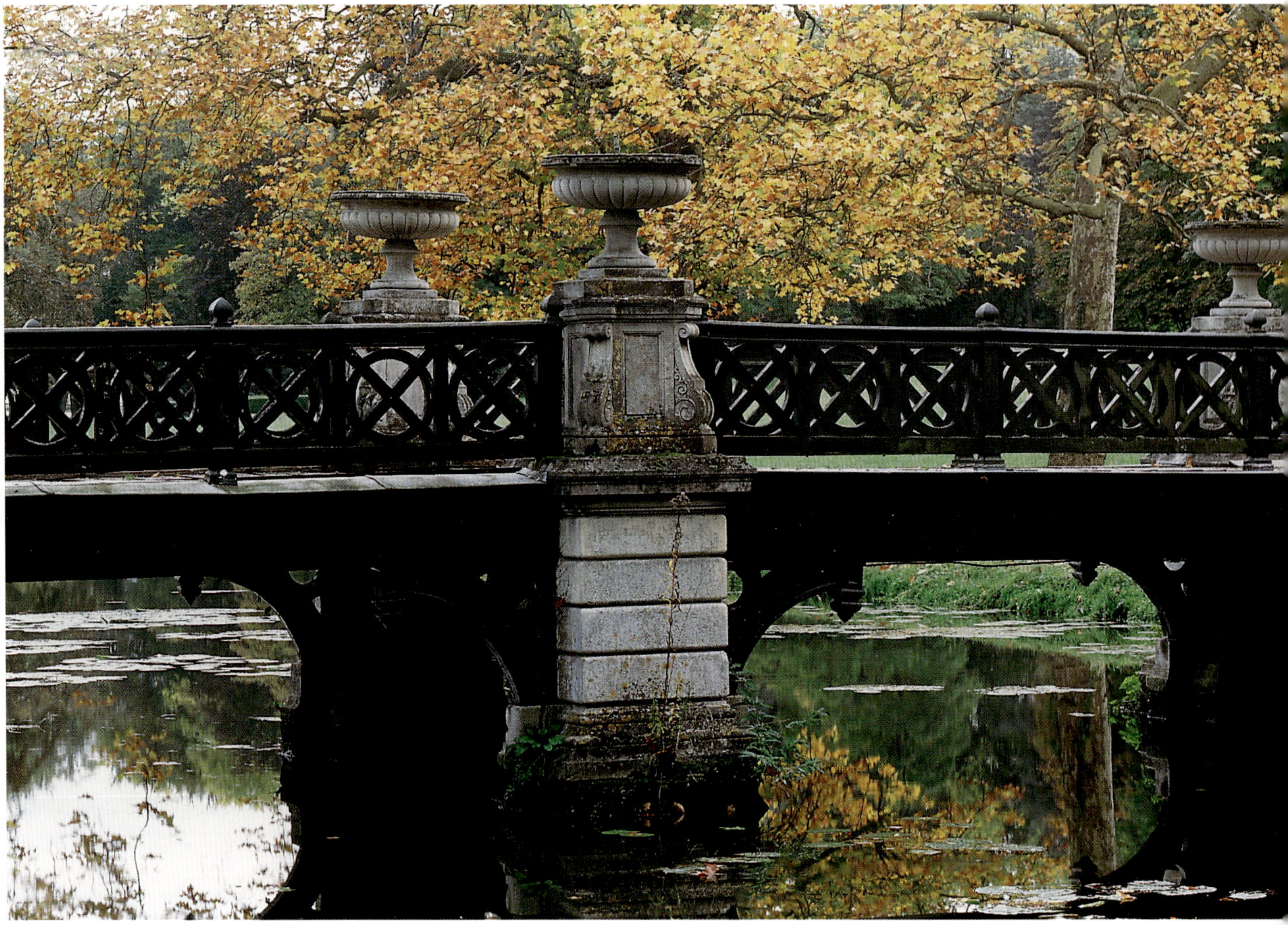

The Pont des Grands Hommes
This bridge was built across the river in the Jardin Anglais, possibly for the duc de Bourbon.

the *parterres* and removed the ruins of all the buildings, terraces and fountains – only the Cascades de Beauvais were preserved – in order to plant a second Jardin Anglais (1817-19), a counterpart to the one that had been laid out the previous century in the eastern sector, around the Hameau.

This garden was to be embellished by several buildings of which only a few vestiges remain, the columns of the temple of the Callipygian Venus and the rock grotto arranged on the site of Bucamp. The tip of the Île d'Amour was provided with a new pavilion made of trelliswork and masonry and again dedicated to Venus, and the nearby banks were planted with poplars. The bridge known as the Pont des Grands Hommes, leading towards the Vineuil road, is probably also a legacy of the duc de Bourbon, if we are to believe the marble plaque engraved with hammered coats of arms; it is equipped with basins for the spurting water and framed by stone columns which at one time supported

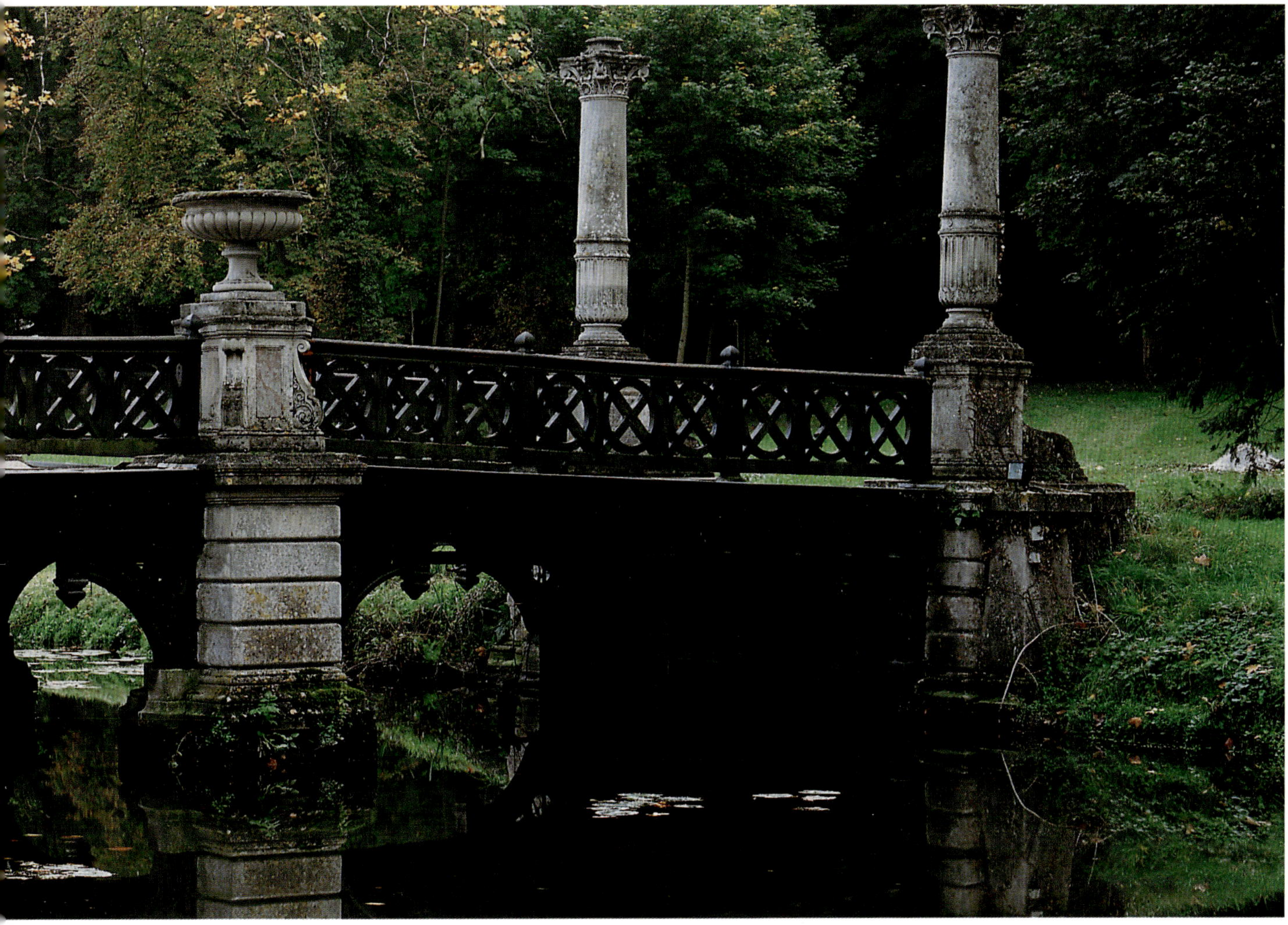

outdoor lights. As for Le Nôtre's parterres and ornamental ponds at the bottom of the Grand Degré, they were ruthlessly sacrificed, making way for commonplace rectangular lawns framed by tall species of trees planted in quincunx (alternate rows of clumps of five) which radically altered the landscape as they grew. Other buildings in the latest styles were erected further north, a Neo-Gothic chapel near the main Pont de Vineuil, which has now gone, and a charming Palladian-style pheasantry between Vineuil and Apremont, which still stands.

At the same time the prince set about recovering works that had belonged to him from the public repositories of the state: pictures, sculptures, furniture, tapestries, books and archives. There was lively resistance, but most of the objects were found and brought back to adorn the Petit Château and the gardens, as well as the Hôtel de Lassay in Paris, which Condé had selected for himself after agreeing to let the Palais-Bourbon to the Chamber of Deputies. However, time was running out for the old man, and on 13 May 1818 he died in the arms of his natural daughter, the comtesse de Rully, the only member of the family to treat him with unfailing affection to the end of his days.

The last duc de Bourbon

After accompanying his father's body to Saint-Denis, Louis-Henri-Joseph, duc de Bourbon, was sole master at Chantilly. He kept his title, refraining from taking that of Prince de Condé, such a heavy burden to carry, and almost an anachronism. The duke was in fact very much subject to the wishes of the imperious Sophie Dawes, who ruled over those around her without brooking any dissent. As she had to be given a socially acceptable reason for coming to France, she was married to Lieutenant-Colonel Feuchères, who was soon made a baron and aide de camp to the prince, without the reason behind these favours being revealed to him; but it did not take her husband long to find out, and he immediately withdrew, with great dignity.

Once again, for a period of twelve years Chantilly served as the setting for the parties and receptions which were so well-suited to the grand hereditary lifestyle of the Condés. These renewed pleasure pastimes brought back some life and activity to the nearby town and were very welcome, for after feeling the full impact of the departure of the residents of the château, the town had also been struck by a new disaster, the financial ruin of the Richard-Lenoir spinning mills. At the château, Bourbon had some building work carried out to improve the awkward layout of his abode. In 1821 Dubois was instructed to fill in the moat which had separated the two buildings from the very start. The platform of earth so obtained made it possible to enlarge the courtyard of the Petit Château as far as the footings of the large one, and move the entrance into the courtyard from the low approach terrace to the north, by throwing a second bridge across, duplicating the one leading to Bullant's portico. At the same time, the old gallery wing was extended by three bays so it joined the remains of the Grand Château, thus making it possible to move directly between the two, while the vaults of the rooms and corridors in the earth platform of the Grand Château, damaged by infiltrating water due to the watering of the garden, had to be covered with an ornamental tiles. The basement was refurbished and a theatre installed. The baronne de Feuchères had the pleasure of performing on several occasions.

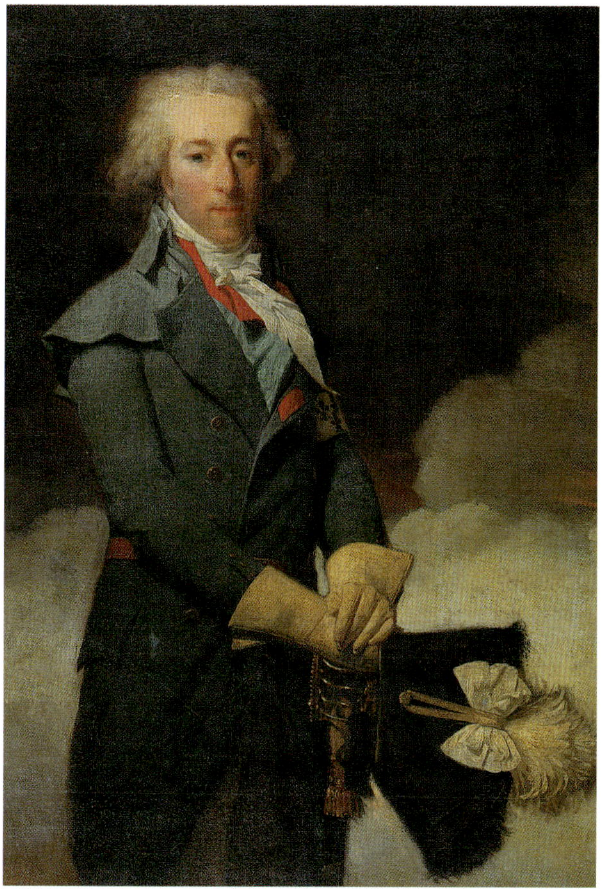

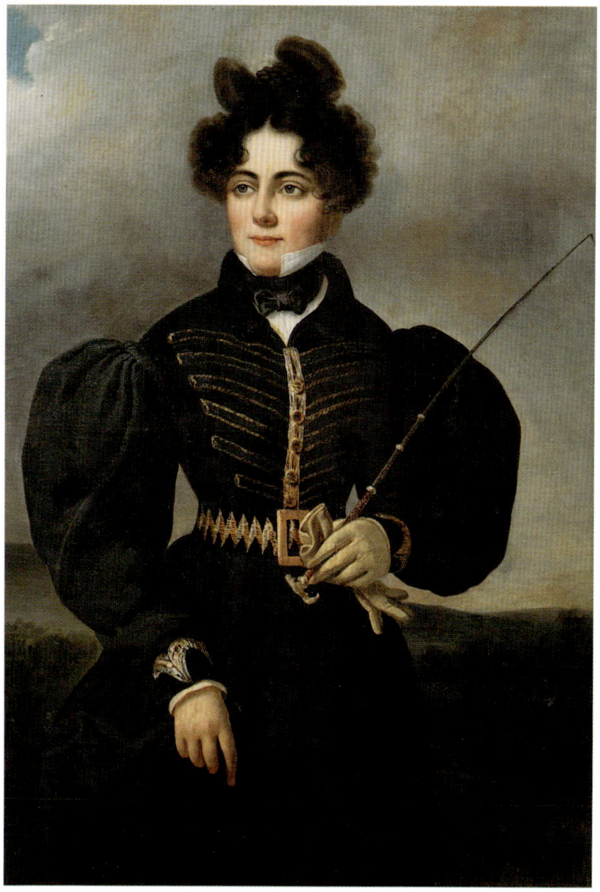

However, the duke's main expenditure related to the reinstatement and even enlargement of the estate of his forefathers. So he bought back the Jeu de Paume, the meadows near the Canal and the Hameau, the land at Saint-Maximin, Courtillet, Saint-Firmin and Avilly, as well as woods and heath lands in the forests of Chantilly, Pontarmé and Coye seized from religious establishments during the Revolution. These huge areas enable him to assuage his passion for hunting which had not diminished with age. "There is no way of getting him to listen to reason on that subject," Madame de Feuchères wrote in October 1829. The most spectacular of these hunting exploits were the subject of commissions placed with the painter Ladurner, so that their memory would be preserved. Hunting was also behind a new building at the Commelles ponds, where it was convenient to have a meeting-place available. Dubois was instructed to adapt the former Moulin de la Loge for that purpose and build a belvedere on top of it so that they could enjoy the view of the forest and the ponds. "His Royal Highness requests that the architecture of the belvedere

Louis-Henri-Joseph duc de Bourbon
This portrait of the new duke, the son of Louis-Joseph, was painted during his time as an émigré by Henri-Pierre Danloux.

Sophie Dawes baronne de Feuchères
The imperious Englishwoman who for a long time shared the duke's life had her portrait painted by Alexis Valbrun in 1830.

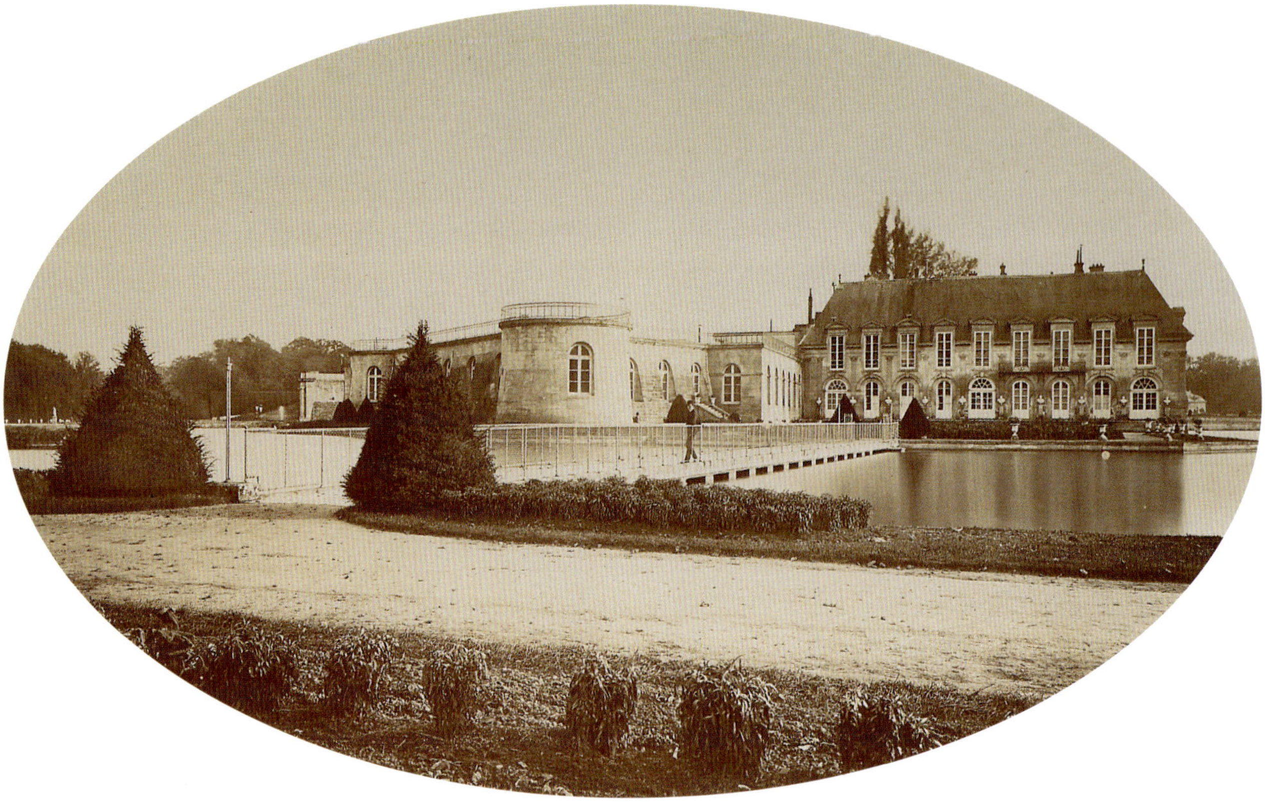

The château of Chantilly seen from the Volière
This view by Claudius Couton is one of the first photographs of Chantilly. It is part of the photographic account the duc d'Aumale commissioned from him in 1872 before undertaking his first building work. We see the Petit Château with its nine-bay façade, the Pont de la Volière, and the Grand Château reduced to a simple platform topped by a garden in the form of a terrace.

should be in the same Gothic style as the building," the architect was told; he successfully acquitted himself of the task in 1826. We do not really know why, but this charming troubadour-style manor was known as the château de la Reine Blanche after an old legend according to which Blanche de Castille and the future Saint Louis were frequent visitors (Cambry, *Description du département de l'Oise*, 1803).

Just one month after the July Revolution, public opinion was knocked sideways by the dramatic events of 27 August 1830. The body of the unfortunate duke was found hanged from the espagnolette of the window of his bedroom at the château of Saint-Leu-Taverny, which he had bought in 1821. Murder or suicide? No official explanation was forthcoming. At Chantilly, the prince was well-liked and sincerely mourned, and his heart was laid in the parish church at the inhabitants' request, but Madame de Feuchères, suspected of having some share in this mystery, had to return to England where she died ten years later.

The inheritance of the last representative of the house of Condé, who had no descendants, had inevitably been coveted, and negotiations had been started

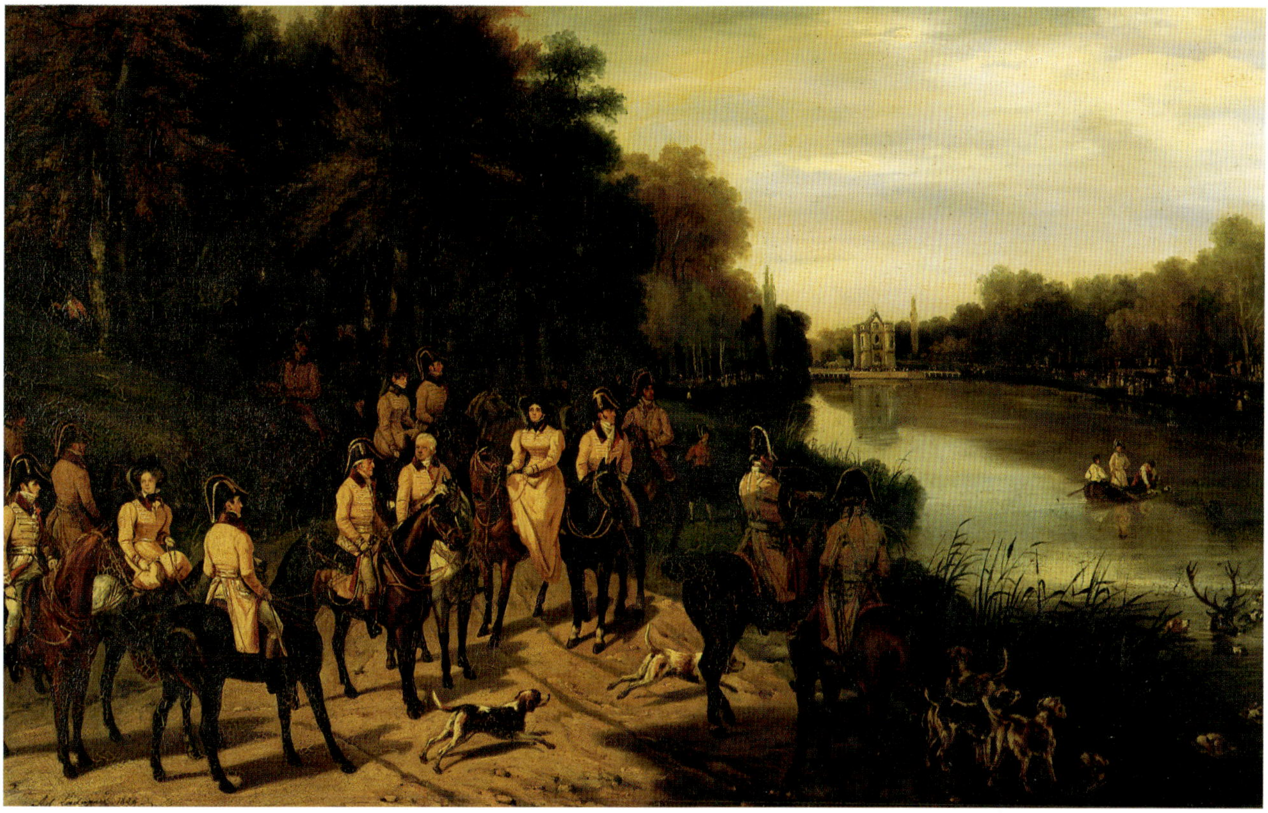

with Louis-Philippe when he was still only duc d'Orléans, and head of a house that had already accumulated the estates left by other branches of the royal blood, the Penthièvres and the Contis. The financial interests at stake were huge and the baronne de Feuchères had every interest in guiding the duc de Bourbon towards choosing the Orléans family, who would know how to reward her, rather than Charles X or his children. So she acted as an emissary to the court at the Palais-Royal, and in particular with the two princesses whose opinion could be crucial in influencing Louis-Philippe, Marie-Amélie and Adélaïde, his wife and his sister. The discussions begun in May 1829 did not fail in their objective and in his will dated 30 August the old duke named one of Louis-Philippe's sons, the one who was his godson, his universal legatee, subject to the guarantee of a special legacy rewarding the good offices of the go-between. A year later Louis-Henri-Joseph de Bourbon gave his approval, very muted admittedly, to his cousin, at the time of the events of July 1830 which made Louis-Philippe king of France and forced Charles X and the senior branch of the Bourbons into exile.

The Mort at the Étangs de Commelles
This painting by Adolphe Ladurner shows us the duc de Bourbon in 1829, one year before his strange death. The work belonged to the baronne de Feuchères, who is featured in it.
In the background is the château de la Reine Blanche, a meeting place for the hunt rebuilt in 1826 by Victor Dubois on the site of the old Loge de Viarmes.

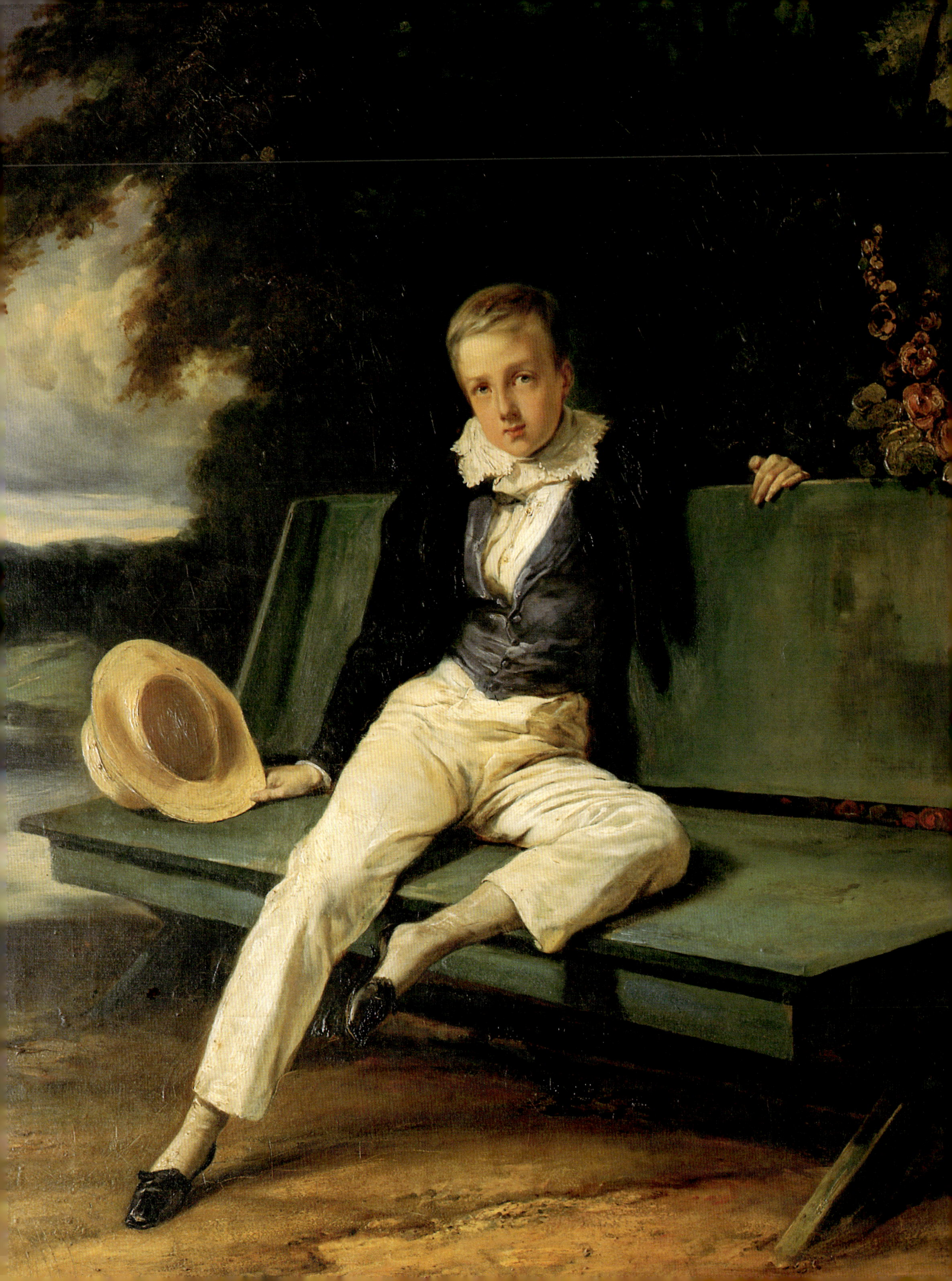

A new Renaissance prince: the duc d'Aumale

The Orléans family at Chantilly - The young duc d'Aumale's first building projects (1846-48)

Chantilly could not have fallen into better hands. Blind destiny guided by an adventuress ensured the glorious perpetuity of the site in its entirety, because the man who came into the inheritance combined passion with scholarship and determination with wealth, the four cardinal virtues of a good owner.

Henri d'Orléans, who held the title of duc d'Aumale, a name inherited from the Lorraine-Guise family, another estate that had passed to the Orléans family, was the fifth and second youngest son of Louis-Philippe d'Orléans and Marie-Amélie de Bourbon-Sicile.[1] He was born on 16 January 1822, and was eight years old when two major events transformed his existence. The Paris revolution on 27-29 July 1830 lifted his father on to the throne, and the death of the duc de Bourbon on 27 August made him the owner of Chantilly and the Palais-Bourbon. The future promised him an exceptional career, and he fulfilled this potential with unusual strength of character.

In the first years family discipline could not let the young lad's imagination drift into thinking about the huge inheritance that had just been bequeathed him, so the sound educational programme provided for the princes, traditional in the Orléans family ever since the lessons given by Madame de Genlis to Louis-Philippe as a child, was applied without interruption, and Aumale like his brothers distinguished himself in literary studies as a pupil at the Collège Henri IV, with the support of a learned tutor, Cuvillier-Fleury. He showed special aptitude for literature and history, as was recognised in an open comradely manner by his brothers, though they too had done well in their studies of the humanities. Aumale was "far more of an academic and much better read than me", the Prince de Joinville wrote in 1842 in his *Vieux souvenirs.* In fact in

The duc d'Aumale at the age of nine
Painted by Robert-Fleury in 1831, this is the young schoolboy who had just inherited the Chantilly estate from his uncle and godfather, the last duc de Bourbon.

The Races at Chantilly
Pierre Vernet has depicted the races held in May 1836 for the Prix d'Orléans. Like his entire family the duc d'Orléans, the duc d'Aumale's eldest brother, was captivated by English fashions, and instituted horse-racing on the Pelouse at Chantilly.

View of the château in 1845
No doubt Nicolas Barbier has depicted the reception given at Chantilly by the duc and duchesse d'Aumale in 1845, on their return from Naples where their marriage had been celebrated.

his tastes and character he was most like his eldest brother Ferdinand, duc d'Orléans, who had an inquiring, independent mind and associated with artistic and literary circles in the capital. While waiting for Aumale to grow up, his father the king set up a family council responsible for managing his property while he was still a minor, and his mother oversaw Chantilly, strictly but generously.[2] We know that he made a few appearances on his estate as a youngster, in 1833, in 1834 with four school friends, and again in 1837 and 1838.

Festivities at Chantilly were not interrupted for all that, and the young duc d'Orléans, a brilliant horseman, presided over the first horse races[3], officially opening the race course that had been laid out in front of the Écuries in May 1834; the last duc de Bourbon who like his forefathers had been a great lover of horse-riding had not failed to have the stables restored. The great hunts were resumed with all the ceremony of earlier times: the stag taken at the ponds, the quarry by torch-light, plays, illuminations, concerts on the water, one following the other, "as if the divinities of these beneficent waters had woken from their long sleep to celebrate, with enthusiastic, loving voices, this poetic, royal renaissance of old Chantilly" (Cuvillier-Fleury, 1841).

As soon as he left school, Aumale like all his brothers embarked on a career in the army, and the Algerian campaign gave him the opportunity to demonstrate his military qualities – courage, determination and generosity. Starting off as his brother Ferdinand's orderly, he quickly proved to be a brilliant commander, fighting alongside Nemours and Joinville and against the legendary Abd-el-Kader. A lieutenant at the age of fifteen, a captain at seventeen, a colonel at nineteen, and a general at twenty-one, he distinguished himself in the Affroun and Col de Mouzaïa expeditions, and even more by capturing the retinue of Abd-el-Kader at Taguin on 16 May 1843, an outstanding feat that earned him the rank of lieutenant general, popularised by the huge canvas commissioned from Horace Vernet and exhibited at the château of Versailles.

That same year the victorious young soldier met his cousin Marie-Caroline, Princess of Salerno, while visiting the Bourbon-Siciles in Italy; as well as being the niece of both Queen Marie-Amélie and Empress Marie-Louise, she was the grand-niece of Queen Marie-Antoinette. Once the next campaign was over, he married her in Naples on 25 November 1844, and this brilliant marriage finally put him in a position to take a personal interest in Chantilly, carrying his young bride back there at the end of the year. Great family celebrations were

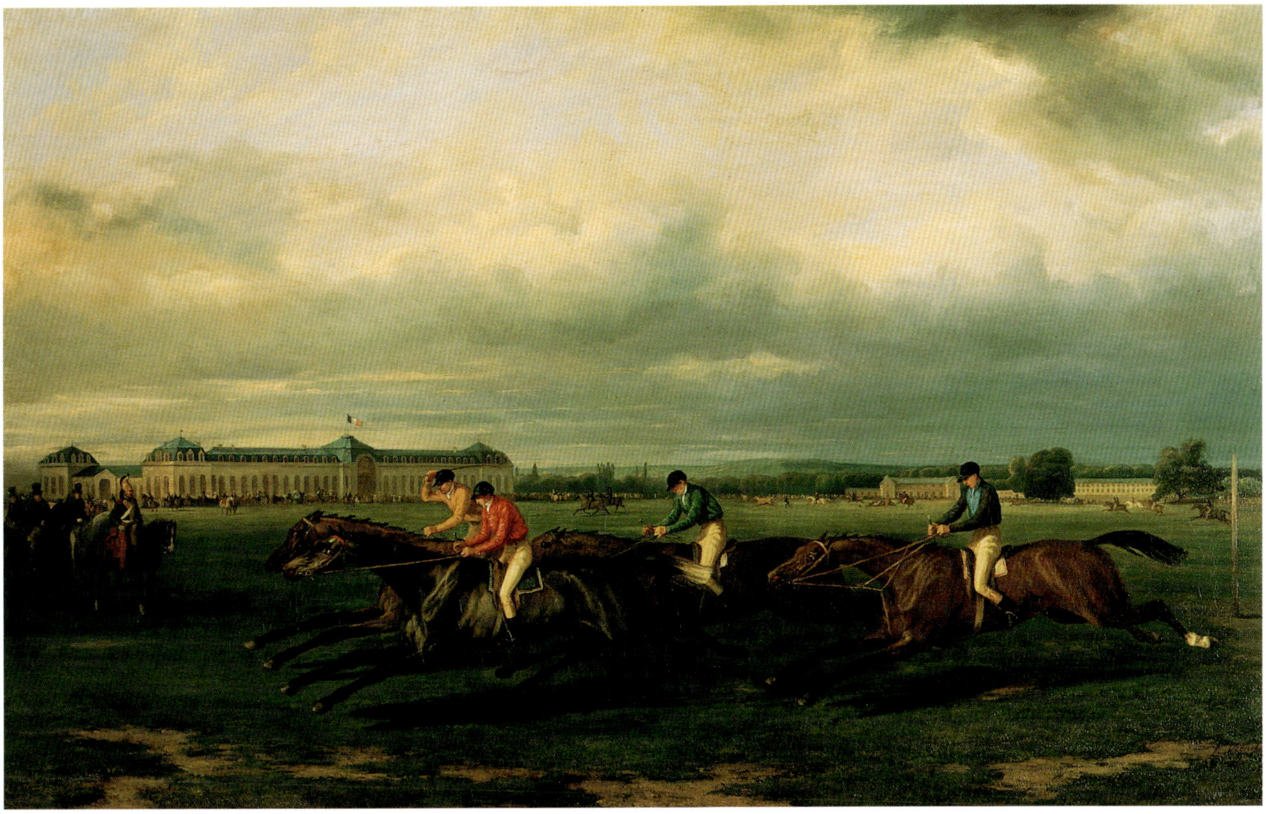

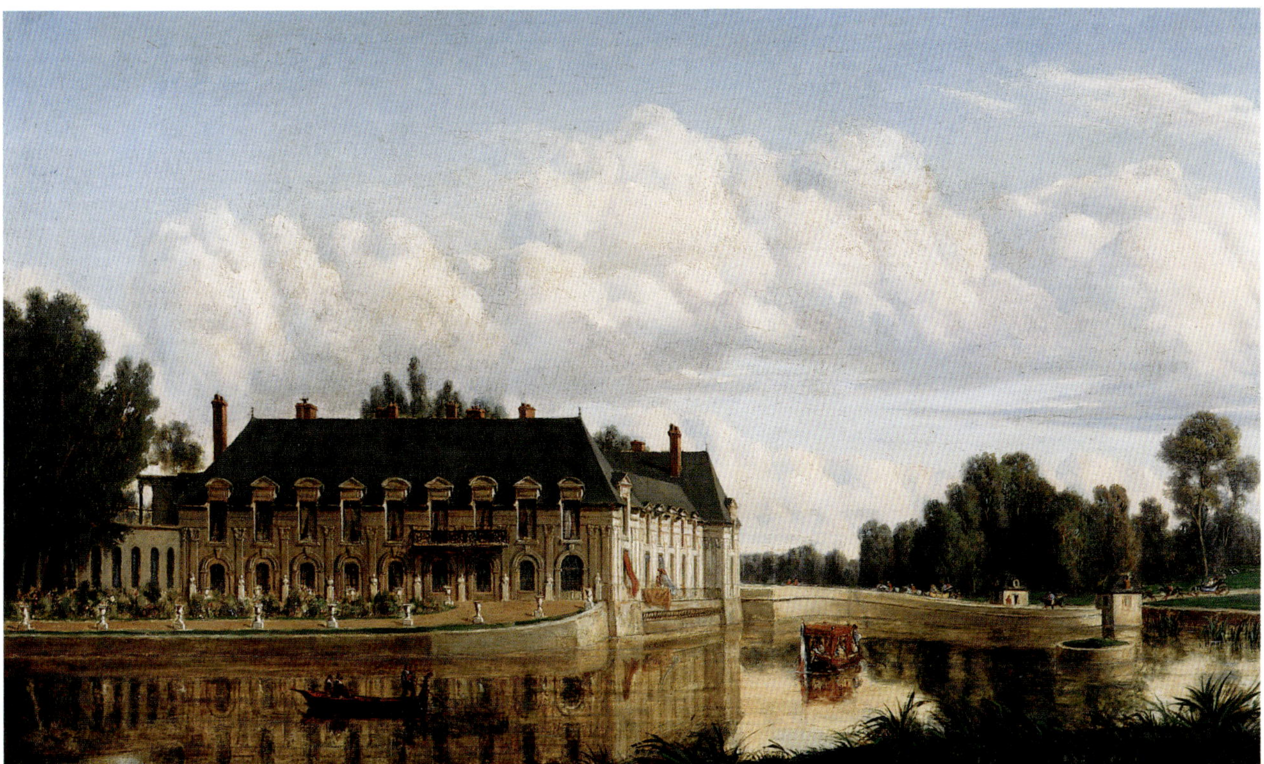

held there in May 1845, bringing together the Orléans princes and princesses with their wives and husbands. This was the apotheosis of the new dynasty, successfully allied to the main courts of Europe by a clever matrimonial policy. The duc d'Aumale's fortune was then estimated at an income of two million francs. Now master of his property, he could undertake his first expenditure, beginning with the essential work to improve and modernise the rooms where he wanted to house his young family; four daughters and four sons were born there, of whom only two boys survived infancy. Straight away he displayed the enlightened taste for architecture and the passion for building that were hereditary in the Orléans family. Looked at with the new eyes which he brought to his estate, Chantilly appeared in all the awkward reality of its two châteaux built on to one another: a small boat floating at the side of an unmasted ship, as Françoise Boudon so aptly put it.[4]

Before reinstating the masts on the ship, the small boat had to be put to rights, and the architect Dubois was invited to refurbish the ground-floor rooms of the Renaissance Petit Château, which over the centuries had remained the only permanent feature on the site.[5] Eugène Lami, a fashionable painter and loyal servant of the Orléans family who had been the drawing teacher of the duc de Nemours from before 1830 and had just decorated the rooms of the duc d'Orléans and the duc de Nemours at the Tuileries palace, was brought in to work with him. As was to be expected, Lami completely took over, and Dubois found himself forced to resign in 1846, leaving his nephew Grisart[6] as the site architect.

Left in sole charge of the site, Lami did the work to the prince's complete satisfaction. Since the loss of the Tuileries palace and the château at Neuilly and the majority of the suites of rooms at the Palais-Royal, Eu and Randan, these rooms at Chantilly now represent the last surviving evidence of the decorative schemes carried out for the Orléans princes in the second quarter of the nineteenth century, which were marked by a pleasant, vivacious eclecticism, but always laden with historical references. Here Lami took on the role of a virtual arts supervisor[7] for his young client, drawing the decoration of the rooms and having it carried out, recruiting artists, ordering furniture and rummaging around everywhere to find pictures and objets d'art that could be bought to embellish the suites of rooms, where they joined the historic furnishings transferred from the Hôtel de Lassay in Paris, since that building had finally

The duchesse d'Aumale's bedroom
The silks and bosses are part of a Louis XV-Louis XVI decoration dreamt up by Eugène Lami. On the ceiling is a bird holding a garland of flowers, painted by Narcisse Diaz.

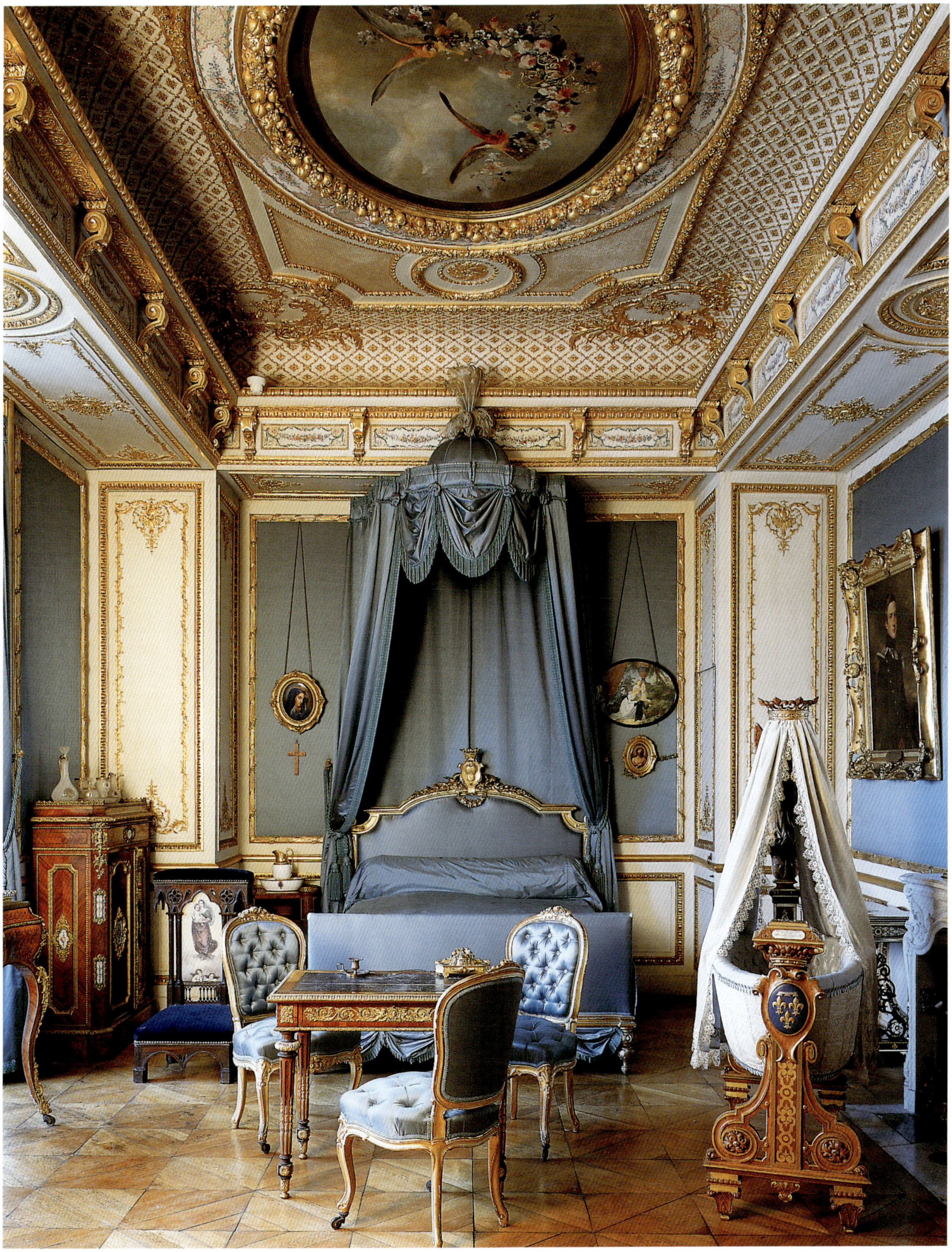

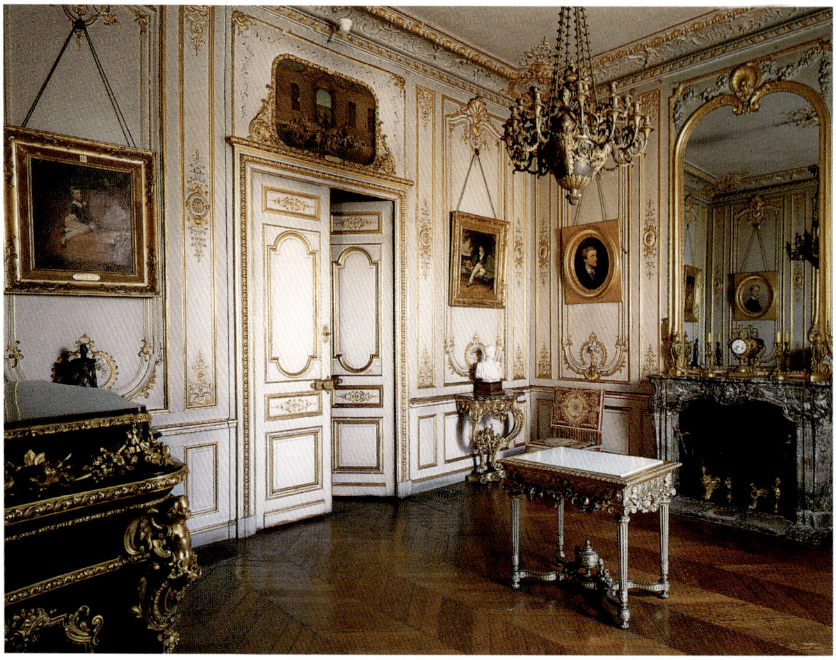

The Salon de Guise
Portraits of members of the Orléans family are hung on the wainscoting of this room in Louis XIV style. As an overdoor, *The Pack Emerging from the Stables* by J.-M. Claude.

been assigned to the state along with the Palais-Bourbon. The marrying of historical styles and the taste demonstrated in the fabrics and colours thus give a special, very "Louis-Philippe" flavour to these schemes devised by Eugène Lami, different from the far less discreet ones he carried out later for the Rothschilds during the Second Empire (1850-76). For instance, he adopted a Louis XV-Louis XVI compromise for the duchess's bedroom, fitted with elaborately shaped marquetry furniture, under an attractive ceiling depicting a bird holding a garland of flowers painted by Narcisse Diaz; Louis XIV style for the Salon de Guise; Louis XV style for the Salon des Dames[8], a round room with rosewood panelling and purple and silver satin brocade curtains, embellished with biscuit ceramic medallions by Alexandre Schoenewerk and a ceiling painted by Godefroy featuring the abduction of Hebe; Louis XIV style again for the Salon de Condé, with red damask wallpaper, fitted with Boulle furniture and a monumental Renaissance chimney-piece copied from one at the château of Villeroy; and finally Henri II style for the dining-room (or library), whose marble tiling was inspired by a portrait of Henri IV by Pourbus. Above the doors, paintings evoke life at Chantilly over the centuries: they are by Lami himself, Roqueplan, Baron and Français.[9] The same style can be recognised in the rooms fitted out on the ground floor of the former Bullant gallery (including the bedroom of Queen Marie-Amélie). Another suite of rooms was arranged on the first floor

Opposite
The Salon Violet
This is the ladies' room in Louis XV style which ended the duchesse d'Aumale's suite of rooms. Eugène Lami handled this decoration with particular refinement.

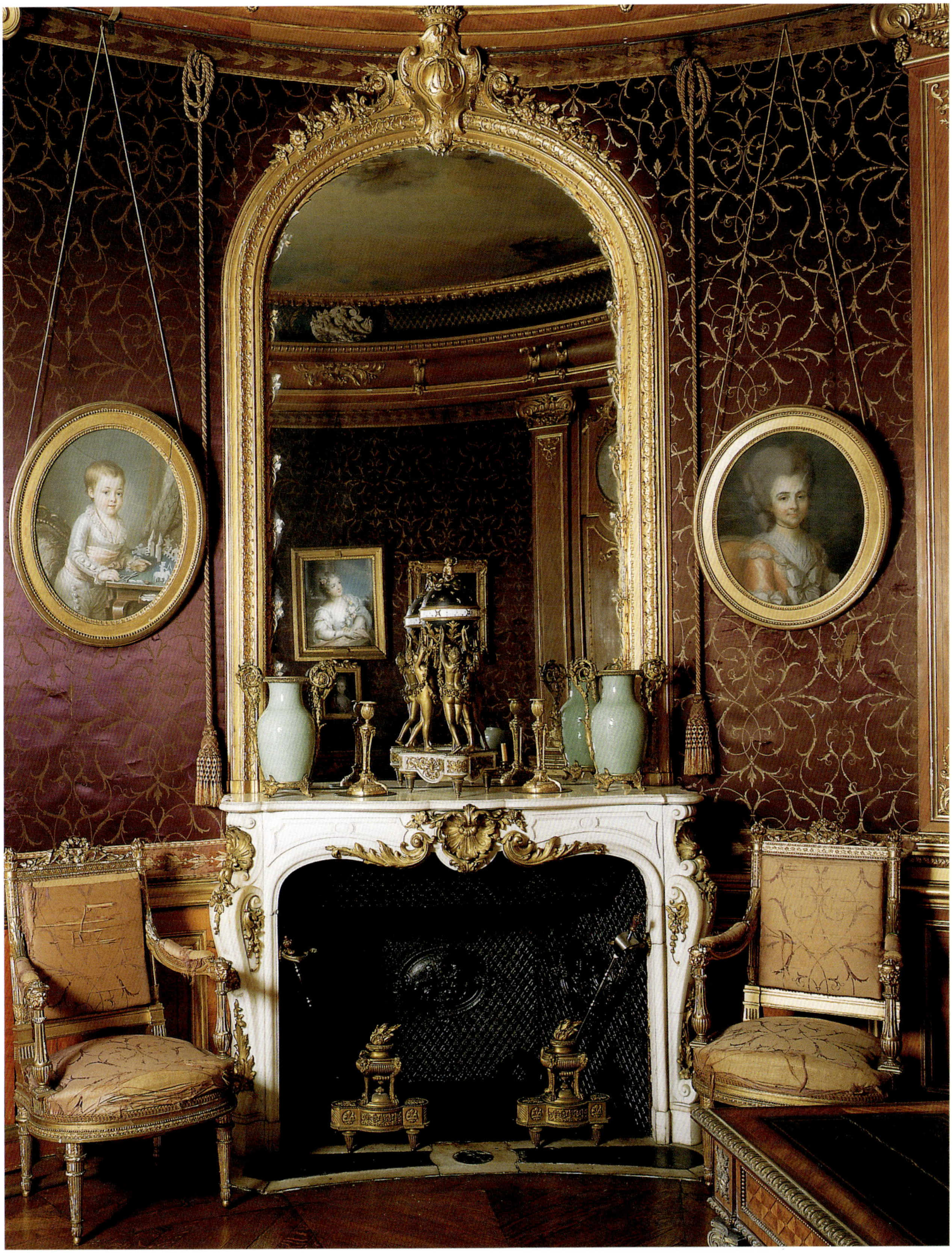

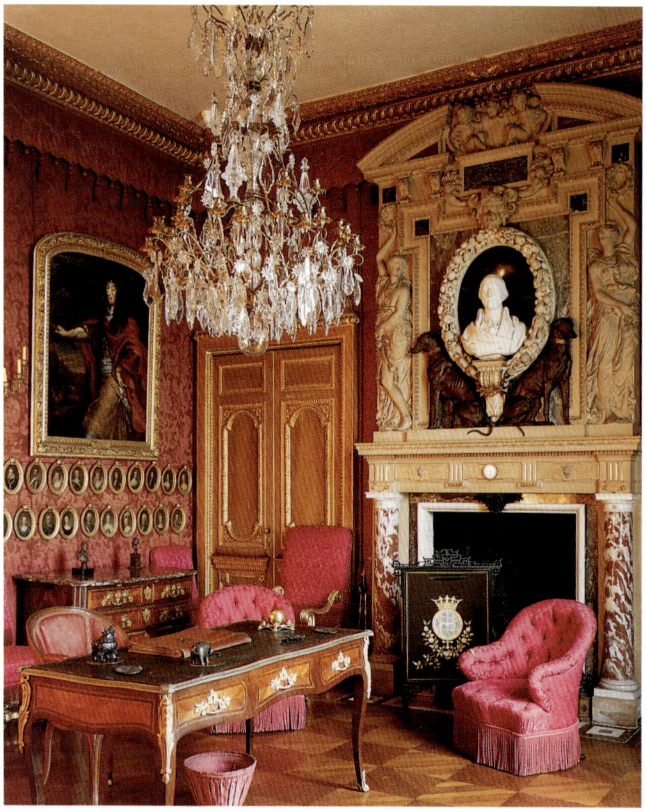

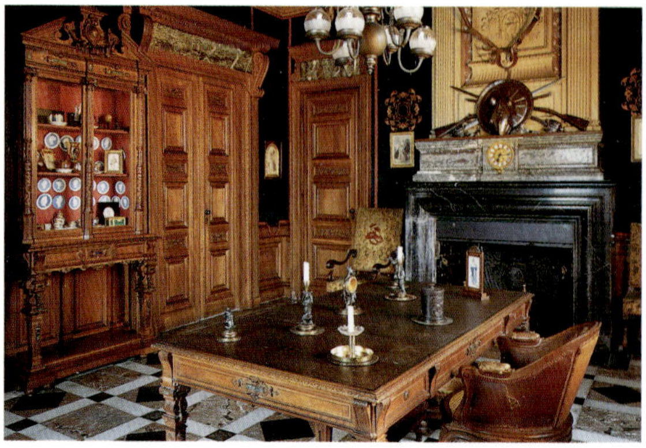

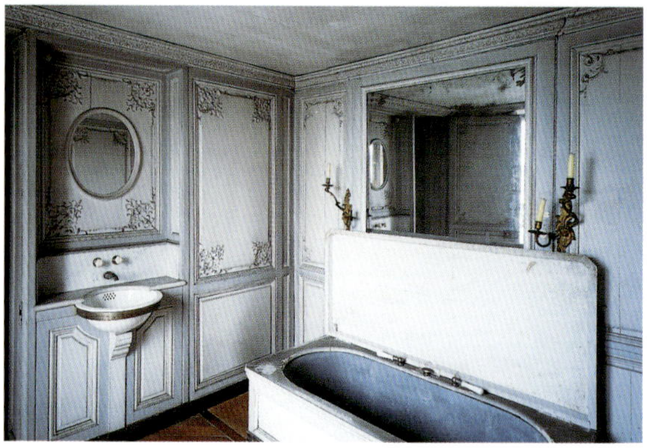

The Salon de Condé
The chimney-piece copied from one at the château of Villeroy, the original now being in the Louvre, is ornamented with a bust of the last Prince de Condé. On the wall are the Great Condé and medallion portraits of the Condé line.

The dining-room known as the Marble Room
In this room in Henri II style, the marble flooring reproduces the floor Pourbus painted with a portrait of Henri IV.

The bathroom
English-style comfort had been introduced in both the duke's and the duchess's suites of rooms.

Opposite

The duc d'Aumale's bedroom
In front of the big Louis XV wainscot panels embellished with images conjuring up Chantilly in the sixteenth, seventeenth and eighteenth centuries painted by Eugène Lami, Henri Baron and Camille Roqueplan, a large desk in incontrovertibly Louis-Philippe style occupies pride of place.

of the entrance wing on the site of the Cabinet d'histoire naturelle – natural history collection – of the duc de Bourbon who had been a Minister of Louis XV[10]: the so-called Jean Bullant bedroom and sitting-room, later the rooms of the comtesse de Clinchamp, the duchesse d'Aumale's companion.

Because they took account of the comfort demanded by those who favoured modernity – bathrooms, mezzanine rooms for servants in the personal service of the duke and duchess – the alterations highlighted even more clearly the inconvenience of these intercommunicating rooms leading off one another. So Lami suggested lining the façade facing the court with a ground-floor level gallery acting as a passageway, lit by a series of geminate round arches between Doric pilasters, in the openings of which he suggested integrating the stained glass panels illustrating *The Story of Psyche* that came from the château of Écouen. This cold neo-classical appendage was not to Aumale's liking. It was a truly architectural project he was after.

The duke had dismissed Dubois with an authoritative statement of intent: "One of our finest prerogatives as a prince and a wealthy man is to be able to encourage the arts," hence to secure the services of the best creative artists of

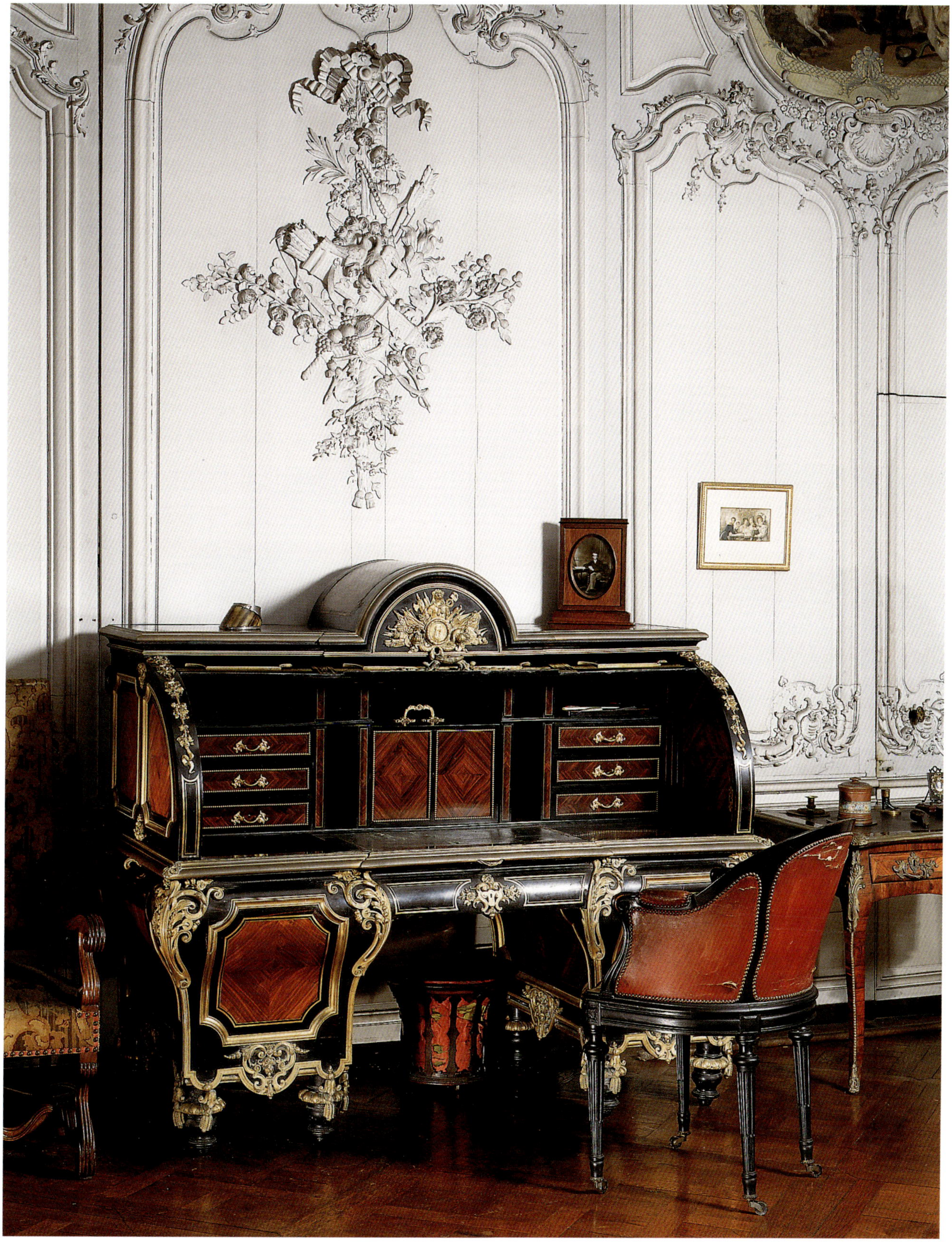

Scheme for the wooden gallery at the Petit Château
This design by Félix Duban for the corridor gallery designed to serve the suites of rooms in the Petit Château (1847) was preferred to one by Eugène Lami.

the day. Now two men had made their mark working on major Paris sites: Louis Visconti, the builder of fountains and the organiser of festivities for the July monarchy, and Félix Duban, whose École des Beaux-Arts (completed in 1843) and Hôtel Pourtalès were much admired, as was his brilliant restoration work at the châteaux of Blois and Dampierre and the Sainte-Chapelle. Duban won the day in the spring of 1846, and was instructed to look into rebuilding the Grand Château, but in the immediate term he came up with a rival scheme for a corridor gallery for the Petit Château, made of richly carved wood like a finely wrought piece of furniture in a very strongly "Henri II" style, which had the advantage of masking Jean Bullant's façade less and fitting in better with his structuring. Started in 1847, the gallery was completed in the middle of the following year, in spite of the Revolution in February.[11]

The Duban proposal for the reconstruction of the château

But Duban had been taken on for a far more ambitious undertaking: the reconstruction of the Grand Château, a recurrent theme that had hung over succeeding generations since the seventeenth century. Off his own bat, Lami had timidly put forward his ideas for the grand design: an open court on the side near the Petit Château, bordered on the east by an arched portico with a monumental doorway, inspired even then by the Baptistery gate at Fontainebleau, and at right angles at the back and on the right a "High Renaissance" château consisting of a main block and square pavilions topped by high roofs. The duke disregarded these suggestions and spent a long time consulting with Duban during the winter of 1846-47 before coming up with a far more elaborate proposal.[12] The biggest constraints came from the adherence to history insisted on by the young prince: not only taking account of the awful triangular ground plan but also reusing the bases of the round mediaeval towers, as Lami's proposal had failed to do; this ruled out any scheme of the type seen at Écouen.

It was at this juncture that Aumale's father, the king, decided to intervene. Anxious to study the proposals on the spot and to put a brake on his son's appetite for spending money, on 7 May 1847 Louis-Philippe came out for a big family outing during which he gave vent to some lively criticisms. The architect was so deeply scarred that seventeen years later he wrote a detailed account of what had happened. Louis-Philippe had become heated with his son regarding the proposed arrangements. Before dinner, he drew Duban into a recess

Interior view of the Duban gallery
The gallery is taken from the area of the court, and runs along the large Bullant wing; it is built of very carefully made joinery work and fitted with stained glass panels with the arms of the various lords of Chantilly.

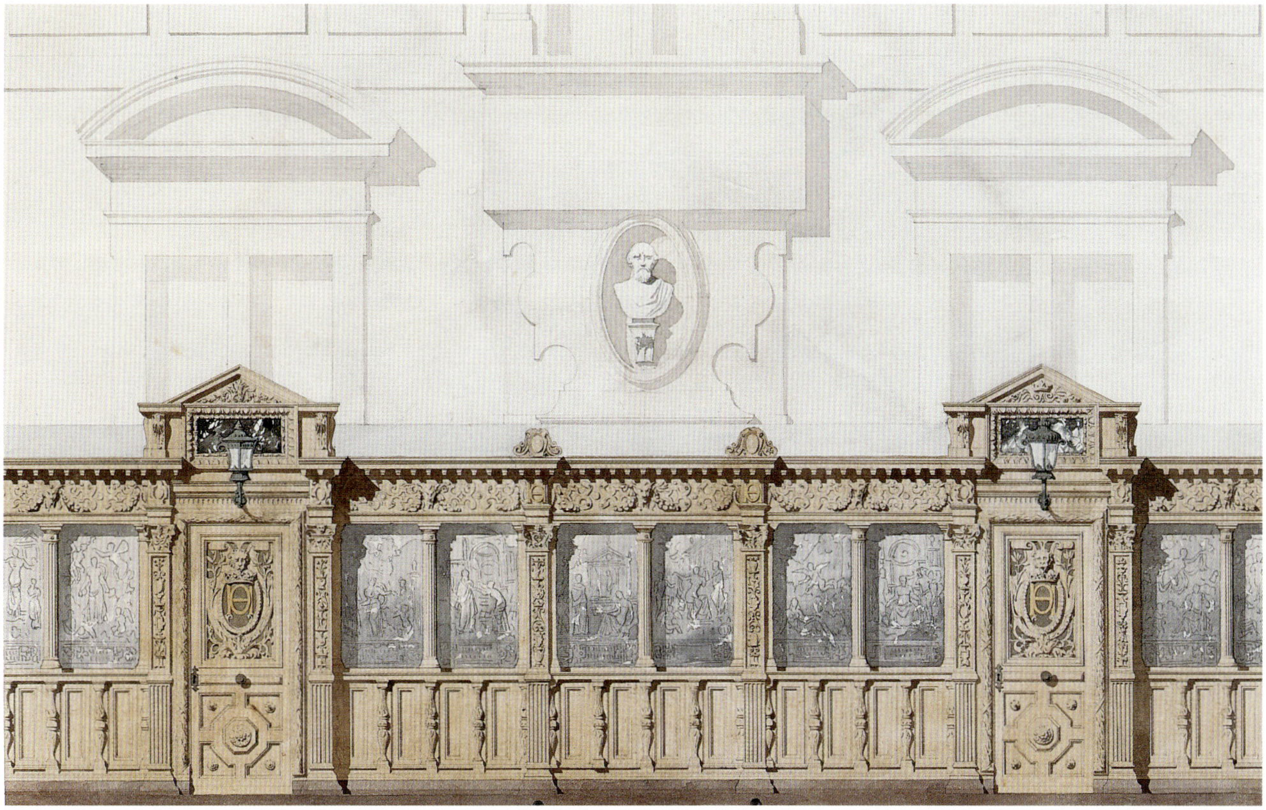

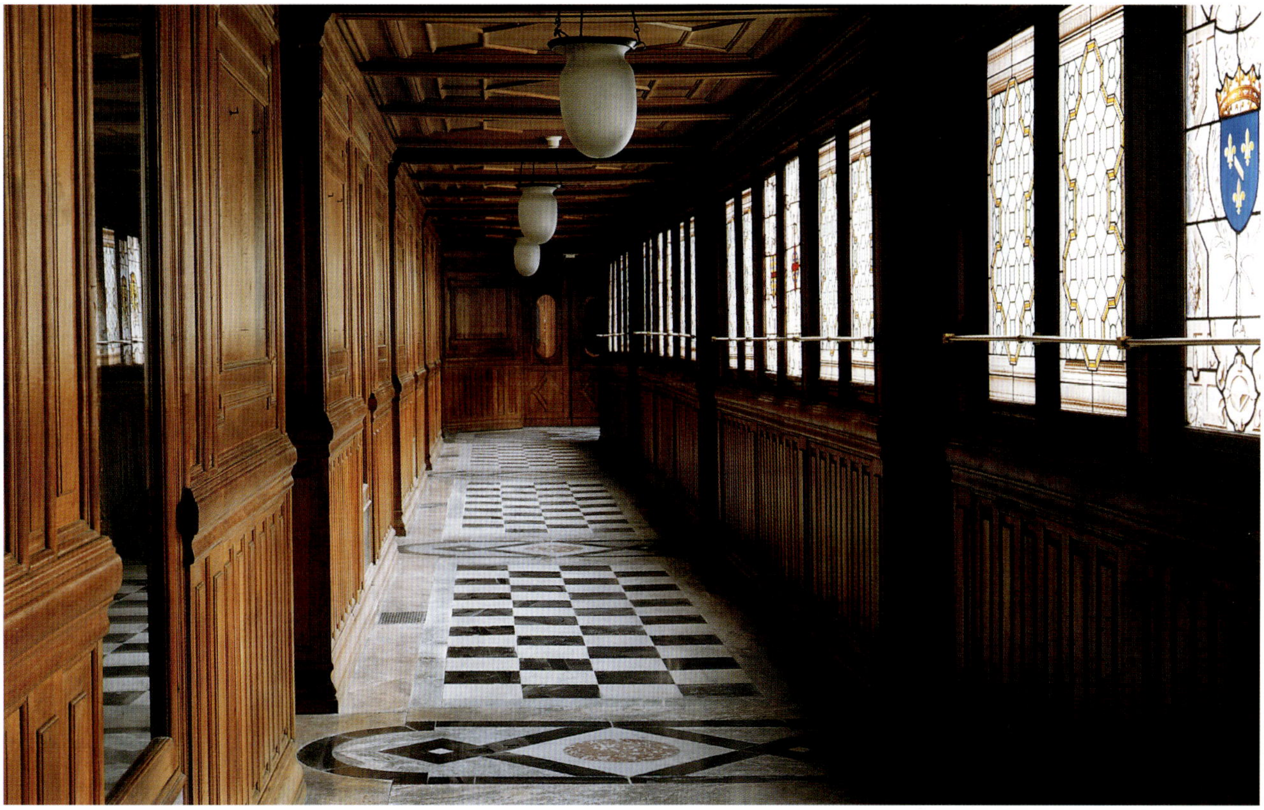

and said: "You seem to me to be an honest man, don't drag Aumale into a great deal of expenditure. His fortune is not yet available as ready cash, and he is young." He went on: "Like my son, I love building, and the Palais-Royal is proof of it. I was richer than him at the time when I embarked on that building. Well, I can tell you, but for the compensation paid to émigrés, the Palais-Royal would be unfinished and covered with straw, as it was for a long time." Later on in the evening, Duban was invited to explain his approach to the sovereign from the ghostly platform of the Old château, by moonlight.[13]

Aumale had not been deterred by his father's reservations – the latter would have preferred to see the duke investing in the château of Châteaubriant to gain the support of the people living in the West – and in July 1847 he officially instructed Duban to proceed with the reconstruction of the Grand Château. After being appointed Governor General of Algeria in September, however, he had to leave Chantilly, but in the autumn the architect submitted a draft project which was accepted, and received the order to start work at the end of the winter. This 1847 scheme is known to us in three variants which make it

Duban's schemes for the entrance façade (below) and for the north façade (opposite)
Unlike Lami, Félix Duban respected the round towers and the triangular ground plan. These two drawings very carefully treated with watercolours show the exterior façades (1847). On the right, above the gallery, his project for a library with a cupola visible on other drawings is absent.

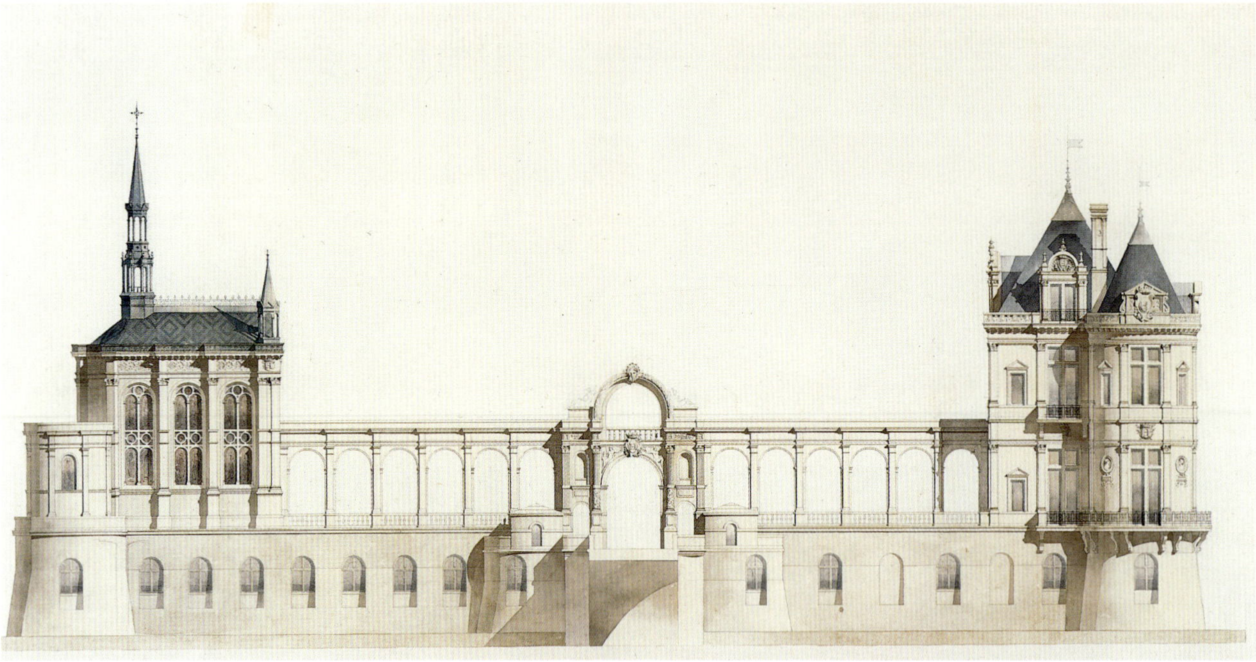

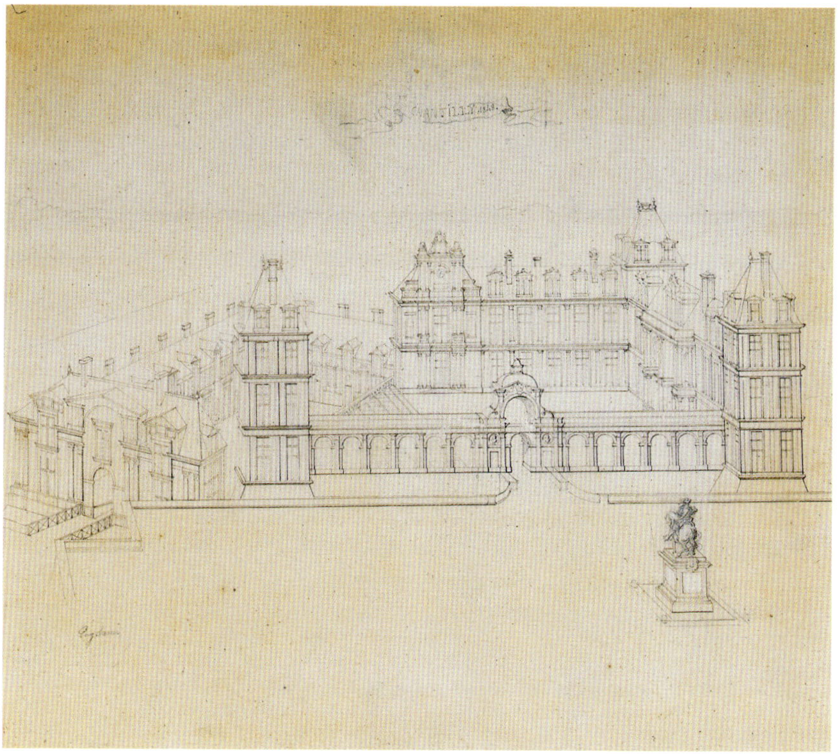

Lami's scheme for the Grand Château of Chantilly

For the reconstruction of the Grand Château, in 1848 Eugène Lami proposed a tall Renaissance château, the square pavilions of which would have entailed destroying Chantilly's ancestral round towers. But for the centre of his low entrance wing he already had in mind a pavilion inspired by the Baptistery at Fontainebleau.

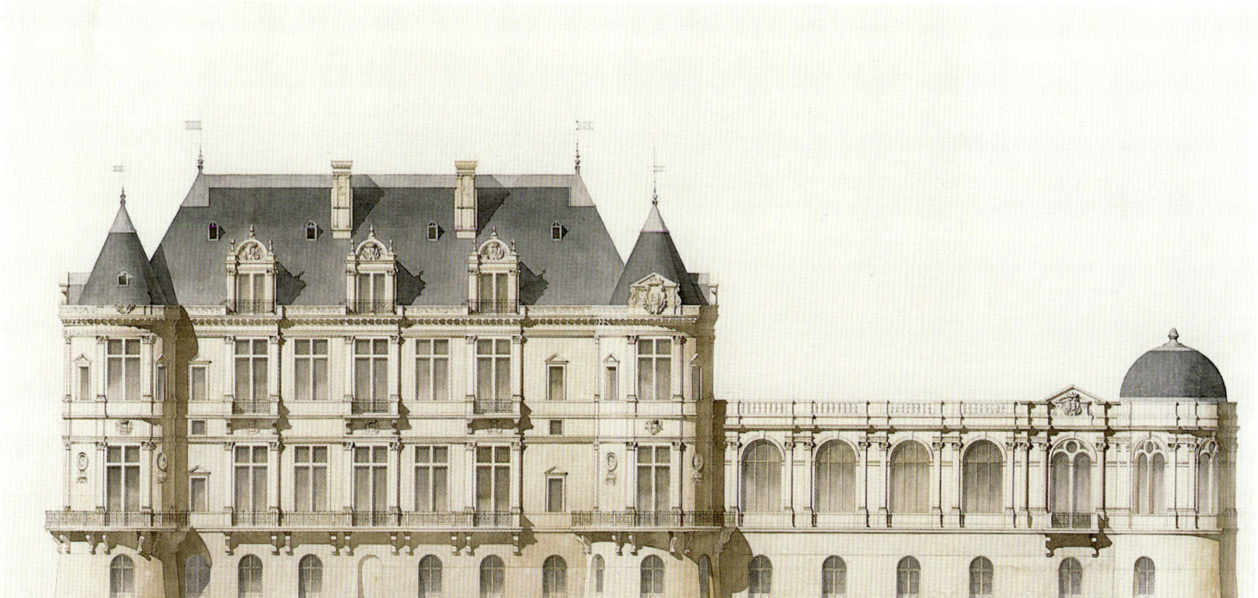

quite clear of the programme: a series of private suites of rooms, reception rooms (including the vast dining-room that had already featured on Dubois's designs), a chapel, a painting gallery and a library, proof that the prince's tastes as a collector and book-lover were already firmly established. The architecture was modern, elegant and open, strongly influenced by the Renaissance but not in academic thrall to it, a fine piece of work by Duban which circumstances precluded from becoming a reality.

Aumale in exile

Again events happened in a rush. Revolution broke out in Paris in February 1848, while Aumale was detained in Alger by his responsibilities as Governor General. Forced to abdicate, Louis-Philippe decided to retire to England with his family, and his sons were invited to join him with their wives and children. For the time being that was the end of major schemes for Chantilly, and the Orléans dynasty followed the Bourbons into exile. For how long?

With his sound pragmatism, while continuing to be responsive to all the events that stirred France, Aumale settled down comfortably in England to lead the life of a prince and aesthete, with a house in the residential suburbs of London – Orleans House in Twickenham – and a country house at Woodnorton, where the pictures, books and archives sent from Paris and Chantilly were amassed. The leisure he enjoyed in exile enabled him to devote himself to his work as a historian, making use of his priceless Chantilly archives to write the *Histoire des princes de Condé* – he would complete the seventh and final volume in 1895 – and his new passion for books, printed matter, incunabula and manuscripts: "I am beginning to think that I am suffering from bibliomania," he wrote to Cuvillier-Fleury as early as 28 November 1848.

Through his correspondents he kept himself informed about all the major sales in England and on the continent, and continued to enrich his personal collections which were to be among the most important ever known. The most fabulous of his acquisitions of manuscripts was agreed in 1855 at a boarding school in Genoa for eighteen thousand francs: it related to the *Très Riches Heures du duc de Berry*, the most beautiful manuscript in the world.

As for paintings, if we can believe G. Macon, who tended to embellish the story[14], Aumale had started buying while still at school, using his pocket money to buy *Soldier of the Republic* by Bellangé and *Standard-bearer of the Republic* by

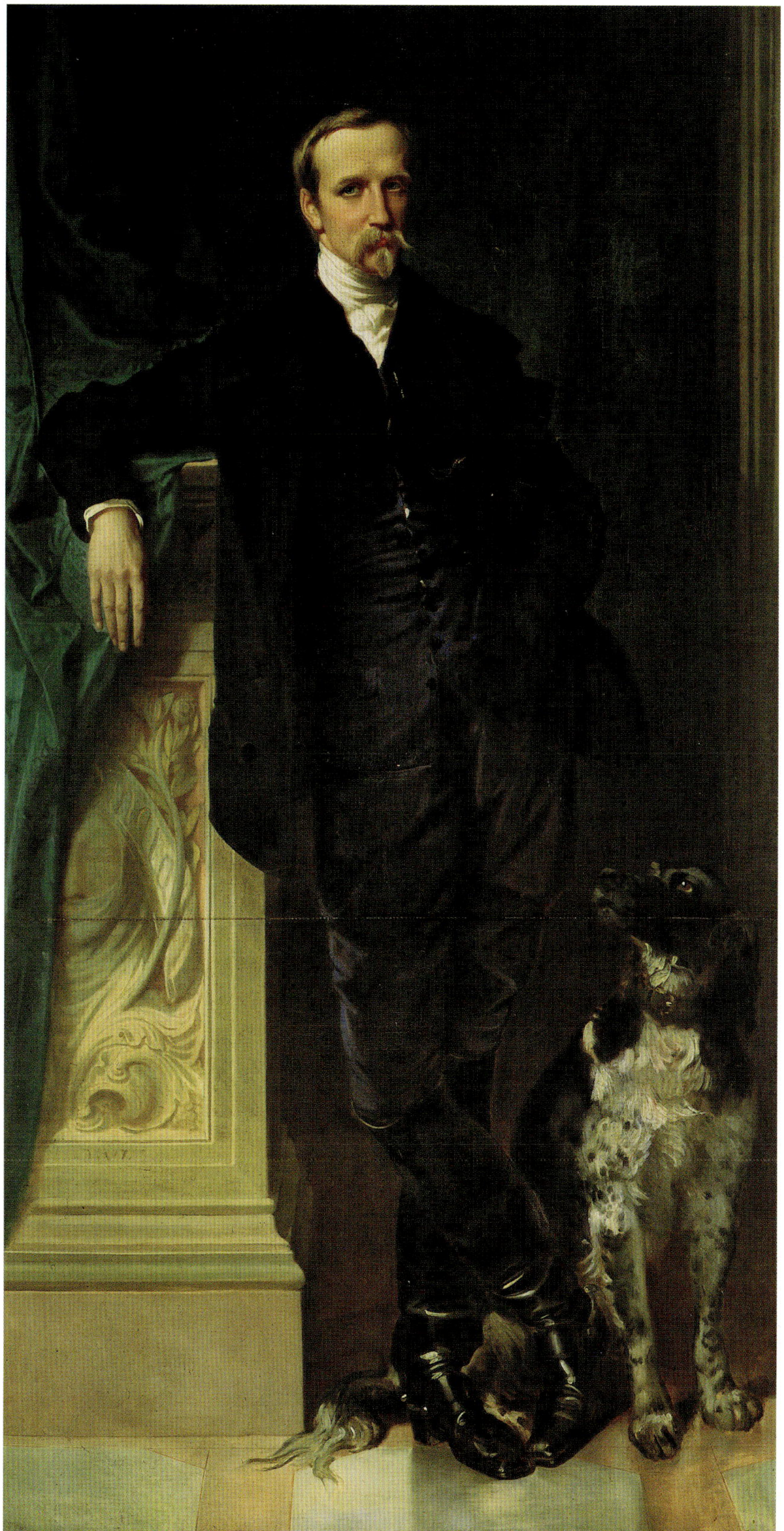

The duc d'Aumale at the age of twenty-seven
This portrait was painted in 1850 by Victor Mottez during his exile at Claremont Castle in England where the duke lived with his father before taking up residence at Twickenham following Louis-Philippe's death.

Charlet, two works with a strong symbolic content attesting to his early taste for history painting and military episodes relating to the French Revolution of 1789. From London the prince who had become known on the international art market was able to take advantage of the great sales of his day, first and foremost those involving his family: first were his father's collections, sold on the old man's death in 1850 (in particular the pictures and books from the former Standish collection); next the sale of furniture from the château of Neuilly in 1851, when he was able to acquire the tapestries of the *Emperor Maximilian at the hunt*; the sale of the property of his father-in-law, the Prince of Salerno, including paintings and antiquities (1852-54); the gallery of his brother Ferdinand d'Orléans sold by his widow in 1853; that of the château of Eu in 1857; and many others such as the Soltykoff sale and the sale of drawings from the Reiset collection in 1861. A few single masterpieces by Poussin, Titian, Perugino and Raphael were also acquired in these years of exile.

Daumet instructed to build Chantilly V

In January 1852 decrees issued by the Second Republic, doubtless inspired by the Prince-President, the future Napoleon III, had ordered the forcible alienation of the prince's property within a very short time, subject to confiscation, and on 30 October the duc d'Aumale had proceeded with the sale of his estate to Coutts and Co. bank, with an option to buy it back. The château was then rented to the British Ambassador Lord Cowley, and subsequently to come Duchâtel and his son-in-law, the duc de La Trémoille. The years of the Second Empire went by in this way until the disaster at Sedan. As a fervent patriot, the prince would have liked to played a role in defending French national territory, like his brother Joinville and his nephew Chartres, but he was too well known for his anonymity not to have been immediately unmasked.

The Republican regime set up on the ruins of the Empire quickly decided to abolish the laws of exile (8 June 1871) and the duke immediately returned to France. He could think sadly back on the family misfortunes that had hit him so cruelly over the past twenty years, the death of his eldest son the Prince de Condé at the age of twenty-one, carried off in May 1866 by typhoid fever on a journey to Sydney, and in December 1869 the death of his wife, the duchesse d'Aumale, deeply affected by the death of their son. A new sorrow was soon to be inflicted on him with the loss of his last child, the duc de Guise, carried

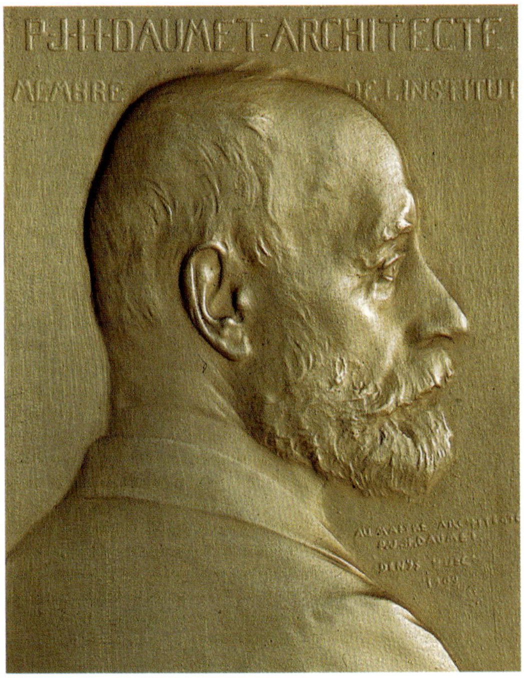

Honoré Daumet, architect
This little bas relief by Denis Puech (1909) shows the effigy of the architect, whose career had been crowned with success. He was a member of the Institut de France.

off in his turn on 25 July 1872, at the age of eighteen. The death of his heir changed the outlook for the future, but in no way lessened the prince's determination to serve his country. The Republic had given him back his rank as general, and he was once again able to devote himself to his military vocation. Hence he presided over the council of war responsible for judging Field-Marshal Bazaine, then assumed command of the Seventh Army corps at Besançon. Besides this he had been elected to the Chamber of Deputies as the member for Oise in 1871, as well as being elected a member of the Académie Française. Within a few months he had become one of the most prominent figures of the new regime, a Republic favourably disposed towards the monarchy with a legitimist soldier as its President in the person of Field-Marshal MacMahon, and he was the centre of attention. Edmond de Goncourt drew a famous word portrait of him in 1874: "There is only one way to describe the duc d'Aumale: he is an old colonel of the light cavalry. He has the typical slim elegance, the ravaged look, the grey goatee beard, the thin hair and the bald spot; he has the same voice, a voice broken by command." In some opinions, Orleanism represented by an extremely dignified and very experienced prince might be the best resort to combat the radically minded Republic, and why should he not take on the role of President of the Republic when MacMahon had served his term?

Following pages

Ground plans of the different levels of the château
These two plans drawn by Honoré Daumet (c. 1875) are the best guides for visiting the building and understanding the junctions that link the Petit Château to the Grand Château at several levels.

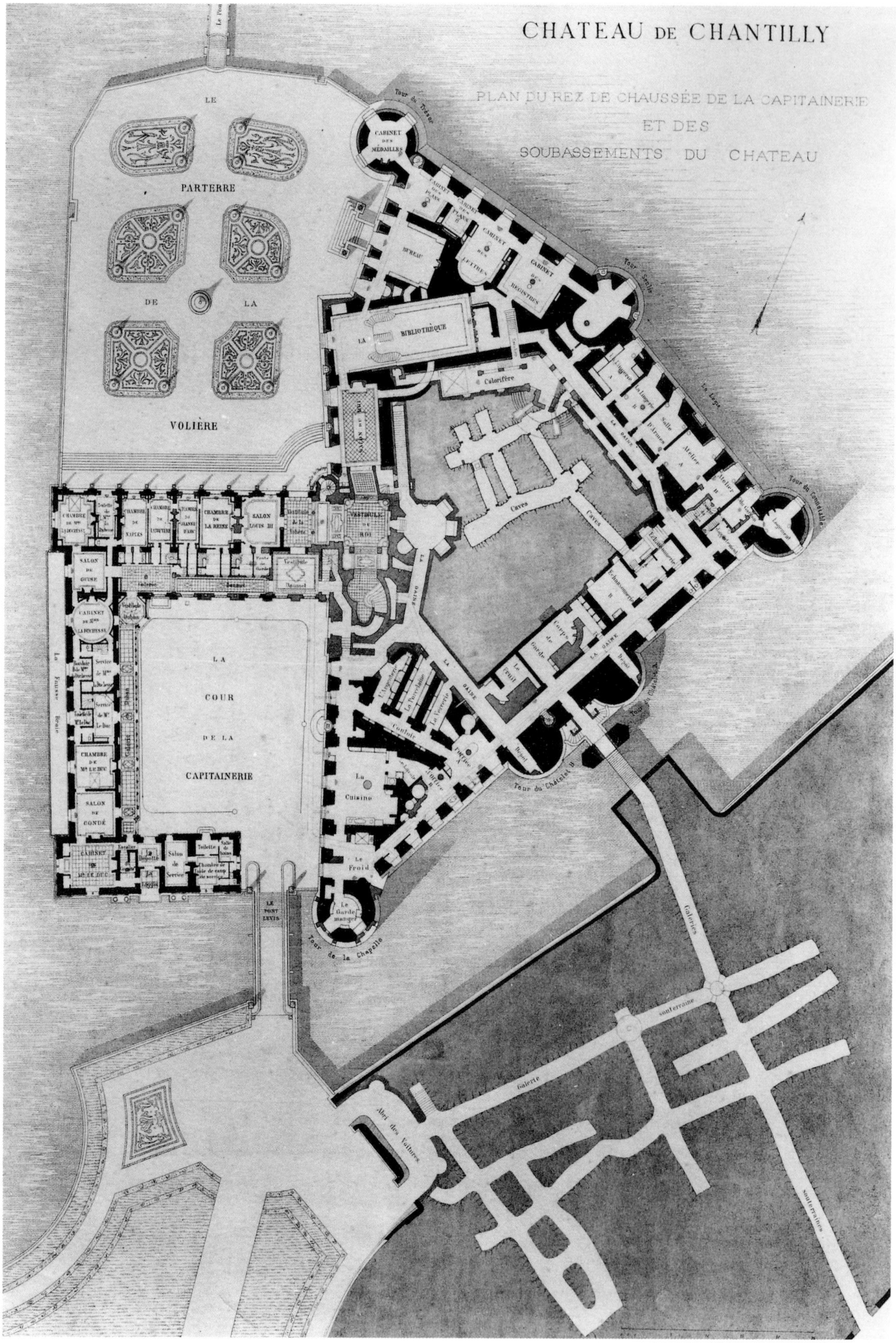
CHATEAU DE CHANTILLY
PLAN DU REZ DE CHAUSSÉE DE LA CAPITAINERIE
ET DES
SOUBASSEMENTS DU CHATEAU
LE
PARTERRE
DE LA
VOLIÈRE
CABINET DES MÉDAILLES
BUREAU
CABINET DES LETTRES
CABINET DES REGISTRES
LA BIBLIOTHÈQUE
Calorifère
Caves
VESTIBULE
SALON LOUIS XIII
CHAMBRE DE LA REINE
CHAMBRE DE NAPLES
SALON DE GUISE
LA COUR DE LA CAPITAINERIE
CHAMBRE DE Mr LE DUC
SALON DE CONDÉ
CABINET DE Mr LE DUC
Salon de Service
LE PONT LEVIS
La Cuisine
Le Froid
Le Garde manger
Tour de la Chapelle
Tour du Châtelet
Tour du Connétable
Tour du Trésor
Galerie souterraine
Abri des Voitures

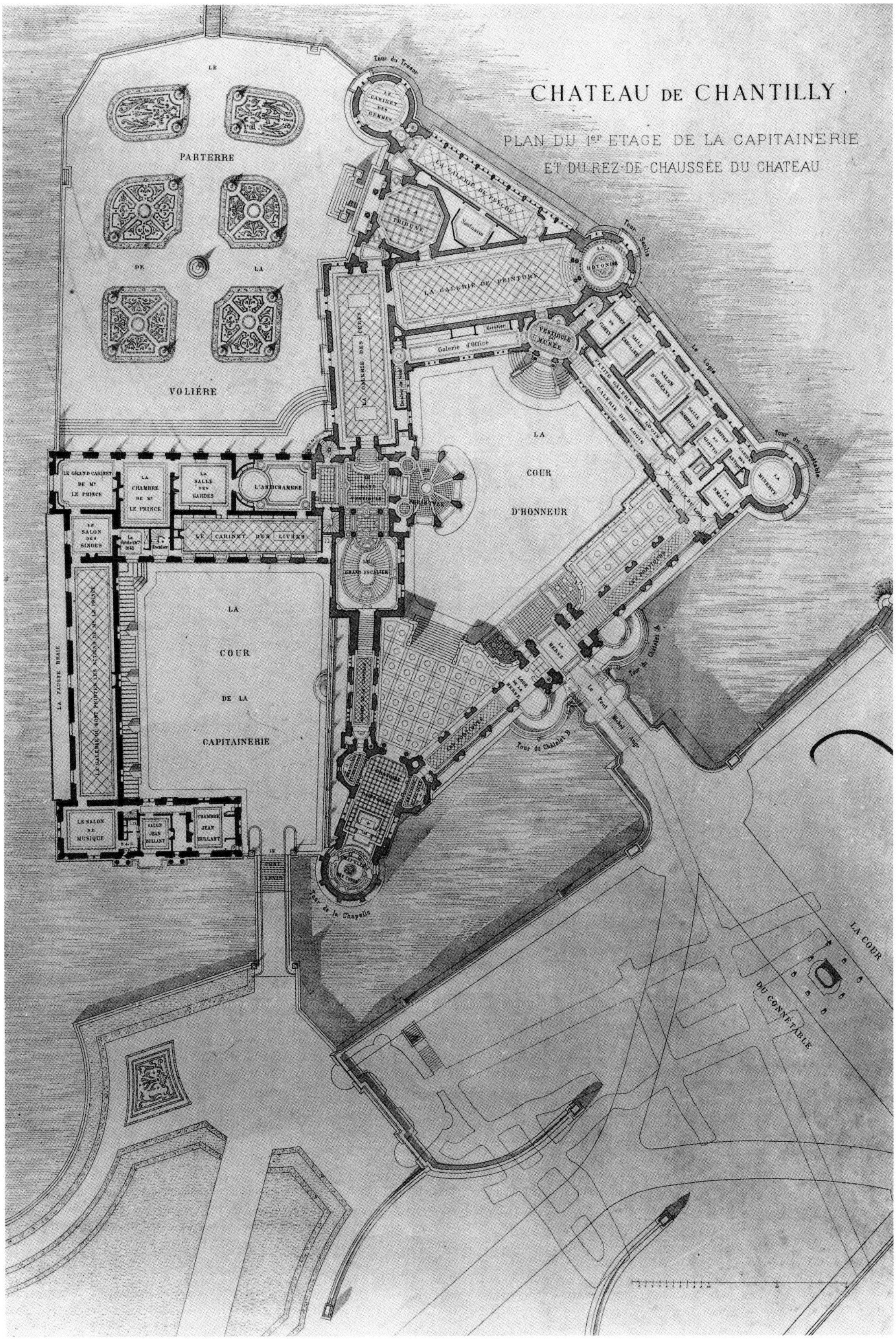
CHATEAU DE CHANTILLY
PLAN DU 1er ETAGE DE LA CAPITAINERIE
ET DU REZ-DE-CHAUSSÉE DU CHATEAU
LE PARTERRE DE LA VOLIÈRE
LA COUR D'HONNEUR
LA COUR DE LA CAPITAINERIE
LA COUR DU CONNÉTABLE
LA GALERIE DE PEINTURE
Galerie d'Office
L'ANTICHAMBRE
LE CABINET DES LIVRES
GRAND ESCALIER
LA FAUSSE BRAIE
LE SALON DE MUSIQUE
LE SALON DES SINGES
LE GRAND CABINET DE Mr LE PRINCE
LA CHAMBRE DE Mr LE PRINCE
LA SALLE DES GARDES
SALON JEAN BULLANT
CHAMBRE JEAN BULLANT
TRIBUNE
LA ROTONDE
LA MINERVE
Tour du Trésor
Tour de la Chapelle
Tour du Châtelet B

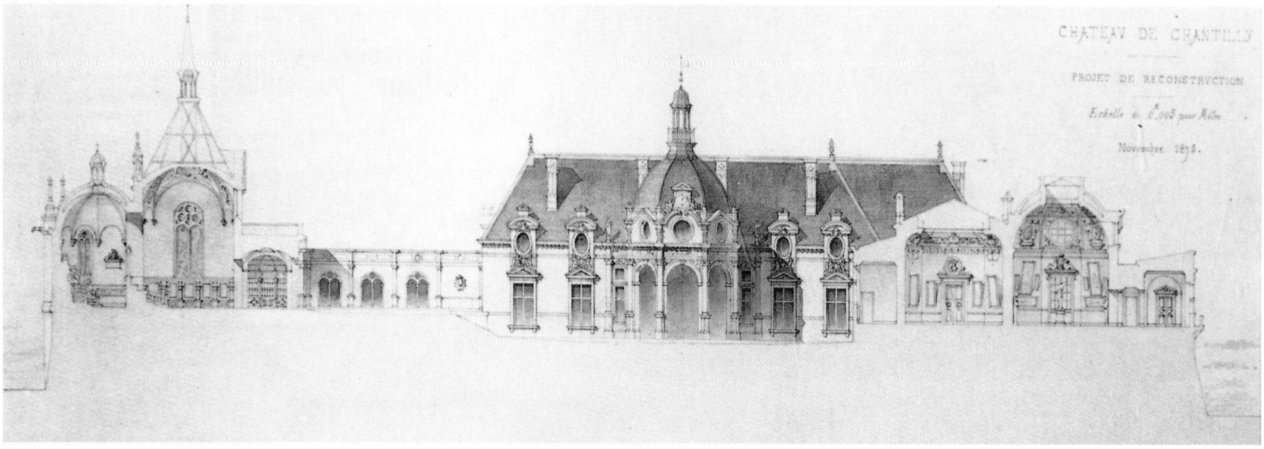

Daumet's façades
These schemes dated November 1875 and carefully presented as a fair copy represent the final state: on the left the main court, on the right the entrance wing.

The prince wisely stood aloof from these discussions, resuming the task that had been interrupted by exile. The repatriation of his fortune in 1874 enabled him to reorganise his services and pick up his grand design for Chantilly again. Living in the former mansion of the banker Achille Fould in Paris at number 129 faubourg Saint-Honoré near the Élysée palace, he set about his arrangements for having a new château built on the mound used by the Bouteillers and the d'Orgemonts: it would be the fifth château.

As his dear Duban had died during the war in 1870 while taking refuge in Bordeaux, he had to look for an architect yet again. Aumale had provisionally entrusted the upkeep of his property to a young architect called Léopold-Auguste-Marie George, who took care of his house in Paris and supervised a few jobs at Chantilly (closing off Bullant's door into the Petit Château by means of an opening with a balcony), but the task was too heavy for his slender shoulders, and a star performer had to be found as quickly as possible. Those who would have come under consideration included Charles Garnier, the architect of the Opéra, Hippolyte Destailleur, Sanson and Aldrophe, great specialists in private town houses and châteaux, or else Hector Lefuel, the architect of Napoleon III's Louvre whom the duke consulted early in 1875, without taking it any further. "First of all it was necessary to find a man with an open mind, still young, who without being bound to narrow theories by his past had nonetheless already given proof of a fine talent, and shown promise of a brilliant future," Gustave Macon wrote. It may also be assumed that the prince, who had Duban's plans to hand, the outcome of their lengthy discussions, meant them to serve as an inspiration for the ideas of any newcomer, which required that person to

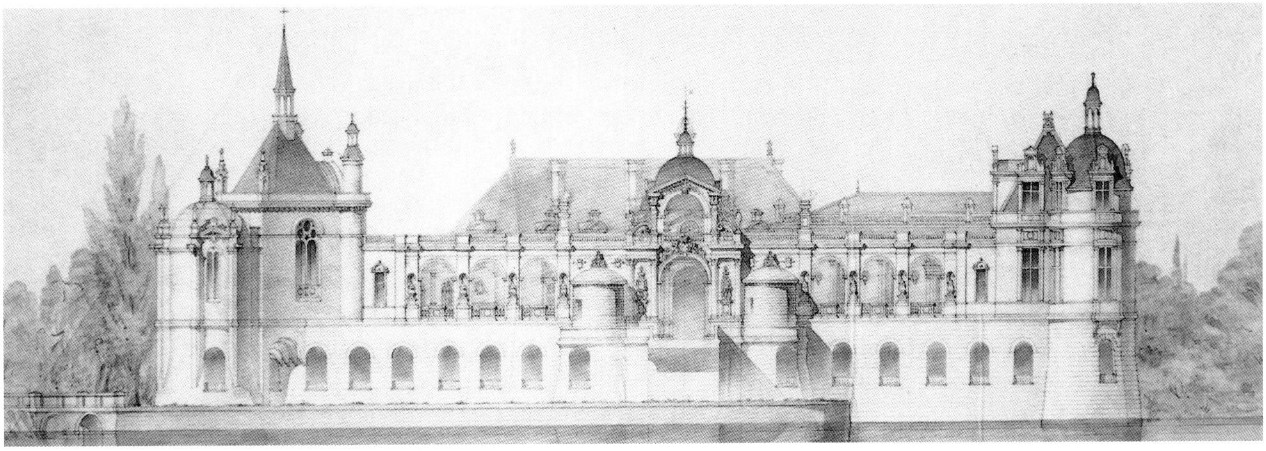

be very flexible and adaptable. Still undecided, the duke confided in one of his colleagues at the Institut de France, the art historian Anatole Gruyer[15], who recommended the name of Daumet. The interview between the two men on 23 August 1875 was decisive.

Pierre-Jérôme-Honoré Daumet, winner of the Grand Prix de Rome in 1855, combined all the requisite qualities. Born in 1826 in very modest circumstances, he had quickly made his name through his talent and his merits: he was hard-working, conscientious and determined. His participation in archaeological missions to the Villa Adriana at Tivoli, then on the site of ancient Pharsalia in Macedonia, had given him a direct knowledge of antique architecture, and his collaboration with Louis Duc on the building of the Palais de Justice in Paris had given him practical experience of monumental eclecticism in large public buildings. On his own he built the Chapel of the Ladies of Sion in Jerusalem and the Palais des Facultés in Grenoble, and in Paris he ran a highly reputed private studio which trained nine winners of the Grand Prix de Rome over twenty-five years. Together with his qualities as an ideal site architect, he had great skill as a draughtsman. His merits were widely recognised, and ensured him a very brilliant career, bringing commissions, honours, and the chairmanship of committees, as well as the recognition of his peers, who included his father-in-law the architect Questel, the creator of the neo-Romanesque style at Saint-Paul in Nîmes and the restorer of the château of Versailles. Thus all the conditions prerequisite to the reconstruction of Chantilly – the largest private building site in France – had come together: it was a true architectural event, and would be recognised in 1882 by a prize awarded by the Institut de France, of which Daumet was elected a member three years later.[16] Agreement between the two men was reached at the interview in August 1875, and Daumet immediately carried out the necessary alterations at the Petit Château so that the duke could move back in on 6 December. The day before that the architect presented his plans for the Grand Château, and they were approved. It was a hard task: "It was not easy to comply with the programme imposed by the duc d'Aumale: the builder had to construct the new buildings on the old foundations; consequently to respect an exceedingly awkward triangular ground plan, and to make reference to the style of the Petit Château, the only vestige of the ducal abode left standing; to give unity to buildings grouped in earlier times without any consideration for the overall effect. Along with that, vague documents, contradictory pieces of information, no measured drawings and an extremely intelligent client, a good judge, a learned archaeologist, a distinguished collector, but where architecture was concerned possessing a half-knowledge a thousand times worse than ignorance."[17]

Aumale had swept aside the advice given by friends that it would be better to rebuild the Terrasse du Connétable on an empty space which would make it possible to adopt the traditional configuration of a castle, replying that "all those who had planted their house on the same spot for nine hundred years knew what they were doing, and an isolated castle on that large site would be sad and monotonous; and finally, as in the old days, all the buildings had to be turned into a single entity by linking the Grand Château to the Petit Château."[18]

The operation undertaken went well beyond the construction of a private abode. In the 1870s, when the political future of France was under debate, Aumale had understood that he had a role to play, but in his own way, not by hectoring ministerial cabinets, the parliamentary assemblies or the electors, but by letting his presence be felt through a very widely recognised moral authority, and protecting his princely independence in a residence located at some distance from the capital. As in the time of the Great Condé, Chantilly again became a kind of Versailles, or rather an anti-Versailles. Recent circumstances had reinforced that plan. The death of his son recalled Aumale to some extent to his role as a special uncle, the uncle of the comte de Paris, born in 1838. The young prince was the head of the house of Orléans and the son of Aumale's beloved eldest brother; the "merger" negotiated in 1873 with the comte de Chambord

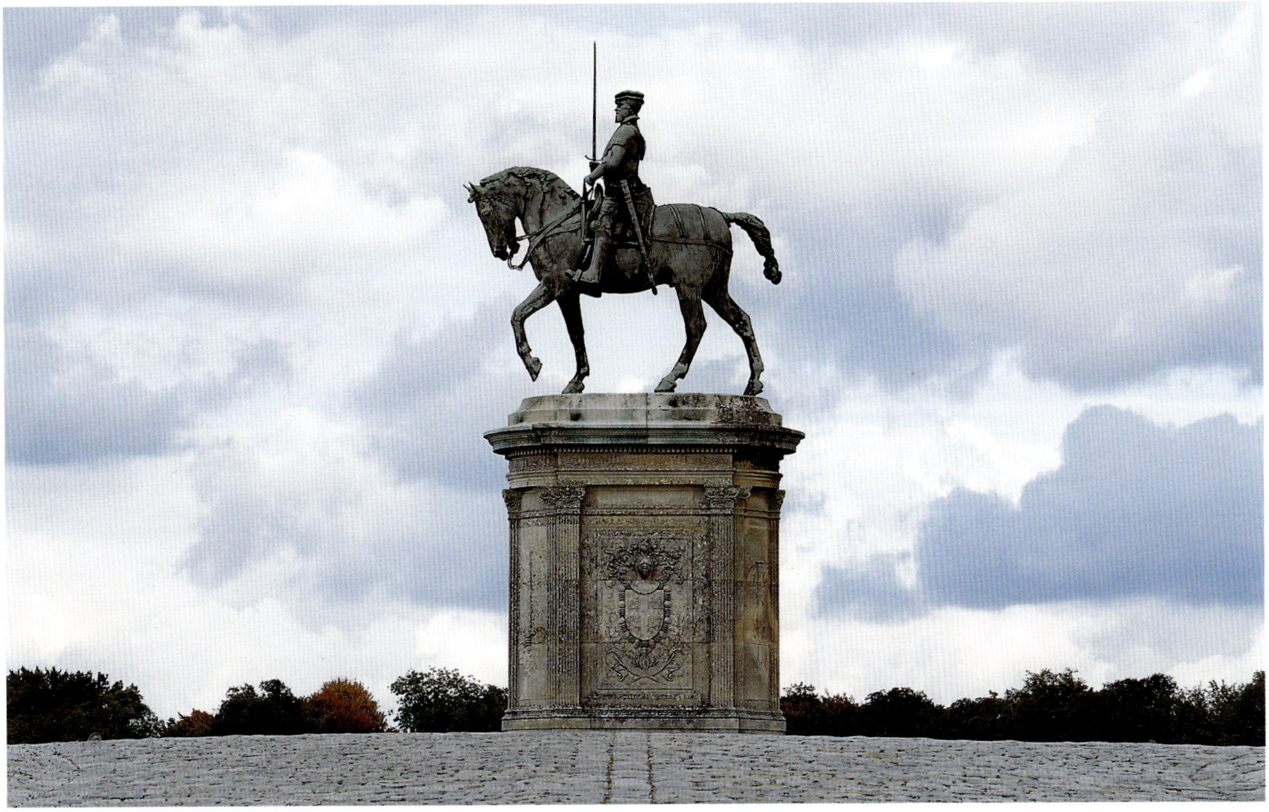

and the legitimists meant he would be the heir presumptive to the throne after the death of Charles X's grandson. But as the monarchists were losing ground daily, this had to be seen as a conceivable course of action, and Chantilly had to be made available as a residence to the young prince and his wife, Princess Isabelle, the daughter of the duc de Montpensier. Therefore Daumet's architecture had to take on the aspect of a manifesto.

The programme imposed by the brief went so far as to take account of this political dimension in the choice of style. Ruling out the classicism of Mansart, thc garb of the senior branch of the Bourbons which the 1814-15 Restoration had made unpopular, the architect turned rather to the Renaissance of the Valois kings, the period of Francis I and Henri II – had not Louis-Philippe been born duc de Valois? – Fontainebleau, Anet, and Écouen, to which he resorted in search of actual quotations, a very fashionable genre at the time.

Thus on the age-old triangle it was necessary to accommodate: 1 – A chapel standing apart from the residential blocks, a clear signal of the dynasty's unswerving faith, into which the bronze monument containing the hearts of the Princes de Condé, erected earlier (1648-63) by the sculptor Jacques Sarazin in the Jesuit

The statue of the Constable
The equestrian statue of Constable Anne de Montmorency, commissioned from Paul Dubois, was erected on the terrace of the château opposite the entrance in 1886. The same sculptor later carved the recumbent figure of the duc d'Aumale for his tomb in Dreux.

Following pages
The entrance façade

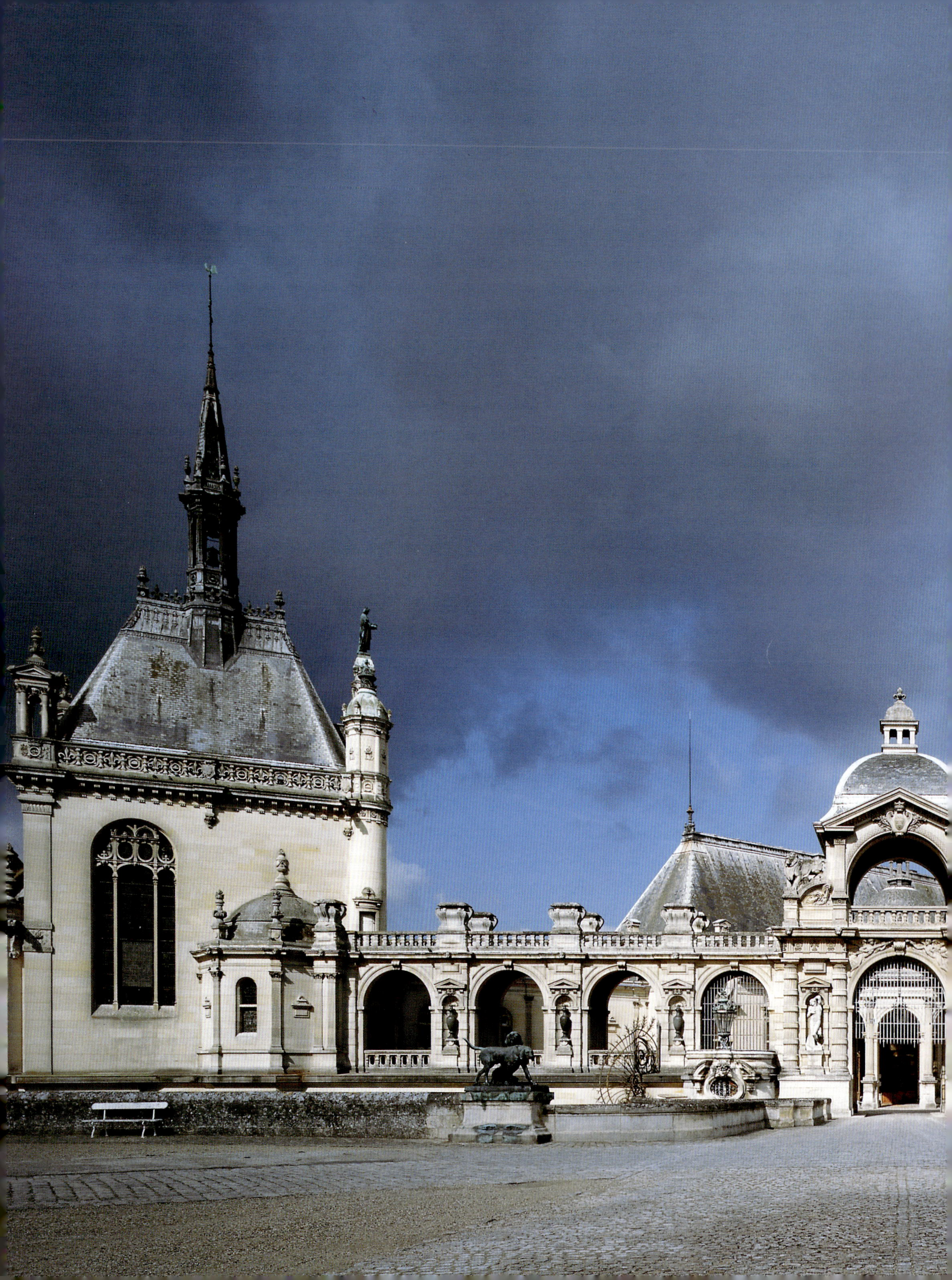

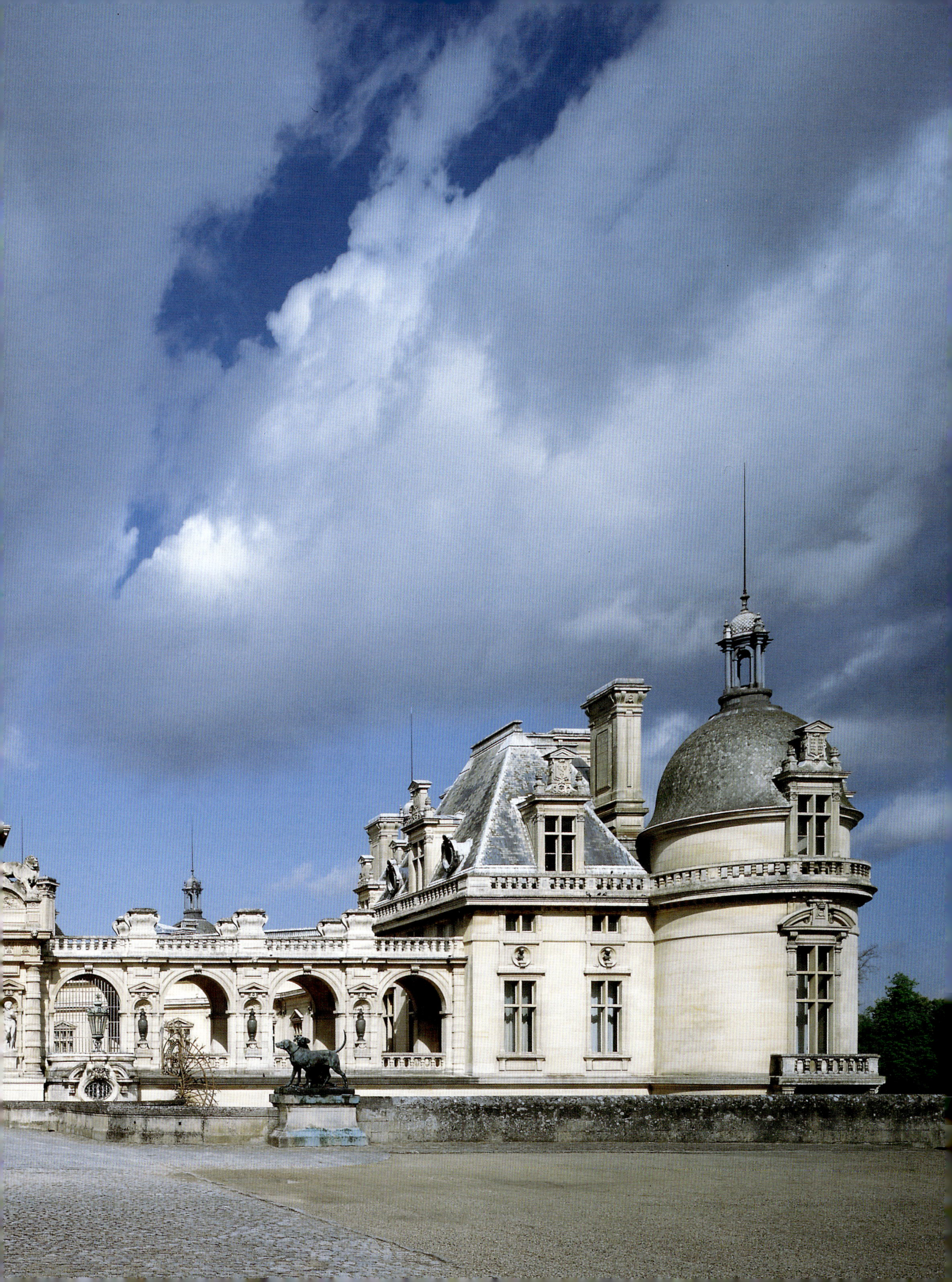

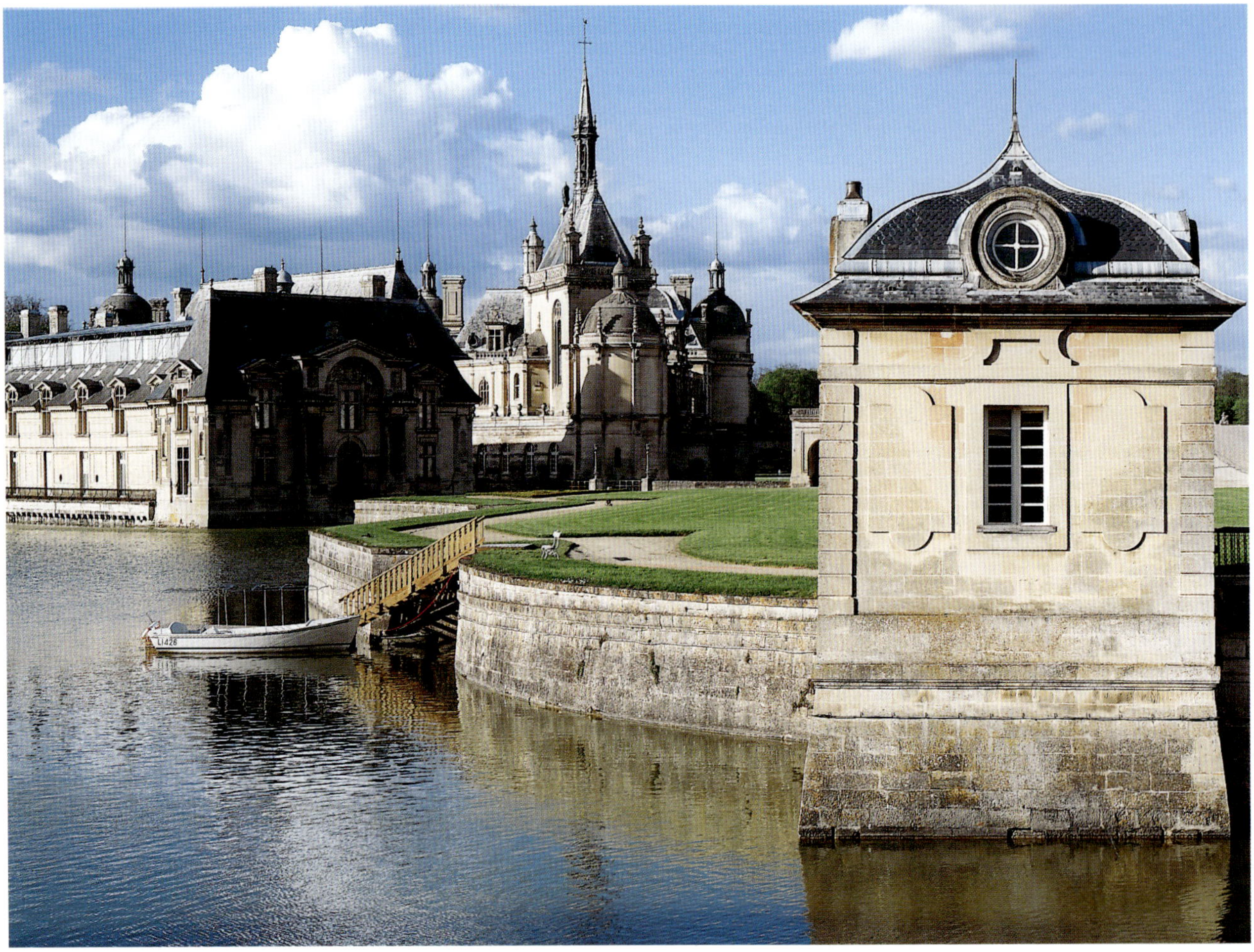

Entrance to the forecourt
One of the watch towers flanking the entrance railings.

church in Paris (Saint-Paul-Saint-Louis) and preserved from destruction in the Revolutions, had to be incorporated, as did the altar, marquetry woodwork and the two family stained-glass windows from the chapel of the Montmorencys at Écouen, dismantled at the time of the Revolution. 2 – A large residential block to house the rooms of the comte and comtesse de Paris. 3 – Reception rooms, in particular a large dining-room which was to be hung with the tapestries of *Emperor Maximilian at the Hunt*, woven in the eighteenth century and purchased in 1852. 4 – Museum rooms to accommodate the prince's collections which he had brought back from England and which were certain to increase, to which a gallery with windows would be added to house the set of stained-glass panels illustrating *The Story of Psyche*, brought from Écouen.

The château of a royal prince during the Republic

Daumet acquitted himself of his task with great skill, bearing in mind vistas and the balancing of masses, although he did pile on architectural gestures with excessive eloquence and somewhat garrulous erudition. We sense the close collaboration with Aumale in the principles adopted: the individualisation of each building pushed to the extreme – this had already been a characteristic of the buildings by Chambiges; the linear and in some way cohesive development of the rooms, English in manner; a consummate technique in dealing with links and levels to the point of making the drawings difficult to read; and perpetual reminders of the historical references associated with Chantilly, the finest examples being the huge bell-tower of the chapel, obviously inspired by the one that had soared above the loggia by Chambiges, and the name Galerie des Cerfs given to the dining-room, in memory of the very first building erected by Anne de Montmorency in the gardens.

Work started in 1876, the structural work was completed in 1882 and the decoration and finishes in 1885, before the second phase of alterations which we will talk about later on. The ground plan, volumes and layout were guided by an unswerving logic. At the centre of Le Nôtre's grand terrace, Aumale had the equestrian statue of a Constable re-erected, no longer Henri de Montmorency but Anne de Montmorency, commissioned in 1884 from the sculptor Paul Dubois and installed two years later. "*Hic stat, pro aedibus suis renovatis, Annas Momorantius.*" This is the crucial signal, visual, historical and political, designating the man whose true heir Aumale wished to be at Chantilly, and in a way it was the château of the Constable, the steadfast supporter of the Valois monarchy, that Daumet was called upon to resurrect, with its moats, drawbridge, portcullis, spiral staircases and tall towers, four out of seven reconstituted to punctuate the jagged, subtopean silhouette so characteristic of the new Chantilly. To underline this dedication even further, the duke had copies of Michelangelo's *Slaves*, the pride of the Constable's château at Écouen, placed in the niches of the entrance pavilion. Opposite the bronze horseback figure which dominates the landscape from on high stands the low entrance wing, a gallery rendered transparent by its eight wide arches and interrupted at the centre by a pavilion with a domed roof, a real set piece echoing Bullant's portico that can be seen lower down on the left; it is very directly inspired by the gate known as the Porte du Baptistère at the château of Fontainebleau, the

Following page

The chapel seen from the main court

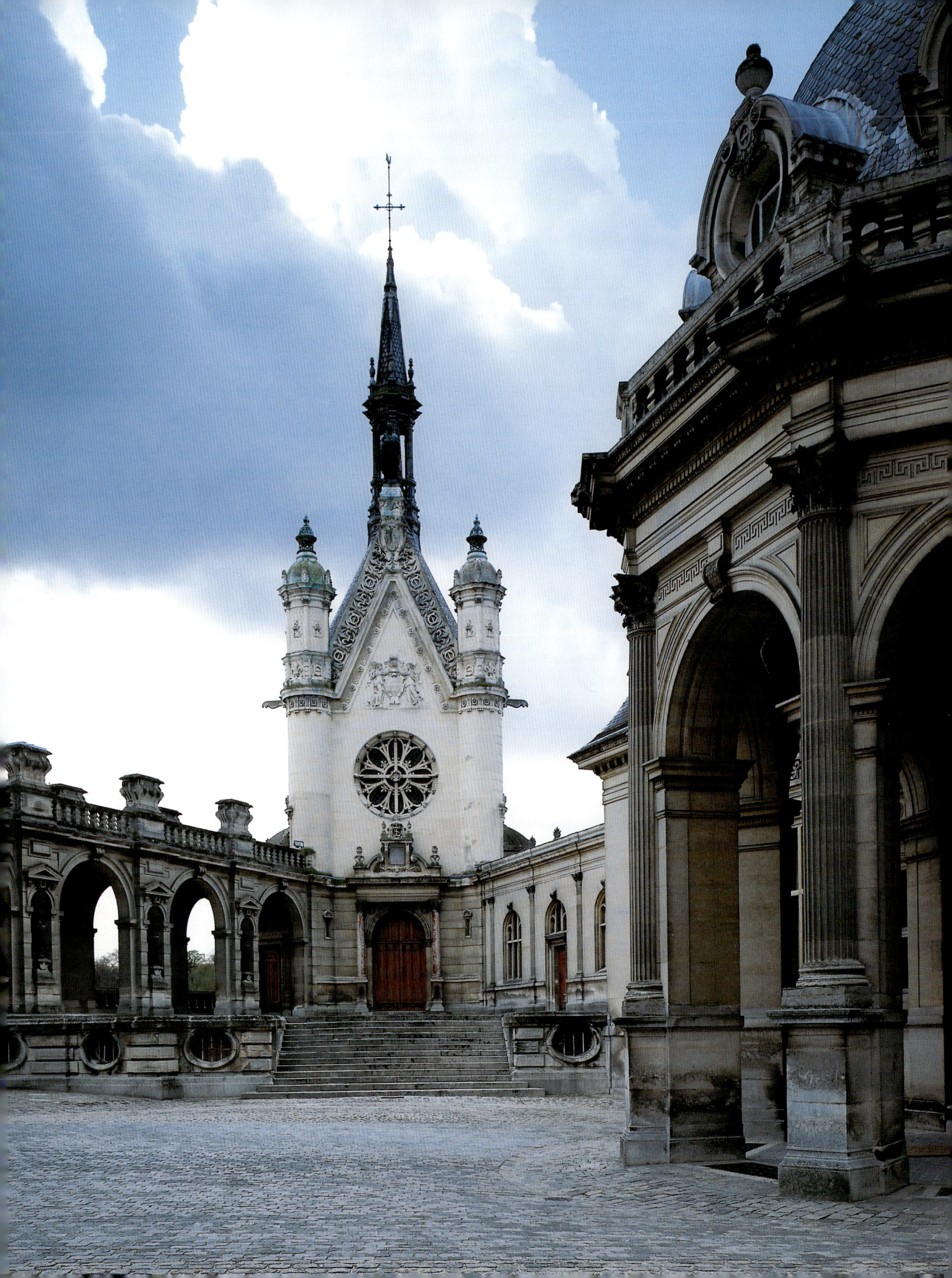

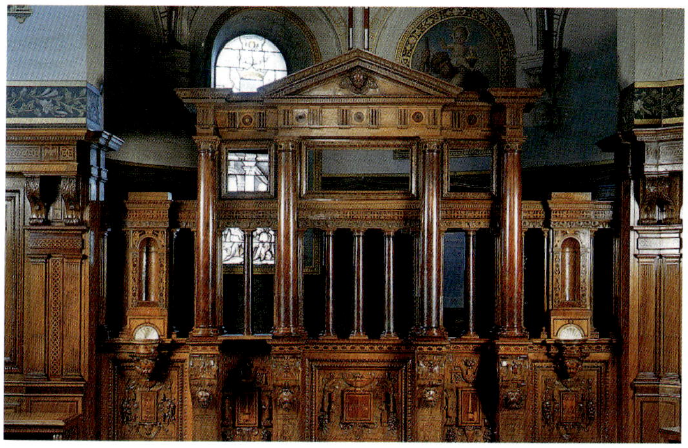

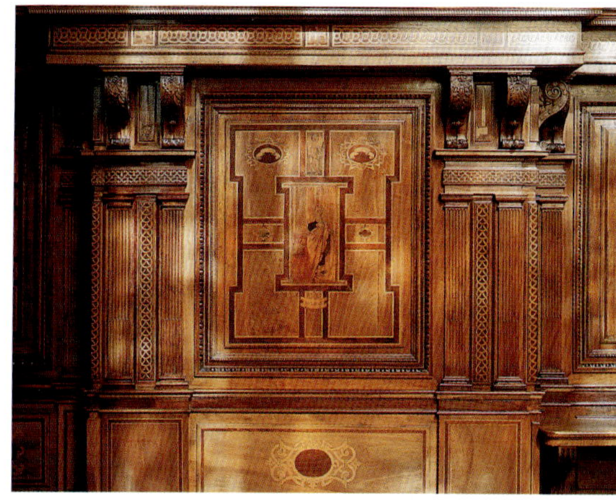

Enclosure in the chapel
This railing closes off one of the two side-chambers of the chapel.

Marquetry panel from Écouen
Like the altar and the windows (see p. 29), valuable marquetry panels depicting the Apostles (1548) came from the chapel of Écouen.

The tombs of the hearts of the Condés
Made after models by Jacques Sarazin installed in the church of Saint-Paul-Saint-Louis in Paris in 1663, the bronze Virtues from the monument were installed in the Tour de Paris behind the chapel by Honoré Daumet.

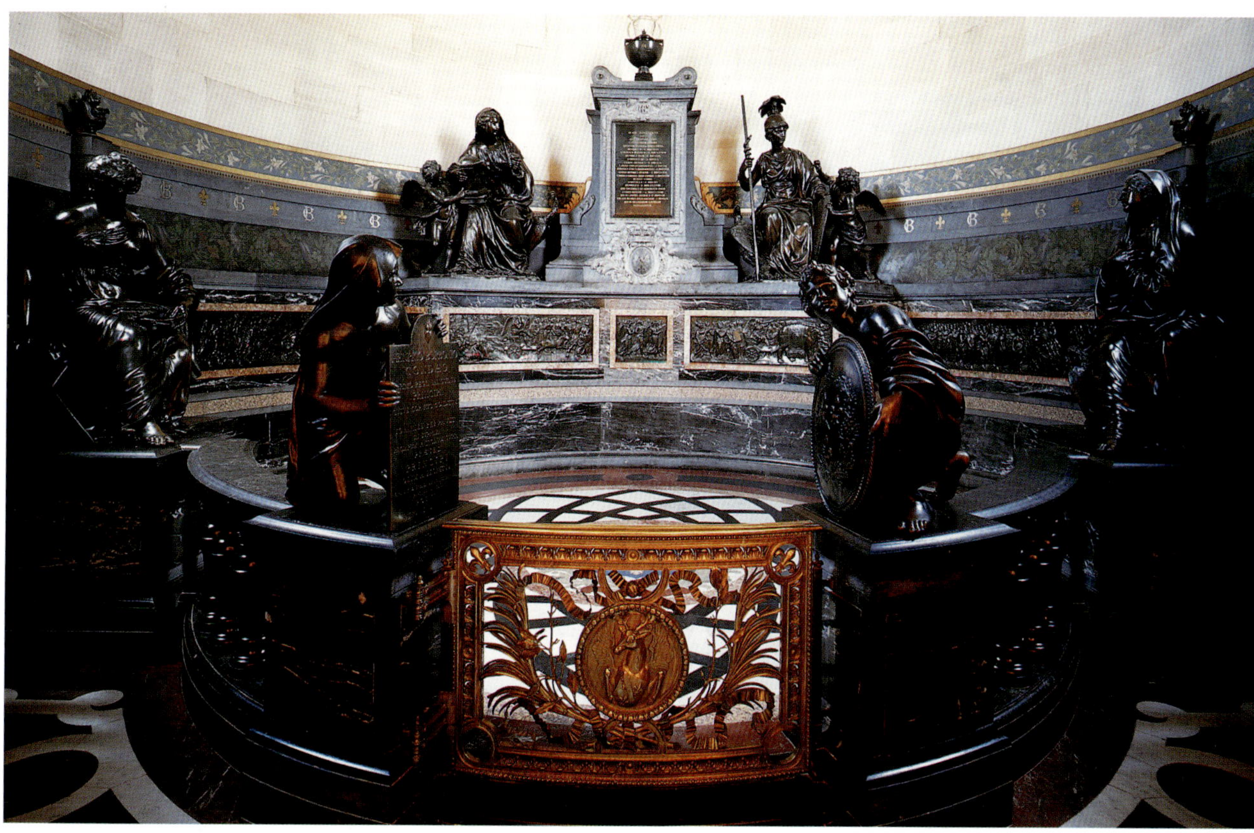

work of Primaticcio rebuilt in earlier times by Henri IV, which Eugène Lami had already considered copying at this spot.[19]

The entrance wing is framed by the taller masses of the residential block on the right and the chapel on the left. Duban had already planned to erect the chapel on the acute point of the triangle, where the main eighteenth-century staircase had been, on the base of the old kitchens, but he was uncertain of which side of the angle to centre it on. Daumet happily hit on a third solution, bisecting the angle and cleverly softening the link with the gallery by means of a corbelled oratory, which has a symmetrical counterpart on the south side. Thus the chapel can present its façade axially to the main court, where it rises at the back of a triangular parvis standing twelve or so steps above the level of the main court. Dedicated as was only fitting to Saint Louis, whose statue in bronze by Marqueste (1878) tops the gable, it follows the same rectangular ground plan as the chapel of Écouen, and at the far end leads into a second smaller chapel serving as an apse, erected on the circular base of the Tour de Paris (or Tour de la Glacière) and topped by a stone cupola. This was intended to become the funerary chapel of the Condés, and receive the monuments of their hearts brought from Saint-Paul-Saint-Louis.

Daumet's consummate skill can be recognised in his handling of the court; the differences in level enable it to act as the central hub of the entire arrangement for all floors. Opposite the entrance, a polygonal pavilion with a domed roof, which again picks up one of Duban's ideas, provides the undercover alighting point for carriages which was a recent added conveniences in the architecture of publics and private buildings, at Garnier's Opéra for example, although it was already an old idea advocated by Bernini at the time of his famous journey to Paris in 1665.

From the pavilion there is level access to the main vestibule, magnificently decorated, which leads on the level to the first-floor rooms of the Petit Château. Daumet radically altered the internal layout of Bullant's château, which was still the residence of the duke. Thus in the connecting bays constructed by the duc de Bourbon at the beginning of the century, he fitted out the first rooms that preceded the Grande Chambre: the Salon de l'Antichambre which ends in an apse and the Salle des Gardes or Salon d'Europe, thus named because of the mosaic from Herculaneum depicting the rape of Europa which came from the estate of the Prince of Salerno and was inserted above the Renaissance-style chimney-piece. The former service rooms located on the south-east side were

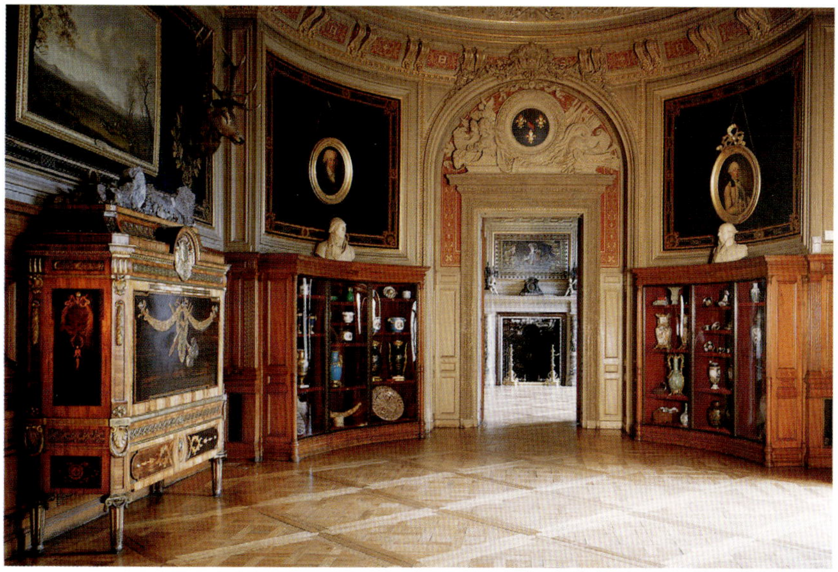

The Antechamber
This room is located in the extension of the Bullant building built in 1821 above the moat. On the left we can recognise the mineralogical cabinet. On the display cabinets are busts of the Prince de Conti and the duc de Bourbon.

replaced by the Cabinet des Livres, which was fitted out in a way reminiscent of the library used by the prince during his exile at Twickenham. Here he could house the most precious of his books and manuscripts, under the commanding eye of the Great Condé whose bust by Coysevox adorned the chimney-piece. On the ground floor, to make the suites of rooms more convenient, Daumet created a gallery along the court which joined the gallery installed at right angles by his predecessor Duban. From the level of the main vestibule, a deep hole had been dug in the rocky ground to ensure the vertical links required. A staircase with an oval stairwell, taking up the ground plan of Jean Aubert's chapel in the eighteenth century at a place where Dubois had already considered installing a staircase, made it possible to go down to the lower vestibule towards the billiard room, known as the Salon du Roi, and the vaulted rooms of the old castle. It also made it possible to reach the lower level of the Petit Château: on the one hand the Daumet gallery which provided access to the suites of rooms, and on the other the Jardin de la Volière which, since the moat had been filled in, extended right to the foot of the Grand Château and was linked with it by means of an enormous flight of steps.

From the main vestibule there was access on the left, via the two arms of the upper landing of the staircase, to an enclosed portico which led under cover to the chapel. Opposite that, as we have said, was the entrance to the suites of rooms in the Petit Château. On the right a few steps led into the large hall forming the dining-room, known as the Galerie des Cerfs; its decoration was inspired by the

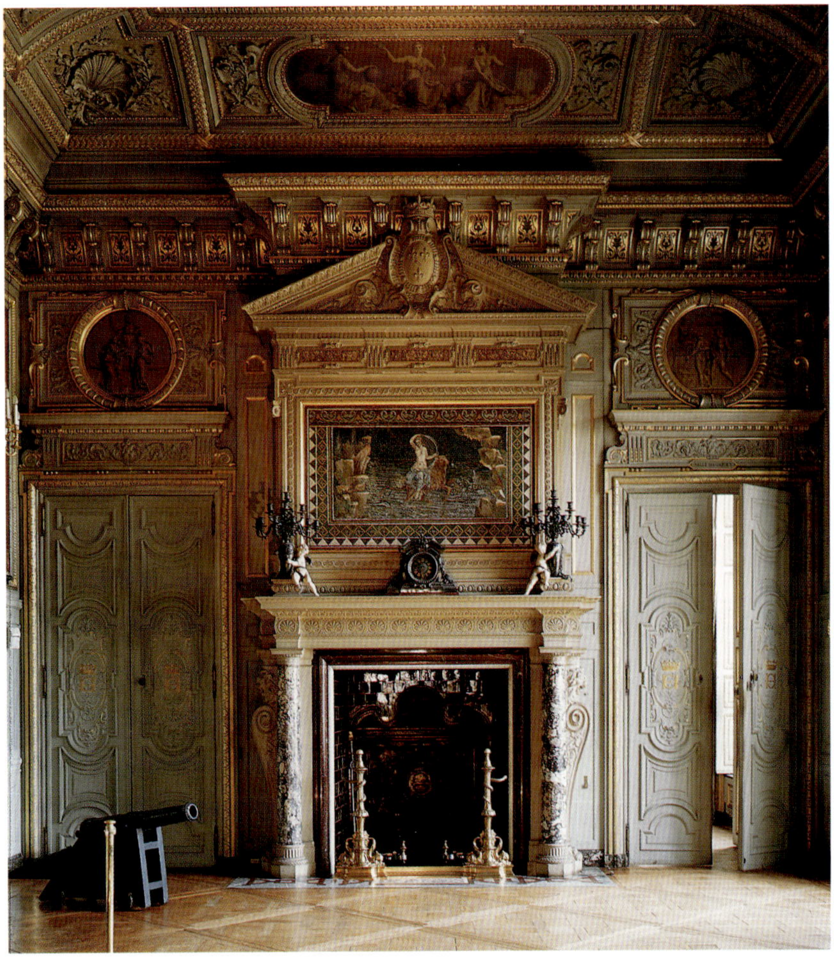

The Salle des Gardes
Above the fireplace is a mosaic from Herculaneum portraying the rape of Europa.

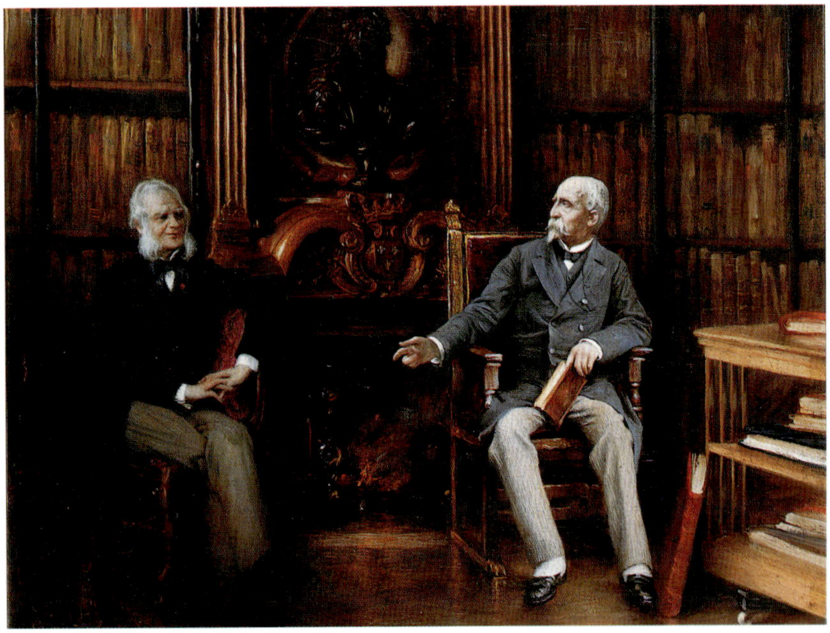

The duc d'Aumale and Cuvillier-Fleury
This domestic scene painted by Gabriel Ferrier around 1880 shows the two men in the Cabinet des Livres: the prince with his former tutor who had become his scholarly collaborator.

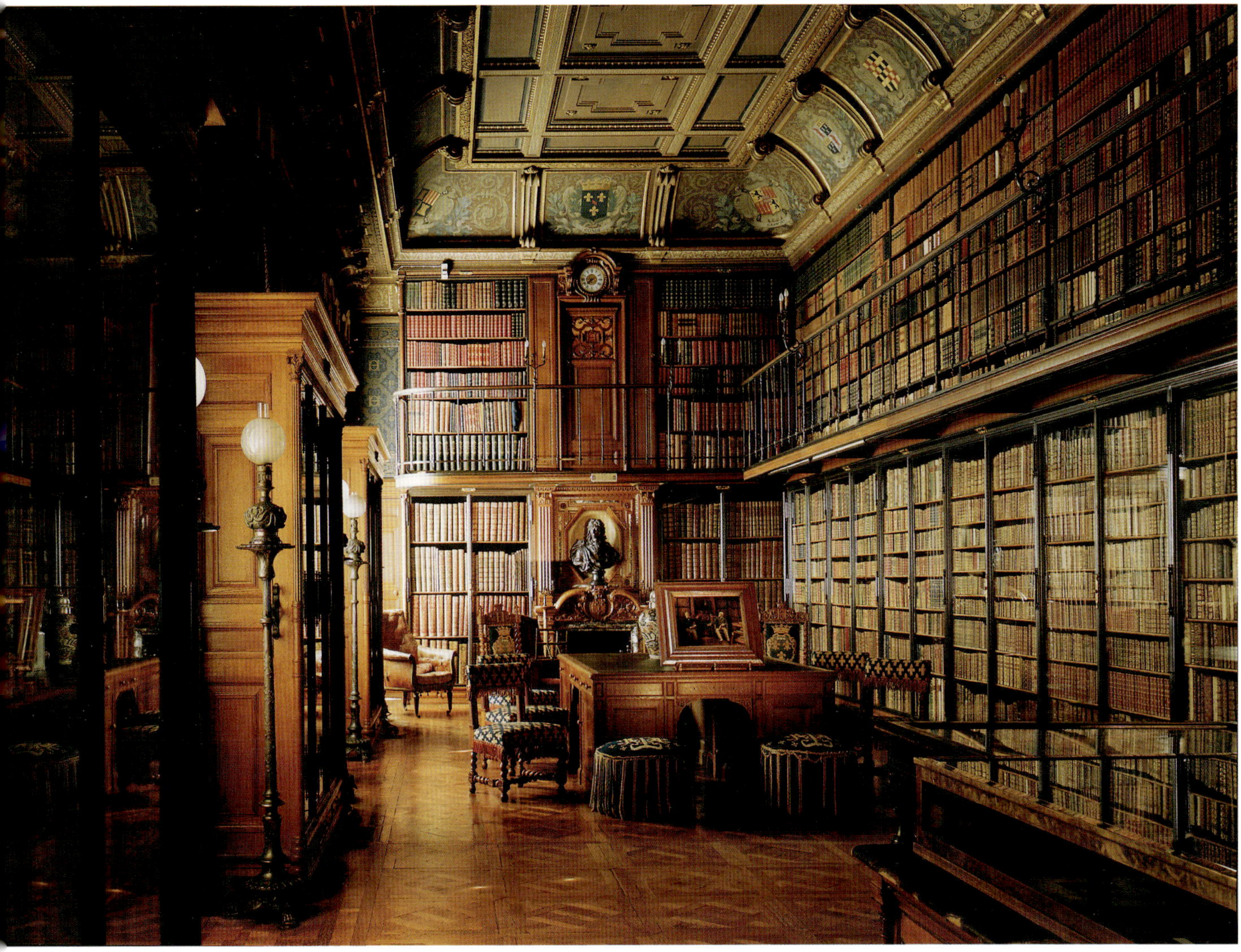

The Cabinet des Livres

The book room was arranged to hold the treasures that the prince, an astute book-lover, had accumulated throughout his life:
13,000 volumes, including 2,000 manuscripts.

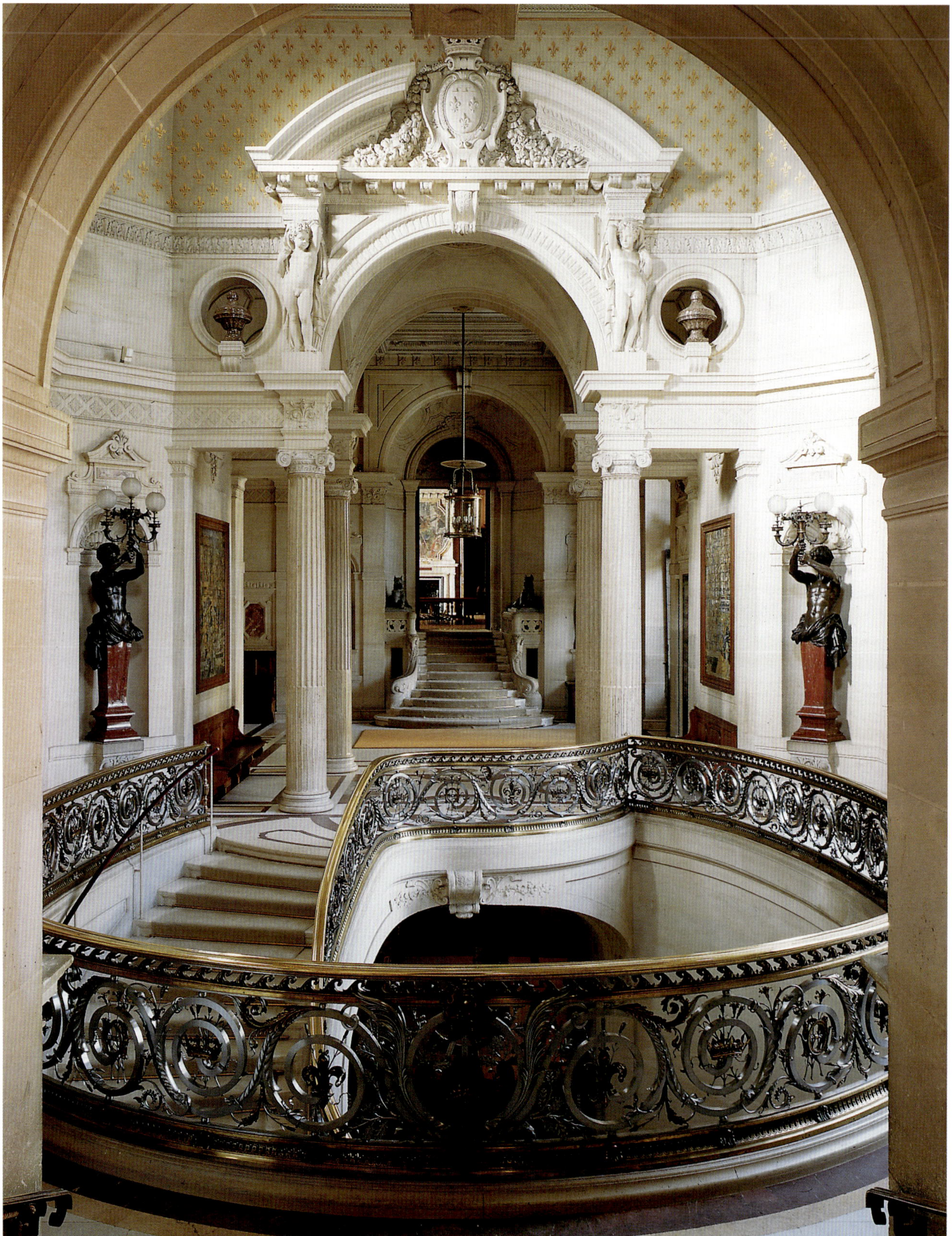

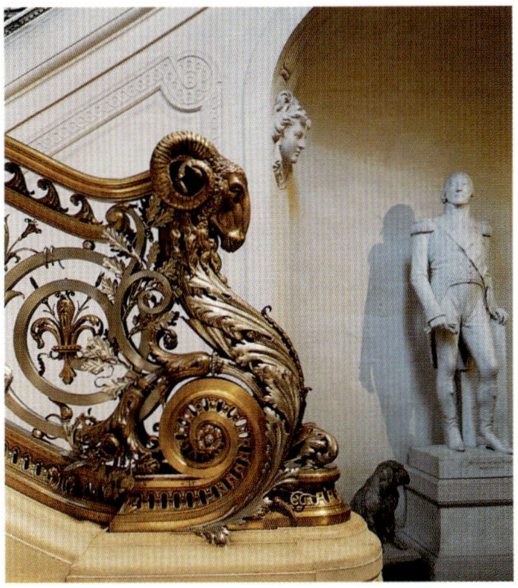

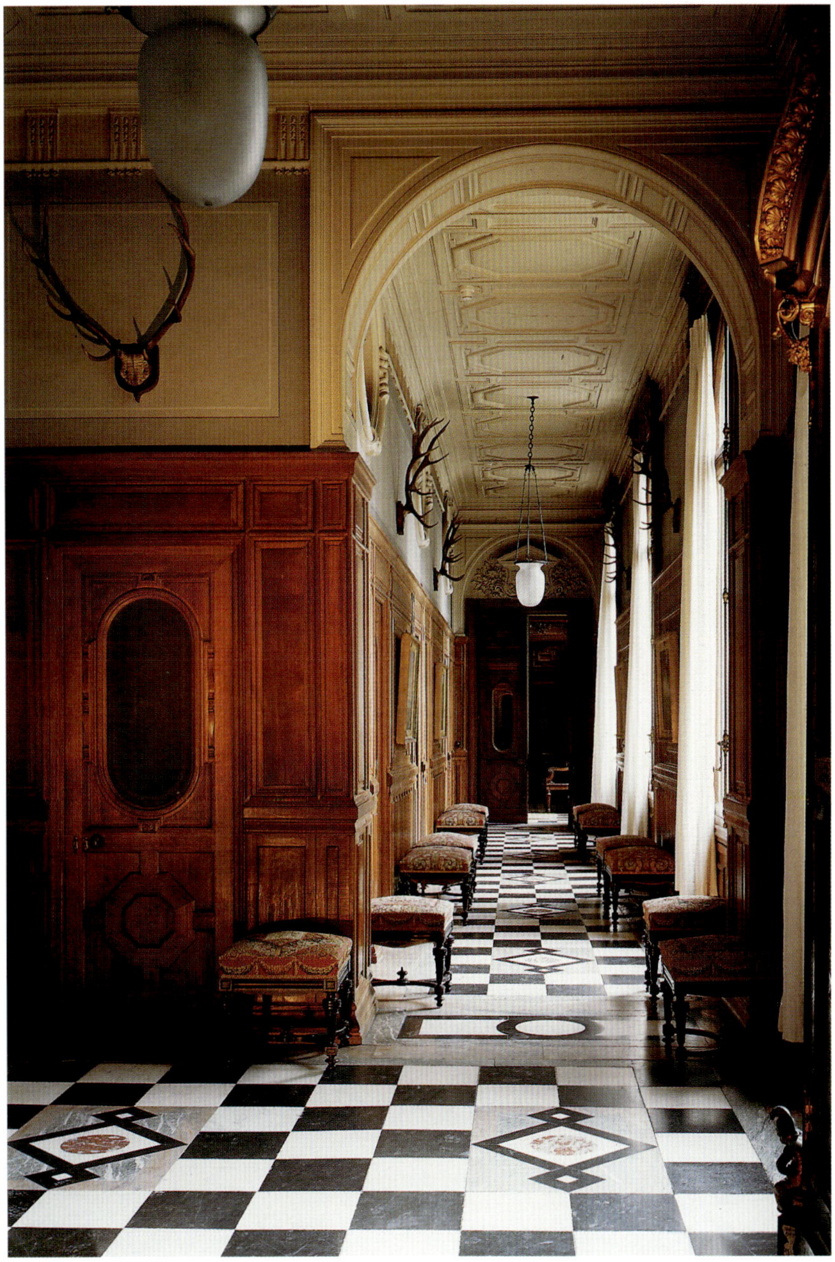

The bottom of the handrail
At the foot of the staircase stands a statue of the duc de Bourbon, a copy in marble by Ch. Jonchery after the plaster statue by P.-J.-H. Lemaire.

The Daumet gallery
This joins up with the Duban gallery to connect the suites of rooms in the Petit Château to the lower vestibule of the grand staircase.

The grand staircase
The magnificence of the handrail and the grace of the figures bearing candelabra, cast from a drawings by Chapu, are admirable.

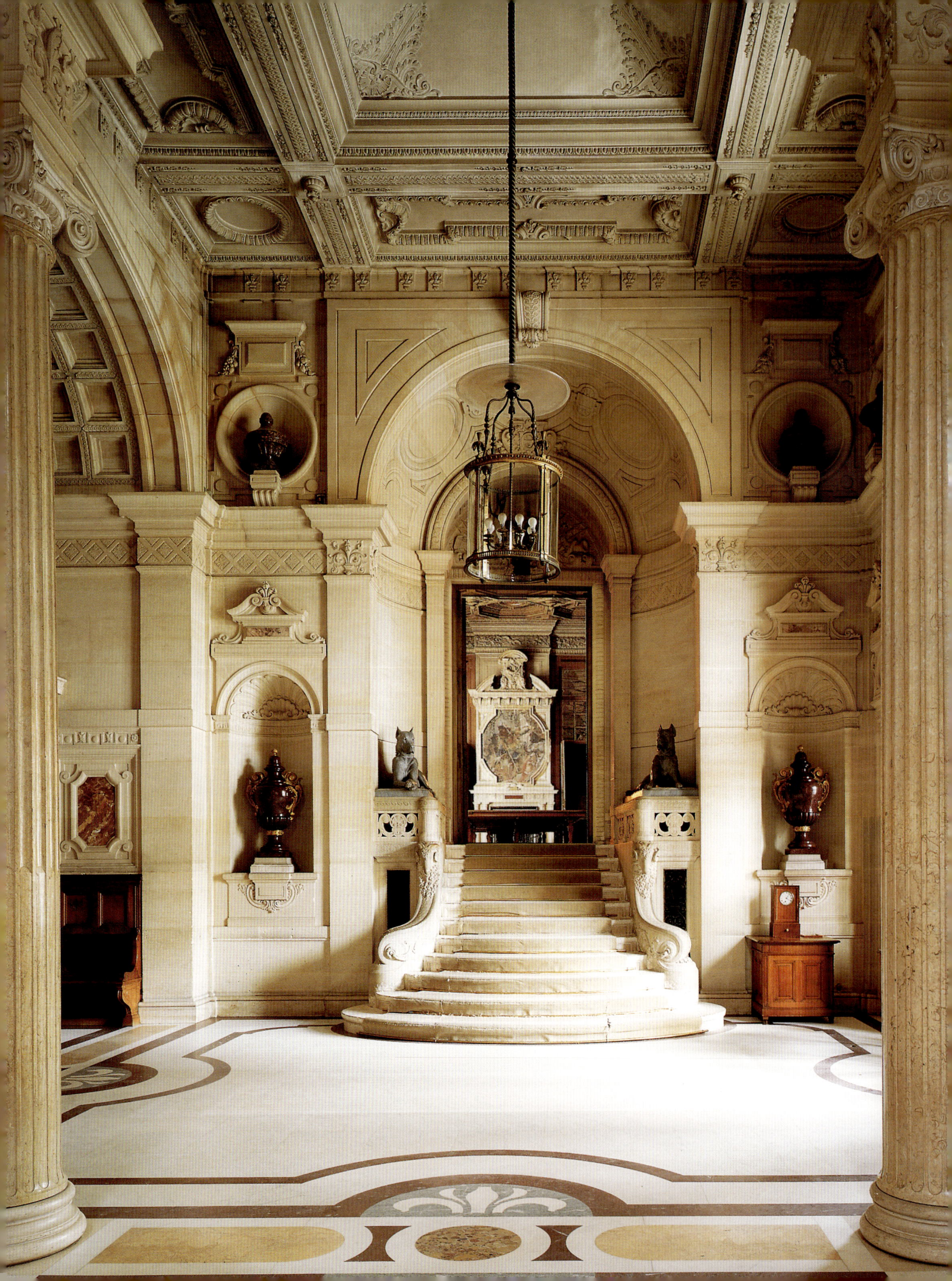

Opposite

The main vestibule
The grand style of Renaissance and classical-period palaces was chosen for the vestibule, which serves the entire château. In the background is the Galerie des Cerfs.

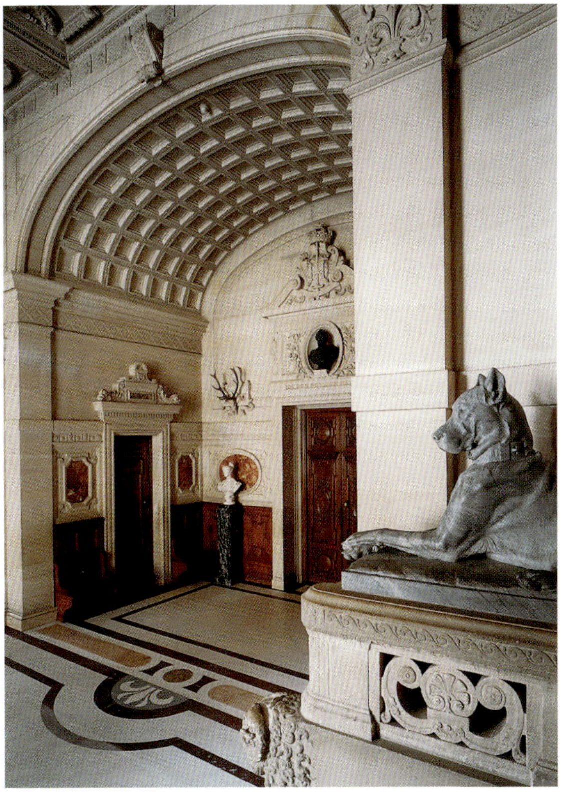

The entrance to the main suites of room
The main vestibule leads through to the Antechamber under a coffered arch.

The Galerie des Cerfs
The large dining-room bears the name of the first structure the Constable built at Chantilly. On the walls hang the tapestries of *Emperor Maximilian at the Hunt.*

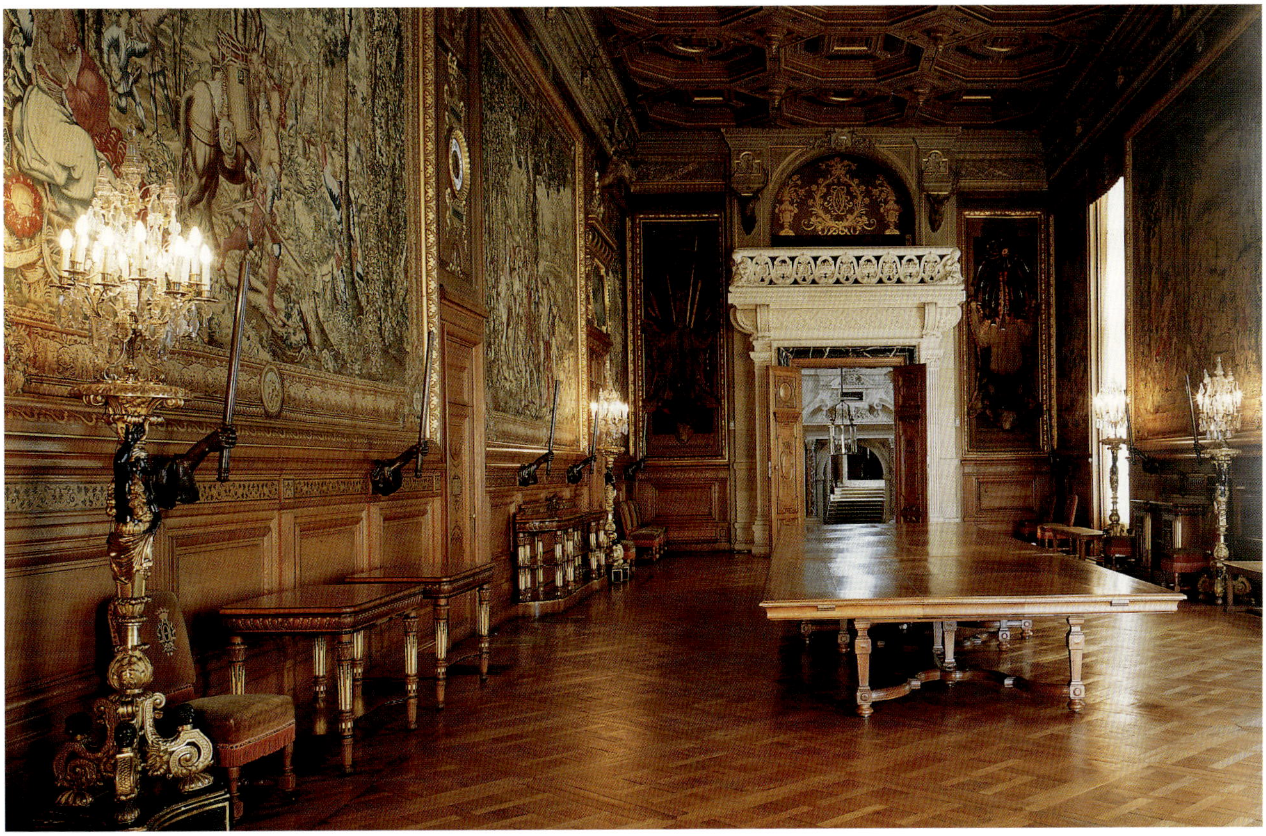

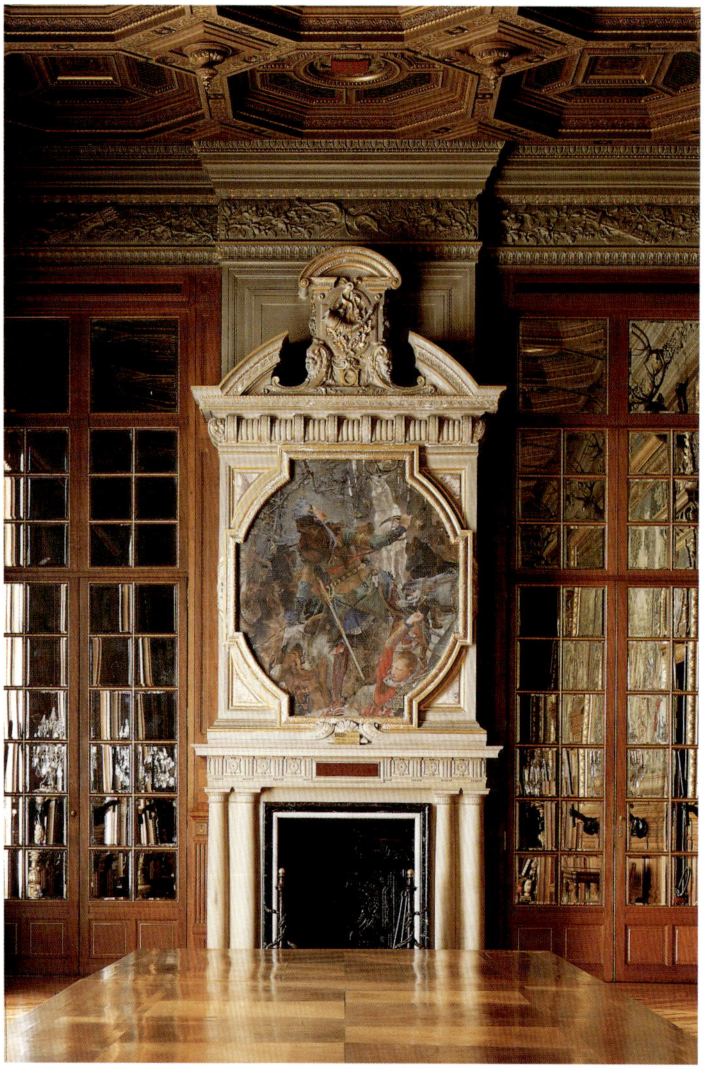

The chimney-piece in the Galerie des Cerfs
In 1882 Paul Baudry painted *The Vision of Saint Hubert* in which the figures of the duc de Chartres and the duc d'Orléans, the brother and the son of the comte de Paris, can be recognised.

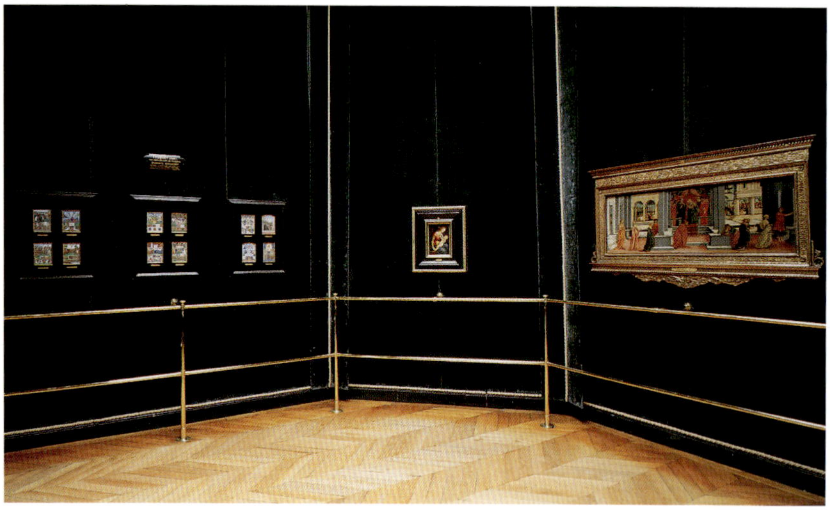

The Santuario
Decorated in dark velvet, this small pentagonal room was intended to house prints.

ballroom at Fontainebleau, with high wainscoting under the tapestries, a chimney-piece, a musicians' gallery and a coffered ceiling. At the far end it leads into the exhibition rooms of the museum, the domain of the collector. The handling of the west tip of the platform at Chantilly, which forms an irregular triangle running between the Tour de Vineuil and the Tour du Trésor and the projecting end of a residential block (now the dining-room) always caused architects great difficulty, for it was impossible to make any court worthy of the name at its centre. Duban had suggested using the central space as a library with a circular ground plan and top lighting, an interesting innovation which was not followed up as it seemed preferable to have the library closer to the rooms of the book-loving prince and keep more space for pictures. But Daumet retained the idea of using the centre of the triangle for individually designed pavilions with top lighting, looking to Italian architecture for inspiration, though they are reminiscent of the layout of some English country houses, also designed to present collections of pictures. The small *Santuario* was intended to house prints, and today we can admire the priceless works of Raphael and the miniatures of Fouquet, while the larger octagonal *Tribune*, with windows overlooking the Jardin de la Volière on the smallest side of the triangle, houses some of the major works in the collection, by Poussin, Van Dyck, Champaigne, Watteau, Delacroix and Ingres. The ceiling cove was decorated with paintings depicting abodes and childhood places which had fond memories for the prince.

To the east, the long side of the triangle is filled by the large volume of the Painting Gallery, backing on to the main court; on one side it opens into the Galerie des Cerfs and on the other into the Tour de Vineuil (also known as the Tour de Senlis). It is handled as a rotunda and brightly lit from windows overlooking the park. Finally between the Tour de Vineuil and the Tour du Trésor, the latter containing the Cabinet des Gemmes, the last side of the triangle is occupied by another gallery whose windows hold the forty-four stained glass panels illustrating the *Story of Psyche*. This low gallery is obviously inspired by the one in the château designed by Chambiges, which had likewise been picked up in Duban's scheme; it made it possible to open up the view of the internal volumes of the triangle from the outside.

On the north side of the main court, decorated with the coats of arms of all the families who had owned Chantilly, stands the block intended as a residence for the comte and comtesse de Paris, two suites of rooms at ground-floor level

Following pages

The Painting Gallery and its rotunda

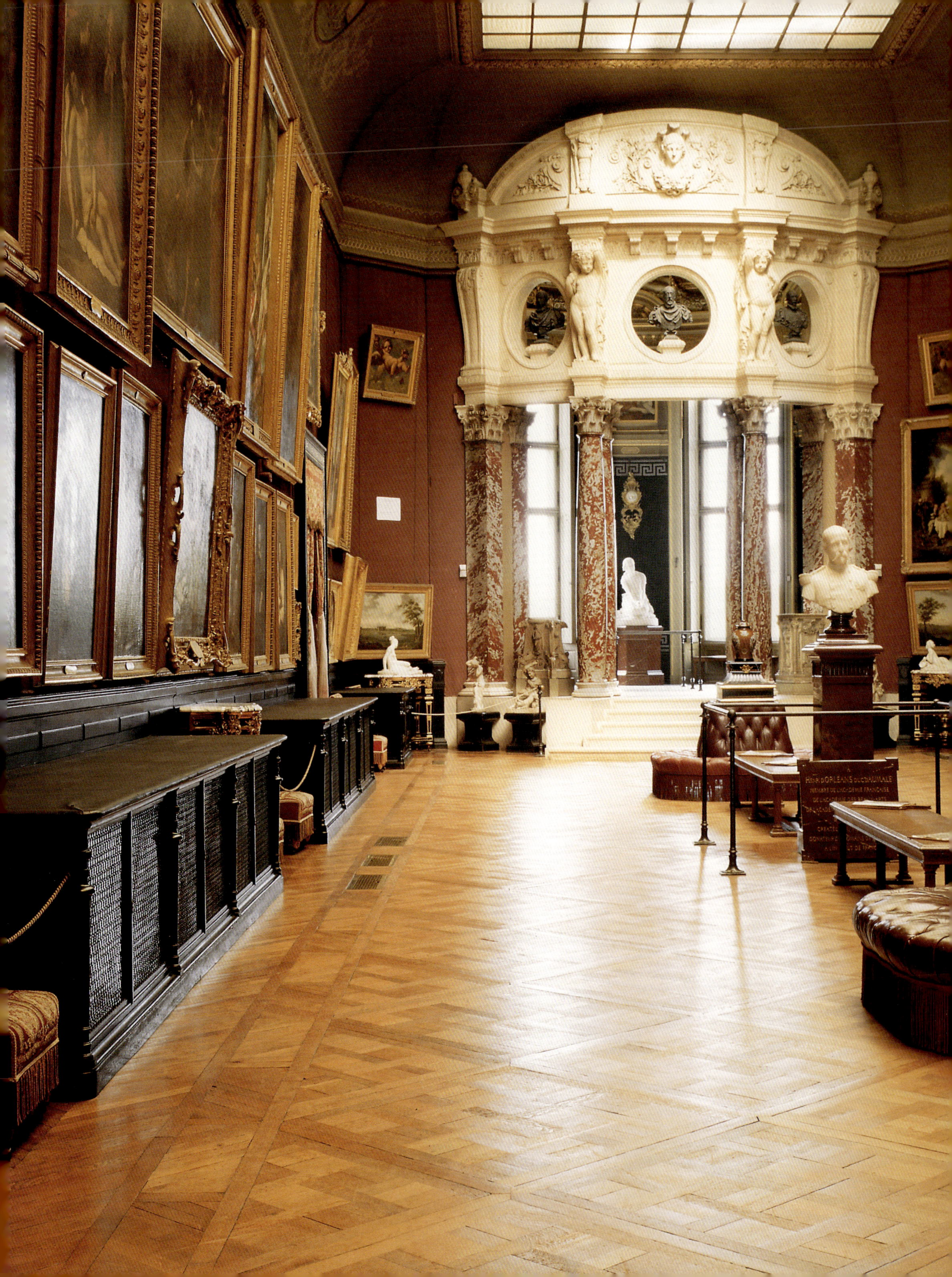
A
HENRI D'ORLEANS DUC D'AUMALE
MEMBRE DE L'ACADEMIE FRANÇAISE

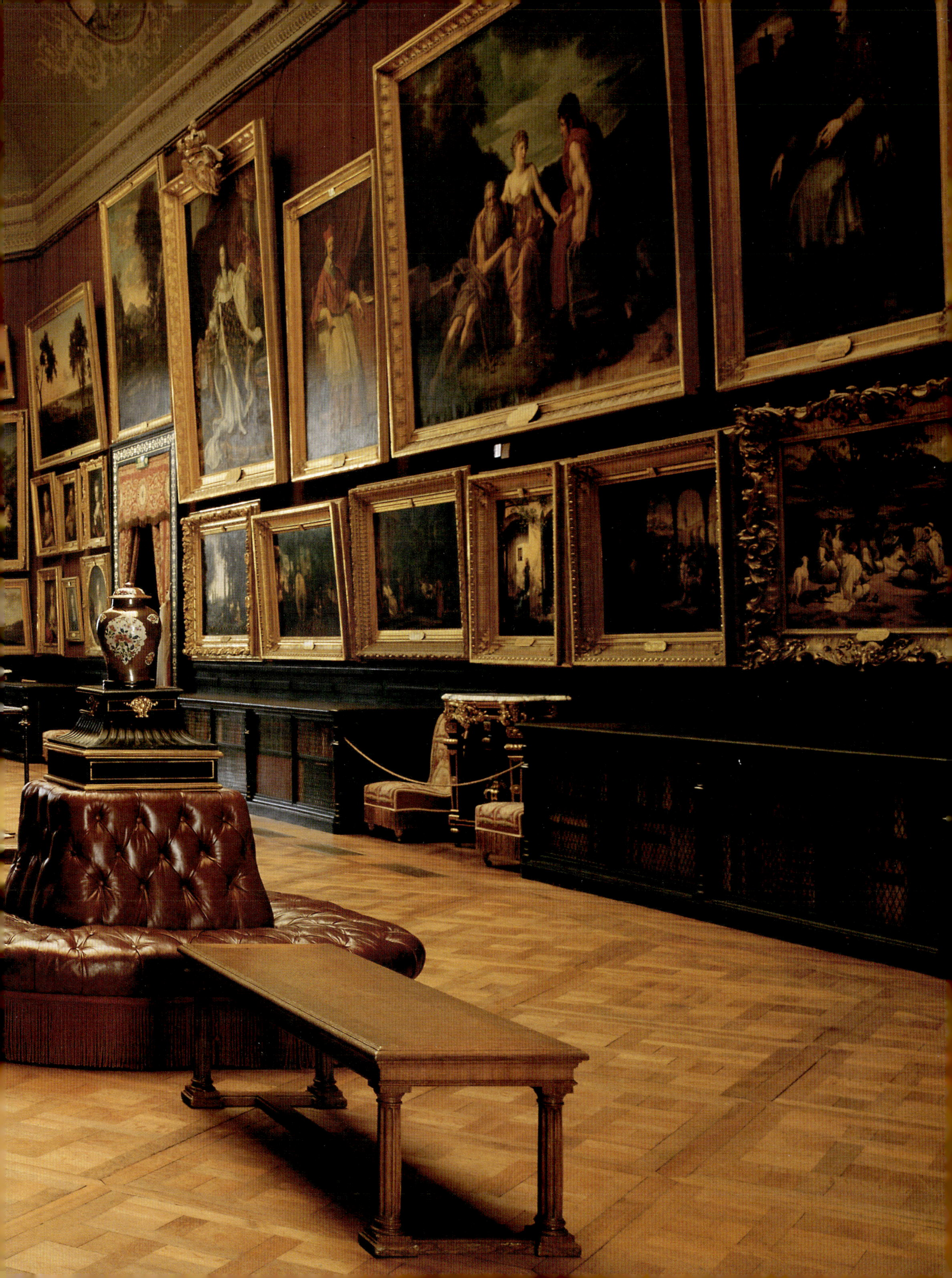

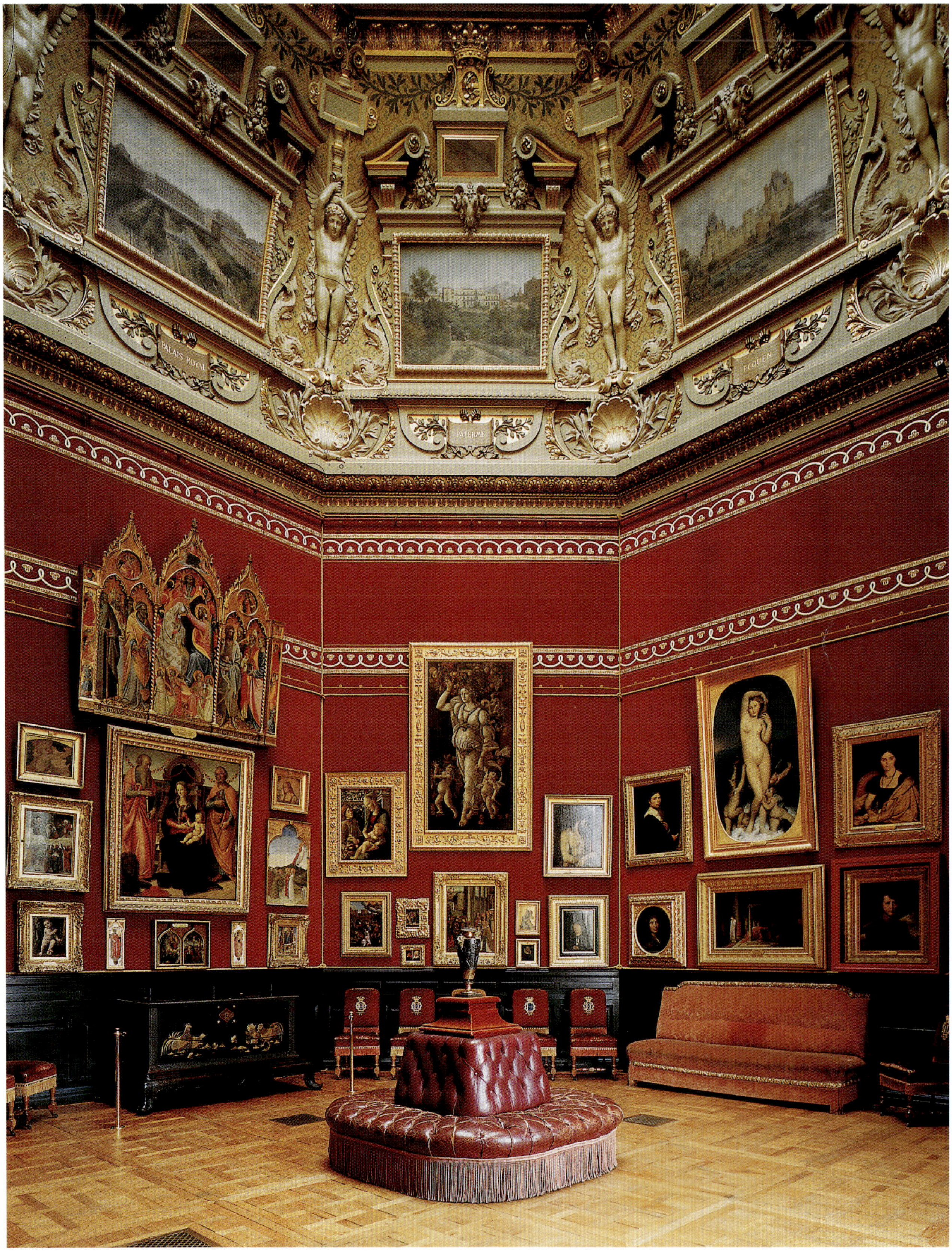
PALAIS ROYAL
PALERME
ECOUEN

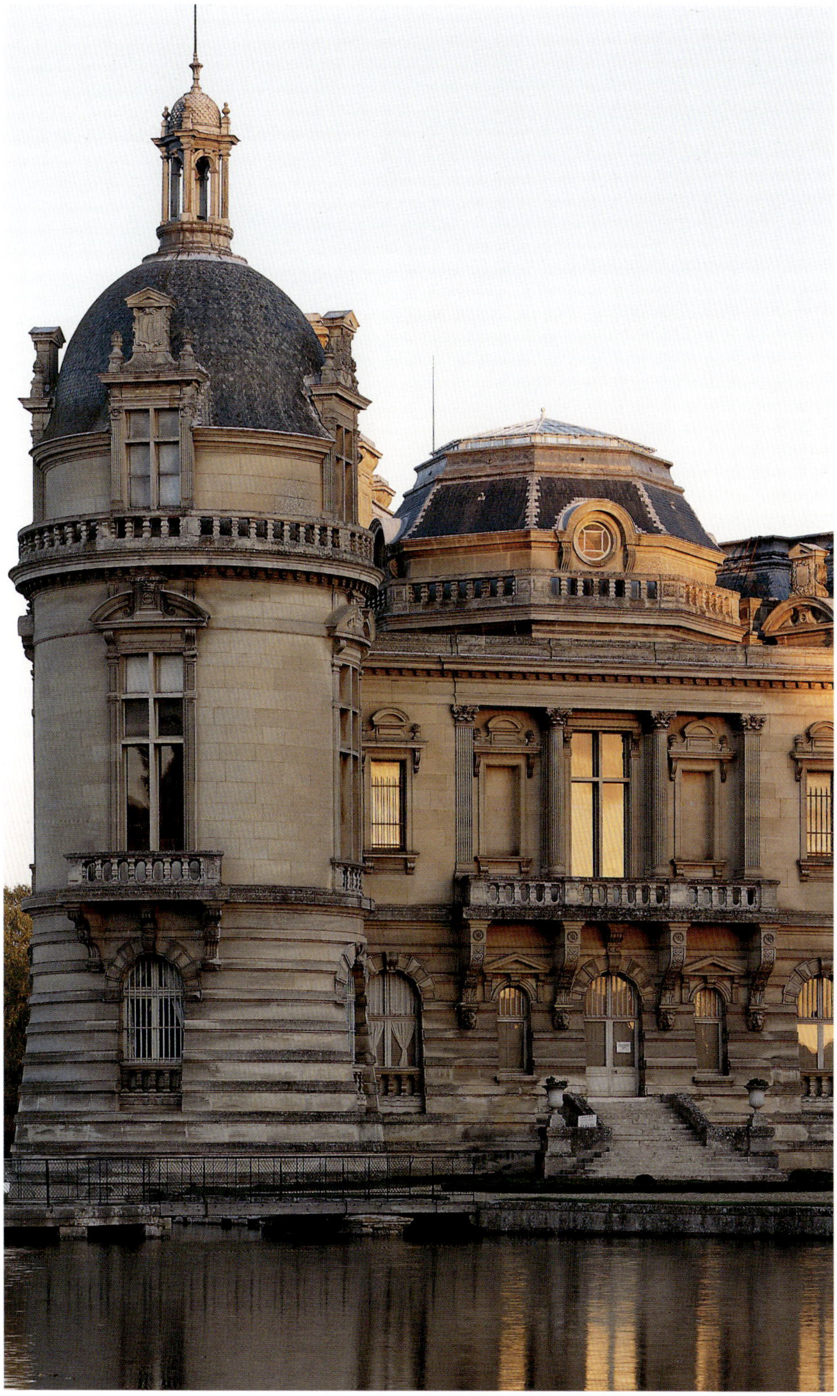

The Tour du Trésor and the Tribune
Below the Tribune, a perron provides access to the Jardin de la Volière.

The Tribune
The masterpieces from the collection, irrespective of schools and centuries, are hung here beneath the high coving on which the prince commissioned Armand Bernard to depict the places dearest to him.

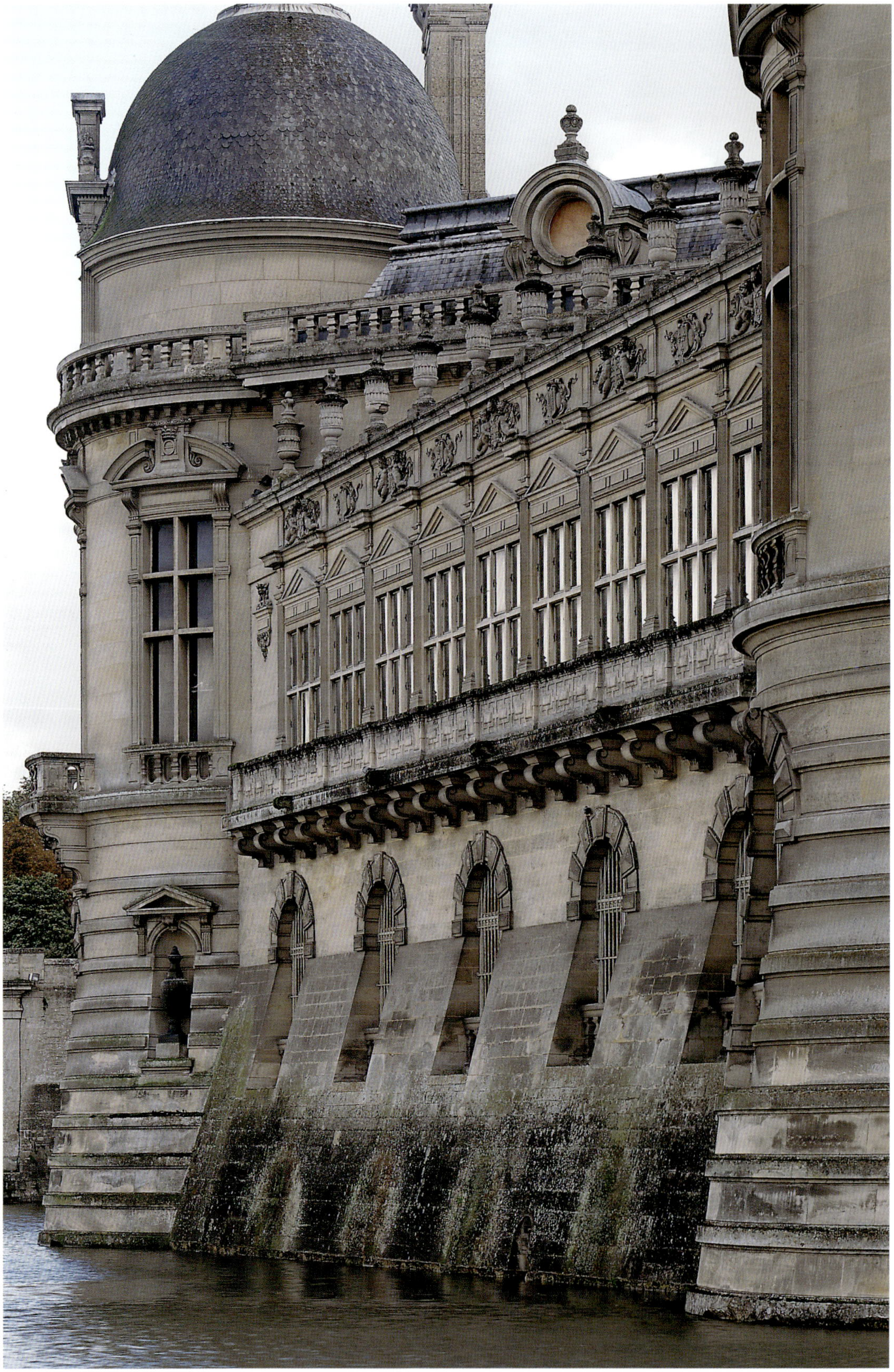

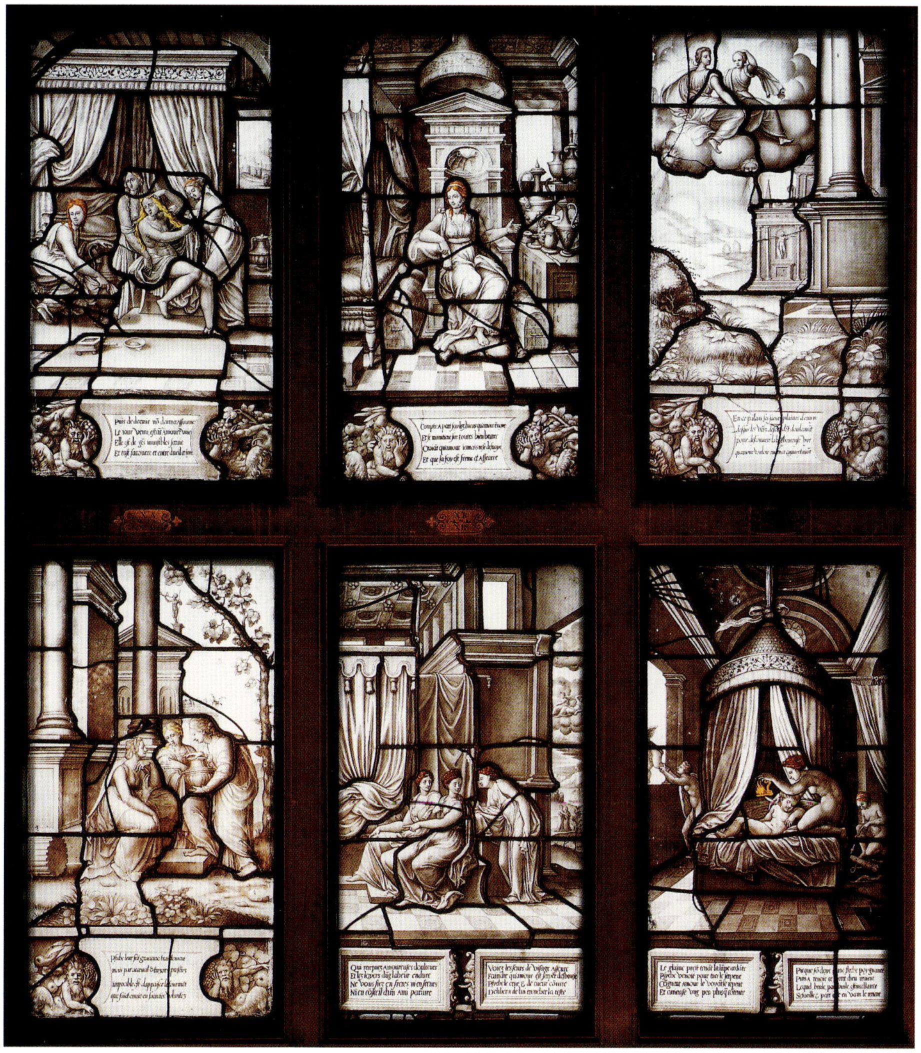

The stained glass panels with *The Story of Psyche*
Made in 1541-42 for the château of Écouen, these panels were remounted by Honoré Daumet in a gallery with northern light, specially designed to house them.

Opposite

The Galerie de Psyché
Lying between the Tour de Senlis and the Tour du Trésor, this gallery is inspired by the old gallery designed by Pierre Chambiges.

Following pages

The Logis
This main residential block stands between the entrance wing and the Galerie de Psyché.

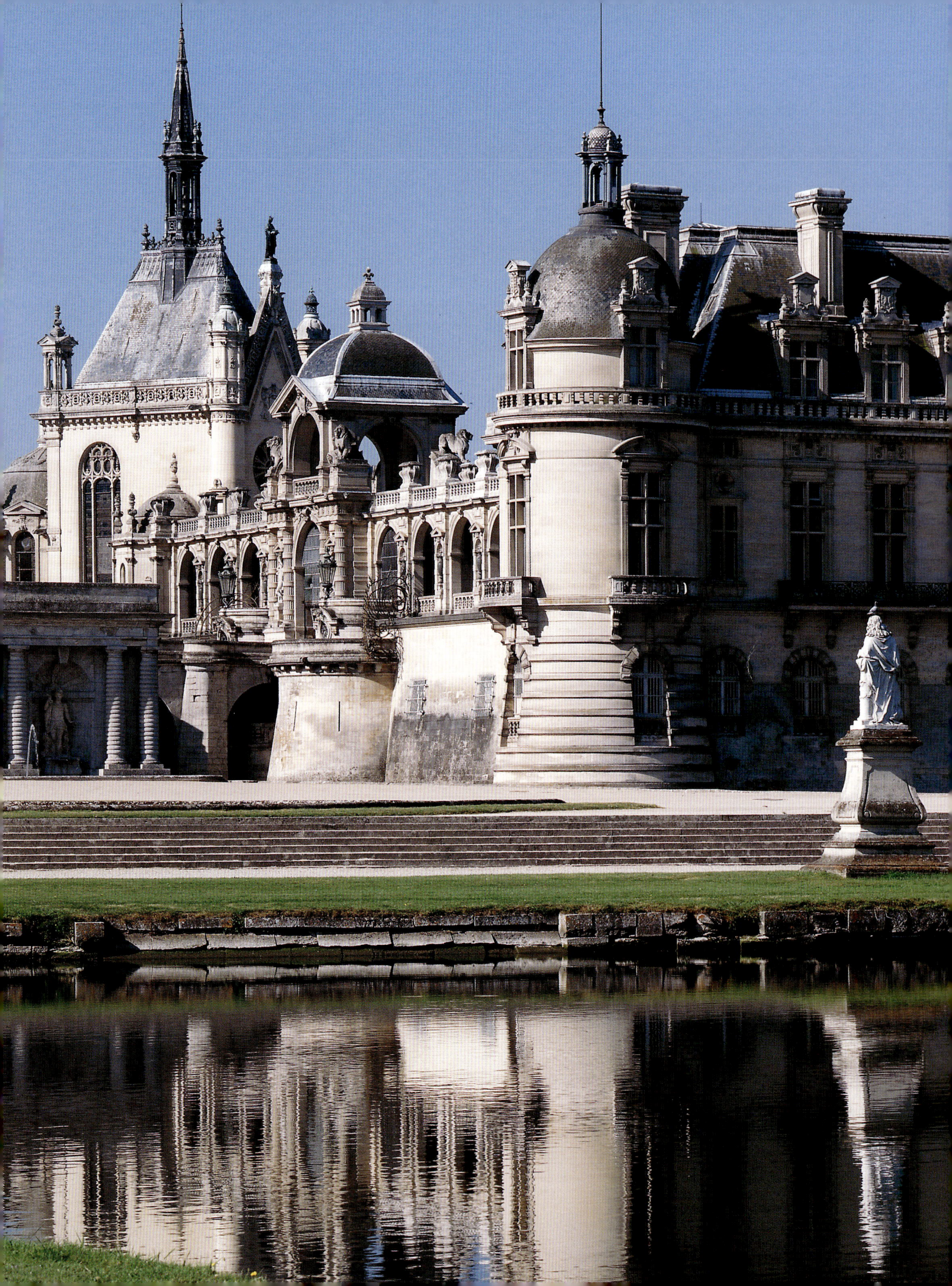

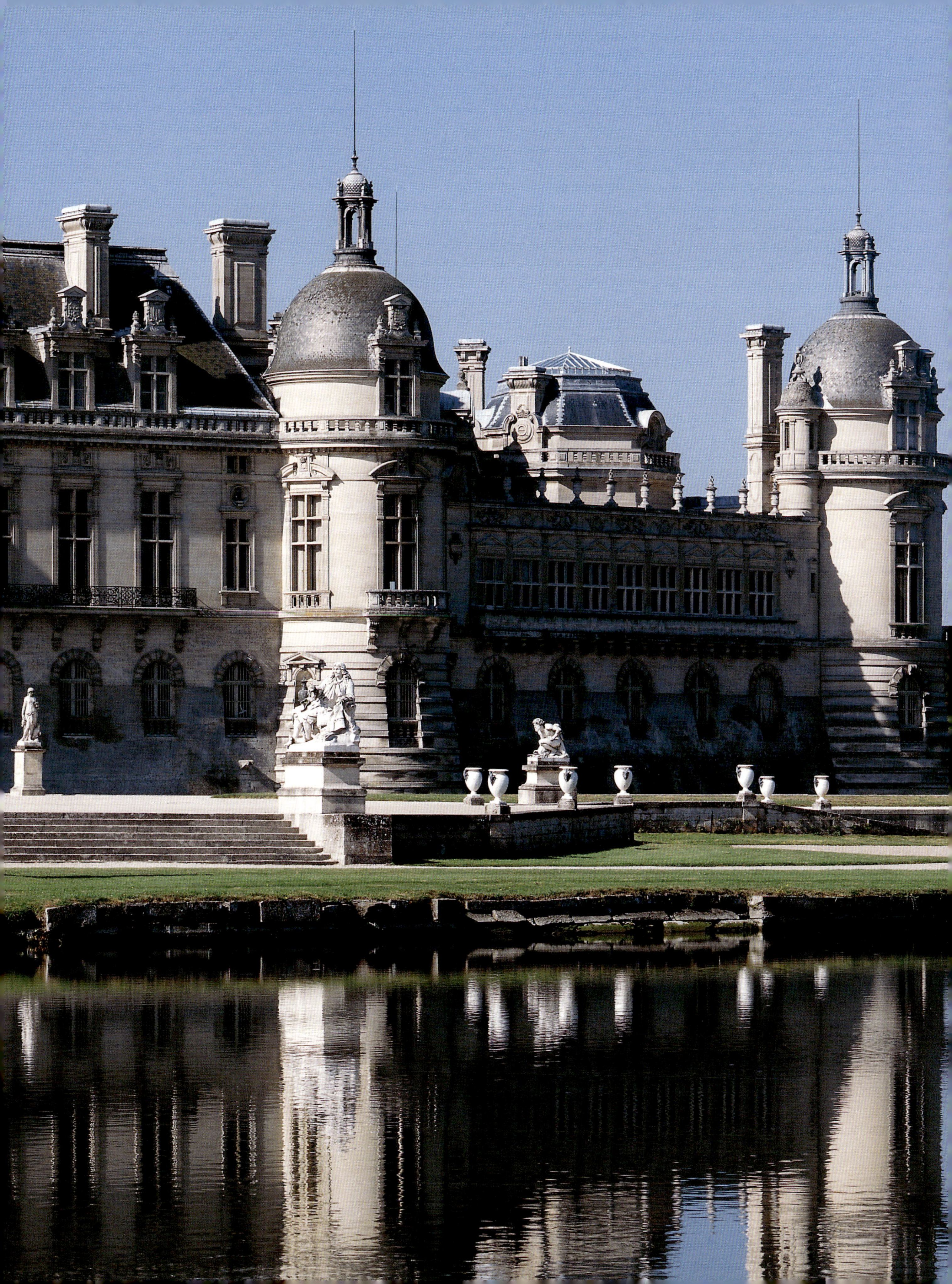

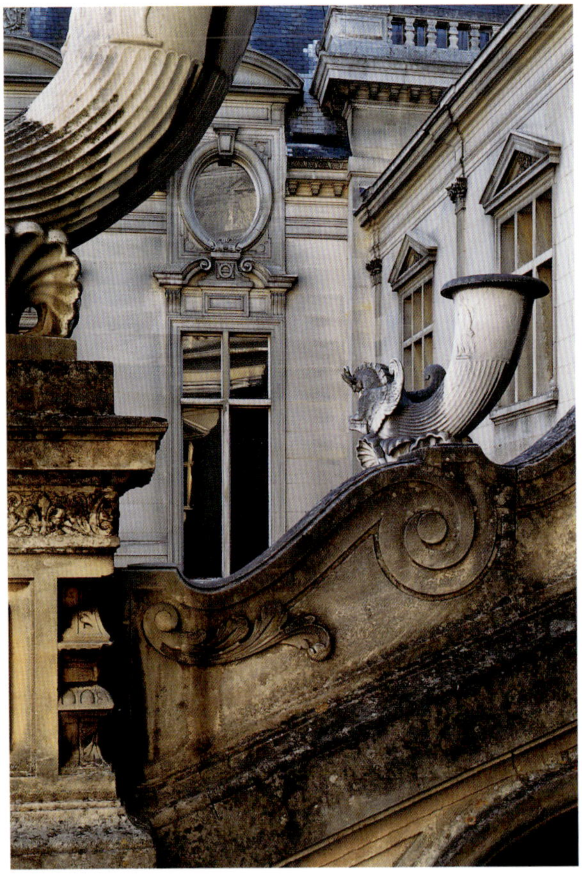

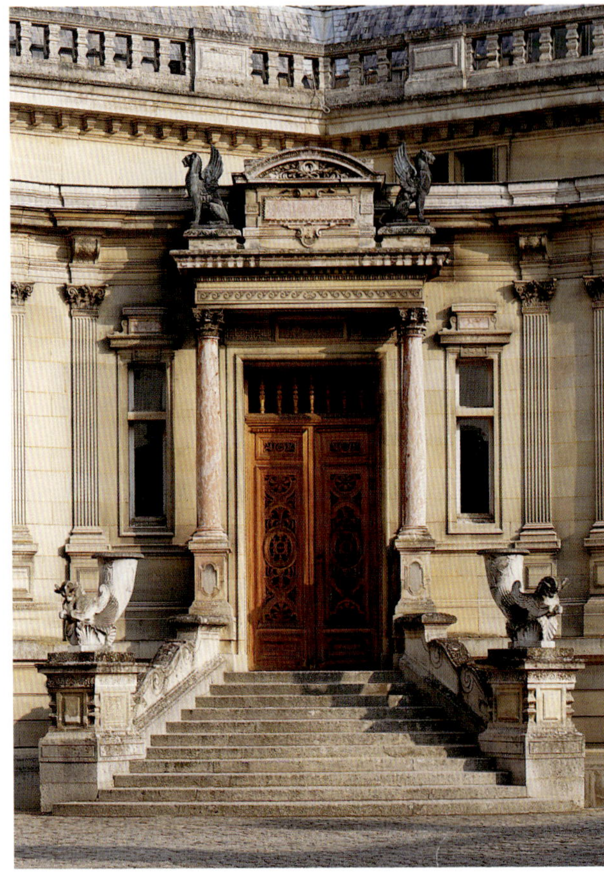

The door of the Musée Condé
The entrance on the right of the main court was intended for the residents of the Logis, the comte and comtesse de Paris. After the law imposing their exile, the duc d'Aumale had new museum rooms laid out, and a plaque was inserted above the door with the inscription MUSÉE CONDÉ.

The Tourelle de l'Horloge
At the junction between the Grand Château and the Petit Château, this turret has a lavish sculpted decoration in honour of the man who renovated Chantilly.

and servants' quarters above, which were in use until 1886. It could be reached under cover from the entrance pavilion, thanks to a portico at right angles skirting the dining-room and the Painting Gallery, and also through a door with marble columns at the top of a semi-circular flight of steps framed by monumental rhytons. For the residential wing, Daumet chose a style very close to Duban's scheme, a Renaissance style from the Loire valley with vertical bays, modernised by the addition of balconies, whereas the buildings on the west tip have very tall window apertures topped by pediments that are more reminiscent of the architecture of Jean Bullant. The sculpted decoration made possible by the use of fine stone from the Oise quarries was spread around with indiscriminate profusion, the prince's monogram and arms, allegorical figures and motifs on the pediments and in the niches, flame ornaments, chimney stacks ending in a tomb shape as at Anet. The small clock tower built to house a spiral staircase at the junction of the Petit Château and the Grand Château, facing the Jardin de la Volière, was decorated with special care, as the personal signature of the man who had renovated Chantilly, with the date MDCCCLXXVIII.

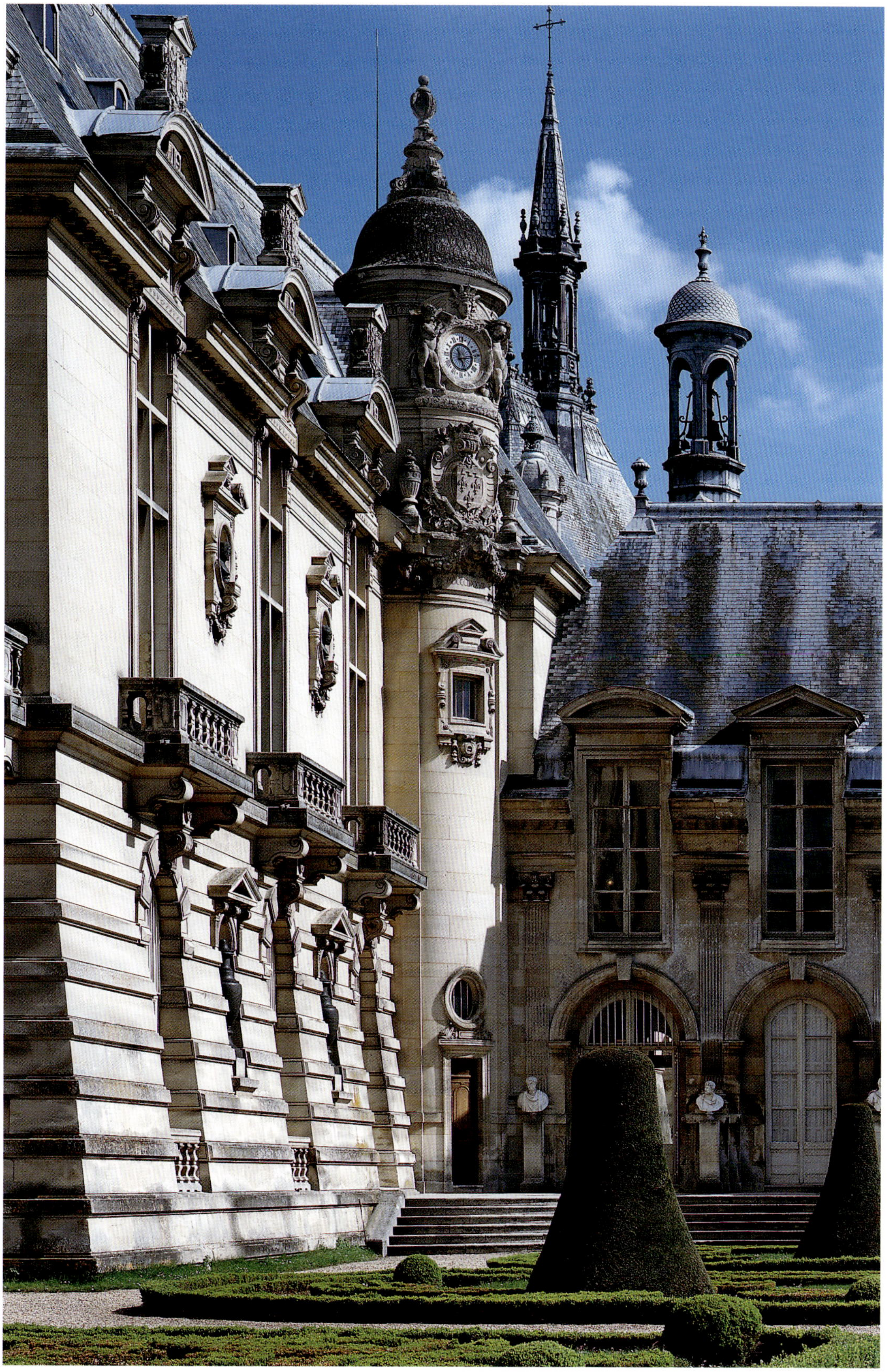

Opposite

The balustrade of the grand staircase
Made to Honoré Daumet's design, this balustrade is one of the masterpieces of nineteenth-century ironwork.

The finest artists were brought in to take part in the work, under the vigilant eye of Daumet. Paul Baudry who had done wonders at the Paris Opéra painted the *Legend of Saint Hubert* on the chimney-piece in the Galerie des Cerfs, near which the *en camaïeu* paintings by the same artist from the Hôtel Fould were relocated, and *The Abduction of Psyche* on the ceiling of the rotunda of the Painting Gallery. Other fashionable painters were brought in, such as Lechevallier-Chevignard, the great master decorator (in particular he designed the windows in the chapel intended as settings for the stained glass panels brought from Écouen), Guifard, responsible for restoring the monkey paintings by Huet, Bernard, a landscape painter, the sculptors Chapu – who made the atlantes bearing candelabra on the staircase – Marqueste, Gardet, Jonchery and Barthélemy, the bronzesmiths Jabœuf, Marchand and Lanson and the goldsmith Froment-Meurice. The banister of the grand staircase, designed by Daumet and made in 1884 by the iron-worker Le Berry at the Moreau workshops in Paris, with its admirable running foliage decoration in wrought iron and cast bronze, embellished with hammer-finished and carved motifs in copper sheet and brass – fleurs-de-lis, crowns and the prince's monogram – is a major masterpiece both in composition and technique[20]. As a great Renaissance prince, the duke wanted the finest materials everywhere: porphyry and granite vases in the vestibule and the porticoes, elsewhere bronze busts. Nothing was too costly. The archives allow us to know exactly[21] what the total cost of the work carried out between 1872 and 1897 was: 5,365,758 gold francs and 17 centimes, about 20 per cent of which was for the art work and the furnishings, and 6 per cent for the architect's fees.

Even so, the prince had not curtailed his budget for enhancing the collections that were to make him one of the greatest collectors of all time. To the major series he had negotiated to purchase, portraits in oil and pencil (the Clouets) from the collection of Alexandre Lenoir, drawings by Carmontelle, and paintings from the Reiset collection, he also added famous paintings, snatched individually from rival bidders, by Raphael, Filippino Lippi, Delacroix and Corot, and again in 1891 the miniatures by Fouquet for the *Livre d'heures d'Étienne Chevalier*, and in 1892 the *Psalter of Queen Ingeborg*. The total amount spent by the duc d'Aumale throughout his entire life on purchases for his collections and his library is estimated at 7,500,000 gold francs.

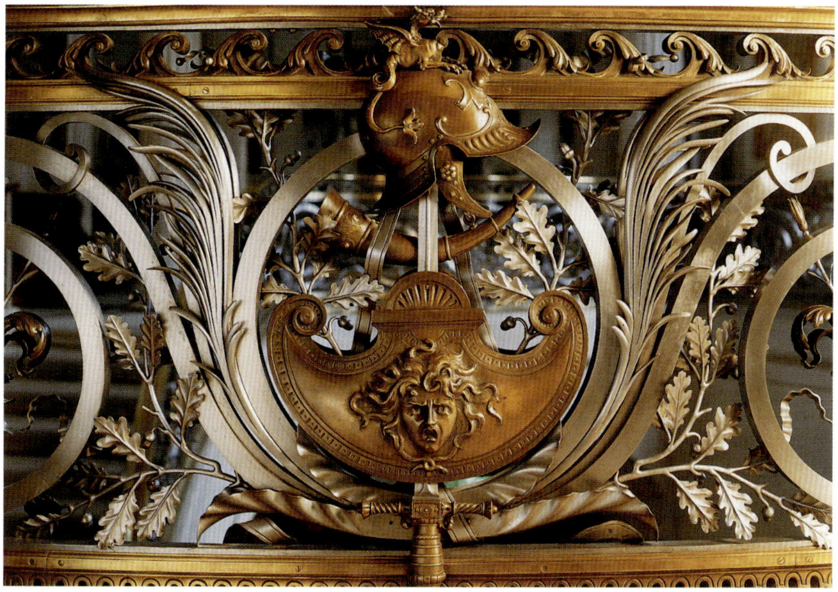

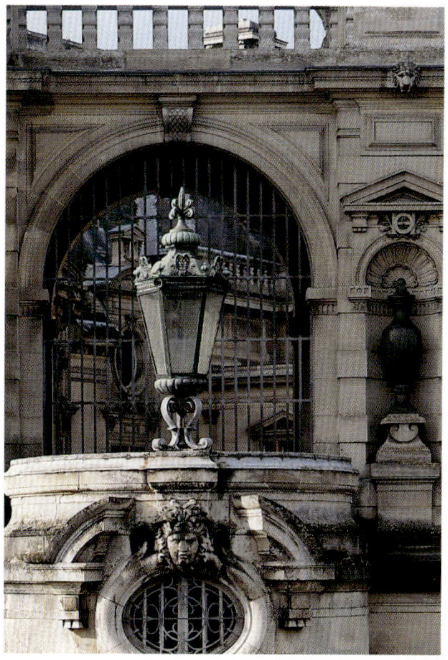

The decoration of the main court
Porphyry vases, lanterns and sculptures are intended to give an impression of princely abundance.

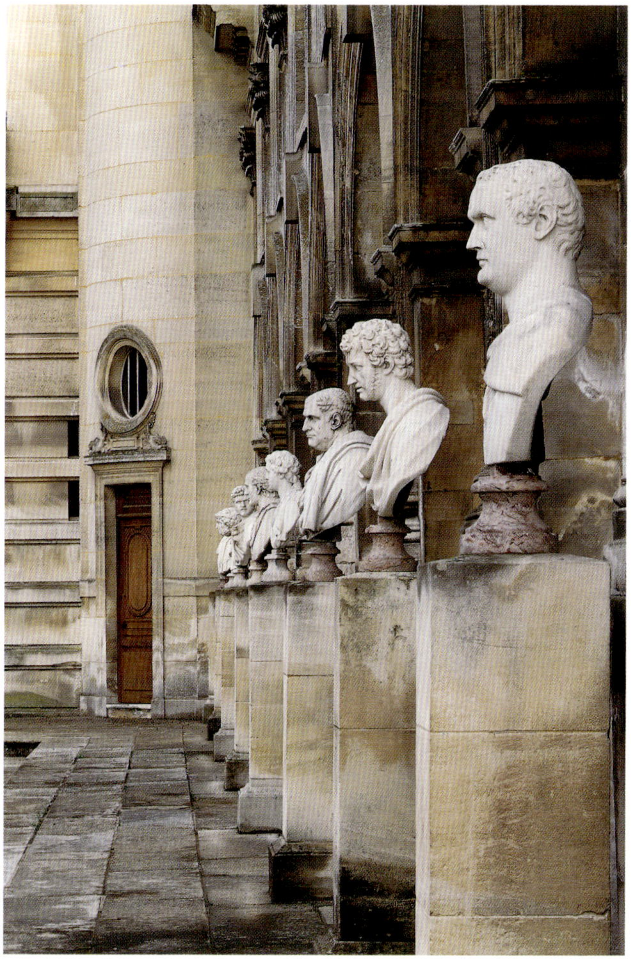

The busts on the Petit Château
It is the duc de Bourbon who had these Roman emperors' heads, copies of antique busts, placed on the façade; their presence there is attested in 1822 on the inventories and in 1845 on the painting of Nicolas Barbier (page 171).

The ceiling of the grand staircase
This painting was first commissioned from J.-E. Delaunay shortly before his death. His sketch inspired Diogène Maillart to carry out the ceiling painting, *Hope Holding the Flag of France*, in 1892. The memory of the loss of Alsace-Lorraine is perhaps tinged with the hope that France will turn again to the Orléans family, who hold aloft the tricolour flag.

The heroic donation[22]

The death of the comte de Chambord at Frohsdorf in August 1883 made the comte de Paris heir to the French crown ("Philippe VII"), but meanwhile developments on the political front had ruled out any plans for restoration of the monarchy for a long time. In the radical Republic dominated by Jules Grévy and Jules Ferry, the duc d'Aumale continued to live up to his rank with his customary independence, holding receptions, races and hunts to which the widest variety of representatives of French society were invited, along with the empress of Austria or the grand-dukes of Russia. It is hardly surprising that the Republicans looked darkly at these dynastic jollifications. The engagement of the Duke of Braganza, the heir to the throne of Portugal, to Princess Amélie, the daughter of the comte de Paris, celebrated at the Hôtel Galliera (now the Hôtel Matignon) on 25 and 26 January 1886, proved to be the final straw, and on 11 June the deputies voted to bring in new laws of exile; at the same time, princes were excluded from serving as officers in the army.

Wounded to the core by this second measure, the duc d'Aumale wrote a letter of eloquent protest to the President of the Republic; as he well knew, this was tantamount to an act of rebellion since he stated that he would hold on to his stars as a general of a division. He then set out for the frontier of his own accord, and on 14 July in his house of Le Nouvion-en-Thiérache he received notification of the expulsion decree. The following day he went into exile once more: Brussels, and yet again London.

For the prince, old, cut off and deprived of any political role, a new chapter of his destiny still remained to be written. He played his part nobly, and without showing any resentment towards the country that had again excluded him from its soil, confiding his thoughts to his book on the Great Condé where he condemns the hero's rebellion. "The blows that strike me do not cloud the calmness of my judgement […] A well-intentioned man has a duty to protest at all costs against a tyrannical act which through his person harms the public; to resist, to fight even, if by risking his life he can put an end to the oppression of all; he does not have the right to disrupt his country, tear it apart and involve it in war to avenge a personal affront." More than that, he speeded up the conservational measures he had taken to settle the fate of Chantilly. To be sure, he had no shortage of nephews to whom he could have left his property, but how was it possible to believe that the inestimable heritage he had assembled

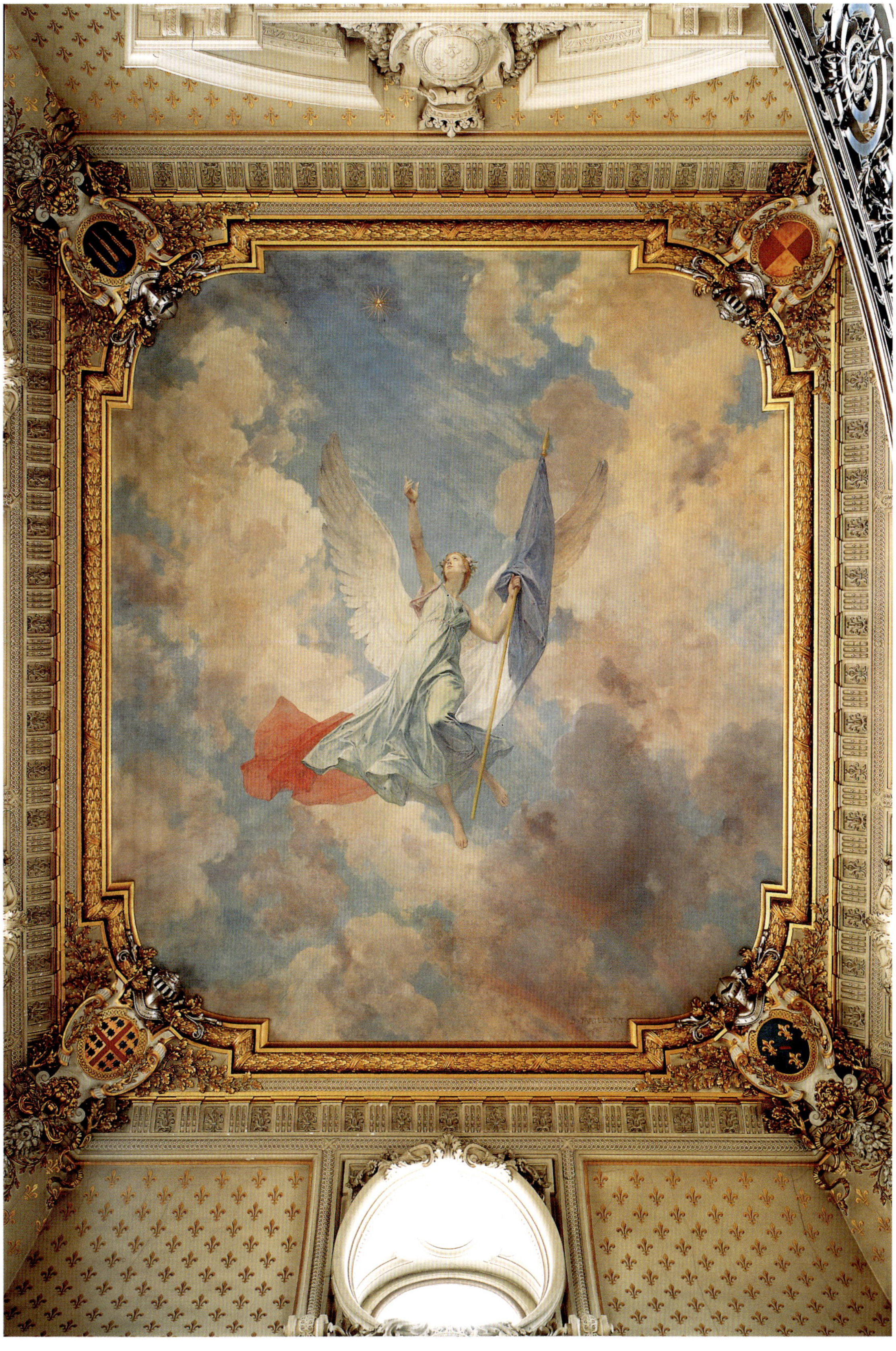

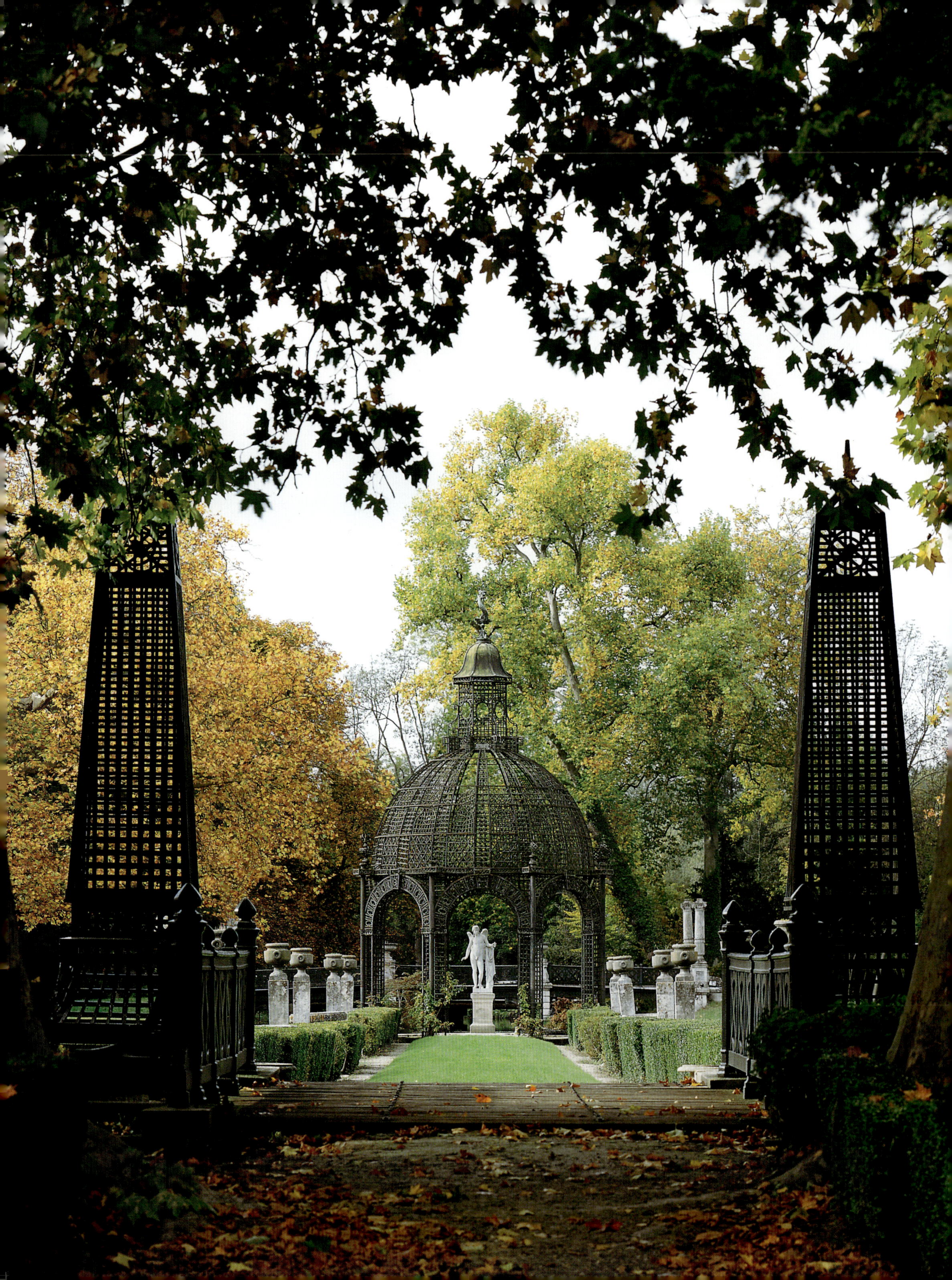

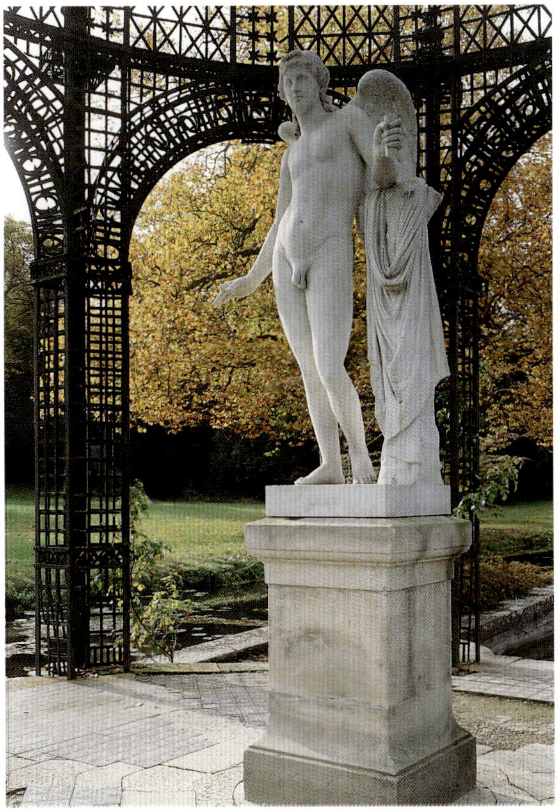

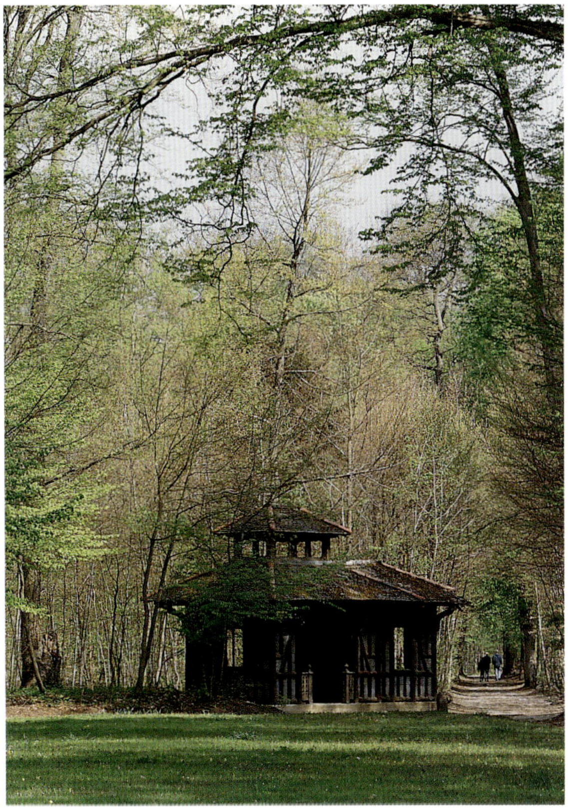

The statue of Eros
This copy of an antique statue commissioned from Jonchery was installed beneath a new bandstand on the Île d'Amour.

The Pavillon du Pas de tir
Located in the Parc de Sylvie, this pavilion bears witness to the duc d'Aumale's keen love of hunting.

The Rocher
This artificial pile of rocks stands at the junction of Le Nôtre's *parterres* and the Jardin Anglais.

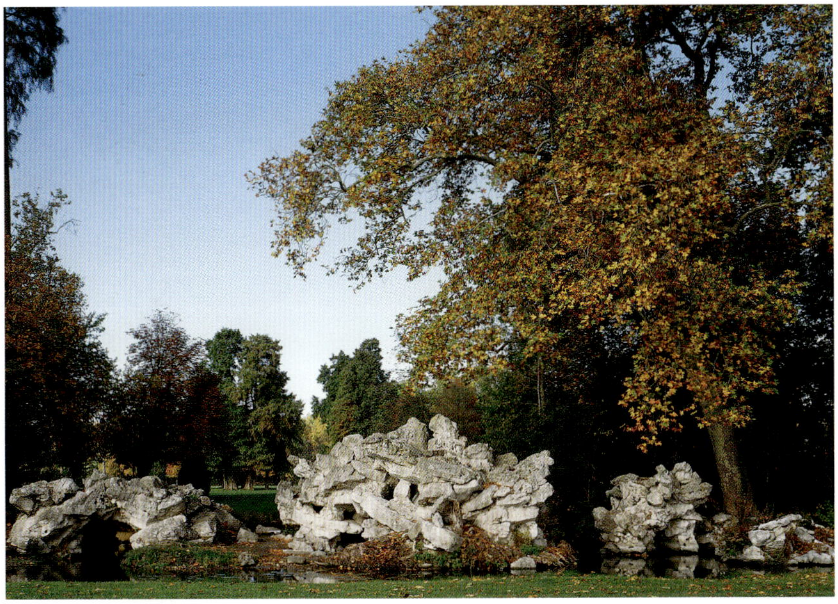

Opposite

The Île d'Amour
Le Nôtre's old Île du Bois Vert reduced to its end point.

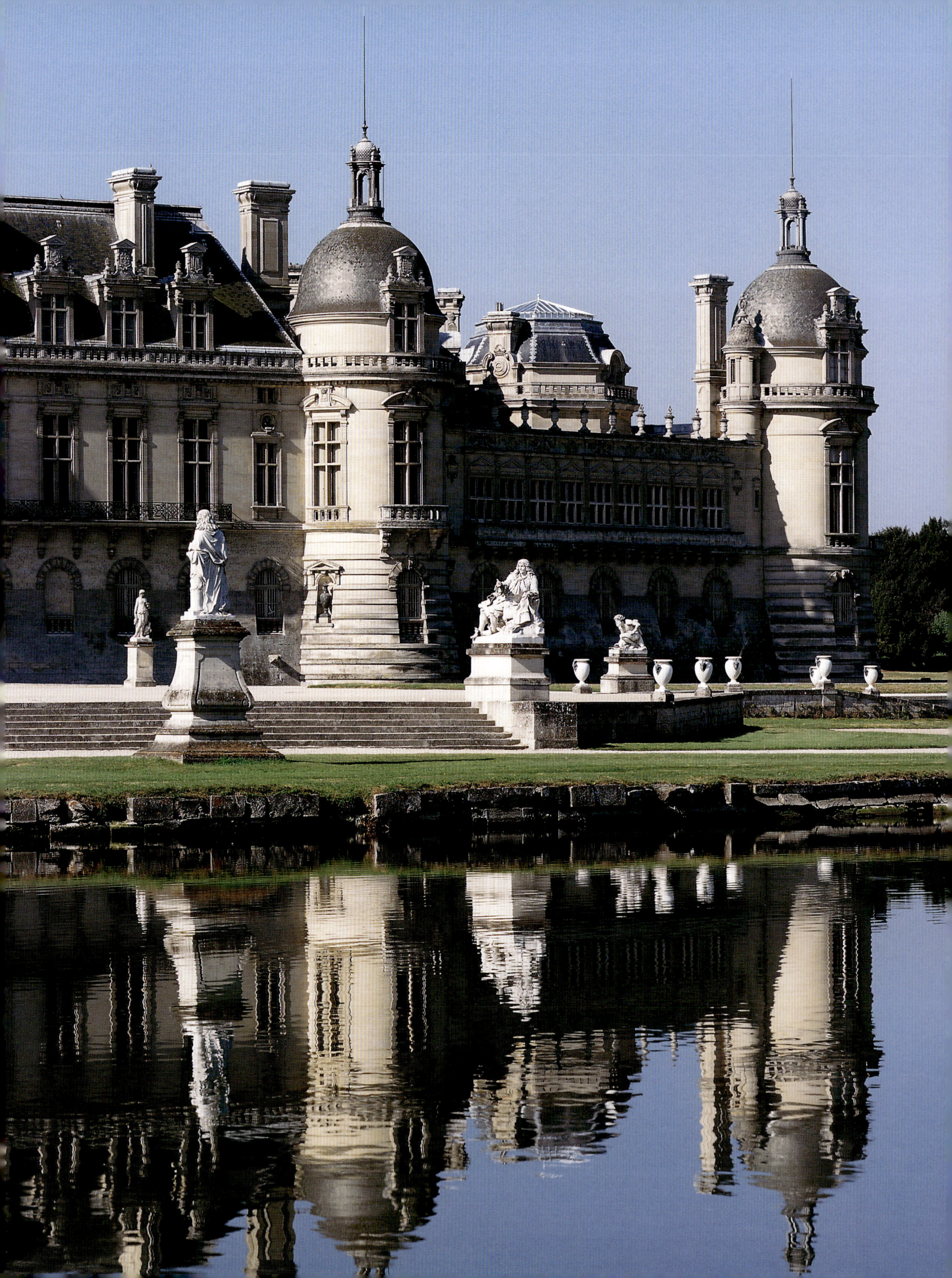

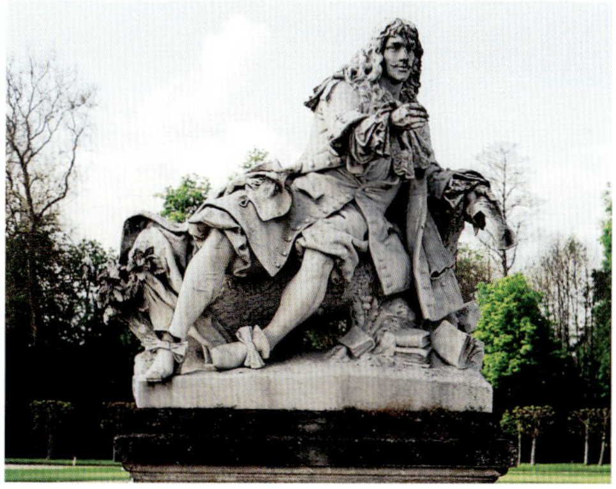

Molière **and** ***Le Nôtre***
These two great seventeenth-century figures by Tony-Noël evoke the memory of illustrious men of Chantilly.

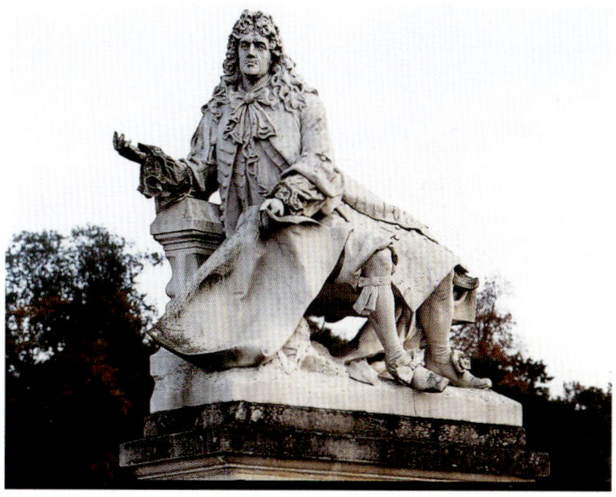

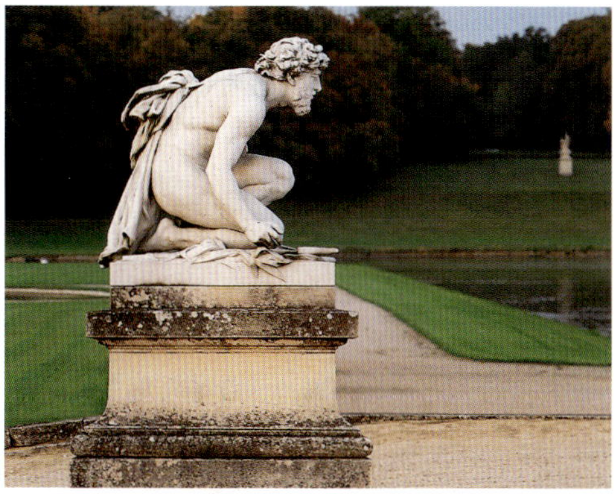

Pluto **and** ***Proserpine***
Chapu leaves us to imagine the abduction a few moments before it takes place. Crouching like a cat, the god of the underworld watches the goddess of fertility as she picks a narcissus.

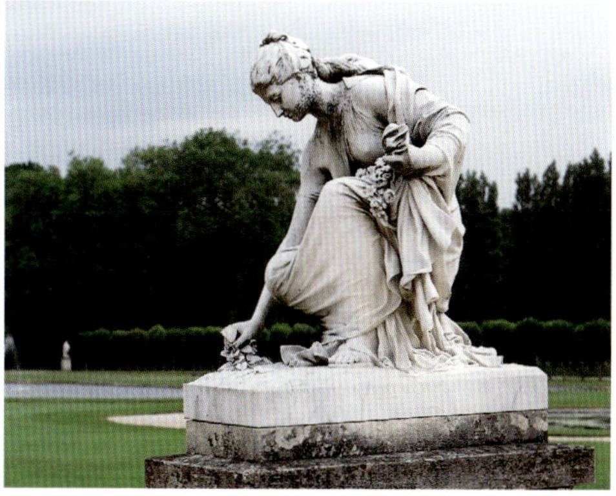

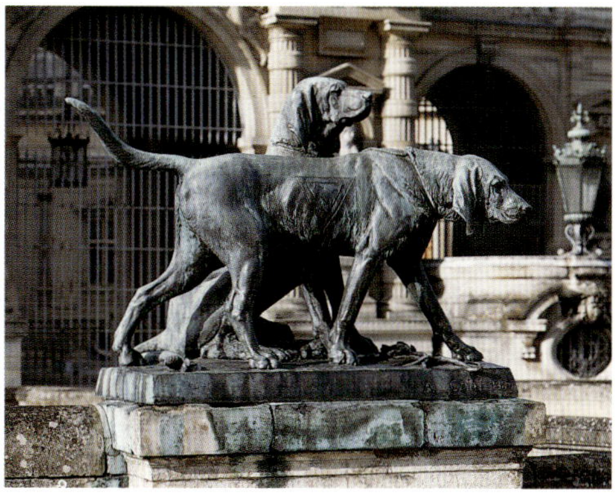

Pairs of dogs
These two pairs of hunting dogs by the great animal sculptor Auguste Cain guard the entrance to the château.

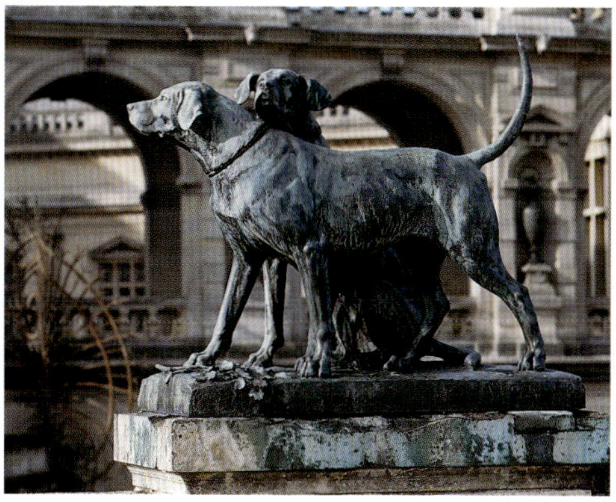

Opposite
Statues and vases
These decorative elements embellish Le Nôtre's reconstituted *parterres.*

could be kept intact by a prince on the territory of a Republican France? The young Prefect of Oise, Justin de Selves, is credited with having advised Aumale to bequeath his estate to the Institut de France, an institution that could offer him all the guarantees of respect and conservation that he wished for. The duke had been a member of the Académie Française since 1871 and of the Académie des Beaux-Arts since 1880, and he would be elected to the Académie des Sciences Morales et Politiques in 1889. He valued that advice, and when a serious attack of gout impaired his health, he drew up his will to that effect, on 3 June 1884[23]. Exile did not lead him to change his mind: on the contrary. Believing that in those uncertain years the situation should be made clear in his own lifetime, on 25 October 1886 he transformed the arrangements made in his will into an irrevocable donation inter vivos, with the reservation of usufruct.

The terms of his will deserve to be repeated here: "Wishing to preserve for France the estate of Chantilly in its entirety with its woods, lawns, waters, buildings and everything they contain, trophies, pictures, books, archives, objets d'art, this whole assembly which virtually forms a complete and varied monument of French art in all its branches and of the history of my native land at times of glory, I have resolved to entrust its safekeeping to an illustrious body that has done me the honour of calling me to join its ranks on two counts, and which, while it is not immune to the inevitable transformations of society, is exempt from the spirit of faction and excessively sudden upheavals, preserving its independence amidst political fluctuations."

The magnanimity thus expressed struck many a chord in France, and a sector of public opinion spoke up in favour of the prince's return; it was listened to by the Council of Ministers which in March 1889 decided unanimously to ask him back. By 11 March he was at Chantilly again, welcomed by acclamations – "slept at home", he wrote in his diary –[24] and on 12 March he was at the Élysée paying his respects to President Carnot. During his thirty-two months of exile, the prince had continued to take an interest in Chantilly from a distance, increasing his collections and commissioning Daumet to carry on with the work made necessary by the new situation. Since the heir to the throne could no longer live in France, his suites of rooms served no further purpose. The architect removed the fireplaces and doors, did away with the dressing rooms, and fitted out the whole block as a new museum of painting, at the centre of which the Salon d'Orléans was equipped with showcases to accommodate the collections of drawings and prints (today Chantilly porcelain and lace). Daumet was also instructed to fit out a research library in the vaulted hall of the former theatre, while the adjacent areas housed the rooms displaying medals, plan drawings, letters and registers. The painting of the chapel was completed, and once he had returned in 1892 the duke gave instructions to proceed with the final phase of the internal decoration, the ceiling of the grand staircase, which was commissioned from Maillard on a patriotic theme that referred to the loss of Alsace-Lorraine, *Hope Holding the Flag of France.*

From the start of his building projects at Chantilly, the duke had not failed to remember the gardens and the park. He first concentrated his attention on reinstating Le Nôtre's *parterres*, but also on carrying on with laying out the Jardin Anglais by repairing the Canal Saint-Jean and the Île d'Amour. Here a new trelliswork arbour was provided to house a statue of Eros, a copy of an antique statue commissioned from Jonchery, and it once again welcomed the Medici Venus. He was also responsible for constructing rustic bridges across the winds of the river, and the river's junction with the west *parterre* was marked by a romantic pile of blocks of stone called the Rocher. A new hydraulic machine was constructed in the Pavillon de Manse, while the Jeu de Paume was turned into an annexe of the museum, housing the tent of Abd-el-Kader and other military trophies. In the eastern sector, the Maison de Sylvie was refurbished and – unfortunately – enlarged by the addition of an octagonal salon arranged to accommodate the eighteenth-century wood panelling removed from a hunting lodge in the forest of Dreux. Paintings commissioned from Luc-Olivier Merson evoke the time spent there by Sylvie. The wooded area of the park was again enlarged, set off to advantage, and the changes required by the big hunts for which the prince had retained a very keen liking were carried out.

New statues filled the parterres and woodland avenues. Sculpted portraits of Molière and Le Nôtre by Tony-Noël, La Bruyère by Thomas and Bossuet by Guillaume are a reminder of the court at Chantilly that surrounded the Great Condé, represented by the statue by Coysevox which was put back in the middle of the *parterre.* Chapu provided a new version of the myth of the abduction of Proserpine in the form of two crouching figures opposite one another, the goddess picking a narcissus while Pluto watches over her. The terrace, château and park were embellished by animal sculptures, made in particular by the great specialist in that field, August Cain.

The duc d'Aumale
Paid for by subscription by the town of Chantilly and executed by the painter and sculptor Jean-Léon Gérôme, this equestrian statue was erected in 1899 in front of the west façade of the Écuries.

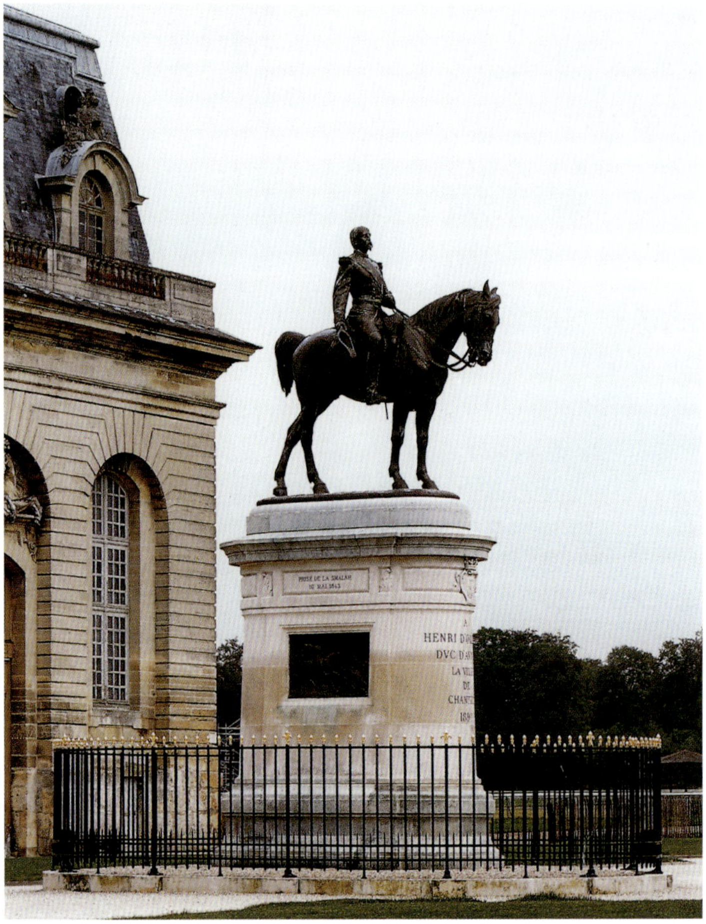

The Musée Condé or the Musée d'Aumale?

The duc d'Aumale's final years passed serenely, with countless demonstrations of esteem; he was especially touched by his appointment as President of the Red Cross and his third election to the Institut de France. Family celebrations and ceremonies continued right to the end, as did his purchases of books and works of art, reverently recorded by Gustave Macon, his secretary and confidant. On 26 October 1895, he was delighted to welcome the members of the five academies that constitute the Institut de France who had come to Chantilly by special train as part of its centenary celebrations. Daumet was at his side, and was warmly congratulated. For the prince, it was a final source of delight. He was known to have a weak heart. On 7 May 1897 he died while visiting his Zucco estate in Sicily. He was seventy-five years old.

Everything had been provided to ensure continuity, and the most detailed instructions had been given regarding the management of the entire estate under the control of an administrative body composed of three curators who were members of the Institut[25] and one deputy curator living on the spot – this was Gustave Macon. The property necessary for ensuring the upkeep of this virtual principality – forests, farms, buildings – had generously been included in the will, and in return an extremely formal obligation was imposed on the Institut de France to open these treasures to the public, but without making any changes to the external and internal architecture of the château or to the arrangement of the works of art, which thus became irremovable fixtures. On 20 December 1886, the date of the presidential decree accepting the donation to the Institut, the prince had a marble plaque placed above the entrance to the residential block, now reserved for visitors to the Musée Condé, the name he had expressly chosen for his collections to indicate his loyalty to the princely lineage to which he owed Chantilly.

These arrangements were scrupulously adhered to. Once the last objets d'art had been arranged in accordance with his wishes by the executors of his will, the Musée Condé was opened to visitors on Sunday 17 April 1898. Staff still wearing the livery of the House of Orléans acted as museum attendants. Three entire trains brought several hundred visitors from Paris, and the success of the venture was confirmed in the following years. In accordance with the prince's stated wishes, the Museum was then open two days a week for six months of the year, with greater freedom of access for students, men and women of letters and artists. Ever since, the Institut de France has shouldered its task with constancy and integrity, conscious of having to maintain one of the richest jewels in the French national heritage, a unique and profoundly original collection at the heart of which the powerful personality of the donor is still magnificently present. It today includes 1,000 paintings, 2,500 drawings and an equal number of engravings, 250 sculptures, 800 mediaeval manuscripts and a library of 30,000 works. Its success has proved enduring, with visitors coming in their hundreds of thousands every year, and while essential restorations to the works, gardens and architecture have been carried out with all the requisite knowledge and tact, Chantilly has indeed remained as the duc d'Aumale wished to leave it to his country.

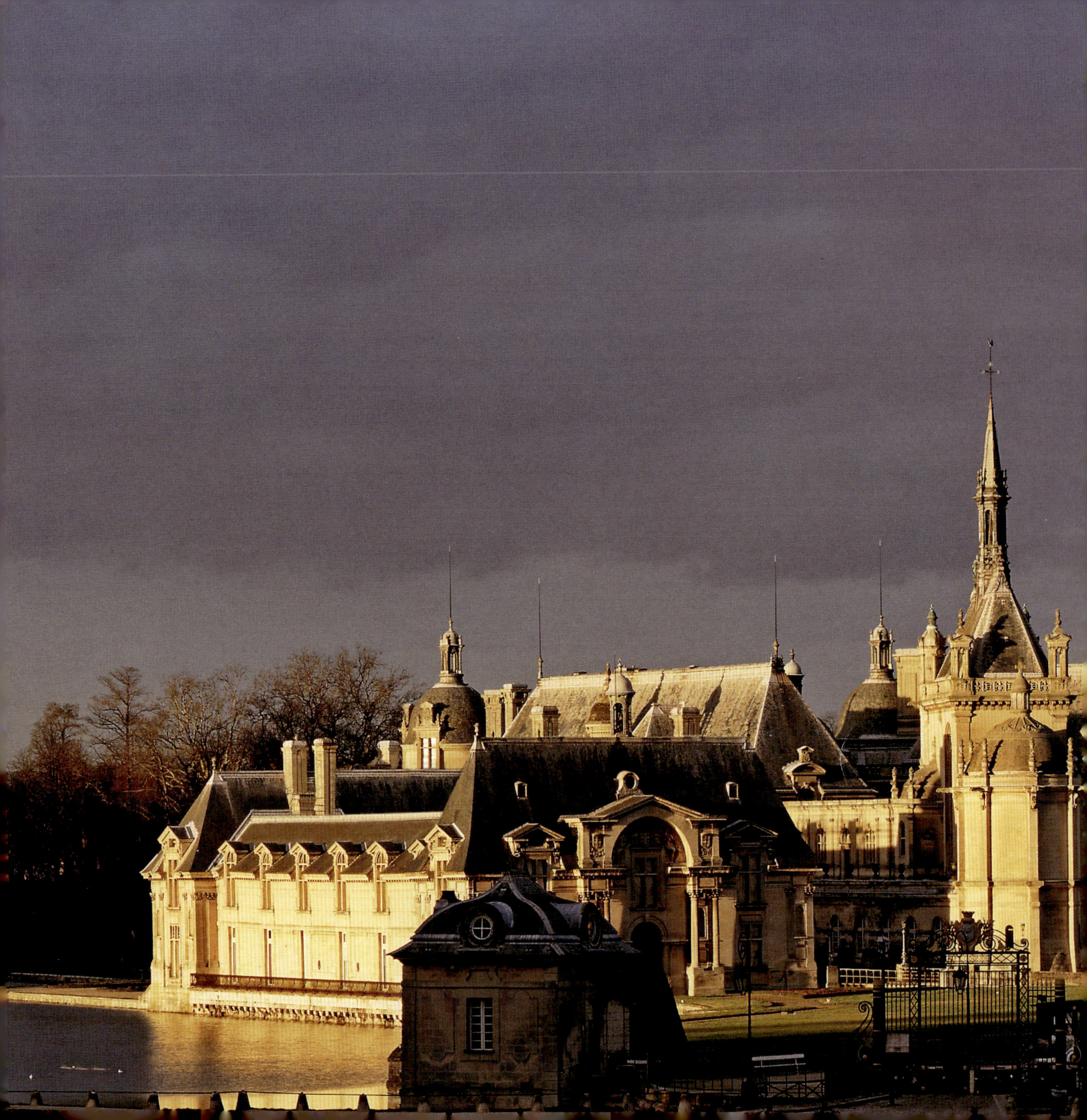

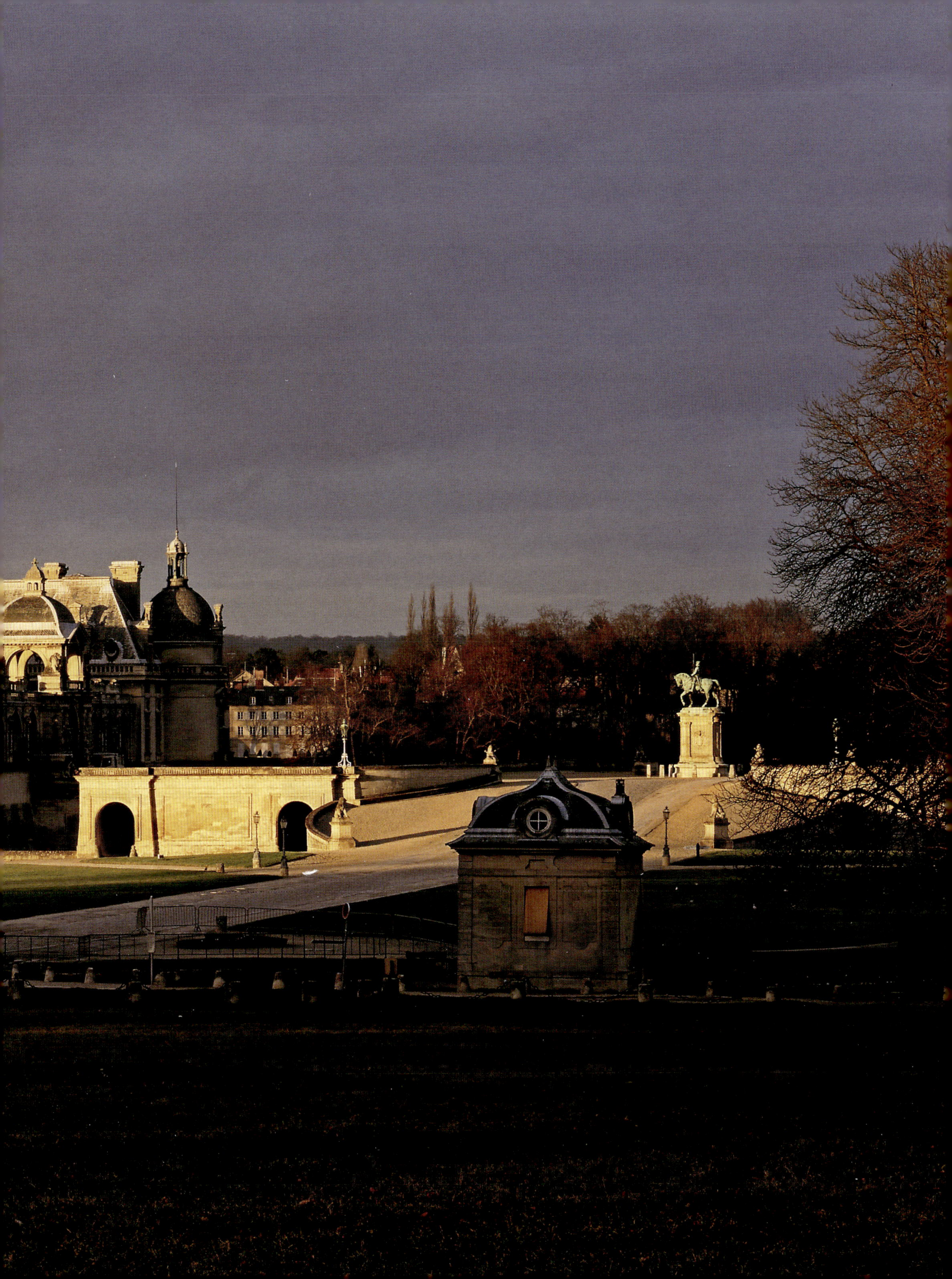

NOTES

CHAPTER I
Pages 16-25

1. G. Macon, *Chantilly et le Musée Condé*, Paris, Laurens, 1910. This book has not dated at all, and is still the main source to which we will have occasion to refer constantly. Tribute should be paid to the work carried out by the eminent curator and historian of Chantilly using the exceptionally rich archives preserved at the château.
2. In the seventeenth century A. Duchesne wrote a *Histoire de la Maison des Bouteiller de Senlis*, published by L. Sandret in 1879.
3. E. Vignon, "Autour de Senlis. Trois grandes forêts: Halatte. Chantilly. Ermenonville". *Talk to the Société d'histoire et d'archéologie de Senlis*, 10 November 1938 and 9 March 1939.
4. The lands of the Priory of Commelles were given to the Abbey of Chaalis in 1136 by Louis VI and c. 1160 by Guy II le Bouteiller. The monks dug out the ponds. In the late Middle Ages there was a tanner's mill, and later on, in the Prince de Condé's time in 1765, a mill for wheat. In the French Restoration period the architect Victor Dubois decorated the building there known as the Loge de Viarmes in the troubadour style; ever since it has been known as the "Château de la Reine Blanche".
5. According to testimony reported by Piganiol de La Force, the body that was found enclosed in a lead coffin was clothed in a shirt made of fairly fine white material, the arms bound at the wrists by a silk cord, in an envelope of waxed grey cloth, tied up with a short piece of rope. Cf. G. Macon, *Les Arts dans la Maison de Condé*, 1903, p. 66.
6. R. Cazelles, "Quand le Roi Jean achetait Chantilly", *Le Musée Condé*, no. 22, 1982, pp. 1-6.
7. Guillaume IV le Bouteiller died in 1360 after selling the lordship to his cousin Jean Herpin, lord of Erquery, who died the following year, leaving it to another cousin, Jean de Laval, lord of Attichy, who in 1376 gave it as a gift to his nephew Guy de Laval. It was Laval who sold Chantilly along with the Tour de Montmélian to Pierre d'Orgemont on 28 May 1386 for the sum of 8,000 *livres* (minted at Tours).
8. L. Mirot, *Une grande famille parlementaire aux XIVe et XVe siècles. Les d'Orgemont*, Paris, 1913.
9. H. Sauval, *Histoire et recherches des antiquités de la ville de Paris*, Paris, 1724 (pub. posthumously), vol. II, p. 147.
10. In fulfilment of this agreed price, the mason Jean Quatrehommes and his journeymen received the sum of 5,625 francs and 4 *sols* (minted in Paris) on 4 March 1389. Cf. G. Macon, *Chantilly et le Musée Condé*, op. cit., p. 12. Quotations are reproduced from that book.
11. A letter from Villeroy to Montmorency dated 23 April 1530 clearly proves that the "old walls of the moats" had been kept intact as high as their upper level as a base for the new buildings.
12. These names are taken from an "avowal and enumeration" of 1426 published by G. Macon, op. cit., pp. 65-72.
13. The feudal documents stating the original configuration of the estate had been burnt at the time of the Jacquerie uprising in 1358, and Amaury assembled a new collection of charters of which he had an inventory drawn up in 1400. These documents, still preserved at the Musée Condé, constitute the first nucleus of the "Cabinet des titres". The estate purchased by Pierre d'Orgemont amounted to 1200 *arpents* (approximately equivalent to acres), and he subsequently bought a further 900.
14. Guillaume came to live at Chantilly with Anne Pot, a rich Burgundian heiress he had married as soon as the division of 14 July 1484 was agreed. His uncle lived with them until his death in 1492.

CHAPTER II
Pages 26-65

1. The duc d'Aumale had two stained glass panels depicting the Constable's sons, his wife and his daughters that came from the chapel at Écouen (1544) remounted in the chapel at Chantilly, built in 1882. Let us mention again that Guillaume de Montmorency had rebuilt the collegiate church of Saint-Martin at Montmorency, the choir of which was completed in 1525, at the beginning of the sixteenth century. The church, later provided with a nave built for the Constable by Jean Bullant, is lit by windows where the members of the family are again depicted as donors.
2. These drawings from the Destailleur collections, nos. 28 to 32 (Bibl. Nat. de France, Prints, Ve 26 i) are reproduced here on pp. 36-37 except for no. 31 (external north face). As B Jestaz correctly saw, they are copies made c. 1788 (captions of no. 29) of drawings that were a century older. For the court they are complemented by a watercolour by Lieven Cruyl (1686) and an engraving of the same date in N. Langlois.
3. This is also the view of W. Prinz and Kecks in their article on Chantilly, *Das französische Schloss der Renaissance*, 1985, pp. 512-519.
4. G. Macon, *Chantilly et le connétable Henri de Montmorency*, Senlis, 1903.
5. Several biographies have been devoted to Anne de Montmorency, some time ago by Decrue (1885), more recently by M. Blancpain (1988) and B. Bedos-Rezak (1990); the last places special emphasis on his role as a patron of the arts.
6. The tiles were delivered in September 1529. Montmorency is known to have taken an interest in the products of the Rouen ceramicist Masséot Abaquesne for the paving of his châteaux at Écouen and Fère-en-Tardenois from 1542. Those still in existence at Écouen enable us to picture the magnificent compositions that must have been present at Chantilly too.
7. On 29 September 1530 Pierre Chambiges undertook to complete work in two months.
8. The decoration of the gallery was subsequently enriched. In Sauval (op. cit., vol. II, p. 143) and the *Mercure françois* of September 1688 (vol. II, p. 179) we read that in addition to the figures of stags it was possible to admire a fresco of *The Story of Psyche* made by Nicolo dell'Abate. This was commissioned by Montmorency in 1556, four years after the arrival of the painter from Modena in France at the same time as the decoration of his mansion in Paris. A drawing held at the Ashmolean Museum in Oxford, *Zephyr and Psyche*, may be a proposal for the gallery at Chantilly. Exhibition catalogue for "L'École de Fontainebleau", Paris, Grand Palais, 1972, no. 13.
9. Bibliothèque Nationale de France, Prints, Va 60, vol. 12, R. de Cotte 198.
10. R. Cazelles, "Le jeu de paume de Montmorency", *Le Musée Condé*, no. 14, 1978, pp. 1-4. The old Jeu de Paume can be seen on an engraving by Israël Silvestre and on a drawing at the British Museum. Its walls were articulated with round arches with projecting keystones. The new one would be built in 1756.
11. G. Macon, "Les architectes de Chantilly au XVIe siècle", op. cit. M. Vachon, *Une famille parisienne de maîtres maçons aux XVe, XVIe, XVIIe siècles: les Chambiges*, 1907. The work by Chambiges for the king was done between 1539 and his death in June 1544. Cf. F. Meunier, "Martin Chambiges", *Positions des thèses de l'Ecole nationale des Chartes*, 1999, pp. 297-300, as well as F. Gebelin, *Les Châteaux de la Renaissance*, 1927, pp. 75-78, and J.-P. Babelon, *Châteaux de France au siècle de la Renaissance*, 1989, pp. 210 and 445.
12. R. Cazelles, "La cour du château de Chantilly après les travaux de Pierre Chambiges", *Le Musée Condé*, no. 6, 1974, pp. 5-8.
13. B. Bedos, op. cit., p. 315.
14. The loggia overlooking the garden at Nantouillet may date from the first years of the 1520s. The course decided upon at Chantilly was repeated with variants in the Loire region, c. 1535, at Villesavin and Châteaubriant.
15. When the roof timbers of the building were finished, it was realised that the measurements had been made wrongly and that the roof was three feet higher than the roof of the keep. Grolier wanted to lower it, but Guillaume de Montmorency was against doing so because of concern over the cost (letters of 15-25 November 1530). The difference is clearly visible in the engravings and drawings.
16. Anne enlarged the wooded estate by buying the 2,000 *arpents* forming the forest of Pontarmé, and it is then that he had the fine emblazoned boundary stones put in place (1537-46) several of which have been preserved; the duc d'Aumale reverently had them erected on the terrace, round the statue of the Constable. J. Peloye, "Les bornes armoriées", *Le Musée Condé*, no. 55, 1998.
17. G. Macon, "Les architectes de Chantilly au XVIe siècle", op. cit., p. 22.
18. F.-C. James, "Jean Bullant. Recherches sur l'architecture française du XVIe siècle", *Positions des thèses de l'École nationale des Chartes*, 1968, pp. 101-109.
19. This letter-report was published in particular by G. Macon, "Les architectes de Chantilly au XVIe siècle", op. cit., pp. 39-41.
20. Another local mason, originating from Saint-Maximin (Oise), Pierre Desilles is often described as the "master of the Constable's masonry works". He had been in his service since at least 1552. He had his home at Chantilly, but worked on the building sites at his châteaux, at the churches of Montmorency and Nantouillet; later, in 1578, he would be the mason of the Pont Neuf in Paris.
21. The Capitainerie buildings can be clearly distinguished on an engraving by Israël Silvestre.
22. The arms and figures which had been defaced with a hammer at the time of the Revolution were reinstated on the orders of the duc d'Aumale.
23. A few subsidiary jobs are mentioned in 1575, at the main bridge of the château, "mended" by a carpenter, in the bedroom of Mgr and Mme de Montmorency (glazing) and at the heronry. P. Héliot, "Textes inédits relatifs à l'architecture française du XVIe siècle", *Bulletin de la Société nationale des Antiquaires de France*, 1945-47, pp. 183-187.
24. G. Macon, *Chantilly et le connétable Henri de Montmorency*, op. cit., p. 7.
25. The mystery was still a matter of speculation at the time of the Great Condé and caused people to believe in the appearance of a mysterious "white lady". Constable Henri, who was temperamentally unsuited to withstanding a second period as a widower, got involved in a third marriage to a young aunt of Louise's, Mme de Dizimieu, but he subsequently decided to discard her, exiling her from one château to another. She died in 1654 at the age of 83.
26. P. Vitry, "Documents inédits sur Pierre Biard, architecte et sculpteur du connétable de Montmorency", *Gazette des Beaux-Arts*, April 1899.
27. It was a decidedly fragile piece of work as in 1876 Daumet again had to put chains through the north-west part, above the duchesse d'Aumale's bedroom. R. de Broglie, *Chantilly*, 1964, p. 206.
28. The pictures are mentioned in place in a description dated 1619. Repaired and put on new canvas in 1679 by the painter Charles Mauperché, they continued in existence until the Revolution.
29. At Notre-Dame-du-Grau, near Agde, in 1609. The Maison de Beauvais had been built by Anne de Montmorency in 1540 on the spot where the territory of the bishopric of Beauvais started. It can still be seen opposite the parish church of Chantilly.
30. His attraction to Chantilly was also explained by the proximity of the château of Verneuil-en-Halatte where the king went to visit his mistress Henriette d'Entraigues, marquise de Verneuil.
31. We have a lot of information through

exchanges of letters (including correspondence with the steward Girard du Thillay) and the descriptions (from the avowal made to the king in 1582 to the *Memoirs* of Lord Herbert of Cherbury) used by G. Macon, op. cit.

32. The time spent there by Louis XIII brought no changes to Chantilly, except for the building of a house in the park, known as "La Caboutière" because the Great Condé had a flower garden created there by a great Parisian botanist, the advocate Henri Caboud. That house still exists, and is occupied by the CAUE (Commitee for Architecture, Urbanism and the Environment) of the Oise department.

Chapter III

Pages 66-107

1. B. Pujo, *Le Grand Condé*, Paris, 1995. S. Bertière, *Le Grand Condé. Le héros foudroyé*, Paris, Fallois, 2012.
2. K. Béguin, *Les Princes de Condé. Rebelles, courtisans et mécènes dans la France du Grand Siècle*, 1999.
3. It was in 1661 that he was able to exchange the duchy of Albret for the duchy of Bourbon with the king, and thereafter it was part of the Condé heritage.
4. J.-M. Pérouse de Montclos, *Vaux-le-Vicomte*, Paris, 1997.
5. P.-A. Lablaude, *Les Jardins de Versailles*, Paris, 1995.
6. Daniel Gittard (1625-86) was born at Blandy-lès-Tours near Vaux. He worked at Chantilly without a break from 1670 until his death, after playing an important role at Vaux. J.-C. Petitfils, "Une œuvre inconnue d'un architecte parisien: Daniel Gittard et Vaux-le-Vicomte", paper read at the Commission du Vieux Paris on 5 May 1998. By the same author, *Fouquet*, Paris, 1998, p. 176. Gittard took a major share in the building of the church of Saint-Sulpice, the Condés' parish in Paris. His son Pierre, an architect and engineer, carried on his father's work at Chantilly in 1686, and married the daughter of the caretaker of the château, Claude Richard.
7. G. Macon, "Le Nôtre à Chantilly", paper given at the Académie des Beaux-Arts on 18 June 1927, *Institut de France, Publications de l'année 1927*, 1928, no. 18, p. 1. By the same author, *Les Arts dans la Maison de Condé*, 1903. Chantilly accounts predating 1676 have not been kept. In that year Le Nôtre received 2,200 *livres* as his annual wage, Gittard 550, and Desgots a fixed monthly sum of 200 *livres*. See also the books published in 2013 for "The year of Le Nôtre": P. Bouchenot-Déchin, *André Le Nôtre*, Paris, Fayard, 2013; N. Garnier-Pelle, *André Le Nôtre et les jardins de Chantilly au* XVII*e et au* XVIII*e siècle*, Paris, Somogy, 2013; J.-P. Babelon (introd.) et J.-B. Leroux (photographs), *Le Nôtre*, Paris, Imprimerie nationale, 2013.
8. K. Woodbridge, *Princely Gardens: The Origins and Development of the French Formal Style*, London, 1986, p. 253.
9. G. Macon, *Histoire du domaine forestier de Chantilly*, 2 vols., Senlis, 1905-06. B. Lefebvre, "Histoire de la forêt", *Le Musée Condé*, no. 32, 1987, pp. 15-20, and no. 33, 1987, pp. 2-10. The Chantilly forest today covers 6,300 hectares.
10. The name of Serrurier which is always given to the expanse of water located to the right of the Grand Degré was attached to a pond fed by the Nonette which was alongside the causeway leading to Vineuil; beside the gate that defended the causeway stood the porter's house, in which a family of locksmiths ("serruriers") by the name of Aubry had lived since 1586. When the 1665 building programme was carried out, the workshop was transferred to Chantilly, to the Cour de Quinquenpoit, where it was still operating in 1903 if G. Macon is to be believed.
11. The king had already come to Chantilly in 1666, and would go back in 1684.
12. To give some idea of comparison, the Grand Canal at Versailles is 1,670 metres long, and the canal at Vaux approximately 1,000 metres.
13. G. Weber, *Brunnen und Wasserkünste in Frankreich im Zeitalter von Louis XIV*, Worms, 1985, pp. 212-216.
14. An association founded in his name set out to reconstruct the big wheel dating from the seventeenth century and to put the hydraulic machinery reinstated for the duc d'Aumale in the nineteenth century back into working order.
15. The starting point of the old causeway was at the site of the present Grille de l'Abreuvoir, to the west of the Grille d'Honneur (main gate).
16. From the correspondence that has been kept, we know that before setting out on campaign Condé had had discussions with Le Nôtre on the outlines of the forecourt and its surroundings which were to respect the existing buildings in the direction of the Pelouse. Le Nôtre took a few liberties with these instructions, which did not please the duc d'Enghien. Provisionally the old causeway, a few nearby buildings and the menagerie were kept, until a new menagerie was built at Vineuil.
17. Vauban was consulted in 1683 with regard to installing the new bascule bridge for the château.
18. Plan drawings dating proposals by Mansart to 1684 (Bibliothèque Nationale de France, Prints, R. de Cotte 180, and Chantilly, Musée Condé, 83 K 14). The same layout appears on an engraved seventeenth-century view (in Langlois). From the various plan drawings we see that the bank of the pond on the Orangerie side remained in its old state for some time, with a very irregular outline, before being given the regular shape we now see.
19. B. Jestaz, "Documents sur l'œuvre de Jules Hardouin-Mansart à Chantilly", *Bulletin monumental*, vol. 149, 1991, pp. 7-75.
20. However, the Prince de Condé must have known the architect, as he had used the services of his father, Raphaël Hardouin, in 1661. K. Béguin, op. cit., p. 332.
21. However, the curved openings towards the south post-date the photographs taken by Claudius Couton in 1872 where they do not appear. *Le Domaine de Chantilly vu par les photographes du* XIX*e siècle*, exhibition catalogue by N. Garnier-Pelle, Chantilly, Musée Condé, 1993.
22. The various plan drawings, sometimes annotated by Mansart, are kept in the R. de Cotte collection, nos. 194 and 197-199 (Bibl. Nat. de France, Prints), as well as at the Musée Condé in Chantilly (83 K 29), where the princes' correspondence is also located.
23. Mansart announces its dispatch in a letter dated 26 November, concerning the "little château of Chantilly for your suite of rooms". At that date Gittard was still acting as general architect for wages of 550 *livres*, while Mansart received 4,400.
24. It has not been proved that the preparatory drawing purchased by the Musée Condé regarding a proposal for the layout of a gallery with the prince's annotation: "This is the design I want. Louis de Bourbon" relates to the gallery at Chantilly. It may relate to the Hôtel de Condé in Paris. *Le Musée Condé*, no. 3, October 1972.
25. We are adopting the spelling advocated by Christine Laroche in her art history master's dissertation, *Le Petit Château de Chantilly. Architecture intérieure et décor sous les princes de Condé au* XVII*e siècle* (Paris IV Sorbonne, 1998). The son of the painter Meiffren Conte, he was born in Marseilles c. 1660 and died in 1694. A. Châtelet et al., *Chantilly. Musée Condé. Peintures de l'École française.* XV*e*-XVII*e siècles*, 1970.
26. We possess a very detailed printed account of that visit which gives an invaluable inventory of Chantilly at that date: *La Feste de Chantilly*. To be complemented by the account in the *Mercure français*.
27. 1,300 *livres* was paid for the first picture, and 1,200 for the subsequent ones.
28. The first and last of these compositions are copies made by Armand Bernard in the 19th century, after the originals held at the Musée de Versailles.
29. It was a modest building that was enlarged c. 1725 by the addition of side aisles and an extra bay on the nave in front of which the doorway was erected. This is the parish church we are familiar with G. Macon, *Les Édifices du culte à Chantilly*, Senlis, 1902.
30. A 1684 plan drawing in the R. de Cotte collection at the Bibl. nat. (no. 2286. Va 66, vol. 12) is marked: "Menagerie for marine animals. Menagerie for the various species of hens". With reference to the menagerie at Chantilly, see the chapters by G. Macon in G. Loisel, *Histoire des ménageries*, Paris, 1912, pp. 278-363.
31. R. de Broglie, "Le hameau et la laiterie de Chantilly", *Gazette des Beaux-Arts*, October-December 1950, pp. 309-324.
32. The Menagerie with its sculpted groups of fabulous animals and the Bassin de Narcisse is shown on various seventeenth-century engravings as well as on the eighteenth-century water colours of the du "Jeu de Cavagnole".
33. Mansart's plan drawings are held in the R. de Cotte collection at the Bibl. Nat. de France, nos. 178-193. In 1688 Mansart had put forward to the prince a proposal for enlarging the Palais des États de Bourgogne at Dijon, a scheme that was implemented throughout the eighteenth century. It was hereditary for the Condés to be governors of Burgundy, and the fame of the Great Condé was also celebrated in the new decoration of the Salle des Festins in 1780. Y. Beauvalot, "De la salle de l'École de dessin à la salle des Festins", *Bulletin de la Société de l'histoire de l'art français*, 1997 (1998), pp. 217-238.
34. Removed in 1735 by the duc de Bourbon to ornament the landing of his new grand staircase at the château, it was broken up by the National Guards in 1792, and the pieces scattered. Bought back by the Prince de Condé at the Restoration and entrusted to the sculptor Deseine who reinstated the missing parts, in particular the head, it once again stands in the middle of the parterres.
35. These works which were very worn by the duc d'Aumale's day were replaced on his orders by a casting of the Diana and copies of the sphinxes and mastiffs by Watrinelle and Jonchery. New dogs sculpted by Auguste Cain decorate the balustrade.

Chapter IV

Pages 108-151

1. As H. Malo puts it, in his *Les Chroniques de Chantilly*, Paris, 1934.
2. A thesis written for the École Nationale des Chartes in 1999 by M. Sébastien Lanoye is devoted to the "Duc de Bourbon, premier ministre de Louis XV".
3. Some are held in the National Museum of Stockholm in the Tessin collection (THC 6335 and 7501).
4. F. Souchal, "Jean Aubert, architecte des Bourbon-Condé", *Revue de l'art*, no. 6, 1969, pp. 29-38. His date of birth is not known (c. 1680?). He was the son of Jean-Jacques Aubert, architect and contractor for carpentry work for the king's buildings. Aubert's name was put forward to the Académie d'Architecture by Mansart in 1709, but he only took his seat there a few months before his death, which occurred on 13 October 1741. The duc de Bourbon had bequeathed him a pension of 1,000 *livres* in recognition of his services, which was paid to his widow.
5. There are still a few remnants of the accounting papers from this period at Chantilly, as well as an anonymous handwritten description of the building work carried out between 1718 and 1740.
6. A booklet written by Louis de Sarrobert, Capitaine at Chantilly. Quoted by G. Macon, *Chantilly et le Musée Condé*, p. 133.
7. Piganiol de La Force, *Description de Paris, de Versailles… et de toutes les autres belles maisons et châteaux des environs de Paris*, new ed., Paris, 1742, vol. VIII, p. 303.

8. For knowledge of it as it was built, we have the plan drawings engraved by Mariette in 1727.
9. One of the most notable results of his period as prime minister was the marriage of Louis XV to Marie Lesczinska in 1725. The Polish princess had the duke to thank for her position and tried to keep him in power.
10. B. Pons, in his book *De Paris à Versailles. 1699-1736. Les sculpteurs ornemanistes parisiens et l'art décoratif des Bâtiments du roi*, Paris, 1986, defined this new creative impulse, in which the suites of rooms at Chantilly occupy a distinguished place. By the same author, *Grands Décors français 1650-1680*, Paris, 1995, p. 211.
11. N. Garnier-Pelle, *Chantilly. Musée Condé. Peintures du XVIIIe siècle*, Paris, 1995, p. 102.
12. The paintings may have been intended for the rooms of Mlle de Clermont, the duc de Bourbon's sister, at the Petit Luxembourg. Their presence at Chantilly in the "billiard room" (the prince's bedchamber) is attested in 1822. There are others on the wainscoting in the suite of Mme de Clinchamp, formerly the natural history rooms of the duc de Bourbon, following the music room. Cf. N. Garnier-Pelle, op. cit., p. 83.
13. X. Salmon, "Christophe Huet, peintre de singeries", *Le Musée Condé*, no. 51, 1996, pp. 43-44.
14. N. Garnier-Pelle, op. cit., p. 65. G. Macon, op. cit., p. 148.
15. This was the case in the private suites of rooms of the Prince and Princess de Soubise in their mansion in the Marais. The shared room, decorated with wainscoting carved with the Fables of La Fontaine (c. 1738), was reassembled at the Hôtel de Rohan-Strasbourg, rue Vieille-du-Temple, not far from the Cabinet des Singes of Cardinal de Rohan. Re the Petite Singerie, cf. N. Garnier-Pelle, op. cit., p. 77.
16. The wainscoting in the duc d'Aumale's bedroom decorated with trophies of musical instruments and gardening implements contrasts markedly with the authentic decorations at Chantilly dating from the 1720s, in the way it is made and its non-symmetrical design.
17. G. Macon, *La Ville de Chantilly*, Senlis, 4 vols., 1908-12.
18. Memorandum by L. de Sarrobert, 1760. The Chantilly factory had a very brilliant reputation throughout the eighteenth century, in particularly for its pieces that were Korean in inspiration, as well as for its imitations of Chinese, Sèvres and Saxony porcelain. After the death of the duc de Bourbon, workers from Chantilly founded the factory of Vincennes, subsequently transferred to Sèvres under royal patronage, but Chantilly continued in production until the French Revolution. A private factory then took over, from 1803 to 1870.
19. *Les Écuries royales du XVIe au XVIIIe siècle*, a collective work edited by D. Roche, preface by J.-P. Babelon, Versailles, 1998.
20. F. Souchal, op. cit. There was an engraved collection of the *Élévations, coupes et profils des écuries du château de Chantilly appartenant à S.A.S. Mgr le duc de Bourbon, commencées à bâtir sur les dessins de M. Aubert, architecte du Roi, en l'année 1719, et terminées en 1735.* A ground plan and four elevations in the hand of Jean Aubert are held at the Bibl. nat. de France, in the R. de Cotte collection (201 to 204, Va 60, vol. 12), and there are others in the Musée Condé at Chantilly.
21. R. de Broglie, *Chantilly*, Paris, 1964, p. 70.
22. Piganiol de La Force, op. cit., pp. 308-332.
23. Admittedly this is the work of Charles Girault, the beloved pupil of Honoré Daumet, the man who built the new château of Chantilly.
24. E. de Ganay, "Les jardins de Chantilly au XVIIIe siècle", *La Gazette illustrée des amateurs de jardins*, 1923, pp. 10-15. He reproduces 6 of the 15 watercolours by Delagardette.
25. G. Bazin, "Éléments du Jeu de l'oie retrouvés dans le parc", *Le Musée Condé*, no. 29, 1985, pp. 1-6, and no. 31, p. 23. The game of goose at Chantilly inspired Louis XV to install a similar arrangement at Choisy.
26. See the *Traité concernant l'entretien des parterres de l'Orangerie, de la Volière, de l'Isle d'Amour, de Bucan et du nouveau potager*, 1783. Acquired by the Musée Condé, *Le Musée Condé*, no. 12, April 1977. F. Vergne, "Le parc du château de Chantilly", ibid., no. 36-37, 1989.
27. R. de Broglie, "Le théâtre de Chantilly", *Gazette des Beaux-Arts*, March 1961, pp. 155-166.
28. Leroy succeeded his father in the job as inspector of buildings at Chantilly, then at Brice-le-Chauve as architect. Cf. G. Macon, *Les Arts dans la maison de Condé*, p. 98.
29. R. de Broglie, "Le hameau et la laiterie de Chantilly", *Gazette des Beaux-Arts*, October-December 1950, pp. 309-324. Le Camus de Mézières, *Description des eaux de Chantilly et du Hameau*, Paris, 1783.
30. F. Vergne, "Le départ des princes de Condé ou la naissance de la première émigration", *Le Musée Condé*, no. 34, 1988, pp. 2-15.

Chapter V
Pages 152-167

1. An inventory of the remarkable or precious objects relating to the sciences, literature and the arts was drawn up by the Commission for Monuments on 18, 27 and 29 April 1793 with a view to their being sent to the Muséum de la République. Cf. *Le Musée Condé*, no. 16, May 1979.
2. These drawings illustrate his recollections, "Les loisirs de ma détention", dated 1794, the manuscript of which was lost in a fire in June 1940. Fortunately photographs of it have been preserved and they have taken on the value of originals. R. Cazelles, "Chantilly pendant la Révolution", *Mémoires de la Société historique de Senlis*, 1970, pp. 215-228. A. Sorel, *Le Château de Chantilly pendant la Révolution*, Paris, 1872.
3. G. Robert, "Les architectes à Chantilly pendant la première moitié du XIXe siècle", *Le Musée Condé*, no. 20, March 1981, pp. 7-13.

Chapter VI
Pages 168-231

1. R. Cazelles, *Le Duc d'Aumale*, Paris, 1984.
2. H. Lemonnier, "Le petit château de Chantilly pendant la jeunesse du duc d'Aumale (1830-1848)", paper read at the Académie des Beaux-Arts on 15 December 1923, *Institut de France. Publications de l'année 1923*, Paris, 1924, vol. 93, no. 33a.
3. J. Stern, *Les Courses de Chantilly sous la monarchie de Juillet*, Paris, 1913.
4. F. Boudon, "Le château de Chantilly, projet de reconstruction et travaux", *Félix Duban, 1798-1870. Les couleurs de l'architecte*, Paris, 1996, p. 159.
5. At this period a habit was adopted of referring to the Petit Château as the "Capitainerie", a name attached historically to the buildings beyond the moat overlooking the approach to the bridge leading to the Petit Château which disappeared in the course of the building work carried out by Le Nôtre.
6. In 1838 Victor Dubois (1779-1850) had provided the plan drawings for the new buildings housing the Archives of the kingdom, adjoining the Palais Soubise, but he was dismissed in 1841. His nephew Jean-Louis-Victor Grisart (1797-1877), winner of the Grand Prix in 1823, would be the architect of Compiègne in the reign of Napoleon III, and subsequently architect of the Archives of the Empire.
7. P. Prévost-Marcilhacy, "Eugène Lami. 1800-1890", *Le Musée Condé*, no. 53, September 1997, exhibition catalogue of "Un prince et ses architectes. La reconstruction de Chantilly par le duc d'Aumale", pp. 2-7.
8. The site of the room where the duc d'Enghien was born.
9. V. Bosc, *La Peinture décorative au château de Chantilly. Achats et commandes du duc d'Aumale*, DUT's dissertation, reported in *Le Musée Condé*, no. 49, December 1995, pp. 21-23.
10. Following the music room; it consisted of three rooms, one each for the animal, vegetable and mineral kingdoms. It was there that the famous mineralogical piece of furniture given by the king of Sweden to the Prince de Condé was kept.
11. Duban also worked on other alterations at Chantilly, on the Pont du Petit Château, a series of picturesque buildings in the park including a stable and a cow shed, drawings of which, still in existence, can be attributed to him, as well as bridges over the canal and the river, equipped with iron balustrades and lights. Work quoted in note 8, p. 26. Later on the prince who had formed a bond with the architect based on profound respect commissioned work from him for his exile in Britain: a funerary chapel and a library study at Twickenham (1859) and furnishings for the chapel at Woodnorton (1865).
12. F. Boudon, "Félix Duban 1798-1870", work quoted in note 7, pp. 8-17. By the same author, "Le château de Chantilly, projet de reconstruction et travaux (1846-1848)", *Félix Duban*, op. cit., pp. 159-166.
13. Document purchased by the Getty Museum in 1989, reproduced by F. Boudon, op. cit.
14. Cf. N. Garnier-Pelle, *Musée Condé, Peintures du XIXe et XXe siècles*, pp. 55 and 84.
15. Inspector general of museums and a member of the Académie des Beaux-Arts, Gruyer had established his reputation as a specialist on Raphael from 1859. He was appointed as one of the three curators of the Musée Condé on the death of the duc d'Aumale, and continued in this role until his own death in 1909, in particular writing the catalogues of the collections of painting at Chantilly.
16. M.-A. Baranes, *La Reconstruction du grand château de Chantilly par l'architecte P.-J.-H. Daumet à travers les fonds d'archives et de photographies du Musée Condé*, master's dissertation at the Paris IV university, 1995, used in: M.-A. Baranes and F. Hamon, "Honoré Daumet. Un prince et ses architectes. La reconstruction du château de Chantilly par le duc d'Aumale", *Le Musée Condé*, no. 53, September 1997, pp. 18-24.
17. *La Construction moderne*, 21 March 1891. Quoted in the work mentioned in note 17, p. 23.
18. A. d'Arenberg, *Notice sur M. le duc d'Aumale*, quoted by R. de Broglie, *Chantilly*, 1964, p. 205.
19. The entrance pavilion proposed by Duban was both more composite and more classical; it is perhaps possible to recognise in it the influence of a château that is not very far from Blois, Selles-sur-Cher, where a long wall-screen (structured with blind arches on the courtyard side) is broken through by a large entrance motif, and on the right joins the main block, the outline in silhouette of which is not unreminiscent of the main building at Chantilly. Cf. J.-P. Babelon, in *Congrès archéologique. Blésois et Vendômois*, Paris, 1986, pp. 392-404.
20. The invoice was for 37,500 francs, but the sum finally paid by the prince to demonstrate his satisfaction with the quality of work was 70,000 francs.
21. M.-A. Baranes, op. cit. in note 7.
22. I have taken this heading as well as the estimated figures preceding it from R. de Broglie, *Chantilly*, op. cit., p. 227.
23. A. Damien, *L'Institut de France*, "Que sais-je?" coll., 1999, pp. 82-88.
24. Quoted by M.-A. Baranes in his master's dissertation, op. cit. in which he transcribes all the prince's diaries and correspondence.
25. This administrative body or college is made up of two members from the Académie Française and the Académie des Beaux-Arts plus a third chosen from among the other bodies of the Institut de France, either the Académie des Inscriptions et Belles Lettres or the Académie des Sciences Morales et Politiques.

BILIOGRAPHY

Unless otherwise indicated the place of publication is Paris.

Album du Comte du Nord, Collection of the plans of the châteaux, parks and gardens of Chantilly dating from 1784 (after the manuscript at the Musée Condé in Chantilly) edited by Jean-Pierre BABELON, éditions Monelle Hayot, 2000.

BABELON, Jean-Pierre, *Châteaux de France au siècle de la Renaissance,* 1989, pp. 210-212 and 445-450.
- Contribution to *Jules Hardouin-Mansart,* edited by Alexandre Gady, 2010, p. 326-331 and 456-457.
BABELON, Jean-Pierre (Foreword) et Jean-Baptiste LEROUX (Photographs), *Le Nôtre,* Imprimerie nationale, 2013.
BARANES, Marc-Alexis. See: *Un prince et ses architectes.*
BEDOS-REZAK, Brigitte, *Anne de Montmorency, seigneur de la Renaissance,* 1990.
BÉGUIN, Katia, *Les Princes de Condé. Rebelles, courtisans et mécènes dans la France du Grand Siècle,* 1999.
BERTIÈRE, Simone, *Le Grand Condé. Le héros foudroyé,* 2012.
BOUCHENOT-DECHIN, Patricia, *André Le Nôtre,* 2013.
BOUDON, Françoise, "Le château de Chantilly, projet de reconstruction et travaux", *Félix Duban, 1798-1850. Les couleurs de l'architecte,* 1996, pp. 159-166. See also: *Un prince et ses architectes.*
BROGLIE, Raoul de, *Chantilly. Histoire du château et de ses collections,* 1964.

CAZELLES, Raymond, *Le Duc d'Aumale, prince aux dix visages,* 1984.
"Chantilly", Beaux-Arts special issue, n.d. Articles by M. Schumann, C. d'Anthenaise, J. Coignard, A. Lefébure, N. Garnier and F. Vergne.
CHATELET, Albert, PARISET, François-Georges and BROGLIE, Raoul de, *Chantilly. Musée Condé. Peintures de l'École française. XVe-XVIIe siècles,* 1970.

DU CERCEAU, Jacques Androuet, *Les Plus Excellents Bastiments de France,* 2 vols. 1576 and 1579. New edition with an introduction and commentary by David Thomson, 1988, pp. 242-255. New edition by Jean Guillaume and Peter Fuhring, 2010.

FOSSIER, François, *Les dessins du fonds Robert de Cotte de la Bibliothèque nationale de France: architecture et décor,* 1997.

GANAY, Ernest de, "Les jardins de Chantilly au XVIIIe siècle", *La Gazette illustrée des amateurs de jardins,* 1923, pp. 10-15.
GARNIER-PELLE, Nicole, *Chantilly. Musée Condé. Peintures du XVIIIe siècle,* 1995.
– *Chantilly. Musée Condé. Peintures des XIXe et XXe siècles,* 1997.
– *Le domaine de Chantilly vu par les photographes du XIXe siècle,* 1993.
- *André Le Nôtre et les jardins de Chantilly au XVIIe et au XVIIIe siècle,* 2013.
GEBELIN, François, *Les Châteaux de la Renaissance,* 1927, pp. 75-78.

HAMON, Françoise. See: *Un prince et ses architectes.*
HAUTECŒUR, Louis, *Histoire de l'architecture classique en France,* vols. Ia and Ib, 1963-65.

JAMES, François-Charles, "Jean Bullant. Recherches sur l'architecture française du XVIe siècle", *Positions des thèses de l'École nationale des Chartes,* 1968, pp. 101-109.
JESTAZ, Bertrand, "Jules Hardouin-Mansart au château de Chantilly", *Bulletin monumental,* vol. 149-1, 1991, pp. 7-75.
Le Musée Condé, twice-yearly newsletter, since 1971.

Le Domaine de Chantilly, special issue of *Monumental,* December 2013, p. 4 à 61, articles by 25 authors.

MACON, Gustave, *Les Architectes de Chantilly au XVIe siècle,* Senlis, 1900.
– *Les Arts dans la maison de Condé,* 1903.
– *Chantilly et le musée Condé,* 1910.
– *Chantilly et le connétable Henri de Montmorency,* Senlis, 1903.
– "Le Nôtre à Chantilly", *Institut de France, Publications de l'année 1927, Académie des beaux-arts,* 1928, no. 18.
MALO, Henri, *Les Chroniques du château de Chantilly,* 1934.
– *Le Château de Chantilly,* 1938.

PRÉVOST-MARCILHACY, Pauline. See: *Un prince et ses architectes.*
PRINZ, Wolfram and KECKS, Ronald, *Das französische Schloss der Renaissance,* Berlin, 1985, pp. 512-519.

ROBERT, Georges, "Les architectes à Chantilly pendant la première moitié du XIXe siècle", *Le Musée Condé,* no. 20, March 1981, pp. 7-13.

SOUCHAL, François, "Jean Aubert, architecte des Bourbon-Condé", *Revue de l'art,* no. 6, 1969, pp. 29-38.
Un prince et ses architectes: la reconstruction de Chantilly par le duc d'Aumale, special issue, *Le Musée Condé,* n° 53, September 1997, articles by P. Prévost-Marcilhacy, F. Boudon, F. Hamon and M.-A. Baranes.

VACHON, Marius, *Une famille parisienne de maîtres maçons: les Chambiges,* 1907.

WOERTH Éric, with Laurence DEFFAYET, *Le duc d'Aumale, l'étonnant destin d'un prince collectionneur,* L'Archipel, 2006. Foreword by Alain DECAUX, of the Académie Française, postface by His Highness the AGA KHAN.

CHRONOLOGY

Late 10th century
First mention of the Chantilly estate, property of Rothold, lord of Senlis and Ermenonville.
Late 11th century
Gui de Senlis, lord of Chantilly, is appointed cup-bearer by King Louis VI. A first castle is built on the small rocky island, overlooking the Picardy road.
1227
Division of the estate of Gui III Bouteiller de Senlis. His second son, Guillaume, inherits Chantilly.
1340
Guillaume III is buried in the castle.
1358
Jacquerie uprising. Chantilly is sacked.
1386
Chantilly is sold by the heirs of the Bouteillers to Pierre d'Orgemont, who has the castle rebuilt.
1389
Death of Pierre d'Orgemont. His son completes the building work in 1394.
1398
The park is enclosed by walls.
1421
Chantilly is handed over to the English-Burgundian side.
1484
Pierre III d'Orgemont assigns Chantilly to his nephew Guillaume de Montmorency.
1507
Guillaume de Montmorency has the chapel of the castle rebuilt.
1515
Anne de Montmorency at Marignano.
1522
Guillaume de Montmorency divides his property and assigns Chantilly to his son Anne.
1524
Start of building work on the Galerie des Cerfs, completed in 1530.
1525
Defeat of Pavia, captivity of Francis I.
1528
Pierre Chambiges is chosen to rebuild the château. Work completed in 1530.
1538
Appointed Constable, Montmorency has the château of Écouen built.
1540
Visit by Emperor Charles V to Chantilly. Montmorency falls from favour.
1547
Death of Francis I. Accession of Henri II. Montmorency back in favour.
1557
Defeat of Saint-Quentin. Montmorency held prisoner by the Spanish.
1558
Jean Bullant starts building the Petit Château.
1567
Battle of Saint-Denis. Anne de Montmorency dies of his wounds.
1579
Death of François de Montmorency. Chantilly passes to his younger brother Henri, Governor of Languedoc.
1589
Accession of Henri IV to the throne.
1594
Henri de Montmorency is appointed Constable of France.
1601
Start of building work by Pierre Biard.
1612
The equestrian statue of Constable Henri is erected on the terrace.
1614
On the death of the second Constable, Chantilly passes to his son Henri II.
1623
Théophile de Viau is concealed by the duc de Montmorency.
1632
Henri II de Montmorency is condemned to death. Chantilly is confiscated by Louis XIII.
1643
Death of Louis XIII. The young Prince de Condé defeats the Spanish at Rocroi. Chantilly is handed back to his mother, Charlotte de Montmorency.
1648
Start of the Fronde. Initially a defender of the Queen and young Louis XIV, Condé becomes leader of the princes rebelling against Mazarin.
1654
Condé is condemned as a rebel.
1659
Peace of the Pyrenees. Return to favour of Condé.
1662
Condé calls on Le Nôtre to redesign the gardens at Chantilly.
1668
Molière puts on *Tartuffe* at Chantilly. Conquest of Franche-Comté by Condé.
1671
Visit by Louis XIV. Death of Vatel.
1672-73
The Grand Canal is dug out. Building work on the forecourt is completed.
1674
Victory by Condé at Seneffe.
1681-84
Construction of the Grand Degré.
1684-86
Jules Hardouin-Mansart renovates the Petit Château.
1686
Death of the Great Condé. His son Henri-Jules succeeds him at Chantilly.
1687
Mansart undertakes the reconstruction of the Grand Château.
1688
Visit by the Grand Dauphin.
1709
Death of Henri-Jules de Bourbon, Prince de Condé. His son Louis III survives him by one year.
1710
Louis-Henri, duc de Bourbon, becomes master at Chantilly.
1715
Death of Louis XIV. Accession of Louis XV. Regency of the duc d'Orléans.
1718
The duc de Bourbon has the reconstruction of the Grand Château continued by Jean Aubert, and the suites of rooms in the Petit Château decorated.
1721
Jean Aubert undertakes the construction of the Grandes Écuries.
1723-26
The duc de Bourbon is Prime Minister.
1735
Completion of the Grandes Écuries.
1740
Death of duc Louis Henri. His son Louis-Joseph, Prince de Condé, succeeds him.
1756
Construction of the Jeu de Paume.
1762
The Prince de Condé victorious at Johannisberg (Seven Years War).
1767
Construction of the theatre, known as the Salle d'Oronthée.
1769
Start of construction of the château of Enghien" by J.-F. Leroy.
1772
Work starts on creating the Jardin Anglais.
1775
Official opening of the Hameau at Chantilly.
1782
Visit of the Count and Countess of the North (the future Tsar Paul I).
1785
Demolition of the Galerie des Cerfs.
1789
14 July, storming of the Bastille; 17 July, departure of the Prince as émigré.
1793
Chantilly is used as a prison.
1799
The Grand Château is demolished.
1804
The duc d'Enghien is executed at Vincennes.
1811
Chantilly is included in the apanage of Queen Hortense.
1814
Abdication of Napoleon I. First Restoration.
1815
Waterloo. Second Restoration. Final return of the Prince de Condé to Chantilly.
1817
Proposal for reconstruction of the Grand Château by Dubois, who starts laying out the western Jardin Anglais.
1818
Death of the Prince de Condé. His son Louis-Henri-Joseph, duc de Bourbon, succeeds him.
1821
The duc de Bourbon has the moat between the Petit Château and the Grand Château filled in.
1829
The duc de Bourbon makes a will in favour of his nephew and godson, the duc d'Aumale, son of Louis-Philippe, duc d'Orléans.
1830
The July Revolution puts Louis-Philippe on the throne. On 27 August, death of the duc de Bourbon in Saint-Leu.
1843
Capture of the retinue of Abd-el-Kader by the duc d'Aumale.
1846
The suites of rooms in the Petit Château are decorated by Eugène Lami.
1847
To rebuild the Grand Château the duc d'Aumale selects Félix Duban.
1848
February Revolution. The duc d'Aumale joins Louis-Philippe in exile in London.
1855
Purchase by the duc d'Aumale of the *Très Riches Heures du duc de Berry.*
1871
After the collapse of the Empire, the duc d'Aumale returns to Chantilly. He is elected to the Académie Française.
1875
The duke chooses Honoré Daumet for the reconstruction of the Grand Château.
1876
Start of building work, completed in 1885.
1883
The death of the comte de Chambord makes the comte de Paris the pretender to the French throne.
1884
On 3 June the duc d'Aumale draws up his will in favour of the Institut de France.
1886
New laws passed by the Republic force the duke into exile on 15 July. On 25 October he turns his bequest into a donation.
1889
Return of d'Aumale. Final building work.
1895
The duke receives the Institut de France at Chantilly.
1897, 7 May
Death of the duc d'Aumale in Sicily.
1898, 17 April
The "Musée Condé" is opened to the public.
2006, 1th of January
Created in 2005 by His Highness the Aga Khan, the "Fondation pour la sauvegarde et le développement du Domaine de Chantilly" (the "Foundation for the Safeguarding and Development of the Domain of Chantilly"), was granted the responsibility to preserve and promote this large historic site.

The Montmorencys

Jean II de Montmorency
grand chambellan
(† 1447)
ép. - 1 - Jeanne de Fosseuse - 2 - Marguerie d'Orgemont fille de Pierre II d'Orgemont

- (1) Jean de Nivelle
- (1) Louis de Fosseuse
- (2) Guillaume de Montmorency († 1531) *ép.* Anne Pot
  - François de La Rochepot
  - Anne duc de Montmorency connétable (1493-1567) *ép.* Madeleine de Savoie
    - 12 enfants dont :
      - François duc de Montmorency (1530-1579) *ép.* Diane, légitimée de France, duchesse d'Angoulême
      - Henri Ier duc de Montmorency, connétable (1534-1614) *ép.* - 1 - Antoinette de La Marck - 2 - Louise de Budos
        - (1) Hercule comte d'Offémont
        - (1) Charlotte *ép.* Charles de Valois (bâtard de Charles IX)
        - (1) Marguerite *ép.* Anne de Lévis duc de Ventadour
        - (2) Charlotte-Marguerite (1594-1650) *ép.* Henri II de Bourbon prince de Condé
          - Anne-Geneviève (1619-1679) *ép.* Henri d'Orléans duc de Longueville
          - Louis II de Bourbon duc d'Enghien puis prince de Condé dit le Grand Condé (1621-1686)
          - Armand de Bourbon prince de Conti (1629-1668)
        - (2) Henri II de Montmorency maréchal de France (1595-1632) *ép.* Marie-Félice des Ursins
      - Guillaume seigneur de Thoré († 1594)
      - Jeanne *ép.* Louis de La Trémoille duc de Thouars
        - Charlotte-Catherine *ép.* Henri Ier de Bourbon prince de Condé
      - Éléonore *ép.* François II de La Tour vicomte de Turenne
        - Henri de La Tour d'Auvergne vicomte de Turenne
          - Henri de La Tour d'Auvergne vicomte de Turenne maréchal de France (1611-1675)
  - Louise *ép.* - 1 - Maréchal de Maillé - 2 - Gaspard II de Coligny
    - (1) Madeleine *ép.* Charles de Roye
      - Eléonore de Roye *ép.* Louis de Bourbon-Condé
    - (2) Odet cardinal de Châtillon
    - (2) François d'Andelot
    - (2) Gaspard III de Coligny amiral de France

The Bourbon-Condés

Louis Ier de Bourbon prince de Condé
(1530-1569)
ép. - 1 - Éléonore de Roye - 2 - Françoise d'Orléans Longueville

Henri Ier prince de Condé
(1552-1588)
ép. - 1 - Marie de Clèves - 2 - Charlotte de La Trémoille

François prince de Conti
(1558-1614)

Charles cardinal de Bourbon
(1562-1594)

Charles de Soissons
(1566-1612)
ép. Anne de Montafié

Henri II prince de Condé
(1588-1646)
ép. Charlotte de Montmorency

Anne-Geneviève
(1619-1679)
ép. Henri d'Orléans
duc de Longueville

Louis II prince de Condé dit le Grand Condé
(1621-1686)
ép. Claire-Clémence de Maillé-Brézé
(1628-1694)

Armand prince de Conti
(1629-1666)

Henri-Jules de Bourbon duc d'Enghien, puis prince de Condé
(1643-1709)
ép. Anne de Bavière

10 enfants dont :

Louis III de Bourbon Monsieur le Duc
(1668-1710)
ép. Louise-Françoise de Nantes
(1673-1743)
fille de Louis XIV
et de Mme de Montespan

Marie-Thérèse
(1666-1732)
ép. François-Louis de Bourbon
prince de Conti

Louise-Bénédicte
(1676-1753)
ép. Louis-Auguste de Bourbon duc du Maine
fils de Louis XIV et de Mme de Montespan

Marie-Anne
(1678-1718)
ép. Louis-Joseph
duc de Vendôme

Louis-Armand II prince de Conti
(1696-1727)
ép. Louise-Élisabeth de Bourbon

Marie-Anne
(1689-1720)
ép. Louis-Henri duc de Bourbon

9 enfants dont :

Louis-Henri de Bourbon
prince de Condé
Monsieur le Duc
(1692-1740)
ép. - 1 - Marie-Anne de Conti - 2 - Caroline de Hesse-Rheinfels

Charles de Bourbon
comte de Charolais
(1700-1760)

Louis de Bourbon
comte de Clermont
(1709-1771)

Marie-Anne
mademoiselle
de Clermont
(1697-1741)

Louise-Élisabeth
(1693-1713)
ép. Louis-Armand
de Conti

Louis-Joseph de Bourbon prince de Condé
(1736-1818)
ép. - 1 - Charlotte-Godefride de Rohan-Soubise - 2 - Marie-Catherine de Brignoles princesse de Monaco

Louis-Henri-Joseph de Bourbon
(1756-1830)
ép. Louise-Marie-Thérèse-Bathilde d'Orléans

Louise-Adélaïde
(1758-1824)
bénédictine

Louis-Antoine-Henri de Bourbon duc d'Enghien
(1772-1804)

The Orléans family

- Charles de Bourbon duc de Vendôme
  - Antoine de Bourbon duc de Vendôme
    - Henri IV
      - Louis XIII
        - Louis XIV
        - Philippe d'Orléans (1640-1701)
          - Philippe II d'Orléans le Régent (1674-1723)
            - Louis Ier d'Orléans (1703-1752)
              - Louis-Philippe d'Orléans (1725-1785)
                - Louis-Philippe-Joseph d'Orléans, dit Philippe Égalité (1747-1793) *ép.* Marie-Adélaïde de Penthièvre (1753-1821)
                  - Louis-Philippe (1773-1850) roi des Français 1830-1848 *ép.* Marie-Amélie de Bourbon-Sicile (1782-1866)
                    - 8 enfants dont :
                      - Ferdinand-Philippe duc d'Orléans (1818-1842) *ép.* Hélène de Mecklembourg
                        - Philippe comte de Paris (1838-1883)
                        - Robert duc de Chartres (1840-1910)
                      - Henri-Eugène duc d'Aumale (1822-1897) *ép.* Marie-Caroline de Bourbon-Sicile (1822-1869)
                        - Louis-Philippe prince de Condé (1845-1866)
                        - François duc de Guise (1854-1872)
                - Louise-Marie-Thérèse-Bathilde (1750-1822) *ép.* Louis-Henri-Joseph, duc de Bourbon
  - Louis de Bourbon prince de Condé

LIST OF ILLUSTRATIONS

All the works depicted are held in the Musée Condé at the château of Chantilly unless otherwise stated. The photographs are by Georges Fessy except for those where the copyright is indicated.

Chapter VI
A new Renaissance prince : the duc d'Aumale

INDEX

Index of proper names appearing in the text:
names of people in normal typeface, place names in bold

Photoengraving : Bussière, Paris
Printed in France by Alpha, Peaugres. Binding by Façonnage Alain, Félines.
Legal deposit : January 2014